Mountain Biking Britain

Chris Moran

Contents

↘ Introduction 4
↘ How do I use the book? 5
↘ What kind of rider am I? 6
↘ Terrain breakdown 7
↘ What kind of bike should I be riding? 8
↘ Terrain and terminology 10
↘ Facility breakdown 270
↘ Index 285
↘ Credits 288

Southwest England

↘ Overview 16
↘ Abbeyford Woods & Goldburn Northshore 18
↘ Asham Woods 19
↘ Ashton Court (The Timberland Trail) 19
↘ Aveton Gifford DJ 20
↘ Bath BMX Track 20
↘ Bradford Hollow 20
↘ How to pack your bike for trips 21
↘ Blandford UK Bike Park 22
↘ Buckland Rings 24
↘ Buriton Chalk Pits 24
↘ Canford Heath & Pit DH 25
↘ Cann Wood Trails 25
↘ Cheddar BMX 26
↘ Combe Sydenham 26
↘ Dartmoor National Park 27
↘ Decoy BMX 27
↘ Forest of Dean 28
↘ Haldon Forest Park 30
↘ Hidden Valley DJs 32
↘ Hook DJs 32
↘ Hundred Acre Wood 32
↘ Island Trails 33
↘ JLC Trails 33
↘ Leckhampton 33
↘ Leigh Woods 34
↘ Nationwide DJs 34
↘ Oasis DJs 35
↘ Patchway BMX DJs 35
↘ Pines Ridge 35
↘ Maddacleave Woods 36
↘ Mineral Tramways Project 38
↘ Poldice Valley Trails 40
↘ Portland Bill Quarries 41
↘ Local riders, Paul Blackburn 42
↘ Portsdown Hill 44
↘ Puddletown Woods 44
↘ Queen Elizabeth Country Park 45
↘ Randwick DH 46
↘ Red Hill Extreme 46
↘ Rogate 46
↘ Sandford DJ & DH 47
↘ Sheet DJs 47
↘ Still Woods 48
↘ 5 tips for trail etiquette 49
↘ Stoke Heights 50
↘ Stoughton Trails 50
↘ Stoke Woods 51
↘ The Track 52
↘ Triscombe DH 54
↘ Watchmoor Wood Bike Park 54
↘ Woodbury Common 55

London & Southeast England

↘ Overview 60
↘ Aston Hill 62
↘ A10 DJs 64
↘ Bengeo Bumps & Waterford Quarry DJs 64
↘ Bedgebury Forest & Freeride Area 65
↘ Blean Woods 66
↘ Bluebell Hill 67
↘ Braintree BMX 67
↘ Brockwell Park BMX Track 68
↘ Bushy Park 69
↘ Chazey Woods & Northshore 68
↘ Chicksands Bike Park 70
↘ Crowborough – The Bull Track 72
↘ Crow Trails 73
↘ Danbury Common 73
↘ Local riders, Ben Wain 74
↘ Devils Drop DJs 76
↘ Devils Dyke DH & XC 76
↘ Devils Dyke Nonsuch DJs 77
↘ Donkey Island DJs 77
↘ Esher Shore 78
↘ Epping Forest 80
↘ Friston Forest 81
↘ Fearnley DJs 82
↘ Gunnersbury DJ 82
↘ Harrow Skatepark & DJs 82
↘ Hayes Hawks BMX Track 83
↘ Highgate DJs 83
↘ Highwood DJs 83
↘ Holmes Place DJs 84
↘ Ipswich BMX track 84
↘ Kuoni Trails 84
↘ Leith Hill 84
↘ Limpsfield DJs 85
↘ Look Out Gulley 86
↘ M3 DJs 86
↘ Mereworth Woods 86
↘ Mousehold Trails 87
↘ Nature Jumps & Gog Magog XC 87
↘ PORC (Penshurst Off Road Club) 88
↘ Normandy Hill DH 90
↘ Peaslake 90
↘ Peckham BMX Track, and Burgess Park BMX 91
↘ Rayleigh 91
↘ Redlands 92
↘ Shoreham DJs 93
↘ Shorne Wood Country Park & DJs 93
↘ Sidley Woods 94
↘ Slindon Quarry 94
↘ Swinley Forest 95
↘ Sloughbottom Park 96
↘ Teddington DJs 96
↘ Thetford Forest 97
↘ Tilgate Forest & St Leonards Forest 98
↘ Track 40 98
↘ Tring Park 99
↘ Warley DJs 99
↘ Whiteways 99
↘ Wild Park 100
↘ Willen Lake BMX Track 100
↘ Wisley Trails 101
↘ Woburn Sands 102

The Midlands

↘ Overview 108
↘ Bringewood 110
↘ Brackley DH 111
↘ Cauldwell Woods DJs 111
↘ Cannock Chase 112
↘ Cheshire Ghost Rides BMX Track 114

- Deeping BMX 114
- Eastridge Woods 115
- Hopton Castle 116
- Keele Woods & DJs 118
- Leamington Spa 4X Track & DJs 118
- Ribbesford DH 119
- Perry Park BMX 120
- Rutland Water Cycle Way 120
- Sherwood Pines Forest 121
- Swithland Woods 122
- Tiny BMX Track 123

The North

- Overview 128
- Carlton Bank DH & XC 130
- Broomley Trails (DJs) 131
- Calverley Woods 131
- Chesterfield BMX/ 4X Track 131
- Chevin Forest Park 132
- Chester-le-Street spots 133
- Chopwell 134
- Delamere Forest 135
- Dalby Forest 136
- Devils Cascade DJs 138
- Elland Park Wood 139
- Gosforth Park DJs 139
- Gisburn Forest 140
- Greasborough Trails 141
- Great Ayton Quarry DJs 141
- Greenway DJs 142
- Guisborough Forest 142
- Hartlepool 4X 143
- Hookstone Woods DJs 143
- Local rider, John Storey 144
- Hamsterley Forest 146
- Hulme Park DJs 148
- Hurstwood Trails 148
- Ilkley Moor 149
- Iron Bridge DJs 149
- Kielder Water & Forest Park 150
- Ladybower Reservoir 152
- Lee Mill Quarry (aka The Adrenaline Gateway) 153
- Little Switzerland 154
- Longridge Fell 154
- Lyme Park 154
- Manchester Road DJs 155
- Meltham Skills Trails 155
- Midgley Woods 155
- Park Bridge 4X 156
- Ramsden Lane DH 156
- Roman Lakes Leisure Park 158
- Scratchmere Scar Freeride Bike Park 157
- Silton Forest DH 158
- Setmurthy DH Trails & Cockermouth XC 159
- Stainburn 160
- Sticks Norden 162
- Storthes Hall DH 162
- Temple Newsam 163
- TNF Grizedale 164
- Wassenden DH 166
- Wiswell Wood 166
- Woodbank DJs 167
- Whinlatter Forest 168
- Wooler 4X 169
- Yeadon BMX Track 169

Wales

- Overview 174
- Afan Forest Park 176
- Abercarn 178
- Aberhafesp Woods & DH 179
- Caerphilly DJs 179
- Brechfa 180
- Betws Y Coed (Snowdonia East) 182
- Clarach DH 183
- Clyne Woods 183
- Coed Llandegla 184
- Coed Trallwm 186
- Top riding tips, Josh Bryceland 187
- Coed Y Brenin (Snowdonia West) 188
- Cwm Rhaeadr 190
- Cwmcarn 192
- Foel Gasnach DH 194
- Gethin Woods 195
- Gwydwr Forest 196
- Kilvey Hill 197
- Henblas/ Caersws nr Newton 198
- Llantrisant Woods DH 198
- Llanwrtyd Wells 199
- Maindy Road BMX Track 200
- Moelfre 200
- Mountain Ash DH 201
- Ponciau Banks 201
- Machynlleth 202
- Nant yr Arian 203
- Rheola DH Track 206
- Rudry DJs 206
- Sandjumps 206
- Snowdonia National Park 207
- Wentwood DH 208
- Local riders, Rowan Sorrell 209

Southern Scotland

- Overview 214
- Local riders, Chris Ball 216
- Ae Forest (7Stanes) 218
- Dalbeattie (7Stanes) 220
- Drumlanrig Castle 222
- Glentress (7Stanes) 224
- Glentrool (7Stanes) 226
- Innerleithen (7Stanes) 228
- The Jedforest Trails 230
- Safety, Steve Ireland 231
- Kirroughtree (7Stanes) 232
- Mabie (7Stanes) 234
- Newcastleton 236

Central & Northern Scotland

- Overview 241
- Aviemore 242
- Balnain Bike Park 243
- Carron Valley Trails 244
- Comrie Croft Bike Trails 245
- Fort William 246
- Glencoe 248
- Golspie Highland Wildcat Trails 250
- Isle of Arran 254
- Kyle of Sutherland Trails 254
- Laggan Wolftrax 256
- Learnie Red Rocks 258
- Moray Monster Trails 260
- Pitfichie Mountain Cycle Trails 262
- Pollock Country Park 263
- Strathpeffer 264
- The Fire Tower Trail 265
- The Kelpies Trails 266
- Donkey Hill Dirt Track 267
- Duchany Woods 267
- Dunkeld Downhill 267
- Kirkhill Mountain Bike Park 268
- Best Films, Callum Swift 269

Welcome to Mountain Biking Britain, hopefully the first of such guides to be printed for your riding pleasure. I've written this guide in the hope that everyone who rides a mountain bike (or aspires to) will be able to find a new, fun local spot to explore, and to know what lies out of your immediate geographical sphere in case you fancy a weekend adventure! Here in the UK we are blessed with some of the best riding to be had anywhere in the world. Within an hour's journey of every major UK city we have world-class mountain biking, from some of the best downhill tracks to the most glorious cross country riding (with spectacular views) and some of the most gentle, perfect, family rides through our wonderful countryside. You don't have to own a bike to use this guide – many of the places featured have quality bikes available for hire – all you really need is a love of life and a wish to get out on two wheels to explore our lovely isle.

How did I pick the places? Many are well-known trail centres – places built specifically for mountain biking - while others are little-known, local spots that have grown organically on rarely used areas of the countryside. I spoke to friends, pros, photographers, enthusiasts, magazine editors, mountain bike legends and those I met on the trails themselves. To be honest, I found the majority of the newer routes by chatting with the fantastic network of mountain bike clubs that exists in the UK. Some are little more than an enthusiastic rider with a mobile phone, some are businesses running mountain bike guiding services, and the rest are small groups of riders that have their own websites or pages on facebook, bebo, or myspace and who are so enthusiastic about riding that they wish to share their cherished spots with other, like-minded riders. A huge thanks goes out to all of them.

So why buy a book? Why not just go online or chat to the clubs yourself? Well, I thought long and hard about that, and I've made sure that each spot has detailed information that's either unavailable on the net (directions, sat nav postcodes, phone numbers, tips etc) or much more difficult to present as concise, comparable information, and I've included quick-glance lists for that very reason. Flick through the lists, and you'll find you can skip straight to the places that fit your own particular requirements. For example, do you need a bike wash to end the day? Do you need to hire a bike in the first place? Or do you want a slice of cake at a café on your ride? We all have different wishes and the comparison list should give you a good idea of which trail centres fit your own needs. And lastly, this book should fit in your pocket, glovebox or backpack, so it's always to hand if you need it. The book should be a starting point too, and for each place, I've detailed where you can find much more information – or how to link to the clubs, shops and local companies – online.

All that remains is to wish you all good luck in finding a great new spot to ride. I've tried as hard as I can to make sure that all the information in here is correct, but if I have got anything wrong (or you wish to recommend somewhere that isn't featured in this book), then please feel free to contact me through mountainbikingbritain@gmail.com.

Good luck! Chris Moran.

How to use the book

Feel free to browse through the book as you see fit of course, but when putting it together, we had in mind that it might be used in the following way:

1 If you already own a bike and know what kind of terrain you prefer, simply check out your local area and comparison chart to find spots you might like. If you fancy a longer trip, or want to get involved with a local riding club, then read up on what's out there in the 'more info' sections in each centre.

2 If you're completely new to mountain biking, and just want to dip your toe into the waters (so to speak), then turn to page 6 to determine which kind of riding you'd like to try out. Then all you have to do is find a nearby trail centre with bikes for hire (see the comparison charts at the back of the book to locate one near you quickly), and then make sure that centre fits in with the kind of riding you can see yourself enjoying.

3 If you're a family and want the perfect day out, simply refer to the beginning of each chapter, where we've starred the best five trail centres for each region. These centres feature bike hire, great visitor facilities, maps, and waymarkers so you're unlikely to get lost on your day out. See the 'Terrain Breakdown' page for more information on what kind of surfaces you might wish to start out on.

4 For each riding spot or trail centre we have tried to give an overall impression – one that will give you a 'snapshot' of what the riding has to offer. We've done this so you can quickly work out whether it's what you want. If you wish to find out more information about any of the places featured in this guide, we've tried to include as many links to further websites, clubs and other links as possible on each relevant page. Please remember, this is not an absolutely definitive guide to the riding spots, it is simply here to give you an overall impression of the best spots near you.

5 Once you've found a good local spot, and met some other riders (and feel like you're part of the brilliant mountain biking scene here in the UK), don't forget to let us know about any more of the amazing – and sometimes underground – spots by emailing Chris at mountainbikingbritain@gmail.com and if you have any photographs, we'd love to see them for possible inclusion in the next edition of Mountain Biking Britain.

CHRIS MORAN

Symbols

Cross-country	Bikewash
Downhill	Uplift
Freeride	Map
4X	Waymarked
BMX	Forestry Commission
Dirt jump	Family
Northshore	Visitor centre
Foam Pit	Accommodation
Bike hire	Café
Bikeshop	

What kind of rider am I?

The ultimate mountain bike would be something like this: ludicrously light and stiff, so it's easy to pedal uphill; have loads of gears to help you ascend the most vertical of gradients (and so you can still push hard when you're flying at 50 kph downhill). It would be grippy over mud, rock, wet wood, and sand; and on descents it would have the best ever suspension and geometry to keep you from going over the front of the bike. It would fly over huge jumps, be small enough to take on tight, technical jumps, large enough to attack gaps on downhill courses and be bombproof if you dropped it.

Unfortunately, such a bike doesn't exist, as many of the above requirements completely contradict each other. For example, lightweight rarely (if ever) means strong. And the geometry of a bike that is great going uphill is exactly the opposite to what you want when pointing it downhill. So choosing a bike is a matter of balancing compromises. Our own thinking is that you can break down what kind of rider you are then match the kind of bike or riding that you're after.

What kind of riding do you like?

For those who want to see the countryside, love the aerobic workout from a good ride, enjoy beautiful views and just love being out and about, but aren't too bothered about hard uphill slogs or thrilling descents, a hard-tail XC (cross country) bike is probably a good place to start.

For riders who love pushing themselves aerobically, enjoy (or at least, are not afraid of) uphill climbs, ride a bike because it's a great way of getting out into the countryside, and know that the downhill sections are going to be good fun, then a full-suspension XC bike might be best. If you think you might want to do enduro-style races (or you might want to race your mates!) then you'll want the most lightweight full-suspension XC bike you can afford.

Riders who endure the uphill sections (OK, sometimes they can be a little interesting), love being out in the countryside just so they get to ride the fun, downhill stuff, and like nothing more than to challenge themselves by riding over jumps and over

A flowing Glentress XC switchback.

balance-sections (such as northshore), then a strong XC or a Freeride bike will be best. Freeriding can be categorized in many weird and wonderful ways, but we see it as riding pretty much everything with the enthusiasm of a kid who wants to jump his or her bike in the air, drop off things, and still loves getting out in the countryside for some rambling action (hunting for jumps!).

For those who love the thrilling downhill sections, jumps and tree roots, and are prepared to either push their bikes uphill (or pay for a lift of some sort), then a downhill bike is brilliant. Note, many people who own a downhill bike might also have an XC bike too.

For those who want to ride their bikes on dirt jumps (a kind of funpark or over-sized BMX track – see the Terrain Breakdown page), and love to be in the air more than anything, then a Dirtjump bike could be perfect.

Note – most riders fit somewhere between riding a full suspension XC and a freeride set up, and generally speaking, they push their bike to its downhill limits. If you can afford two bikes, you'd probably want a downhill bike, and a lightweight XC one.

Now skip to the 'What kind of bike should I be riding?' page…

Terrain breakdown

Many of the trail centres are now as organized as ski resorts, with visitor centres, cafés, hire facilities, changing, showers, car parking and bike washes. They also – like alpine resorts – operate a colour-graded system for each trail so you can make a judgement as to how difficult the riding might be. The colours match the same system as used on alpine ski runs and break down as:

1 **Green trails** are the easiest graded trails, and are suitable for all riders including novices and families. Expect the terrain to be gentle, smooth and with the odd fun challenge along the way (such as a small section of up or downhill riding). Often these runs are on old disused railways, or next to canals and run through areas of outstanding beauty. Please note that some areas in the UK use the colour purple for family-graded or forest road trails.

2 **Blue trails** are more difficult, but should still be fairly easy for athletic, adventurous beginners, and should offer more of a challenge than green trails but be gentle enough for most novices to attempt.

3 **Red trails** are for intermediate riders, and the increase in difficulty over blue trails can be for a variety of reasons. Perhaps the trail is much longer (and therefore, more physically demanding), or it might feature some jumps, drops or steeper down and uphill sections. Red-graded trails may still be attempted by adventurous amateurs, but are best ridden by those who have already got to grips with blue-graded trails and have some bike skills.

4 **Black-graded trails** are for advanced riders, and may feature difficult, technical sections where riding skills are needed. For example, there may be tricky downhill sections over rocks and roots, or there may be drops or jumps on the trail that cannot be avoided.

5 **Orange-graded runs**, which are classified as 'funpark' runs, are usually filled with jumps and various man-made or natural structures to ride over. These can be very, very difficult and should be watched before being attempted.

6 **Diamond** (or double diamond) is another imported symbol from ski resorts and designates a particularly hard section of trail. For example, a jump may be classed as diamond (if there is danger associated with not clearing the entire jump), or double diamond if it's a very large jump.

7 Some trail centres feature 'Skills Areas', where different examples of the likely obstacles to be encountered on the trails is presented in a small area. Skills areas are well worth seeking out, as they will help you brush up on your bike-handling technique, and give you a great idea as to what terrain you prefer riding.

Afan's orange, red and purple trails.

CHRIS MORAN

CHRIS MORAN

What kind of bike should I be riding?

If you've read the 'What kind of Rider Am I?' page, here is a rough breakdown for each of the bikes.

If you're thinking of buying a bike on a limited budget, please note that the mountain bike magazines websites have fantastic forums for advice and users are always selling their surplus kit. Ebay is a great place to go (once you know exactly what you're after), or you can always go to a bike shop and ask for either a second-hand model or last year's models. The discounts can often be enormous.

CHRIS MORAN

Right: Cwmcarn's uplift trailer. Most bikes here will be DH rigs.

Freeride/Downhill	
Features	super-sturdy forks (full length usually), plus rear suspension.
Great for	going very fast and riding off large drops.
Pluses	very sturdy great downhill geometry (lots of fork angle forward).
Minuses	very heavy and has wrong geometry to ride uphill.
Travel	at least 7 inches (178 mm) and up to 8 inches (205 mm) on both forks and rear suspension.
Great example	Commencal Supreme DH.
Cost range	£700-3000.

Dirtjump bike	
Features	hard tail, suspension on forks, sturdy materials, and only rear gears. Sometimes dirt jump bikes use the smaller 24-inch wheels instead of the regular 26-inch mountain bike wheel diameter.
Great for	riding over large jumps.
Pluses	strong, can take abuse, low maintenance.
Minuses	bouncy downhill, low seat, not made for comfort, few gears.
Travel	4-6 inches (100-150 mm) on the forks.
Great example	DMR Rhythm.
Cost range	£400-900.

Hardtail XC bike

Features suspension forks, but rigid back end (hence the name).

Great for riding gently uphill and along rough terrain, though nothing super technical.

Pluses easier to maintain than a full suspension bike, and simple to ride uphill.

Minuses it will be very shaky when riding fast over bumpy ground (downhill riding in particular), and the geometry will lean you over the front of the bike.

Travel 2.5-4.5 inches (65-110 mm) of up and down movement on the forks.

Great example Specialized RockHopper.

Cost range £300-500

Full suspension, lightweight XC bike

Features suspension forks, plus a suspension system for the back of the bike. Lightweight materials.

Great for going both uphill and downhill.

Pluses lightweight materials mean it'll be breeze up difficult climbs.

Minuses likely to break if ridden hard downhill. It might need lots of maintenance to keep it tuned.

Travel up to 6 inches (150 mm) of movement on both forks and rear suspension.

Great example Santa Cruz Superlight.

Cost range £800-2000.

XC/Freeride bike

Features suspension front and rear, sturdy materials.

Great for riding hard downhill or over jumps and northshore.

Pluses strong, won't break easily if dropped or ridden hard.

Minuses geometry and weight make it more difficult to ride uphill than a pure XC bike.

Travel Around 6 inches (150 mm) of travel on the forks and up to 7.5 inches (190 mm) of rear suspension travel.

Great example Yeti ASX.

Cost range £600-2500.

Terrain and terminology

Like any new pursuit (sailing, painting and decorating, car racing), there will be a whole load of words, terms and shortcuts to learn. Mountain biking culture is no different, so here is a list of unfamiliar words that you may come across:

Fire-road/forest road This is simply a dirt road that cuts through many of the UK's forest and are used by forest rangers and loggers for access. They are normally closed to the public with locked gates but easily accessible on a bike (and as such, can be used to get to the top of various hills by the quickest route).

Singletrack This is the terrain best suited for mountain biking (one of the UK magazines is simply named 'Singletrack'). It is a snaking path cutting through the terrain that has been hardened by much cycle use and is a clear marker as to which way other riders have been.

Purpose-built singletrack With the opening of more and more trail centres, purpose-built singletrack is increasingly common. It is usually built by mountain bikers and is like regular singletrack, but with the addition of thoughtful features (jumps, rocks etc), as well as a solid surface that – if possible – drains well and won't clog up with mud. Natural singletrack can be fantastic on its own, but purpose-built singletrack is probably what the majority of riders would prefer.

STACEY/THE-TRACK.CO.UK

The Track in Portreath's rhythm section in full effect.

Double track Double track is basically the mark left by off-road vehicles, or can be overgrown forest road. Again, it can be used to ascend hills or to work out where you are.

Bridleways/horse riding paths The UK is criss-crossed with bridleways and which are wider paths for horses, ramblers or other outdoor users. They are generally not as much fun as singletrack routes (as they are normally quite flat and featureless) but are definitely preferable to forest roads. They are often waymarked too.

Waymarked Waymarked routes are simply areas of singletrack or forest road that have posts at strategic places to show you the direction in which to ride.

Dirt jumps Dirt jumps are areas where local riders have built a network of jumps – normally in close proximity to each other – to pack as many into as short a run as possible.

Berm A berm is a banked turn.

Tabletop If you build a jump with a take off, a middle section that you could walk over, and a landing ramp, you've built a table top.

Gap If you remove the middle section from a tabletop (see above), you've now got a gap jump. Think of it as an Evil Kneivel jump with the buses removed.

Hip A hip jump is one in which the take off and landing are around 45 degrees from each other. So you launch heading straight onwards, and land riding to the left or right.

Rhythm section Dirt jumps come in 'sets' (single lines that can be ridden in one go), also known as

CHRIS MORAN

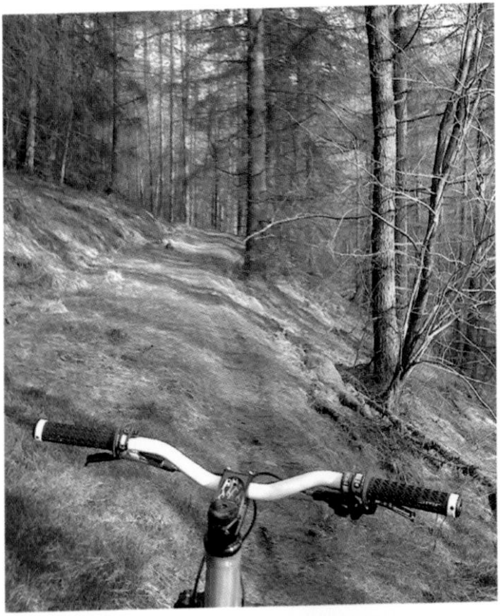

CHRIS MORAN

CHRIS MORAN

'rhythm sections' which means once you start getting air, you'll go again and again and again.

Chicken line This is an 'opt-out' line on where you might wish ride around a difficult section of trail.

Northshore Northshore is purpose-built (normally from planks of wood or felled logs), terrain that can be ridden over in order to test a rider's nerve and balance. The name comes from Vancouver Island's north shore area, where the ground is boggy and the local riders built bridge after bridge over muddy patches on their trails, and noticed they preferred riding the wood structures in the end.

Downhill This is simply singletrack that runs downhill and can feature lots of drops, jumps and tricky rock sections or root sections.

Rock Garden An area of downhill track which is littered with rocks and can be difficult to navigate down. Similar to a mogul field in skiing or snowboarding.

Tracks Tracks are simply trails.

Trails Tracks by another name. The 'path' on which you're riding.

Trials A trial is where potential criminals are put in front of a jury. It's also a style of riding where the idea is to jump your bike from object to object almost always hopping on your back wheel. Not to be confused with a trail (the 'a' and the 'i' are the opposite way around). Trial bikes are basically the 'kick start' of mountain biking.

Above: Singletrack ahead.
Far left: Forest roads can be a great way of getting to the top.
Left: Waymarkers at Drumlanrig.

Southwest England

- Overview 16
- Abbeyford Woods & Goldburn Northshore 18
- Asham Woods 19
- Ashton Court (The Timberland Trail) 19
- Aveton Gifford DJ 20
- Bath BMX Track 20
- Bradford Hollow 20
- How to pack your bike for trips 21
- Blandford UK Bike Park 22
- Buckland Rings 24
- Buriton Chalk Pits 24
- Canford Heath & Pit DH 25
- Cann Wood Trails 25
- Cheddar BMX 26
- Combe Sydenham 26
- Dartmoor National Park 27
- Decoy BMX 27
- Forest of Dean 28
- Haldon Forest Park 30
- Hidden Valley DJs 32
- Hook DJs 32
- Hundred Acre Wood 32
- Island Trails 33
- JLC Trails 33
- Leckhampton 33
- Leigh Woods 34
- Nationwide DJs 34
- Oasis DJs 35
- Patchway BMX DJs 35
- Pines Ridge 35
- Maddacleave Woods 36
- Mineral Tramways Project 38
- Poldice Valley Trails 40
- Portland Bill Quarries 41
- Local riders, Paul Blackburn 42
- Portsdown Hill 44
- Puddletown Woods 44
- Queen Elizabeth Country Park 45
- Randwick DH 46
- Red Hill Extreme 46
- Rogate 46
- Sandford DJ & DH 47
- Sheet DJs 47
- Still Woods 48
- 5 tips for trail etiquette 49
- Stoke Heights 50
- Stoughton Trails 50
- Stoke Woods 51
- The Track 52
- Triscombe DH 54
- Watchmoor Wood Bike Park 54
- Woodbury Common 55

The Forest of Dean's FODCA Trail in full flow. [ANDY LLOYD]

Southwest England

Trails...

1 Abbeyford Woods and Goldburn Northshore
2 Asham Woods
3 Ashton Court
4 Aveton Gifford
5 Bath BMX Track
6 Bradford Hollow
7 Blandford UK Bike Park
8 Buckland Rings
9 Buriton Chalk Pits
10 Canford Heath and Pit DH
11 Cann Wood Trails
12 Cheddar BMX
13 Combe Sydenham
14 Dartmoor National Park
15 Decoy BMX
16 Forest of Dean
17 Haldon Forest Park
18 Hidden Valley DJs
19 Hook DJs
20 Hundred Acre Wood
21 Island Trails
22 JLC Trails
23 Leckhampton
24 Leigh Woods
25 Nationwide DJs
26 Oasis DJs
27 Patchway BMX DJs
28 Pines Ridge
29 Maddacleave Woods
30 Mineral Tramways Project
31 Poldice Valley Trails
32 Portland Bill Quarries
33 Portsdown Hill
34 Puddletown Woods
35 Queen Elizabeth Country Park
36 Randwick DH
37 Red Hill Extreme
38 Rogate
39 Sandford DJs and DH
40 Sheet DJs
41 Still Woods
42 Stoke Heights
43 Stoughton Trails
44 Stoke Woods
45 The Track
46 Triscombe DH
47 Watchmoor Wood Bike Park
48 Woodbury Common

For the purposes of this book, the southwest of England comprises Cornwall, Devon, Somerset, Dorset, Wiltshire, Gloucestershire and Hampshire. Hampshire is perhaps not technically the southwest, but we had to put the border in somewhere, and – to us at least – heading in that direction makes me think of heading on holiday, and the New Forest and many of the beautiful spots in Dorset easily fit into that category.

The southwest of England is a great place to ride a mountain bike, whether you're local to Bristol, Exeter, Plymouth, Bath, Southampton or Portsmouth, or you're on a road trip from elsewhere. In fact, for visitors, mountain biking has become an extra attraction to an area that was already beckoning tourists from all corners of the UK. Witness the brilliant Minerals Tramways Project running through Redruth where the beginnings of a bike-specific tourist attraction much like the successful 7Stanes areas of Scotland are underway. By using the old railway infrastructures that linked the various mines of the area, The MTP offers a linked, family-friendly area that ticks every box on the mountain biker checklist, from the formidable dirt jumping site of The Track in Portreath, to the brilliant freeride and DH paradise of Poldice Valley, while at the same time being a great ride for families. It is also the only place in the UK where you can ride from the north coast to the south coast in a couple of hours. Add in some bike-friendly accommodation, and a trip to this part of the world becomes a must for all UK riders.

Geographically, the southwest has no actual mountains, but its hills are easily big enough to satisfy the local downhill and freeride enthusiasts. For visiting downhillers, it might be best to re-route over to south Wales, but for lovers of beautiful XC riding, great northshore, and for those who use their bikes to access some lovely remote cafés and wonderful vistas, the southwest is a perfect place to head. The spread-out countryside and scattering of small, picturesque villages has one more advantage too: hit many of the spots mentioned in this book through the off-season and you're likely to have them to yourself.

Local scene

From the very tip of Land's End to the Gloucestershire border, and all the way to the eastern edge of Hampshire, there are an untold number of mountain bikers busily building their own perfect trails. Like the rest of England, the land they're using is a mix of unauthorized sites, open access areas, bridleways, national parks, public rights of way, government-owned land, major road and motorway no-man's-land areas, areas of outstanding natural beauty and private land owned by a number of land-management organizations. Perhaps the biggest of these – The Forestry Commission – has been very open to the idea of local riders building their own trails on its land, and a forward-thinking policy that originated at the start of the new century has started to reap real rewards in many areas of the country, not least in the southwest. Abbeyford Woods, Cann Woods, Hundred Acre Wood, Leigh Woods, Puddletown Forest, Haldon Forest, Rogate and Stoke Heights are all examples of this partnership in action and a hearty thanks goes out to the guys and girls at the Forestry Commission for their work. Please respect all signs

Below: Haldon Hill has great views.
Bottom: Portreath's The Track.

CHRIS MORAN

STACEY/THE-TRACK.CO.UK

and closures pointed out by the FC as they are a very cool organization and the rangers almost always have your best interests at heart. Some areas, such as the popular downhill routes at Rowberrow Forest, have been omitted from this guide because the FC doesn't fully own the land used by riders and we have been asked not to include such sites. We do so obligingly.

Hubs

There are pockets of riders all over the southwest, but we'd single out the areas of Exeter, Bristol and Portsmouth as having fantastic local scenes. Bristol riders have the great spots of Leigh Woods, Asham Woods, Ashton Court and Still Woods to choose from, while Exeter's Haldon Park is one of the best sites in the whole of the southwest. Add in Pinesridge Trails, Woodbury Hill and Stoke Woods all within half an hour's drive, and it's one of the best cities for riders in the UK. Portsmouth has the brilliant trio of Rogate (an amazing Forestry Commission freeride and downhill partnership), the incredible Sheet dirt jumps and the very family-friendly Queen Elizabeth Country Park all on its doorstep. On top of this, the stand-alone UK Bike Park in Blandford, Dorset is easily worth a drive from any part of the UK, while the fantastic Minerals Tramway Project should see riders of all abilities and ages push West Cornwall high up the 'must visit' when it officially opens in September 2009.

The Mineral Tramways Project's Coast-to-Coast trail.

XXXXXXXXX

❺ Best rides in the southwest

There are plenty of stand-alone spots to head for in the southwest, but we think these are absolute gems and have to be on your list of places to visit in this area:

❶ The Mineral Tramways Project (incorporating The Track and Poldice Valley), page 38

A perfect, family-friendly route that ticks every box: beautiful scenery, wonderful pit stops and cafés, car-free, great bike-friendly accommodation and bike hire if you need it at The Bike Barn. And for better riders, The Track and Poldice Valley make it one of the best kept secrets in the UK.

❷ Haldon Freeride, page 30

This hill to the south of Exeter has everything - northshore, freeride, downhill, and some beautiful XC in a wonderfully unspoilt part of the country. A great atmosphere makes it perfect for all abilities.

❸ Dartmoor National Park, page 27

Who'd have thought that in an area of such outstanding beauty someone would be thoughtful enough to have started an uplift service? Lazy, XC perfection!

❹ Still Woods, page 48

Riders in Bristol have an embarrassment of choices, but Still Woods is the cherry on the top of a very downhill-rich cake.

❺ Blandford UK Bike Park, page 22

If you like jumping around on your bike, testing your balance skills, and racing fast downhill, then the UK Bike Park in Blandford, Dorset has to be bleeping very loudly on your radar.

↘1 Abbeyford Woods and Goldburn Northshore

XC DH N

Train station Okehampton
Nearest city Exeter
Sat Nav N/A

Location Heading south along the A30 take the first exit to Okehampton town centre and turn right at the first set of lights signposted North Road Industrial Estate. Turn left at the roundabout, then right at the T-junction, then take the first left and follow the road to the top of the hill to Abbeyford car park.

Facilities The riding area is Forestry Commission land and has no on-site facilities. Nearby Okehampton is a large town with plenty of food outlets and pubs, and is home to Moor Cycles (moorcycles.com), the nearest bike shop.

Overview Okefreeriders are a group of mountain bikers from the local area who have worked with the Forestry Commission and built up an impressive array of freeride, XC, downhill and Northshore trails in the area, all graded blue, red or black. Membership to the club costs £15 for the year (through their site okefreeriders.co.uk), which has downloadable trail maps and jpegs of their northshore set up.

XC There are no specific XC routes at Abbeyford, but the Okefreeriders club often meet and head out on rides in the surrounding countryside. There is also a huge amount of singletrack riding to be had in the general area including the cycle paths that criss-cross Dartmoor national park, and the famous Granite Way – a 12 km cycle route which starts in Okehampton and loops around through Lydford.

Downhill Abbeyford's downhill sections are short but sweet with plenty of rootsy, technical sections and interesting features to drop, avoid and ride over.

Freeride There is a tonne of freeride potential here, with new drops and lines being built all the time. The Goldburn Hill Northshore is perhaps the most obvious freeriding attraction, but lack of maintenance and problems with safety mean it is sometimes closed. If you live local, join the club, help maintain the wood and you'll have plenty of NS adventures!

Conditions The singletrack can be muddy in wet conditions and in winter.

ⓘ **More info** okefreeriders.co.uk.

JETHRO LOADER

Left: Banking on some good northshore.

↘2 Asham Woods

DH FR N

Train station Frome
Nearest city Bristol
Sat Nav BA11 4NL

Location Asham Woods are about 8 km to the east of Shepton Mallet on the A361. Turn off the road at Nunney, and go through the village taking Castle Hill Road out. After 250 m take another left (signed Leigh On Mendip), and Asham Woods is 1.5 km along this road on the left. Some signs indicate Torr Works Quarry, which is south-west to the riding.

Facilities No facilities but the nearest village is Nunney with local shops.

Overview There are DH trails, a freeride trail, and even some northshore (and more DH tracks in the woods), but it is infrequently maintained and has no official status so don't expect too much! However, if you're in the area it could be a great place to become involved with and start building on the already cool jumps and singletrack. Plus the quarry has some brilliant natural terrain and obstacles to take on. MBUK recently shot there with pro freerider Darren Bearclaw so there are definitely some good jumps!

Conditions Watch out for mud in winter or when it rains, but even then the quarry should still have some decent riding.

↘3 Ashton Court (The Timberland Trail)

Train station Bedminster Down
Nearest city Bristol
Sat Nav BS41 9JN

Location Leave the M5 at junction 18 and head down the A4 towards Bristol. When you get to Clifton Suspension bridge, cross it and head straight on towards Ashton Court which is well signed.

Facilities Ashton Court is a privately-owned manor house and surrounding area, and is home to concerts and many outdoor events. There are plenty of cafés and refreshment areas in the grounds. Cross back over Bristol's famous Clifton Suspension Bridge at the eastern corner of the park which leads to plenty of shops in Bristol itself.

Overview These trails circle the estate, with the yellow trail being the beginners'/family area and a perfect place for kids to get to grips with their bikes. The pink trail that runs through Fifty Acre Wood is more testing, but anyone looking for hardcore DH or XC action will be disappointed. This is mellow, singletrack territory in one of the UK's most spectacular settings, with

PAUL BLACKBURN

BRISTOLTRAILSGROUP@GMAIL.COM

a little purpose-built wood but generally natural terrain. There are 11 km of trails in total and they can get very busy.

Conditions Mud, concerts, and popular weekends are all potential hazards.

ⓘ **More info** The local scene site is bristoltrailsgroup.com, and there's a great page including a map of the trails at forestofavon.org.uk/out-and-about/cycle-routes/timberland-trail.

S4 Aveton Gifford DJs

DJ

Train station Ivybridge
Nearest city Plymouth
Sat Nav TQ7

Location Aveton Gifford is a tiny village in South Devon, about 5 km north of Kingsbridge. Heading south towards Aveton Gifford on the A379, take a left in the village and head towards the village of Loddiswell. At Loddiswell, from the corner of Village Cross Road and Fore Street, head north on the B3196 for about 100 m. Take the next right and as that road bends sharply to the right the dirt jumps are just next to the road on the left.

Facilities There's a shop in Loddiswell which is less than a minute's ride away.

Overview These dirt jumps are certainly not worth a long journey, but for local riders this is a one-line of DJs that might provide some fun with a couple of gaps and some tabletops.

S5 Bath BMX Track

DJ

Train station Oldfield Park/Bath Spa
Nearest city Bath
Sat Nav BA2 2AX

Location Bath BMX track is just to the south of Bath city centre. From the A36 Lower Bristol Road/ Rossiter Road, take the A367 south towards Peasedown St John. This road is called Wellsway. After 400 m take a right down Bloomfield Road. Bath BMX is about 200 m down this road, turn right at the entrance to Chelwood Drive, go to the far end of the car park and follow the path to the north.

Facilities The track is virtually in the city centre of Bath, so while there are few direct facilities on site, the nearest shops are minutes ride away.

Overview With the help of a £32,000 grant, and the hard work of local riders (particularly Steve at bath.madnutter.com), this is a fantastic, competition-standard BMX track with loads of whoops, berms, tables and gap jumps to practice on. Mountain bikers are welcome but helmets, sleeves and leg coverage are all mandatory.

Conditions The track is open in most conditions and dries out relatively quickly. The gate area is tarmacked and the DJs are purpose -built so perfect.

ⓘ **More info** bathbmx.com.

S6 Bradford Hollow

XC DJ

Train station Yeovil Junction/ Yeovil Pen Mill
Nearest city Bath/Exeter
Sat Nav DT9 6JN

Location Bradford Hollow is 1 km to the southeast of Yeovil. From Yeovil take the A30 in the direction of Sherborne. Cross the railway line, then the river, and take the second right marked Underdown Hollow. The dirt jumps are 100 m up this road on the right.

Facilities There are plenty of shops etc in nearby Yeovil, which is minutes' ride away.

Overview In the middle of a secluded wood, this could be good XC country, but most come here for the DJs in a clearing of the woods. There are several lines with gaps, tables and step ups with lines from medium to difficult. This isn't a place for learners, or worth a long journey, but those local riders with DJ experience will have a ball.

Conditions Avoid after heavy rain.

ⓘ **More info** Bradford Hollow has a few clips on Youtube.

How to pack your bike for trips
Sam Dale

Sam Dale is 19 and already a veteran of two UCI World Cup tours. Since the age of 15 he has been traveling to National Point series, Maxxis Cup and one-off events around Europe and the UK. He knows the inside of a Ford Transit better than the guy who designed it. Here are his 10 tips to packing your bike away for travel.

1 Number one has to be: get a bike bag off eBay. It should cost you less that £100 and definitely get one with a hard base and wheels. Some of those airports are massive, and without a bike bag some airlines won't let you on.

2 If you're going to spend money on anything, spend it on a good lightweight pump, a tool kit with good allen keys and some screwdrivers, and get a good pedal spanner.

3 What do I take apart first? I take the wheels off, then the handlebars and brake calipers, then the rear mech (the de-railer), then the pedals off, then I take my chain off to stop it hitting the frame, then I take the brake levers and the gear shifters off the handlebars too. It all goes in the bag.

CHRIS MORAN

4 Put the pedals in your normal clothes bag, but wrap them in something first, as they can scratch up anything they come into contact with.

5 Cut some stiff pipe big enough to go in the space where the hubs would go, to prevent your swing arm and your forks getting squashed. Keep your axel on for the same reason. You'll also want some cable ties for all the brake and gear cables. If you've got loads then just cut them when you take the bike apart and put new ones on when you put it back together.

6 Put a bit of plastic in between the brake pads so that if the lever gets accidentally squashed, it won't pull the pads together and the pistons won't get pushed out. They're a nightmare to get back in 'cos if there's no air in the brake system you'll have to re-bleed them.

7 Take your brake rotors off to stop them getting bent, and then put them in a bit of cardboard and tape it up to stop any oil or anything getting in there. If they get contaminated they won't be as effective.

8 Take a small bottle of oil to lube the chain with. Make sure it's got a tight top on it so it doesn't leak. Then chuck all your pads, protection wear and rain gear in with the bike to give it extra padding. Not your main clothes though – my sharp suits and going out wear are kept away from all that grease and oil!

9 Deflate tyres. Then cover your bike with all your pads and wet weather gear to give it some padding.

10 Last thing to do before you leave the house: check you're not overwwieght – 32 kg is the max for any one bike bag. You should be able to take in on pretty much all airlines. Easyjet and Ryan Air sting you for sporting luggage though, but BA are pretty good. That's how they make all their money innit?

Sweet, wondrous allen key.

↘7 Blandford UK Bike Park

Train station Gillingham
Nearest city Southampton
Sat Nav DT11 0TF
Opening times The park is run using club memberships so there are no opening times - members ride whenever they feel like it

JETHRO LOADER

JETHRO LOADER

Top: Push...
Above: Push...
Opposite page: ...And ye shall be rewarded.

Location The park, now named UK Bike Park but more commonly known as Blandford Freeride Park, is located at the top of Okeford Hill near Shillingstone in Dorset. Shillingstone itself is a very small village that has a couple of corner shops and traditional pubs, so just enough to make you comfortable for an overnight stay. The current size and nature of the park means that you are unlikely to stop for more than one night at a time. Blandford is on the A350 around 10 km south of Shaftesbury. From Blandford take the A357 north west in the direction of Sturminster Newton. Just after Shillingstone turn left into Shillingstone Lane towards Okeford Fitzpaine. There, turn left again towards Ibberton, and take the next left towards Turnworth. The UK Bike Park car park is about 1.5 km down this road on the right. The park itself is on the left.

Facilities Plenty – this is a purpose built mountain bike centre with a permanent uplift (using army-style trucks), although private hire is for a minimum of 10 riders (there are public days – check the website). Expect to pay around £20 for public use or £30 for private hire.

XC This is not a XC venue as it has no cross country trails; however, due to its multiple size obstacles, it is well suited to XC riders looking to develop their downhill or freeride handling.

Downhill This is a 125-m high hill (perfect height to push a bike up), with lines and options to the four main downhill routes – Big Grin, BTNE (Ben Terrace's Natural Extension), Dark Side and Devils Dyke. All the courses end up at Mix It Up – a natural bowl full of freeride obstacles and jumps to finish on. If you manage to book into one of the very popular uplift days you can link up the various different sections and hit a different route each time. The park is ideal for novice to intermediate riders as all the features have chicken lines for building up confidence. Expert or advanced riders may find that there is not much here to challenge them, but the park is constantly evolving with new lines of all sizes.

Freeride The park is a popular freeride venue and heavily leans towards this style of riding. In the park there are various ladder drops, gaps, a mini A-line style trail, plenty of small to medium jumps, and balance northshore features. The other routes are alternative DH courses or freeride mini trails in their own right. Berm Bandit, X up, Ladder Ally, Log Jam, Dirty Bomb, George and Zippy, Drop Three and Abyss can all be found in the flatter, summit area of the park and at the start of the downhill course.

Not to miss The foam pit will see most people practising their X-games moves.

JETHRO LOADER

Conditions It can get really boggy in the winter months if it's been raining.

Nearest Bike/Hire shop Bikelab (T01202 330011) are found in Poole which is a short drive away from the park; alternatively Torico Performance Bikes in Sturminster Newton (torico.co.uk) has a full range of demo bikes.

Local accommodation Pennhills Farm (T01258 860491) is actually located at the bottom of the freeride park so you couldn't be in a more convenient location. They are more than used to looking after mountain bikers.

Eating There is a range of hot and cold drinks available most days, with burger-style vans coming on weekends and race days.

ⓘ **More info** UK Bike Park, T07881571069, ukbikepark.com has jpeg trail maps which are available in hard copies on site.

> **Lowdown**

Locals do
Book very early to get on the uplift days.

Locals don't
Mind showing you around the trails.

Pros
Good progressive ride venue for novice/intermediate riders.

Good use of the land area.

Ideal day trip or weekend overnight venue.

Cons
Limited space on the public uplifts (but a group can book VIP lifts).

Riding could be exhausted after a couple of days.

↘8 Buckland Rings

DH FR 4X DJ

Train station Lymington Town/Sway
Nearest city Southampton
Sat Nav SO41 8LJ

Location Buckland Rings is on the southern edge of the New Forest, around 30 km to the east of Bournemouth and 30 km southwest of Southampton. From the M27 exit at junction 1 and take the A337 south through the forest towards Lymington. After about 10 km you'll exit the forest and start the approach to Lymington. Before you hit town, take a right onto Sway Road and follow it round to the right. After 200 m take a right and the dirt jumps are near the bottom of this road in the forest to the left and next to the railway line.

Facilities This is public-access forest land with no amenities, Lymington is a few minutes' ride away with plenty of shops for supplies. Nearest bike shop is CycleXperience in Brockenhurst (cyclex.co.uk, T01590 624204).

Overview This probably isn't worth a long journey, but the two disused quarries here have seen lots of work by the local bike scene. The biggest quarry is taken over with tables, gaps, step ups and speed drop-ins, while the smaller quarry is great for freeriders with plenty of Red Bull Rampage-style drops and cliffs. There's a DH trail (short but sweet) behind the woods and even a 4X course. All in all, a neat set-up.

Conditions This is mostly clay tracks and well-packed.

PAUL BLACKBURN

↘9 Buriton Chalk Pits

XC DH DJ

Train station Petersfield
Nearest city Portsmouth
Sat Nav GU31 5SH

Location Buriton Chalk Pits are around 5 km south of Petersfield in Surrey. From the A3, exit at the junction signposted to Buriton and Petersfield on the B2070. Head east off the A road for 100 m before turning right on Greenway Lane, heading towards Buriton. In Buriton village turn right into Kiln Lane and go uphill to the old signposts where there's a car park on the right and an opening to the left where the pits are signed.

Facilities Nearby Buriton has a corner shop, two pubs (the Five Bells and Robert Inn) and is a stunningly beautiful Hampshire village.

Overview This is low-budget downhill territory with some fantastic, empty woods to ride in (with one very obvious DH track from the wood entrance back to

Burton village) as well as the added bonus of a disused chalk quarry which has some dirt jumps built. The local scene are proud of their set up, but this isn't particularly worth a long journey (though it could be combined with a trip to nearby Sheet DJs and the brilliant Rogate DH tracks).

Conditions Chalk clay in the quarry and classic forest for the DH with a well-worn shale track that has re-inforced edges in places. Avoid after heavy rain.

↘10 Canford Heath and Pit DH

XC FR

Train station Parkstone/Branksome
Nearest city Bournemouth
Sat Nav BH21 3BA

CHRIS MORAN

Location Canford Heath and the Pit are just on the north west edge of Bournemouth. From the A31 heading into Bournemouth take the B3073 and then the A31 again towards Wimborne. Turn south at Oakley on the A341, and after 500 m take a left into Queen Anne Drive. Carry on for about 1 km and Canford Pit is behind the grassland on your right.

Facilities There are no facilities at the heath and pit but head into Oakley village which is a short ride away to the north for shops and supplies.

Overview Canford Heath has plenty of chalky and flinty singletrack for the XC enthusiast to explore, and is generally pretty empty. The bombhole and pit are a huge whole that freeriders have built drops, jumps and even some cliff drops around, in and out of. For local riders it's a bonus, but most agree it's not worth an enormous journey for.

Conditions Most routes chalky, but mud can be a problem.

ⓘ **More info** Locals The Dorset Rough Riders regularly ride at Canford, dorsetroughriders.co.uk.

↘11 Cann Wood Trails

DH FR

Train station Plymouth
Nearest city Plymouth
Sat Nav PL7 4DP

Location Cann Wood Trails are just north of Elfordleigh Golf Club, north of the town of Plympton/Colebrook which is east of Plymouth on the A38. From the A38 exit onto the B3416 heading to Plympton; after 1 km take a left into Plymbridge Road, then first right onto Boringdon Road, and follow this to the T junction. Take a right here then follow the road up to the left (Boringdon Hill), and past the Elfordleigh Hotel Golf and Country Club on your left. Park soon after in the Forestry Commission signed car park and Cann Woods are just to the north.

Facilities The Forestry Commission looks after the land, but there are few facilities other than a car park.

Overview Cann Wood Trails are predominantly freeride-based, with plenty of short downhill sections and trails and all sorts of drops and jumps hidden about the 10-mile or so network of trails. There are some easier routes, but the local scene have been riding in the area

PAUL BLACKBURN

for ages, and build increasingly challenging trails. As such, expect plenty of cool drops, interesting features and short but really sweet rides.

Conditions This is all forest land so plenty of roots and singletrack to be had, much of which is prone to mud in the winter due to the popularity of horse-riding in the area, although there are few walkers.

ⓘ **More info** The Cann Woods Maniacs have a Bebo page: bebo.com/CannWoods.

↘12 Cheddar BMX

Train station Worle/Western Milton
Nearest city Bristol
Sat Nav BS27 3DB

Location Broadway House is to the north of Cheddar, around 20 km to the southwest of Bristol. Exit the M5 at junction 22 and follow the A38 Bristol Road in the direction of Bristol. After around 1 km turn right onto the A371 at Axbridge. Head 2 km along this road and Broadway house is on the left, just before the roundabout.

Facilities Broadway House is a fully operational caravan park with showers, launderette, shop, music (and on-site PA when there are comps), food and accommodation (log cabins or caravans). Billed as a bike venue, they have bike wash facilities, a bar, and everything else an overnighter could wish for.

Overview This is a competition standard 4X track, with some decent dirt jumps including berms, gaps, whoops, tables and hips. There's also some fantastic XC in the surrounding hills including the awe-inspiring Cheddar Gauge. The house is home to the Cheddar Challenge.

Conditions The 4X track is purpose-built so works in most weather. Otherwise, much here is open farmland so avoid in the wind of after periods of rain.

ⓘ **More info** cheddarchallenge.com for up-to-date news on the local scene, or broadwayhousepark.co.uk for accommodation.

↘13 Combe Sydenham

Train station Bishop's Lydeard/Taunton
Nearest city Exeter/Bristol
Sat Nav TA4 4JG

Location Combe Sydenham Hall and Country Park estate can be found by exiting the M5 at junction 23, heading through Bridgwater and taking the A39 towards Minehead. About 1 km after the village of Williton, take a left and head down the B3190 towards Huish Barton. Take another left after 1 km, heading towards Monksilver. Combe Sydenham is about 500 m after Monksilver with various parking and facilities off the right of the road next to the manor house.

Facilities CSH&CP is a privately-owned manor house and park which has re-invented itself as a historical centre (Sir Francis Drake stayed there), as well as using its grounds as a 4x4 and mountain bike centre. Food and drinks available but only for group tours on admission.

Overview The DH course here is competition standard. Put £5 in the box at the entrance for the DH area (to the southwest of the car park), head up the fireroad and start the course: the first section is open farmland, dropping into berms and plunging into the forest.

BEN WAIN

The course has lots of features including areas that drop off the fire-road to singletrack through the forest, with great gap jumps – up to 20 ft – (with sneak-round tracks), tabletops, fast, open field sections and plenty of doubles.

Conditions The track can be gravelly and exposed, so avoid in high wind. But the forest sections are well covered, with the only problem being mud and water pipes breaking and flooding the course (it has happened!).

ⓘ **More info** Call before you leave (especially for longer journeys) as they often use the course land for mountain bike and motocross competitions, T01984 656284 or check the Information Britain site page on CSH&CP at information-britain.co.uk.

↘14 Dartmoor National Park

DH XC ...

Train station Newton Abbot
Nearest city Exeter/Plymouth
Sat Nav TQ13 9JQ

Location Dartmoor is a huge expanse of public-access moorland in Devon maintained by the Dartmoor National Park Authority, with plenty of starting and finishing points for the adventurous XC rider. Local riders tend to prefer routes which leave from Bovey Tracey. From the end of the M5, head down the A38 and take the Chudleigh Knighton exit. From there head west on the B3344 (Bradley Road) towards Bovey Tracey, go through the village of Bovey Tracey, cross the A382 and head straight on (the road changes to the B3387, but is the same road you were on), and the DNPA car park is signed first on the right.

Facilities Mountain biking is open to roads, bridleways and dedicated singletrack on Dartmoor with the Dartmoor Freewheeler (a Sunday minibus with trailer operating from April to September) taking riders to the centre of the moorland. The ride home is predominantly gentle downhill for families and learners.

Overview There are plenty of serious XC routes (for a map try the local rider website exmtb.co.uk), and long-distance enduro rides, many well signed. Beginners and families love the area, with the Granite Way (an 11 km scenic route from Okehampton to Lydford) taking in viaducts and areas of spectacular beauty.

Conditions Avoid in the wet; can be boggy for long periods in winter.

ⓘ **More info** dartmoor-npa.gov.uk has a great routes page, or try the Exeter local scene site; Bikus is a fantastic mountain bike shop in Bovey Tracey (T01626 833555, bikus.co.uk) with plenty of local knowledge.

↘15 Decoy BMX

DJ

Train station Exeter/Plymouth
Nearest city Newton Abbot
Sat Nav TQ12 1EJ

Location Decoy is just off Torquay Road, to the south of Newton Abbot town centre.

Facilities Decoy is a BMX track that was completed in 1998, and has a couple of tarmac circuits and some dirt jumps.

Overview This is a great place to practise some bike control, either around the surfaced BMX track itself, or on the dirt jumps which include tables, hips, double jumps, step-ups and some beginner jumps.

Conditions The surfaced track can be ridden in almost all weather apart from rain and the DJs are fine unless it's really muddy.

ⓘ **More info** Decoy has its own website, decoy-bmx.co.uk.

16 Forest of Dean

DH FR ...

Train station Lydney/Gloucester
Nearest city Gloucester
Sat Nav GL16 7EH
Opening times All day, 365 days per year. Free to use

Location The Forest of Dean is west of Gloucester and north of the Severn Channel. From Gloucester head west along the A48, turning towards Littledean at Elton on the B4226 (Elton Road). Carry on along this road and take a right after Speech House onto the B4234. Go up about 2 km and the Forest of Dean entrance is on the left and well signed.

Facilities Cannop Cycle Centre is an old Colliery centre and has a café. The trails are all well marked from the centre, and there is bike hire available from Pedalabikeaway Cycle Centre (although they're fairly basic bikes). Parking costs £3 for the day and food and drinks are also available from nearby Beechenhurst Lodge, all well signed. Trail maps can be purchased from Pedalabikeaway of the Forest of Dean offices in Coleford for 60p.

DARREN EDWARDS (FORESTRY COMMISSION)

XC The Family Cycle Trail runs through former railway lines, specially-laid singletrack and well-marked fireroads. It's a very picturesque route, perfect for families but, as you would imagine, short on challenges for the serious rider. The FODCA Trail (graded Red on the CTC classification and renamed the Freeminer Trail for 2009) is built and maintained by its original namesake, the Forest of Dean Cycle Association (in partnership with the Forestry Commission), and is a 4.5-km loop of challenging singletrack with switchback climbs, drops, root sections, hairpins, and some big jumps, all starting from the Cycle Centre. There's a little northshore but mostly armoured bridges and jump aids and there are plenty of low level cycle paths for simply getting out and about in the woods.

Downhill Although the downhill course at the Forest of Dean is not officially recognised or waymarked by the forestry, it has been in existence and hosting races since back in 1996 and – springing forward over 13 years – it is still a great ride. What the Forest of Dean lacks in vertical drop, it makes up for in variety and ease of sectioning and is good to shuttle, which is perhaps why it has remained a popular place to ride downhill despite the bigger hills of Wales being only one hour away.

Freeride There are quite a few features dotted around the forest built by riders. Near the cycle centre there are some old coal tips with a range of different sized jumps and steep banks to conquer. Up the road you will find The Dips – a prime play spot with a number of bowls with drops, small jumps and a small set of trail (more suited to beginner to intermediate), while just north of the Pedalabikeaway Centre there are some well-maintained DJs with a few tables and gaps – all popular with the local BMX scene.

Easy The Family Trail – perfect scenic rides, even on a hire bike.

Hard The FODCA/Freeminer trail is a must, while there's a new 12 km Enduro trail in the planning stages which could be a challenge for good XC riders.

Not to miss A run of the classic downhill which can be ridden on any of today's suspension trail bikes.

Remember to avoid Some of the features and jumps are badly built so check before you ride.

Nearest Bike/Hire shop Cannop Cycle Centre.

Local accommodation
For B&B try Allary House (T01594 835206) or Lower Perrygrove Farm (T01594 833187). There are plenty of camping and caravanning sites in the forest of Dean – try Bracelands (T0131 314 6505). There are also many cottages and

buildings that can be hired for self catering groups – try Stank Farm (T01594 832203).

Eating Cannop Cycle Centre has drinks and snacks, and nearby Coleford has pubs and shops. The Ostrich Inn (T01594 833260) has hearty meals.

ⓘ **More info** The Forest of Dean has its own page on the Forestry Commission website, forestry.gov.uk; the Forest of Dean Cycle Association has its own site fodca.org.uk, and the Pedalabikeaway Cycle Centre can be found at pedalabikeaway.com, T01594 860026. Coleford Tourist Information centre T01594 812338.

> Lowdown

Locals do

Ride up to the dips and play up there before riding one of the many descents back towards the centre.

Use this as a great night-riding spot as there are plenty of trails that are kind to night riders.

Locals don't

Always ride up the hills – you can shuttle it.

Forget to pay and display – the money will benefit the cycle facilities.

Pros

Super family riding area, with expansive flat routes.

Fun short trails, lots of good singletrack.

A great place for XC riders to sample downhill as the courses are not too technical.

Cons

Lots of roads in the area to cross.

Not perhaps the same variety for expert riders found in some regions.

There is no formal uplift arrangement at the Forest of Dean but public roads run through the wood and it can be shuttled very easily with your own vehicles, making it a very popular destination.

DARREN EDWARDS/FORESTRY COMMISSION

↘17 Haldon Forest Park

Train station Exeter St Thomas
Nearest city Exeter
Sat Nav EX6 7XR
Opening times This is Forestry Commission-owned land which is open year round, with no time limits. However, please check the website as essential repairs and building work will often close certain trails

CHRIS MORAN

CHRIS MORAN

Location From the M5 head towards Exeter where the motorway ends, and carry on down the A38 towards Plymouth. On the hill as you exit the city, take the turn-off signposted for Exeter Race Course (it's a brown sign with a picture of horses), then turn right (going under the A38) and follow the Forest Park Centre signs. Carry on along this road (past the Haldon sign), and the car park is on the left.

Facilities Where to start? Haldon is a great example of what happens when riders get together with the Forestry Commission and make incredible use of the available land. Haldon is rightly up there as one of the best UK trail centres with something for everyone, whether you're looking for a family day out with the kids and hoping to get them into the sport, you're a freestyle pro or you're taking your first tentative steps on northshore. All done with an ethos of respect for the environment that goes down to the choice of wood used to build obstacles.

XC There is a huge XC scene at Haldon, with around 8 km of virtually purpose-built trails at your disposal. All trails are well signposted and go from gentle sections of rollable singletrack through incredible forest to gentle northshore bridges and armoured crossings over sections of boggy land of small streams, through to fun and challenging rock gardens. There's a downloadable map at the Haldon website. Because of the bridges, the trail stays open throughout most weather conditions. The Family Cycle Trail and the Adventure Cycle Trail have been built with families and intermediates in mind.

Downhill Haldon doesn't offer any specific DH routes, but the Adventure Trail and Red Trail have sections that DH riders would appreciate.

Freeride A freeride haven, Haldon's local scene put much of their efforts into making the designated 'Freeride Area and Trail' the best they can, meaning

CHRIS MORAN

there are plenty of decent jumps, wall rides, berms, skinnis, step ups, platforms, rock drops, and some brilliantly innovative northshore. Currently there's a 15-and 20-ft gap jump, and, if all goes to plan, there'll be plenty of new wood installed for the summer. Again, this is all done with the best interests of the forest in mind, so expect the features to use existing tree routes, natural terrain and to blend in well with the local surrounds. The Freeride Area is classed as double black, meaning it should be for experts only, but there are plenty of jumps on the other parts of the hill to build up confidence in all riders.

Easy Start out on the 'Family Cycle Trail' and work your way up to the

'Adventure Cycle Trail'. Make sure you have mastered what you're riding now before moving onto something much bigger.

Hard The Freeride Area is testing enough for experts.

Not to miss The growing Northshore areas.

Remember to avoid Check the Haldon Freeride website to see if there are any closures before leaving the house!

Nearest Bike/Hire shop Sidwell Bikes in Exeter are the local hardcore mountain bike shop, sidwellcycles.co.uk.

Local accommodation Upcott House is a bike-friendly Edwardian house on the edge of Dartmoor and offers B&B accommodation, T01837 53743, upcotthouse.com.

Eating Haldon has a café at the Forest Park Centre.

ⓘ **More info** Haldon Freeride haldonfreeride.org, Exeter Mountain Bike Club embc.uk.net, The Forestry Commission Haldon forestry.gov.uk.

> Lowdown

Locals do:
Ride amazingly well (as to be expected with this on their doorstep).

Join up as a member and get exclusive stickers and join in on build days.

Locals don't
Build anything illegally.

Leave anything behind in the forest.

Pros
One of UK's great trail centres.

Shining example of co-operation with the Forestry Commission.

Cons
No great DH tracks.

As a co-op organization relying on volunteers, new areas build up slowly.

CHRIS MORAN

↘18 Hidden Valley DJs

XC DH DJ

Train station Hamworthy
Nearest city Bournemouth
Sat Nav BH17 7YR

Location This predominantly freeride area is located on the west side of Bournemouth. Heading out of Bournemouth on the A35 towards Dorchester, take a right signposted Creekmore. Go under the A35 and straight over the next roundabout. This is Longmeadow Lane. Park at the end and enter Upton Heath on the left. Hidden Valley is about 200 m to the east of where you've parked and is a large clay quarry.

Facilities Creekmoor has plenty of corner shops, etc for refreshments.

Overview This area is also known as the Clay Pits, and is popular with the local scene due to the brilliant dirt jumps (featuring some big jumps, step downs, drops, tables, hips and good berms), with great drop-ins on the bowl, which gives it an almost skatepark feel. There are also some short but sweet DH trails and plenty of XC singletrack surrounding the site. Well worth a visit if you're in the area.

Conditions This is mostly clay. Avoid when wet, but great for shaping!

↘19 Hook DJs

DJ

Train station Swanwick
Nearest city Southampton
Sat Nav SO31 9JH

Location Hook DJs are just to the south of Locks Heath, which is around 6 km southeast of Southampton. Leave the M27 at junction 9 and head south on the A3051 towards Locks Heath. At the next roundabout take the A27 towards Titchfield, and after 1 km take a right at the roundabout onto Warsash Road. Follow this road and take a left off after 1 km onto Hook Lane. This turns into Fleet End Road; take another left into New Road. Park after the line of houses and the DJs are just on the other side of the copse to the left.

Facilities Warsash is the nearby village with shops and amenities.

Overview This is council land and the DJs have been built with local permission. They're nothing too spectacular, and not really worth a drive, but local Southampton riders might make use of the couple of lines of gaps, tables and hips on offer.

Conditions This is open grassland next to a copse of trees in a popular dog-walking area. Avoid after rain as it can get muddy.

↘20 Hundred Acre Wood

XC

Train station Fareham/Porchester/Botley
Nearest city Portsmouth/Southampton
Sat Nav PO17 6HS

Location Hundred Acres is around 5 km north of Fareham, Hampshire, between Southampton and Portsmouth. Leave the M27 at junction 10 and head up the A32 Hoads Hill road. At Wickham, turn east (right) onto the B2177 Southwick Road and carry on for 1 km, then take a left into Hundred Acres Road. Carry on down here for 1 km and park at the Hundred Acre Forestry Commission car park.

Overview There are plenty of gentle and fun XC routes that criss-cross this picturesque tract of land in the Hampshire countryside. Many of these are signed by the FC, and cutting off the family routes are plenty of good trails that might be a little more testing for better riders and extend as far as you could wish to ride in a day. Recommended for adventurous riders who like to route-find.

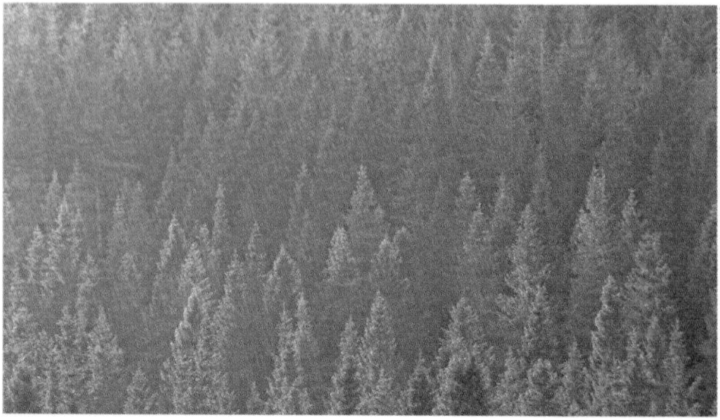

CHRIS MORAN

Conditions Most routes are fantastic singletrack or bridleways and tend to be gravelly and exposed, so avoid in high wind. As always, mud is a frequent problem.

↘21 Island Trails

DJ

Train station Havant
Nearest city Portsmouth
Sat Nav PO11 0ED

Location Hayling Island is just off Havant, to the east of Portsmouth. From the A27 Havant Bypass take the A3023 to Hayling Island. Carry on for 3 km past North Hayling on your left, then through Stoke, then before South Hayling take a right into Station Road. Head along there for 400 m then take a right into Furniss Way. Park at the end and the DJs are in front of you.

Facilities Nearby South Hayling has shops and amenities.

Overview This is a Havant Council supported project and aims to have over 18 well-maintained jumps with 6 lines ranging from intermediate to super pro. Not much time to prepare yourself for the next hit. Well worth a visit if you're nearby and want to improve your dirt jumping skills. There are also some more beginner-oriented DJs if you head back out on the A3023 north. The Esso DJs are just opposite Ave Road which is off to the right of the A3023.

Conditions This is well-drained area that has been purpose-built, but will still be off limits in bad weather.

↘22 JLC Trails

DJ

Train station Polsloe Bridge
Nearest city Exeter
Sat Nav EX1 3DS

Location Take the Honiton Road (the A3015) from junction 29 off the M5 heading towards Exeter. Around a mile from the motorway, turn right into Sweetbrier Lane. At the end of the road, turn left onto Whipton Lane, then immediately right into George Close. There are a series of football pitches at the end of the road and JLC trails are halfway along on the left. Alternatively, find Polsloe Bridge Train station – the park land is directly to the south.

Facilities This is Exeter so there are plenty of nearby corner shops as you would expect in a city centre. However, the trails are hand-built on the side of public parkland and there are no immediate facilities.

Overview JLC are primarily BMX DJs, with lots of gaps, berms and drop-ins all condensed into a small, level area the size of a five -a-side pitch. The jumps are out in the open, and right next to five football pitches in the middle of a big city, so expect it to be busy if you turn up on a weekend. Expect it to be as pikey as any other inner-city skate park or BMX area. This is no place for learners, and respect must be afforded the locals who have put an enormous effort into building the jumps.

Conditions Rain renders the DJs unridable.

ⓘ **More info** jlctrails.net.

↘23 Leckhampton

XC DH FR

Train station Chelthenham Spa
Nearest city Cheltenham
Sat Nav GL53 9QQ

Location Leckhampton DH is around 2 km south of Cheltenham town centre. From the M5 leave at junction 11 and head along the A40 to Cheltenham town centre. When you get there take the A46 south (the Bath Road), and after a few hundred metres take a left onto the B4070 Leckhampton Road. Head down here past the rehab hospital on the left and Leckhampton Woods are straight on, just before Daisybank Road on the left.

Facilities Leckhampton and Cheltenham are right on your doorstep with plenty of shops.

Overview Several downhill trails snaking through the woods and all are short but incredibly sweet, with plenty of drops, step ups, and interesting terrain to ride. There are steep, technical sections on some, with roots and loose ground as well as off-cambers to ride. There's everything here from XC-style riding to difficult DH.

Conditions This is mostly singletrack through forest land. Avoid after periods of rain.

ⓘ **More info** The local riders are rightly proud of their area, and have built the site thecorrective.com to help get council support and to welcome diggers to maintain and increase the scene here, at Cleave Hill and in Cheltenham.

↘24 Leigh Woods

XC DH FR

Train station Bedminster Down

Nearest city Bristol

Sat Nav BS41 9JN (for Ashton Court next door)

Location Leigh Woods are next door to Bristol's Ashton Court and just to the north of Clifton Suspension Bridge on the western edge of the River Avon gorge.

FORESTRY COMMISSION

Facilities Leigh Woods are minutes from Clifton, which has plenty of shops and amenities, and there are often burger vans selling refreshments on site.

Overview There is plenty of well-marked singletrack at Leigh Woods with the impressive Avon Gorge and the famous landmark of Clifton Suspension Bridge to add to a day here. There are three entrances – from North Road, from the Forestry Commission entrance 2 km east of Abbots Leigh Village or by the River Avon trail around 3 km north of Clifton Suspension Bridge. This is the steepest section so it might be worth finishing your day exiting here. There are plenty of XC loops and the occasional bit of DH and freeride fun. It's basically a more hardcore scene than Ashton Court, but still with the emphasis on fun.

Conditions Avoid in muddy conditions.

ⓘ **More info** Check out the Bristolian local scene – bristoltrailsgroup.com.

FORESTRY COMMISSION

↘25 Nationwide DJs

XC DJ

Train station Swindon

Nearest city Bath/Reading/Bristol

Sat Nav SN38 1NW

Location Croft Community Cycle Trail (also known as Nationwide DJs because they're opposite the Nationwide Building Society HQ) are just to the south of Swindon, between the town centre and the M4. Leave the M4 at junction 15 and head north on the A419 Marlborough Road. Take the A4259 – the first left at the roundabout – and then the first left at the next roundabout onto the B4006 (also called Marlborough Road). Take the second left off this road (Piper Way), and the DJs are about 100 m down here opposite the Nationwide HQ.

Facilities Swindon is just up the road and there are plenty of local shops, etc.

Overview There's a 1 km purpose-built XC loop in the woods, put together by a Nationwide employee named Steve Smith, and with help from the building society, local council and a national lottery grant. The XC loop is well signed, and should be expanded to 5 km soon. The current trail is largely tame and built for family cycling, but the dirt jumps are up and running and feature some decent tables, gaps and step-ups.

Conditions This is a purpose-built trail and should work in most weather, but avoid after a period of heavy rain.

↘26 Oasis DJs

DJ

Train station Swindon
Nearest city Bath/Reading/Bristol
Sat Nav SN2 1EJ

Location Oasis is a BMX track with some fairly good jumps in the centre of Swindon. From the M4 leave at junction 16 and head up the A3102 Great Western Way northwards towards Swindon. After 2 km take the B4006 (it's still the Great Western Way) and follow signs for Hawkesworth Trading Estate. Go into the estate and take Newcome Drive all the way to the end. Park here and the DJs are right in front of you.

Facilities Swindon has plenty of shops and cafés on hand. You're right in town.

Overview Certainly not worth a long journey, but the Oasis BMX track is good for local riders to get some dirt jump practice in. The area is popular with BMXers and dirt jumpers, with a decent loop course on hand with plenty of gaps, berms and tables to get air on. There's a gate and drop in too.

Conditions Gravel and dirt – already built with little area for improvement.

↘27 Patchway BMX DJs

DJ

Train station Patchway
Nearest city Bristol
Sat Nav BS32 4UD

Location Patchway is just off the M5 at the north edge of Bristol in the borough of Patchway. Exit the motorway at junction 16, and head south on the A38 Gloucester Road. After 1 km turn off the A38 to the right, and at the roundabout take a right down Coniston Road. After 400 m, take another right down Waterside Drive. The track is just to the right and clearly visible.

Facilities Patchway has plenty of shops and amenities nearby.

Overview Home of Bristol's BMX Club, this is a competition standard track which has been recently renovated to a high standard. The track features plenty of berms, rollers, gaps, tables and a drop-in start gate.

Conditions Well maintained but avoid after rain.

ⓘ **More info** Check out the local scene at bristolbmxclub.com

↘28 Pines Ridge

XC DJ

Train station Lympstone Village
Nearest city Exeter
Sat Nav EX8 5ED (the trails are around 100 m north of this address)

Location From the M5 (junction 30), take the A376 to Clyst St George, where the B3179 (Woodbury Road) splits towards Woodbury. Go through the village and then turn right at the crossroads about 1 km after the village (this will take you onto the B3180 heading towards Budleigh Salterton). Go south down this road for 1.5 km, then take a left onto the next road, in the direction of Yettington. Turn left into the first car park; Pinesridge Trails are through the trees.

Facilities There are no readily available facilities at these trails, but the nearest shops, etc can be found in Yettington.

Overview This is a joint dirt jumping, freeride and XC area, just to the south of Woodbury Common and for the more hardcore riders out there. The tree jump is perfect for learners, and also has a transfer line. There are plenty of drops, gaps and bowls and the hardpack soil is great for building jump lines. The area has been built primarily by a crew of riders from Exmouth and Exeter and has everything from 2-ft learner jumps through to 18-ft gaps. Turn up ready to help build and you're sure to get a fine welcome.

Conditions Avoid if it's been raining.

ⓘ **More info** Check out the Pinesridge mini-site – freewebs.com/pinesridgetrails.

↘29 Maddacleave Woods

XC DH FR

Train station Gunnislake

Nearest city Plymouth

Sat Nav PL19 9DP (for Dartmoor Cycles)

Opening times The trails are on private land and can only be ridden on open days, weekends and holidays and are only available to member riders. Contact Woodland Riders (woodlandriders.com) to join; membership is currently £25 per year, or a day pass costs around £8. Uplift fees are likely to be around £25 for the day. There is no trail map available at present although all trails are shown on the information board at the car park

JACOBGIBBONS.CO.UK

Location From Tavistock, take the A390 west towards Gulworthy. Then head south (taking a left) on the B3257 towards Morwell where the road forks and you take the right-hand road for 500 m. Just after the road turns sharply to the right take a left exit which is the access track to Maddacleave Woods. Be warned though – you must be a member to ride here, so it's best to head to Dartmoor Cycles in Tavistock first or see below.

Facilities The trails are situated on the steep face next to the Tamar river, overlooking Cornwall. The woods are a mixture of plantation and broadleaf and house some spectacular rock formations that jut-out over the severe slope. The trails are cut into this steep slope with several permanent downhill routes; two are aimed at experts whilst the third is more gentle and suitable to ride on both XC and downhill bikes. Trails are constantly being built and the rock here makes up a large proportion of the trails features as there are exposed rock outcrops and loose rock fragments littering the hill.

XC The third red downhill route also acts as a short XC loop as there is a trail to return to the top. Whilst overall distance of this loop is relatively very short, it is packed with interesting features and can be sessioned again and again. There are paths going from this venue out to other general cycle paths in the Tamar Valley that link many of the heritage sites, but they are not designed specifically for mountain bikes. However, there is some excellent XC riding on Dartmoor, which is an expansive moorland National Park. You should not ride out onto the moor without being prepared though, as the weather can change very quickly and it is easy to lose your way. Take a map and compass or GPS and you'll have a great time.

Downhill This is primarily a downhill venue with several courses that will test all riders' abilities including The Corkscrew (an all-weather track which is fast and flowing), and Rich's Course (technical). The black routes should only be attempted by expert downhillers, who will love the challenging features on offer from this hill. It is a national standard competition trail, though many have commented on it being of international competition difficulty. The red trail runs down the hill following much gentler gradients and with less technical features, more suitable for riders with less downhill experience.

Freeride There are no stand alone freeride stunts or trails; however some of the harder lines and bigger jumps on the downhill routes will challenge all but the professional freeriders, so a day's riding using the uplifts will appeal to all freeriders.

JACOBGIBBONS.CO.UK

Easy Ride the red easier trail a few times to learn to cope with the obstacles found on the trail.

Hard For expert riders it will probably take more than a full day's riding to master all the lines and options on the two more technical downhill runs.

Not to miss A run down the red route as it flows perfectly.

Remember to avoid It is an old tin mining site so stick to the marked trails at all times.

Nearest Bike/Hire shop Dartmoor Cycles in Tavistock – (T01822 618178, dartmoorcycles.co.uk).

Local accommodation There is no shortage of B&Bs, either in town or on many of the farmhouses in the area. Try former railway station Brentor Station (T01822 810403) or Sunnymead (T01822 612801).

Eating For something to keep you going when out in the woods stock up on pasties from the Original Pasty House (T01822 616003); they have 13 different flavours to choose from. In the evening try Montery Jack's (T01822 612145) for a range of enchiladas and tacos.

ⓘ **More info** Dartmoor Cycles are the main hub for the centre, although Maddacleave does have its own site at woodlandriders.com.

> Lowdown

☻ Locals do

Use the uplift facility to get the most out of a day on the hill.

Ride within their own abilities.

☹ Locals don't

Ride here when it's very wet – the rock can be very slippery.

Ride on their own or without a phone.

✔ Pros

One of the most technical downhill facilities in the UK.

A well managed facility.

✖ Cons

Riders looking to get some miles under their belt will have to look elsewhere.

Members only and with strict rules (although sensible ones).

↘30 Mineral Tramways Project

XC DH FR

Train station Redruth
Nearest city Plymouth
Sat Nav TR16 5UF

Location The Mineral Tramways Project is a range of sites that make use of the ex-mining railway lines to take in the beautiful countryside in the southwest of Cornwall. For 2009, the best trail to head for would be the Coast to Coast Trail, which starts at the Bike Barn, part of the fantastic Elm Farm Cycle Centre set up just on the outskirts of Portreath. To get to Elm Farm, head down the A30 to Redruth, then take the B3300 New Portreath Road north (right), in the direction of Portreath/Cambrose. After 1 km take a right into Cambrose and through the village on Chapel Hill. Carry along this road for 1 km and the Bike Barn and Elm Farm Cycle Centre are signposted off to the left.

Facilities Elm Farm Cycle Centre is the full set-up, with Cornwall's leading bike shop The Bike Barn (thebikebarn.org), as well as the official Trail Information Centre with info and maps on the Mineral Tramways Project incorporating the Coast to Coast Trail, bike hire, guides, teaching, campsite, B&B, holiday cottages and maps. The MTP has over 60 km of trails, making use of the disused railway lines that fell into neglect following the dismantling of Cornwall's mining industry. The trails can be ridden on their own or used to link up with some of the fantastic downhill sites in the area (such as Poldice Valley Trails), or the brilliant dirt jumping site of The Track in Portreath, plus many kilometres of singletrack offshoots.

Overview This is a fantastic project, linking up several well-known mountain bike sites in the southwest, as well as adding in all the infrastructure needed to bring families down to this part of the world on weekend or week-long holidays. The jewel in the crown is the Coast to Coast Trail, a 15-km ride (or 30 km if you loop it), from the north coast of Cornwall to the south coast town of Devoran (where a stop at The Quay Inn is a must), enabling you to brag that you've ridden from the top to the bottom of England. Much of the trail is very pleasant and easy riding, perfect for families; if you're looking for more adventurous areas they are easily found however and the Elm Farm crew will be happy to point out off-shoot areas that suit your ability level.

ROGER KNIGHT

Terrain The MTP features disused embankment riding, and is mostly level, pleasant family riding. But using the trails to access the singletrack, downhill or dirtjumping facilities nearby will bring you into contact with every grade of terrain from the easiest green trails to the most difficult of black runs.

XC The Coast to Coast trail is the main one here, but the involvement of Cornwall County Council means the project is set to grow and grow. Nothing is waymarked as yet (though maps are available from Elm Farm), but expect this to change in the near future.

Downhill See the Poldice Valley pages.

ROGER KNIGHT

The Coast-to-Coast trail, 12 miles of gentle riding.

Dirtjumps/Freeride The Track in Portreath is one of the UK's best dirt jump sites with every range of jump from beginner, to foam pit, to the most enormous gaps imaginable. See The Track's stand-alone pages for more details.

Not to miss The Coast to Coast Trail is the flagship for 2009, with its grand opening due in September 09.

Remember to avoid Leaving the camera at home – this is beautiful scenery.

Nearest Bike/Hire shop The Bike Barn (thebikebarn.org) is in Elm Farm.

Local accommodation
Elm Farm has a campsite, B&B, and holiday cottages to stay in.

ⓘ **More info** For all info on the MTP and the Coast to Coast Trail, please check out the Bike Barn and Elm Farm websites – bikebarn.org and, elm-farm.co.uk, or get in touch with Roger Knight on T01209 891498, bikes@thebikebarn.org.

> **Lowdown**

Locals do
Use the tramways to get to some of the UK's best dirt jump and downhill sites.

Locals don't
Have much to worry about in this part of the world!

Pros
A fantastic, new venture opening up Cornwall to the possibilities of mountain biking.

Cons
Not fully waymarked (yet, when book went to print).

↘31 Poldice Valley Trails

XC DH FR DJ

Train station Redruth/Perranwell
Nearest city Plymouth
Sat Nav TR4 8QZ (for bike Chain Bissoe), TR16 5UF (for the Bike Barn)

Location Poldice is just to the north of the village of Carnon Downs which is on the A39 halfway between Falmouth and Truro in Cornwall. This is a disused mine and can be accessed from the Mineral Tramways Project. Please call into either The Bike Barn in Portreath (bikebarn.org) or Bike Chain Bissoe near the Old Conns Works (cornwallcyclehire.com) for directions, maps, bike hire and snacks. Or, if you want to head straight to the valley, head south on the A30 towards Redruth, and take the Redruth North exit onto the A3047. At the first roundabout take the first exit almost back on yourself onto the B3298, then take a right off this road (though still following the B3298) after 400 m. Follow this road for 2 km to St Day, then take a left and follow the back roads towards Twelveheads. Poldice Valley is halfway between St Day and Twelveheads, and the backroads are unmarked and unsigned so it's best to ask someone in the village how to get to the entrance.

ROGER KNIGHT

Facilities There isn't much for the visiting rider at the valley DH tracks, just some fantastic trails, but nearby Falmouth can provide lots of entertainment (it's a University town), and a night out in St Ives is always legendary. If you fancy a break you could join the Mineral Tramways Project and hit either of the bike shop/visitor centres above and get a snack.

Overview These are home-built and maintained trails, in the classic wrangle with the local council over land use and – as it's a disused mine – safety issues, but there's a strong group in the area and a great scene. Expect constant improvements. The area is predominantly used by freeriders, with some good DJs and interesting features to ride on and makes a welcome change for those in the SW who have extensively ridden at The Track.

Terrain The red clay soil gives the freeride area the name 'Mars'; elsewhere it can be rocky.

XC There are plenty of loops nearby, and the coastal routes in the area are always popular, but there are no specific XC routes that start and finish here.

ROGER KNIGHT

Downhill The riders are in constant battle with the council over safety, especially in the nearby Unity Woods, but there are some good, short but interesting downhill sections much of the time.

DJs The area is predominantly freeride based, and the Mars area now has a step-down gap, plenty of gaps and lines and many other interesting features for all abilities to ride.

Conditions The XC routes are hard-packed dirt singletrack. The area is popular with walkers but well known as a mountain biking centre so expect to see plenty of bikes.

ⓘ **More info** To get involved with the great local scene, join their Facebook group under the search 'Cornwall Freeriders'.

↘32 Portland Bill Quarries

XC DJ

Train station Weymouth
Nearest city Exeter
Sat Nav DT5 2JT (for the Portland Tourist Information Centre)

PAUL BLACKBURN

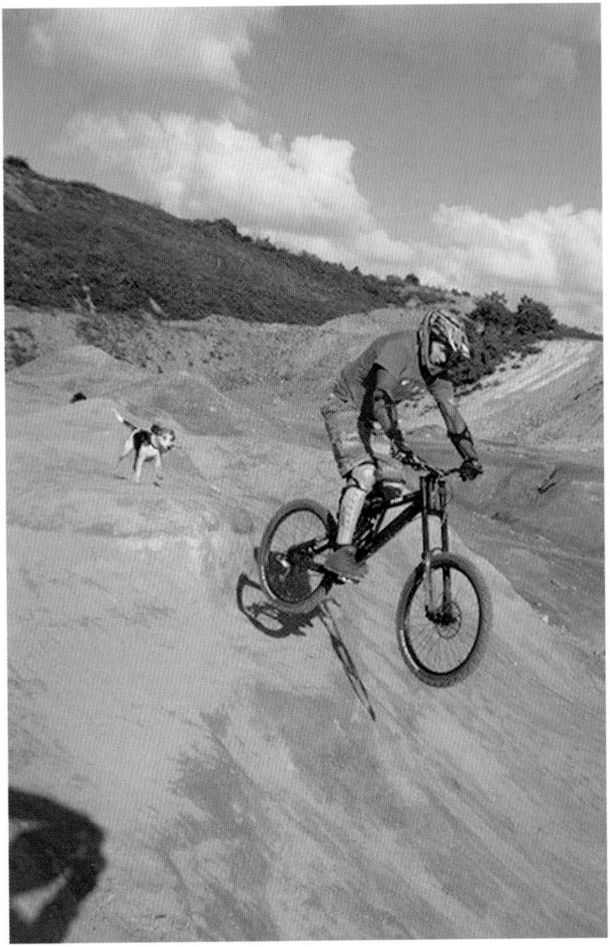

Location Portland Bill is an outcrop of limestone on the south coast of Dorset. It is where much of the stone from the UK's finest buildings has come from, and as such is riddled with quarries. Head south from Dorchester on the A354 and the road goes straight to Portland. Head all the way down to the Portland Tourist Information Centre, located at the lighthouse on the southern tip, and grab a map of the island with the below quarries located thereon.

Facilities There are shops in Portland and plenty of smaller food and refreshment outlets between the spots.

Overview There's the Old Quarry (just to the south of Glacis Road), New Ground (off New Ground Road), The Gore (to the east of where Easton Lane meets Inmosthay), Tout Quarry (200 m to the east of where Weston Road turns into Reforne), and simply, The Quarry (just north of where Weston Road turns into Pennsylvania Road). All are filled with all manner of dirt jumping treasures such as berms, drop-ins, tables, gaps and great for make-shift 4X tracks. It's all totally illegal, but there's a good scene so you're likely to meet others. There is some beautiful XC riding to be had around the coast too.

Conditions This is almost all stone quarry, so it's shaley and dusty and exposed.

ⓘ **More info** portlandbill.co.uk.

Local riders
Paul Blackburn

Bike Commencal Meta 5.5 XT
Local spot Poldice Valley
Club member Cornwall Freeriders
Age 31
Type of rider All Mountain (everything)

Where's the one place you'd recommend above all, for those coming to the southwest?

PB Gawton in Tavistock. There's a mix of double black DH with fast-flowing singletrack descents. It's an amazing place but only for the experienced rider really.

Where has the best XC?

PB Afan in Wales! No, here we've got everything, from epic coast rides from Portreah to St Ives that are amazing; tight and rocky climbs and miles and miles of singletrack with stunning cliff-top views, the open boggy, grassy, rocky trails through Bodmin Moor and the fun blasts through woods such as Cardinham in Bodmin, Tehidy in Redruth or Idless in Truro. All offer rooty, muddy trails tucked away in the deepest part of the wood, so hours of exploring is to be had.

Where is the best Downhill?

PB Gawton in Tavistock is amazing, offering a world-class super steep and tech downhill line called super-tavi with berms, switchbacks, huge jumps (with chicken runs), off-camber rooty sections and flat out sections – it's not for the faint hearted. Also there is a lovely fast-flowing track called HSD that weaves through the trees at a great pace where the only thing holding you back is your own brakes; then there is the Egypt trail which defines the word STEEEEP, also off-camber rooty and full of obstacles, the cause of many an off for me.

The best dirt jumps?

PB The Track at Portreath. We're lucky to have that. Also there's Mount Hawke indoor skate park, perfect for those rainy days.

If you were to take a family out – say a cousin who's visiting with his kids – where would you head?

PB Probably the Minerals Tramway Project, starting at Bissoe is the best – a fairly easy cycle from Bissoe (Devoran) to Portreath. But there's also the Wadebridge Camel Trail – a family-friendly gravel trail winding its way along the coastline to Padstow where you can grab a cream tea and a pasty. Lovely. And both have cycle hire facilities.

What secret stashes do you know about?

PB If I told you it wouldn't be secret now would it!? Look up our group 'Cornwall Freeriders' on Facebook and give us a shout and we'll gladly take anyone along to our secret spots! I will give you this though, our homeground of Poldice is well worth finding with a freeride area, DH line, various singletrack lines and a big natural bowl cut into the landscape – perfect for jumps, etc. Head along Bissoe tramway and keep your eyes to the left, and you'll find it…

If you were a huge fan of cake and wanted to find the best trail with a foodie pit stop, where would it be?

PB I'd say Smokey Joe's in Redruth is a truck stop that serves up a genius full English. Many a rider has sat on its benches and consumed their ballast for a good day's ride. It's halfway along the Bissoe tramway, easy to find, just follow the trucks! Or there is a café at the cycle hire shop at the start of the trail. To be honest, when you ride in Cornwall you're never far away from pubs that serve great food, cafés that dish up glorious cakes or twee little cottages that have all sorts of home-made delights ready to be devoured by a hungry rider.

Where – if anywhere – outside of your area do you often visit with your bike?

PB Afan Forest in Wales is just an amazing place to ride and a trail I try and visit as often as possible. Also Gawton is only an hour away and usually has a Cornwall freerider or two ripping up its tracks; Cwncarn is always a good bet for a mint day's ride too. We're pretty blessed really in that Cornwall has a hugely diverse range of riding for all sorts of cyclists to be kept happy: from the weekend warrior to the road-riding fitness freak, from dirt jumpers to downhillers, from XC whippets to hardtail hackers, we've got it all. And we're always willing to meet new riders and have a laugh, because that's what it's all about.

Which websites have the best info on your local area?

PB Log onto Facebook and hunt out 'Cornwall freeriders' – it has all the info, advice and giggles you'll need. It always surprises me the amount of like-minded bike-obssessed nuts like myself there are on there – bike chat, bike vids, bike photos, bike links, trail info, tech advice, and mum jokes! We've got everything.

Which is the best shop to head to if you're in the southwest?

PB Easy, Clive Mitchell Cycles in Truro (the Capital of Cornwall). A great bunch of lads who are clued up on all riding disciplines and always willing to help and offer advice. They're also the best mechanics in the southwest, which is handy as we're always breaking our bikes. I wouldn't know what we'd do without 'em (there's got to be a free pair of 5.10's in it for me for that glowing praise, ha ha!). Basically, come to Cornwall, ride bikes and eat pasties. What else is there?

↘33 Portsdown Hill

XC DH

Train station Cosham/Portchester
Nearest city Portsmouth
Sat Nav PO6 4DQ

Location Portsdown is an area of land around 3 km north from Portsmouth city centre, next to the town of Paulsgrove. Leave the M27 at junction 12 and take the A3 north for 1 km; turn left onto Allaway Avenue, then right onto Credenhill Road, left onto Ludlow Road, then right onto Leominster Road and finally right into Lime Grove. The trails are all to the north of this area and are easily spottable. Park at the edge of where Leominster Road meets with Lime Grove.

Facilities Paulsgrove has plenty of shops and amenities.

Overview This area of land is narrow – James Callaghan Drive to the north is the border, but it stretches east and west some kilometres with plenty of DH trails that will give some short but feature-full descents. Not the prettiest place in the world, with its views of industrial parks and the M27 to the south, but well worth a visit for local riders who want to get some practice in.

Conditions This is chalky, south downs land, so dries quite quickly but can be lethally slippery when wet.

↘34 Puddletown Woods

XC DH 4X

Train station Dorchester South/ Dorchester West
Nearest city Southampton/ Bath/Exeter
Sat Nav DT2 8QJ

Location Puddletown Woods are around 5 km to the northeast of Dorchester. From there, take the A35 eastwards to Bournemouth. Turn off to the right at Two Droves, around 400 m before Puddletown itself, park at Hardy's Cottage just on Beacon Hill (where the author Thomas Hardy was born), and follow the singletrack from there to all the good stuff!

Facilities Nearby Puddletown has shops, and Hardy's Cottage is just off Two Droves, which is the main parking area for the forest.

Overview There's a fantastic scene at the sleepy Dorset site, and they regularly build and maintain their fantastic DH and XC trails. They have a huge area of natural singletrack, DH sections, a 4X course and plenty of bowls, berms and decent jumps. The Forestry Commission is active in the area, felling trees etc, so the trails are constantly changing, but there's so much natural terrain that there's always something cool to ride. Plus you can cycle on chalk paths and get to see the famous Dorset Chalk Man (the one with the huge club and erect penis), which is an unusual sight on the trails. The area is highly recommended and often relatively empty.

Conditions As always, avoid after periods of rain.

ⓘ **More info** The locals have built the brilliant site ridepuddletown.co.uk.

JETHRO LOADER

JETHRO LOADER

↘35 Queen Elizabeth Country Park

Train station Petersfield
Nearest city Portsmouth
Sat Nav PO8 0QE

Location Queen Elizabeth Country Park is just to the south of Petersfield, itself about 25 km north of Portsmouth. From the A3 heading south from the M25, carry on towards Portsmouth and QECP is clearly signed (with brown 'points of interest' signs on its own turn off from the A3).

Facilities There's a café and visitor centre at QECP which serves hot and cold drinks, food, and has toilets etc. The car park is pay and display (£3 for a day ticket), and the area is very popular with walkers, horse-riders and other mountain bikers.

Overview QECP is prime XC country, with two marked trails (the Queen Elizabeth Country Park Mountain Bike Trails), both 3.5 miles in a loop, and rated Purple and Orange (the purple one for beginners and the orange for intermediate riders). Both are well marked, and feature some lovely singletrack through the delightful forest (though the proximity of the A3 takes a little getting used to at various points on the orange route). There's nothing too strenuous here, but it is lovely scenery with fantastic singletrack in a beautiful setting. On the expert track there is some good climbing,

CHRIS MORAN

and some technical off-camber and rootsy trails, and if you find it's too difficult, the two loops interact frequently so you can pull out. Meanwhile at the north end of the park there are some pretty decent DJs and drops in a disused quarry for the freeriders out there, and there are plenty of easily accessible DH tracks flying off in different directions. All in all, this is a lovely day out for learner/intermediate riders.

Conditions This is well-kept forest and open land, but still prone to muddy areas in bad weather. Much of the purple trail is on forest road which has a flinty base, but expect mud in spots if it's been raining recently or throughout the winter months.

CHRIS MORAN

ⓘ **More info** QECP has its own page on the Hampshire County website at 3.hants.gov.uk/qecp.

↘36 Randwick DH

XC DH

Train station Stroud
Nearest city Gloucester
Sat Nav GL6 6EX

Location Randwick is around 8 km to the south of Gloucester. Exit junction 13 of the M5 and head east on the A419 towards Stroud. Around 2 km from the motorway there's a roundabout with the second exit being the B4008 (the Ebley Road). Take that road then turn left at Foxmoor Lane, then take another left onto Redhouse lane, then another onto Ash Lane which turns into Robbers Road. Randwick is down this road on the left after about 250 m.

Facilities There are some shops in nearby Randwick.

Overview Randwick is a small DH area with some fantastic drops, jumps and berms through the trees. It's short, but definitely sweet. There's a good scene and the area is expected to grow as the local riders add features to their impressive forest and cool natural terrain. Few people ride here so it's friendly.

Conditions Mud is the constant problem, and some of the drops are pretty close to the trees! Good soil surface, if a little loose in places.

ⓘ **More info** Put Randwick Downhill into Youtube to see plenty of clips.

↘37 Red Hill Extreme

XC 4X DJ

Train station Gloucester/Lydney
Nearest city Gloucester
Sat Nav GL14 1JU

Location Red Hill is a purpose-built centre (combined with mountain boarding), near the village of Elton in the Forest of Dean to the west of Gloucester. Take the A48 from Gloucester towards Chepstow, and turn off at Elton on the A4151 towards Cinderford on the Elton Road. Go past the Tudor Racing Stables and Red Hill Extreme is just on the right, as part of Elton Farm.

Facilities Hot and cold refreshments available from the farm.

Overview Red Hill is a purpose-built 4X and DJ site that also doubles as a mountain boarding track. You'll have to pay to use it (full day £8, half £5 and there are discounts for club members) and the price includes uplift to the top of the trails. There are plenty of jumps, berms, step ups and drops on the trail which is short but feature packed. Regularly holds competitions on its 4X track.

Conditions The DJ and 4X trails are open field land so avoid when windy or wet, and it closes when the weather's bad too. Best to call and check.

ⓘ **More info** redhillextreme.co.uk, T01594 827007 or T07877 147636.

↘38 Rogate

DH FR DJ

Train station Petersfield
Nearest city Portsmouth
Sat Nav N/A

Location Rogate is north of Petersfield off the A3. From the M25 head south on the A3 towards Portsmouth and exit at the B3006 heading towards Liss. Follow signs for the village, and at the first T junction, turn right onto Hill Brow Road. Go all the way to the end, then take a right, then immediately left, and go 1.5 km to the next T junction (marked Rogate right, and Rake left). Take the left towards Rake, then park up after a few hundred metres as the road bends to the right (if you've hit the crossroads you've gone too far). Rogate DH tracks are in the woods on the left of this road.

Facilities Hill Brow has a corner shop for supplies.

Overview Rogate is kept by the Forestry Commission and the local riders have done an incredible job of keeping the place clean whilst building some amazing DH and freeriding features. There are six DH trails, each filled with jumps, doubles and drops, while

JTON_DHER

CHRIS MORAN

elsewhere in the woods there are plenty of drop-offs and DJ-style features for freeriders and hardtailers to keep themselves busy. This is a popular site with other riders, although other users (dog walkers etc) seem to be fairly absent. Very impressive set-up and one of the best DH centres of the mid-south.

Conditions This works well in most weather, although busy periods such as holidays might be best avoided. There's quite a young scene who are keen to ride hard.

↘39 Sandford DJs and DH

XC DH DJ

Train station Wareham/Holton Heath
Nearest city Bournemouth
Sat Nav BH20 7AA

Location Sandford DJs are around 5 km to the west of Poole in Dorset. Head out from Poole on the A35 heading towards Dorchester. Just outside of Poole take the A351 towards Wareham. Sandford is around 2 km down this road. As you pass through the village, take a right onto the B3075 (Morden Road); the DJs are around 200 m up this road on the left. Either walk through the woods, or, to drive all the way up to them, carry on up Morden Road for 500 m, and take the first road off to the left. Then first left, all the way back down that road and park at the end.

Facilities Nearby Sandford has shops.

Overview This is a freeride haven, with a pretty decent DJ set-up featuring good gaps, tables and drops, and then on the way out there are some cool – if a little short – singletrack and downhill trails.

↘40 Sheet DJs

DJ

Train station Petersfield
Nearest city Portsmouth
Sat Nav N/A

Location Sheet DJs are just off the A272 on the north edge of Petersfield in Hampshire. Coming south from the M25 head towards Portsmouth on the A3, then exit at the junction marked Petersfield on the A272. Take the first exit at the roundabout (London Road, still the A272). Cross the river, and after 150 m, the A272 turns off to the right, heading to Rogate. Take this road and park immediately on the left. The DJs are on the opposite side of this road in the copse of trees.

Facilities Sheet is the nearest village, just back over the river.

Overall This is an incredible set of DJs nicely hidden off the road with

CHRIS MORAN

some good lines, hips, gaps and tabletops. For those visiting Queen Elizabeth Country Park, Rogate or Buriton, it might be worth a pop in. There's a heavy BMX scene here, and there are constant builds, but mountain bikes can be seen occasionally. Not for beginners, and you'd definitely need to know how to ride tight transitions to even drop in here.

Conditions This is a red-clay soil with plenty of reinforced take offs and landings. These are popular DJs.

S41 Still Woods	
DH FR N	
Train station	Bedminster Down
Nearest city	Bristol
Sat Nav	BS41 9DJ

Location Still Woods are around 3 km to the southwest of Bristol city centre. From the A4 to the west of the city head south and then turn west onto the A370 towards Long Ashton. Before you hit Long Ashton, take a right onto the B3128 (Ashton Road), head west along this road for around 1 km then take a left into Providence Lane. After 150 m park at the Community Centre car park and walk through the park, heading uphill. The woods are in front of you.

Facilities There's nothing at this DH course although you're minutes, riding away from Long Ashton village centre where there are plenty of shops.

Overview Still Woods are owned by Bristol University, and the land is open for anyone who wishes to ride. The university has a great mountain bike scene, and improvements are constantly being made. Currently the set-up consist of a few short-ish DH trails, some great DJs and some decent gaps and tabletops of varying lenghts and heights. There's also a bit of northshore being made, and expect the locals to keep improving the site.

Conditions The forest can get muddy during winter and after periods of heavy rainfall, but there's always something to ride.

ⓘ **More info** There's a mailing list set up to organize digging days. Go to bmbc.4.forumer.com/index.php?act=idx or type 'Still Woods' into Youtube for plenty of clips posted.

PETE TILEY

5 tips for trail etiquette
Sam Reynolds

Sam Reynolds is 17 years old and part of the DMR team. He counts Kingswood's Kech Trails as home, but is equally found on various dirt jumping sites across Europe including the Nissan Qashqai tour. Here's Sam's etiquette tips for when turning up to new trails. As Sam says: "follow these simple tips and hopefuly you'll be invited back to ride again!"

1 If possible, before going to the new trails for the first time, try to find out who owns or digs the jumps and drop them an email asking if it's ok to come along sometime. If you don't know who that is, just turn up and generaly be polite! When you turn up ask the locals if it's ok to ride, and offer to help dig. You can't have all that fun without helping out a little!

2 Wear a helmet! Besides being sensible, most trails have rules in place not allowing you to ride without one.

3 Take the right bike – put on slick dirt/street tyres for most trails, knobbly tyres dont go down too well with the builders 'cos they churn it up. A dirt jump bike or bmx are most suited to trails, so don't expect to be allowed to ride on a downhill bike with chunky tyres.

4 Respect the locals. Probably the most important rule of all is to respect the jumps, riders and the land they are on. Try to skid as little as possible and if you do for whatever reason damage the jumps, get a spade and fix it. Before dropping in to your run, make sure no one else is going, because cutting out in front of someone is not cool. Litter is also a big one: if anyone dropped litter at my trails they certainly wouldn't be invited back. The cleaner the land, the less likely the jumps are to get knocked down, so the happier the locals will be.

5 Lastly – why not dig your own trails? Find a plot of land, preferably ask the land owner if you can use it, and start building. Seeing your own jumps coming to shape is sometimes almost as satisfying as riding them. Also, when you have a few jumps riding you can invite other riders, and they will most likely invite you back to their trails, giving you more and more places to ride. What goes around comes around eh? So get digging!

↘42 Stoke Heights

XC DH

Train station Eastleigh/Hedge End
Nearest city Southampton
Sat Nav SO50 8GL

Location Stoke Heights are around 5 km northeast from the centre of Southampton next to the village of Bishopstoke. From the M3 exit at junction 13 and head east along the A335 towards Bishopstoke. After 1 km you'll hit a roundabout. Take the third exit – Bishopstoke Road (the B3037) and carry on down here for about 2 km, then turn left onto Sandy Lane, then after 400 m take another left onto Harding Lane. This leads to woodland. Park where you can and carry on into the woods on your bike.

Facilities The nearby village of Fair Oak has plenty of shops and amenities.

Overview Stoke Heights is a large tract of Forestry Commission land that has been explored by mountain bikers for years. There are plenty of XC trails criss-crossing the land, and there are some short but sweet DH trails. None have been built officially, but there are some purpose-built jumps and berms that have been strengthened. Again, not necessarily for the travelling rider, but Southampton locals will enjoy. Friendly locals should point out the hidden gems.

Conditions The woods have plenty of roots, and good rock gardens. Avoid if it's muddy, and can be dark in winter. Likely to be fairly empty though.

↘43 Stoughton Trails

XC DJ

Train station Nutbourne/Bosham/Southborne/Rowlands Castle
Nearest city Portsmouth
Sat Nav N/A

Location Stoughton is a small village between Havant and Chichester to the far west of the South Downs. From the A27 Havant Bypass exit at Westbourne and take the B2147 heading towards Racton. Turn off to the left at Walderton heading for Stoughton, and carry along this road after Stoughton village for around 1.5 km until the road turns sharply to the left. Here turn right (ie carry straight on) and park immediately to the right. The DH trails are around 250 m to the northeast.

Facilities This is deep country forest, although Stoughton has a shop for supplies.

Overview This is a locally-built DH track with some good jumps and some care and attention having been lavished on the area. There's a hip jump and some big doubles, and if the local crew carries on this could turn into a good – but relatively small – spot.

Conditions This is unmanaged forest area so expect it to be very muddy and unrideable in the winter months or after heavy rainfall.

CHRIS MORAN

↘44 Stoke Woods

SQEGG.CO.UK

XC DH FR DJ

Train station St James Park
Nearest city Exeter
Sat Nav EX4 7DP

Location Take the A377 north out of Exeter city centre. About 1 km out, and just before the village of Cowley, turn right onto the A396 (Stoke Road). After a couple of hundred metres, Stoke Woods will be on the right. Turn right into Pennsylvania Road and park at the clearing on the right just after you've gone through the woods. The main XC and freeride area starts at this car park, while the DJs are at the other end of the woods, just before Stoke Hill Road heads off into farmland.

Facilities Cowley is just down the road and has plenty of corner shops etc, and the city of Exeter is only 2-3 km away for everything else. On site, there is very little other than a car park (free), and the forest area. No shops or cafés.

Overview For riders out of Exeter, Haldon Freeride Park might be enough to satisfy their every need, but not content to rest on their laurels, Stoke Woods is a similarly impressive set-up. While Haldon has a fancy website, a club, and a very organized set up, Stoke is a more laid-back affair, but with the same approach – take one already cool XC riding area and pour a load of effort, time and trail-building skills into it to create some great freeride and DH tracks. Plus over to the east side of the woods there's a DJ spot with six decent jumps.

Terrain There's plenty of unofficial singletrack, with some purpose-built freeride obstacles. Ground is mostly hard-packed soil with few rocks but the odd exposed tree root.

XC Stoke Woods is predominantly XC singletrack (be careful – this is also popular with walkers and dog owners, but not especially busy). There are loops all over the forest, ranging from super easy to some lovely technical sections. The area is much quieter than Haldon, and being a mere half an hour's ride from Exeter sees plenty of people popping up for a short session. There are plenty of drops, kickers and log rides (the beginnings of northshore obstacles are starting to take hold), and around 10 km of decent riding to be had. The Forest is surrounded by farmland, so you can't get too lost, and practically every acre has networks of singletrack criss-crossing it.

Downhill There are around 6 or 7 short sections of DH in various spots throughout the forest. Most head north from the top of the hill towards the river and link the XC loops.

Dirt jumps There are several lines through the jumps ranging from medium to difficult with tabletops, gaps and doubles. These aren't necessarily for beginners as they will struggle with the size and speed of the jumps.

ⓘ **More info** Exeter Mountain Bikers – exmtb.co.uk. There is a great map with all the routes and ability levels to be found at sqegg.co.uk/stokemap.jpg.

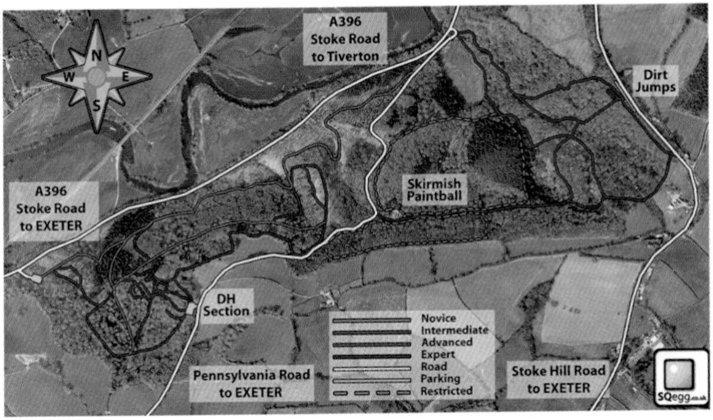

SQEGG.CO.UK

↘45 The Track

XC FR 4X DJ N

Train station Redruth

Nearest city Plymouth

Sat Nav TR16 4HW

Opening times 1500-2100 weekdays, 1100-1800 weekends. The Track is floodlit so riding at night is fine

Location The Track (sometimes known as The Cornish Extreme Centre can be found by heading down the A30, turn-off at the Redruth in the direction of Portreath on the B3300. The turning to The Track is 50 m on the right having just passed Treasure Park. Nearest train station is Redruth; riders exit the station and head towards Treasure Park, which is well signed, around town.

Facilities This is essentially a dirt jumper's paradise, heavily weighted towards the freeriders. What is easy to miss is that for families, it's the perfect setting for kids to progress their riding in a safe environment, while benefitting from plenty of scenic trails around the surrounding area. In fact there is a coast to coast trail running from Portreath that is only 11 miles one way. The dirt at the track is perfect for building and shaping lips and transitions and a full floodlight system, large PA set-up and a viewing platform result in a great atmosphere. There are numerous lines from beginner to pro, a foam pit to learn tricks in, a soft landing area to dial the airs in, and several purpose-built obstacles (wallrides etc) as well as a 4X track.

STACEY/THE-TRACK.CO.UK

XC Whilst the track itself offers nothing to the XC rider other than the opportunity to progress their riding skills on the beginner jumps, there are coastal paths and trails in country parks that can be reached from the Track. There are very few marked rides so to find the more interesting trails it would be worth hiring a guide. Try Mobius trails (T08456 430630) who will assess your ability and take you on a ride to suit.

Downhill The track does not offer any DH riding and Cornwall on the whole is not a good place to ride downhill due to its topography. Any downhiller would do far worse than to spend a few days here on a hardtail brushing up on their jumping skills. Then for real DH riding it's about an hour's drive to the Maddacleave woods DH trails.

Freeride A freeride haven, the track offers so many ways to progress your riding skills with multiple lines of DJs for all abilities. In fact there are over a mile of jumps! In order to learn some of the harder tricks there is a 50 sq m foam pit with multiple ramp and transfer lines, a resi ramp to test your tricks before taking them to dirt and a national standard BMX track to test your speed and aerial prowess. Also under construction is a Kona Slopestyle course. The place is constantly evolving so there will always be some new lines to try. Also in the area are Mount Hawke indoor

STACEY/THE-TRACK.CO.UK

skatepark and Wooden Waves outdoor skatepark in Newquay.

Easy Start out on the beginner jumps – there is so much here that it is definitely a case of building up slowly to make sure you have mastered what you're riding before moving onto something much bigger.

Hard There are plenty of hard lines to try for the more advanced jumper. The only limitation in a place like this is your imagination!

Not to miss The foam pit will see most people practising their X-games moves.

Remember to avoid Travelling here in less than perfect weather conditions. Call before you leave.

Nearest Bike/Hire shop Konas can be hired from The Track (£15 per day).

Local accommodation The Track has camping available (£10 per pitch per night, one person must be over 18), or nearby Elm Farm has B&B and is affiliated with the centre elm-farm.co.uk.

Eating The Track has the onsite 'snax shax' to keep you topped up through your day with burgers, bacon and chips. For a biker's pub meal try the Basset Arms (T01209 842077) or for a gastronomic delight head for Tabb's Restaurant (T01872 262110) in Truro. Just make sure your wallet is fully loaded.

ⓘ **More info** The Track – T01209 211073, the-track.co.uk; Cornwall Tourist Board, cornwalltouristboard.co.uk.

> Lowdown

Locals do
Ride amazingly well (as to be expected with this on their doorstep).

Fix up any cases.

Locals don't
Try and ride the jumps when the sea breeze is strong.

Respect the laws of gravity.

Pros
UK's top DJ facility.

Great chilled, friendly atmosphere.

Cons
Very specific type of riding.

Can be quite exposed to wind and rain.

↘46 Triscombe DH

DH

Train station Bishop's Lydeard/ Bridgwater

Nearest city Bristol

Sat Nav TA5 1HN (for Marsh Mills)

Location Triscombe Downhill is a quiet series of DH lines all facing southeast on a beautiful stretch of Devonshire countryside about 15 km west of Bridgwater. From the M5 exit at junction 23 in the direction of Bridgwater. Then take the A39 towards Minehead. Before you hit the village of Nether Stowey take a left towards Marsh Mills and carry on through the village for a further kilometre, turning at the next right. Carry on along that road and take the left-hand fork. Triscombe DH is about another kilometre along after the fork and is the hill on your right.

Facilities Triscombe is way out in the country with very little other than unspoilt views. The nearest shop is to be found in Over Stowey.

Overview There are six DH tracks to be ridden here, all with fantastic natural features, off-camber berms and, with it being in the forest, plenty of roots to take on. The local riders often build features on the track but seem to be in constant battle with the land owners so you're never sure what will await you until you get there. That said, there are plenty of gulleys, always some great jumps and berms and sometimes some decent gaps.

Conditions Mud is a frequent problem but in good conditions the tracks here are first class.

ⓘ **More info** Type 'Triscombe' into Youtube to see plenty of action.

↘47 Watchmoor Wood Bike Park

XC FR N

Train station Bournemouth

Nearest city Bournemouth

Sat Nav BH24 2ET

Location Watchmoor Wood Bike Park is around 15 km to the north west of Bournemouth. From Southampton or the M27, go west to the end of the motorway and carry along the A31 towards Bournemouth. Take the Ashley Heath turning off the A31 just west from Ringwood, where you'll catch brown signs heading to Moors Valley Country Park. Head through Ashley Heath and the park entrance is on the right just as you exit the village.

Facilities Moor Valley Country Park (part of Ringwood Forest) has a visitor centre with café, bike hire, toilets and car parking, as well as bike maps available for the fun, family-based XC to be found in the forest. Most come for the northshore though…

Overview This is a brilliant family set-up and was perfect for some gentle XC riding; that was before they built a one-hectare

JETHRO LOADER

northshore set-up in the forest which has attracted good riders from far and wide. Everything is here, from super pro down to beginners, though absolute first-timers may be intimidated. Well worth a visit for those in the southeast.

Conditions Brilliantly-built wood with plenty of random lines. Many of the XC routes weatherproofed but as always, avoid after heavy rain.

ⓘ **More info** Moors Valley Country Park has its own website at moors-valley.co.uk, while the Forestry Commission website has a page on the park at forestry.gov.uk.

↘48 Woodbury Common

Train station Exton/Lympstone Commando
Nearest city Exeter
Sat Nav EX5 1JJ

Location From the M5 (junction 30), take the A376 to Clyst St George, where the B3179 (Woodbury Road) splits towards Woodbury. Go through the village and keep on until the crossroads, around 2 miles away. Woodbury Common is the area directly ahead.

Facilities This is prime XC country, with plenty of rambling routes, bridleways and single track to explore. For those looking for a family day out, park for a small fee at Woodbury Castle (signposted from Woodbury village), or for the more serious rider, park for free in Woodbury itself and ride up to the common.

Overview The land is owned by the Clinton Devon Estates and open for the public to use. There are a variety of routes, ranging from short, action-packed loops to longer, enduro rides to be had. Maps to be found online at the fantastic local scene site of: exmtb.co.uk.

Conditions Can be muddy in the winter, but there's always something to ride in all conditions.

ⓘ **More info** See above; for the land website try clintondevon.com.

JETHRO LOADER

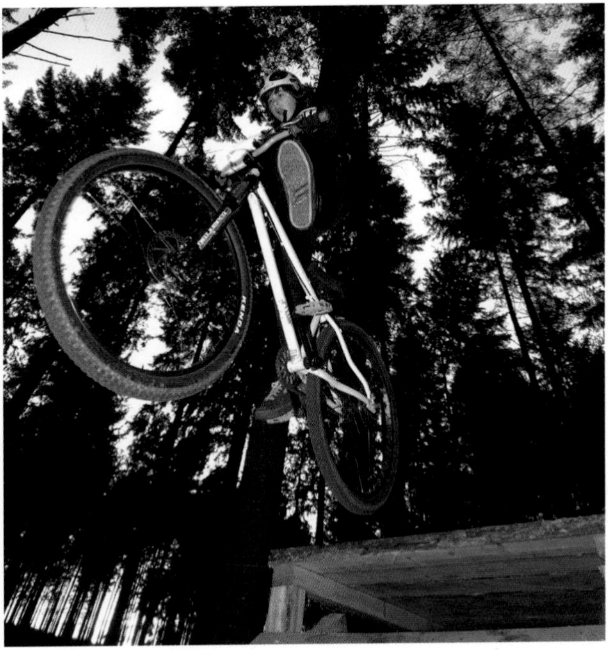

London & southeast England

↘ Overview 60
↘ Aston Hill 62
↘ A10 DJs 64
↘ Bengeo Bumps & Waterford Quarry DJs 64
↘ Bedgebury Forest & Freeride Area 65
↘ Blean Woods 66
↘ Bluebell Hill 67
↘ Braintree BMX 67
↘ Brockwell Park BMX Track 68
↘ Bushy Park 68
↘ Chazey Woods & Northshore 68
↘ Chicksands Bike Park 70
↘ Crowborough – The Bull Track 72
↘ Crow Trails 73
↘ Danbury Common 73
↘ Local riders, Ben Wain 74
↘ Devils Drop DJs 76
↘ Devils Dyke DH & XC 76
↘ Devils Dyke Nonsuch DJs 77
↘ Donkey Island DJs 77
↘ Esher Shore 78
↘ Epping Forest 80
↘ Friston Forest 81
↘ Fearnley DJs 82
↘ Gunnersbury DJ 82
↘ Harrow Skatepark & DJs 82
↘ Hayes Hawks BMX Track 83
↘ Highgate DJs 83
↘ Highwood DJs 83
↘ Holmes Place DJs 84
↘ Ipswich BMX track 84
↘ Kuoni Trails 84
↘ Leith Hill 84
↘ Limpsfield DJs 85
↘ Look Out Gulley 86
↘ M3 DJs 86
↘ Mereworth Woods 86
↘ Mousehold Trails 87
↘ Nature Jumps & Gog Magog XC 87
↘ PORC (Penshurst Off Road Club) 88
↘ Normandy Hill DH 90
↘ Peaslake 90
↘ Peckham BMX Track, & Burgess Park BMX 91
↘ Rayleigh 91
↘ Redlands 92
↘ Shoreham DJs 93
↘ Shorne Wood Country Park & DJs 93
↘ Sidley Woods 94
↘ Slindon Quarry 94
↘ Swinley Forest 95
↘ Sloughbottom Park 96
↘ Teddington DJs 96
↘ Thetford Forest 97
↘ Tilgate Forest & St Leonards Forest 98
↘ Track 40 98
↘ Tring Park 99
↘ Warley DJs 99
↘ Whiteways 99
↘ Wild Park 100
↘ Willen Lake BMX Track 100
↘ Wisley Trails 101
↘ Woburn Sands 102

Chicksands is a freeride paradise. [DANNY MILNER]

London & Southeast England

Trails...

1 Aston Hill
2 A10 DJs
3 Bengeo Bumps and Waterford Quarry DJs
4 Bedgebury Forest and Freeride Area
5 Blean Woods
6 Bluebell Hill
7 Braintree BMX
8 Brockwell Park BMX Track
9 Bushy Park
10 Chazey Woods and Northshore
11 Chicksands Bike Park
12 Crowborough – The Bull Track
13 Crow Trails
14 Danbury Common
15 Devils Drop DJs
16 Devils Dyke DH and XC
17 Devils Dyke Nonsuch DJs
18 Donkey Island DJs
19 Esher Shore
20 Epping Forest
21 Friston Forest
22 Fearnley DJs
23 Gunnersbury DJs
24 Harrow Skatepark and DJs
25 Hayes Hawkes BMX Track
26 Highgate DJs
27 Highwoods DJs
28 Holmes Place DJs
29 Ipswich BMX Track
30 Kuoni Trails
31 Leith Hill
32 Limpsfield DJs
33 Look Out Gulley
34 M3 DJs
35 Mereworth Woods
36 Mousehold Trails
37 Nature Jumps and Gog Magog XC
38 Penshurst Off Road Club
39 Normandy Hill DH
40 Peaslake
41 Peckham BMX Track and Burgess Park BMX
42 Rayleigh
43 Redlands
44 Shoreham DJs
45 Shorne Wood Country Park and DJs
46 Sidley Woods
47 Slindon Quarry
48 Swinley Forest
49 Sloughbottom Park
50 Teddington DJs
51 Thetford Forest
52 Tilgate Forest and St Leonards Forest
53 Track 40
54 Tring Park
55 Warley DJs
56 Whiteways
57 Wild Park
58 Willen Lake BMX Track
59 Wisley Trails
60 Woburn Sands

While the southeast has little in the way of real mountains, it has one of the strongest mountain bike scenes in the country, with a mass exodus from the cities to the nearby forests, jump spots and secret stashes most weekends. Naturally, because of the amount of riders in this part of the country, and with commercial opportunities to cash in on their outdoor expectations, there are plenty of purpose-built sites already in existence, as well as many planned for the near future. London is home to hundreds of thousands of bike riders, so it is unsurprising that its nearest riding spots are the most popular. Hence, if you were to head to Swinley Forest or some of the popular Surrey spots on a bank holiday, you're unlikely to have the run of the trails to yourself. This isn't to say the area is crowded however, and for riders heading to the newly re-named Viceroy's Wood in Kent, Friston Bedgebury and Thetford Forests, or any of the fabulous trio of centres in Bedfordshire (Woburn Sands, Aston Hill and Chicksands), you're in for a lovely surprise: they're as well kept, open, beautiful and as organized as any trail centre in Wales or Scotland.

Local scene

The southeast of England holds the biggest population of riders, but one would presume it has the least facilities for mountain biking. While this is true in terms of real mountains and big descents, there are more than enough world-class trail centres dotted around the counties of West Sussex, East Sussex, Kent, Surrey, Greater London, Berkshire, Oxfordshire, Buckinghamshire, Bedfordshire, Hertfordshire and Essex to keep any rider happy. Like in the southwest, the Forestry Commission plays a huge part in the outdoor experience for many riders here, being behind the fantastic facilities to be found at Bedgebury Forest, Friston Forest and Thetford Forest. But there are also plenty of privately-owned operations here, as well as manor parks, country estates and, in Hampshire, an entire county with a forward-thinking policy on bike riding. Even inside the M25 there are fun places to ride, and naturally

ISOBEL CAMERON/FORESTRY COMMISSION

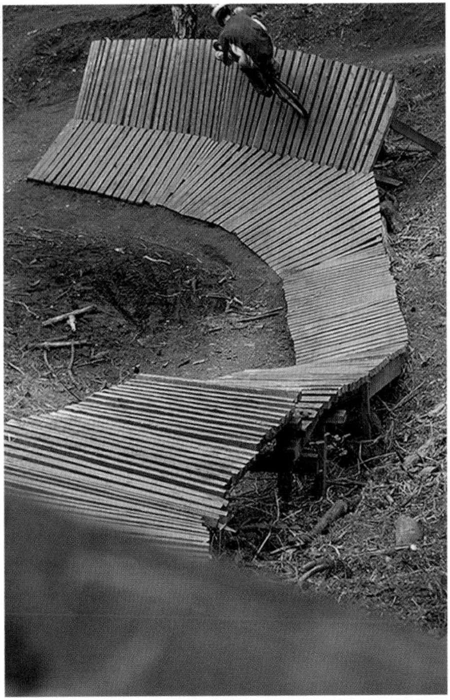

JASON WAIN

Above: Chicksands is perfect for wallrides.
Opposite page: Bedgebury Northshore.

the dirt jumping scene here is huge. We've included many BMX tracks in this guide because for many riders, heading to pure dirt jumping spots can be intimidating, and heading to a BMX or 4X track is a good way to ease into the dirt jumping scene.

Hubs

Where to start? There seem to be three major hubs – those riders in and around Milton Keynes are spoilt for choice with Woburn Sands, Aston Hill and Chicksands on tap, while riders around Tunbridge Wells have The Bull Track, Bedgebury and Viceroy Wood all competing for their attention. Riders in West London, Bracknell and Reading are all within easy reach of the fantastic Swinley Forest, while Surrey and Sussex riders have the incredible South Downs on their doorstep, home to some of the most beautiful XC riding in the country.

⑤ Best rides in London and Southeast England

There are plenty of stand-alone spots in the southeast, but riders who are based here should definitely check out:

① Thetford Forest, page 97

For those who like their XC rambling interesting but not crammed with huge uphill sections, East Anglia's Thetford Forest is a fairly flat, but stunningly beautiful tract of land with the full bike shop and visitor centre set-up. There are tonnes of races too, so check the calendar if you fancy testing your lung capacity.

② Swinley Forest, page 95

If you're in London and fancy trying out mountain biking, Swinley Forest has bike hire, some brilliant XC trails and, in Great Windsor Forest, some of the best woodland in the country.

③ Viceroy's Wood, page 88

Kent's eco-centric mountain bike spot has great food, a brilliant visitor centre, some fun downhill and stunning views. Well worth a look in.

④ Bedgebury Forest and Freeride Park, page 65

In conjunction with the Forestry Commission, the crew at Bedgebury have built some impressive northshore and freeriding fun, all surrounded by beautiful XC riding with a full visitor centre set-up. A great Kentish rival for Viceroy's Wood.

⑤ Esher Shore, page 78

It's in the M25, it's a purpose-built northshore park, and it's got some fantastic dirt jumps. If you're in London and love freeriding, this is your number one destination.

↘1 Aston Hill

XC DH FR 4X

Train station Stoke

Nearest city London

Sat Nav HP22 5NQ

Opening times Weekends and Bank Holidays – 0900-1630. Tuesday and Thursday evenings 1700-2000. Check site for special openings and any closed days

NEIL CAIN

Location Aston Hill is around 5 km east of Aylesbury and 10 km north west of Hemel Hemstead. From the M25 exit at junction 20 heading north to Hemel on the A41. Stay on this road until you pass Tring on the right hand side (around 20 km from the M25). Exit the A41 at Drayton Hollow on the B488 for Dunstable and the 'old A41' for Aston Clinton and Aylesbury. Carry on straight at the roundabout, then after 500 m turn left on the B4009 in the direction of Wendover. After 1.5 km, take a left into the road signposted Aston Hill, Go Ape and Wendover Woods. Aston is 300 m up on the left.

Facilities The current tracks were built by Ian Warby over a 10 year period. Ian had a real insight in to what is now a global phenomenon. For years Aston Hill has been one of the only venues to provide for downhill and 4X in the southeast. The soil type at Aston is quite chalky and is littered with flint, which can make for interesting riding when wet, but the tracks are well maintained, if not manicured, and will test the most proficient of riders. In addition, there are three downhill tracks, a XC downhill, a 4X track and a 10 km XC loop.

XC The XC loop runs along the outside edge of the wood until it reaches the top of the hill where it meanders through a slightly flatter section. The track is very cardiovascular with few places to rest, as well as being technical in places with steep sections, off-cambers and roots galore.

Downhill The three DH tracks are all of similar length and make the best use of the gradient and terrain. The black run is the oldest and has received design input from Rob Warner. There is a steep shoot on the track, which is pure chalk and has been given the name Cocaine Alley. The other two tracks are equally as technical with a mixture of jumps, drops, berms and off-cambers. The new Ultimate Pursuits Downhill is technical and not for beginners.

4X/Freeride Built on chalk the Buckingham Bikes 4X track is almost unrideable when wet but bakes hard and rides very quick in the dry. It features the usual doubles, rollers and tables as well as a road gap. There are plans to surface the track when funds become available.

Easy The XC loop has some fun but challenging areas for beginners.

Hard Virtually all the DH trails are top class with plenty to challenge good riders.

Not to miss The best DH trails in the southeast.

Remember to avoid Travelling here in less than perfect weather conditions. Call before you leave.

Nearest Bike/Hire shop
Mountain Mania in Tring is a 10-minute drive away; they also offer a priority repair service to Aston hill riders and a discount on parts.

Local accommodation
The majority of visitors to the hill just come for the day, but there are a large number of B&Bs, hotels and guest houses within a ten minute drive. For local tourist information you can call Wendover tourist info on T01296 696759 or Tring tourist info on T01442 823347.

Eating The well-named Café in the Woods in the neighbouring Wendover Woods. Wendover and Tring, five minutes' drive away, has plenty of eateries to choose from.

ⓘ **More info** Bike park contact rideastonhill.co.uk or call the tourist Office (above).

> Lowdown

Locals do
Session the road gap on the 4X/

Locals don't
Ride without protection. The flint here is very sharp and can slice your knees and elbows open.

Pros
Good transport links.

Technical trails.

Quality coaching program.

Cons
Difficult to ride in the wet.

No uplift.

NEIL CAIN

↘2 A10 DJs

DJ

Train station Welwyn Garden City
Nearest city London
Sat Nav N/A

Location The A10 DJs are in a traffic island off the A10 near Hertford, itself between Harlow and Welwyn Garden City. From the M25 exit at junction 25 and head north on the A10 for around 10 km, then take the exit signposted for Great Amwell. At the first roundabout, take the first exit – the B1502 Stanstead Road, and go back under the A10. The DJs are in the copse of woods immediately to the right of this road just after you've passed under the A10 bridge.

Facilities Great Amwell has some shops and facilities.

Overview These DJs are right next to the A10, but otherwise are on land used for little else, so expect few visitors other than riders. There are quite a few lines, ranging from some easier lines to pro-standard. This is no place for beginners, however. They would be better off heading to Hertford to ride the Bengeo Bumps.

Conditions This is council land on a traffic island between the busy A10. It's copse woods with few visitors apart from riders. Respect the building that has gone into the trails and fix any casings.

↘3 Bengeo Bumps and Waterford Quarry DJs

DJ

Train station Hertford East
Nearest city London
Sat Nav SG14 3JS

Location 'The Bumps' are in Hertford, between Harlow and Welwyn Garden City. From the A10 heading north from junction 25 of the M25, take the Hertford exit, onto the A414. In town, turn right onto the B158 Port Hill (which turns into Bengeo Street), and head up this road for 1 km. Turn right into New Road, then left in Ware Park Road, then left again into Rib Vale. Park at the end of the road where it loops back on itself. The DJs are in a small area of common land behind the houses on the left.

Facilities Bengeo Street has plenty of shops and amenities and is a few hundred metres' ride away.

Overview This is a very low budget DJ spot between houses that no-one should take a long journey too. But if the A10 dirt jumps are too busy or scary, this might make learners salvage something from the trip. One kilometre further north are Waterford Quarry DJs (the quarry is sign posted), which has a sand landing similar to a foam pit!

Conditions This is a small clearing of land between houses. The quarry is a disused pit area.

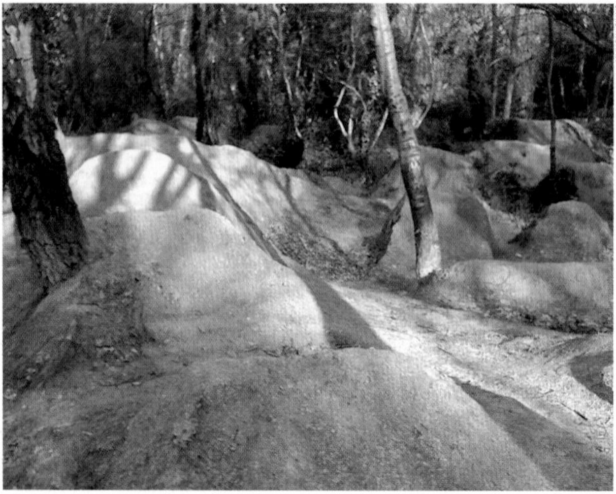

CHRIS MORAN

↘4 Bedgebury Forest and Freeride Area

Train station Wadhurst/Frant
Nearest city London
Sat Nav TN17 2SJ

Location Bedgebury Forest is around 15 km southeast of Tonbridge in Kent. From the M25 exit at junction 5 and join the A21 southbound towards Hastings. Bedgebury is signposted off the A21 on the B2079.

Facilities Bedgebury is the full Forestry Commission deal – visitor centre, café, toilets (and showers), a bike shop (Quench Cycles, T01580 879694, quenchuk.co.uk, they have suspension bikes, as well as disabled or learning difficulty bikes), car parking (though expensive at £7.50 for the day), a museum and the Pinetum area (a designated tree experiment with some impressively tall trees). The area is hugely popular, with lots of riders, walkers, families and other forest users.

Overview Bedgebury used to be (and still is) a fantastic XC venue, with loops heading all over the 800 hectares of ride-able land. The local riders banded together to form the 'Boars on Bikes' Bedgebury Forest Cycle Club (boarsonbikes.co.uk, membership gives free parking and showers etc), and they have built some impressive northshore, as well as creating some incredible XC and freeride trails throughout the forest. Well worth a visit if you're in the southeast.

Terrain Virtually all singletrack, with some great armoured bridges, jumps and work put in to add features and obstacles to the trails.

XC There are 15 km of dedicated, purpose-built trails, and 10 km of family trails for the less experienced or those with kids.

Downhill There are some short sections of DH in the forest but no dedicated DH trails.

Northshore There is a Freeride a+Area, which has some impressive wood-elevated ladders, skinny log rides, drops, see-saws, kickers, berms and a three-way 'combobulator'. The locals are definitely into building, and use sustainable, locally sourced wood to build their park. A good sign for the future. There is a set of DJs too, which is set to expand in the coming years.

Conditions The XC routes are hard-packed dirt singletrack, prone to bouts of serious mud in the winter. However, where the problem areas render the trails un-ride-able, the locals are hitting back with bridges and reinforced wood.

ⓘ **More info** Bedgebury Forest (forestry.gov.uk/bedgebury), Bedgebury Forest Cycle Club (boarsonbikes.co.uk), mudtrail.co.uk/where-to-ride.php also has a page dedicated to Bedgebury.

JASON WAIN

BEN WAIN/JAB-RIDE.CO.UK

↘5 Blean Woods

XC

Train station Canterbury West/ Canterbury East

Nearest city Canterbury

Sat Nav CT2 9BX

Location Blean Woods is just to the north west of Canterbury, Kent. From the M2 (which finishes at junction 7) carry on along the A2 towards Canterbury. Leave the A road after 6 km at Upper Harbledown/the A2050. After 500 m turn off left onto Palmers Cross Hill, and head towards Rough Common. In the centre of the village turn left up New Road, and Blean Woods is 300 m up this road on the right after the playing fields.

Facilities Rough Common has a corner shop and amenities.

Overview This is an enormous stretch of forest and open land covered with mile after mile of singletrack and fire-road, perfect for the rambling XC rider. There's nothing too demanding here, but the three connected woods offer some lovely views, and the occasional bit of technical riding. Not worth a journey to this part of the world but a definite addition to the Kent riding scene. There is no map, but the trails are ridden often enough to be obvious.

Conditions This is relatively wild country, so mud can shut down the trails in winter, but if it's been dry for a while the whole network opens up.

BEN WAIN/JAB-RIDE.CO.UK

↘6 Bluebell Hill

XC DH

Train station Aylesford/New Hythe
Nearest city London
Sat Nav ME5 9SE

Location The charmingly-named Bluebell Hill is around 5 km to the south of Rochester in Kent. From the M25, exit at junction 2 onto the A2 heading to Rochester. This road turns into the M2, then exit at junction 3, the A229. Head towards this A road (which looks like another motorway), but before the entry slip, turn off to the left after 100 m into Maidstone Road. Head down here for 500 m, then turn right onto Common Road. This road crosses the A229. Just after, turn left into the Bluebell Hill car park.

Facilities Nearby Boxley and Walderslade are full of shops and amenities. Bluebell Hill has its own car parking area and dedicated picnic site.

Overview Bluebell Hill is connected to and part of the North Downs Way, and the area is hugely popular with walkers, horse-riders and mountain bikers. There is some fabulous XC riding – although not particularly challenging – with great views to the south. There are also some short but interesting DH trails dotted around, with natural banks, berms and drops. Riders often head off to the east or west for sections of the North Downs Way.

Conditions This is chalky, flint-based riding, so works well in most conditions, but avoid after heavy rain.

RACHEL BESANT

↘7 Braintree BMX

DJ

Train station Braintree
Nearest city London
Sat Nav CM7 9BJ

Location Braintree BMX Track is on the outskirts of Braintree in Essex. From the A131, exit at Braintree and head for the town centre, then head out north on the B1053 in the direction of Shalford/Churchend. On the outskirts of Braintree, turn left into the car park between Churchill Road and Panfield Lane and the track is just on the other side of the trees.

Facilities Braintree has lots of shops and amenities.

Overview This is a fantastic BMX track with regular club meets and a decent course for those looking to brush up their freeride and freestyle skills on some doubles, berms and table tops before going on to some more serious DJs and DH trails.

Conditions This is a well-kept, pro BMX track with drainage, but still avoid during rainy periods.

ⓘ **More info** See Braintree BMX's website, braintreebmx.co.uk.

↘8 Brockwell Park BMX Track

DJ

Train station Herne Hill
Nearest city London
Sat Nav SW2 2YD

Location Brockwell Park is in southeast London, just next to Brixton. From the A23 in the centre of Brixton, loop around the main church and head south on the A204 Effra road in the direction of Tulse Hill. Carry on down this road for 1 km and turn left into Bascombe Street. Brockwell Park is just in front of you, and the BMX track is in the north end.

Facilities Nearby Brixton has plenty of shops and amenities, while Brockwell park has a café, a fantastic open-air swimming pool, tennis and football areas, and a mini train.

Overview This is a competition standard BMX track with well maintained berms, jumps, drop-ins and features. Being central London, it is often busy, and probably best avoided at super busy times. Not worth a huge journey, but worth a shot if you're in the area.

Conditions This is a tarmac/soil track with drainage built in, but still avoid if muddy.

ⓘ **More info**
brixtonbmxclub.com.

↘9 Bushy Park

XC DJ

Train station Teddington
Nearest city London
Sat Nav TW11 0EA

Location Bushy Park is in Teddington, south of Twickenham and Teddington. From the centre of London, take the A308 through Roehampton and Kingston Vale, and head through Hampton on the Hampton Court Road (still the A308). Just after Hampton, the road cuts straight between Hampton Court Palace Gold Club on the left and Bushy Park on the right. Park at the park entrance on Chestnut Avenue.

Facilities Teddington has plenty of shops and amenities, and the park has Hampton Court Palace with a variety of museum and café facilities (for a price).

Overview Bushy Park is a Royal Park which is open to all, although there is a small fee for parking. Cycling is permitted on the roads, and XC rambling is frequent but unofficial, although you're likely to see plenty of riders. To the east of Chestnut Avenue is the Heron Pond, and to the northeast of this is a dirt jumping spot with two lines of small to average sized jumps, though not well maintained. Not worth a long journey, but if you're in the area…

Conditions This is an open grassland park which can get very busy in good weather and be empty and muddy in bad.

ⓘ **More info** royalparks.org.uk/parks/bushy_park/about.cfm.

↘10 Chazey Woods and Northshore

XC DH FR N

Train station Tilehurst/Reading
Nearest city Reading
Sat Nav RG4 7TQ

Location Chazey Wood is a tract of land to the north west of Reading, on the south side of Caversham Golf Club. From the M4 take junction 11 and head north into Reading centre on the A33. Keep straight at all roundabouts as the road changes numbers to the A329 Caversham Road, then turn left at the roundabout onto the A4155, going over the river and left onto Church Road, the A4074. Head along here for 300 m and turn left onto The Warren. Follow this road for 2 km and Chazey Wood is on the right.

Facilities Caversham has loads of corner shops etc for local supplies.

Overview Chazey Wood is a popular DH area and the local riders have even built some pretty impressive northshore. However, this is an unofficial site, and is prone to being shut down. Riders mostly ignore any ban and the area has some great, yet short, DH tracks. It's mostly technical riding, with plenty of drops, berms and jumps; experienced riders will probably make the best of it. There is some good XC riding to be had in the surrounding woods too.

Conditions The northshore can be ridden in most weather, but as ever, mud tends to shut the area down in the colder, wetter months for long spells.

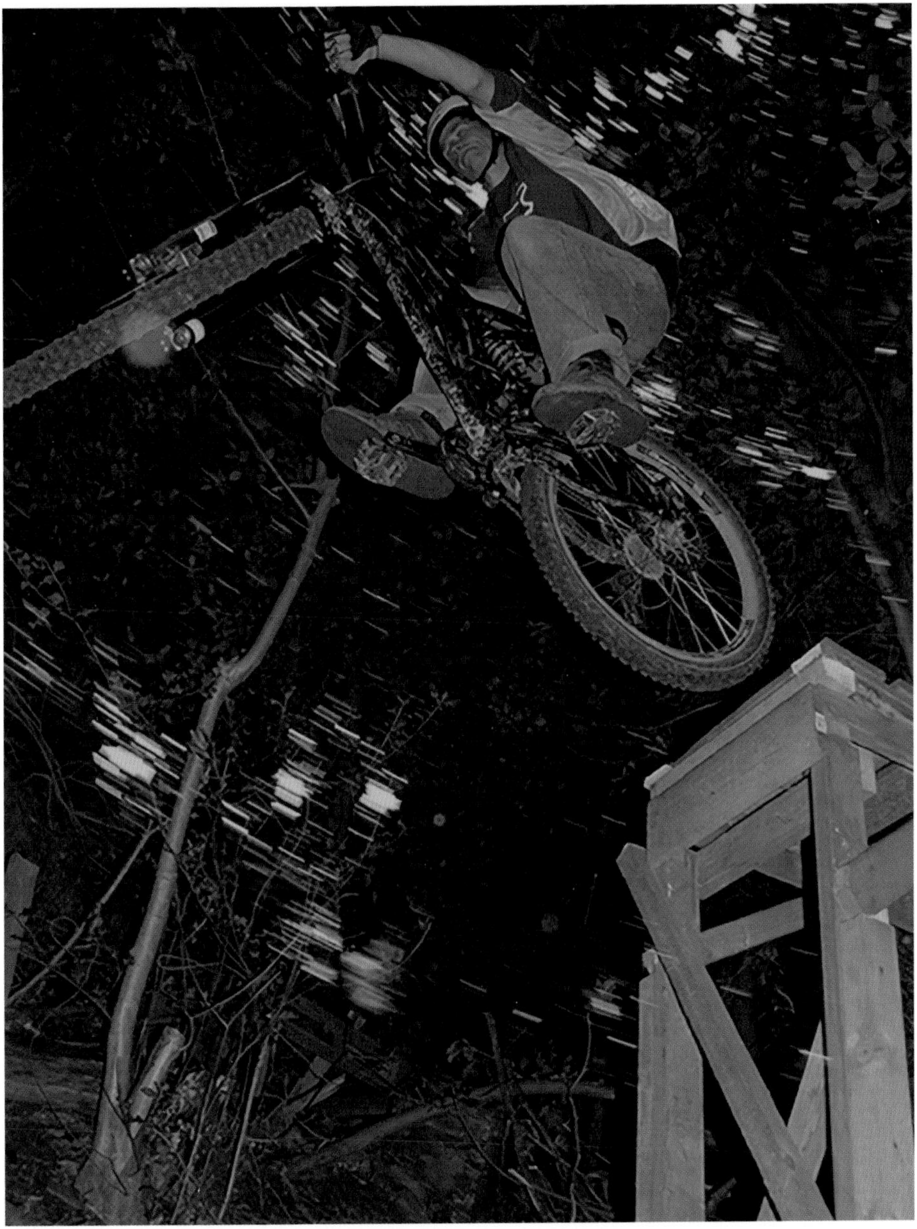

BEN WAIN/JAB-RIDE.CO.UK

↘11 Chicksands Bike Park

Train station Arlesey/Millbrook (Beds)/Stewartby

Nearest city London

Sat Nav SG17 5QB

Opening times Chicksands is only closed on trail-building days or for one-off events. Weekend rides cost £5 per session and weekdays are free. Annual memberships are £50 for seniors, £30 juniors or a family ticket (2 senior, 3 juniors) for £80.

Location Chicksands Bike Park is in Rowney Warren, just north of Shefford and around 15 km to the east of Milton Keynes. From the M1 leave at junction 13 and follow the A507 past Ampthill towards Shefford. At the roundabout with the A600 take the first exit to Bedford, carry on over the next roundabout, and take a left down Sandy Lane and the car park is signposted.

Facilities Formerly most associated with being an RAF base, Chicksands is a small village in the area that contains some great freeride trails on a block of Forestry Commission land where a hugely popular freeride area has been developed. The area is continually changing with both more challenging and easy lines being created to allow all riders to enjoy the site. The soil in this area is perfect for riding bikes all year round – a mix of sand and clay that drains well and sticks together to shape transitions and landings. Branded a Bike Park, this is fantastic jumping and technical skills territory with purpose-built trails, tonnes of northshore, berms and drops, and feature after feature on every bit of singletrack.

XC A trip to Chicksands to purely ride XC would leave you disappointed as despite there being a blue and red XC route, they are both very short (each less than 4 km). However, if these are combined with the jumps and berms of the freeride area there's plenty of fun to be had.

Downhill There's a short DH track but due to the very small hills here the runs are very short and it would be crazy to come here solely for this. Any downhiller would however have great fun on the obstacles provided in the freeride area.

Freeride Chicksands is essentially a freeride hotspot with riders travelling from all around the south of England to ride here. With a good scene and plenty of riding to try out there's something for everyone here, from the tabletops and DJ lines, through the dual slalom to the national standard 4X track and freeride course made up of ladderdrops, step ups and northshore obstacles.

Not to miss Racing your mates down the dual slalom and 4X tracks – a bit of friendly competition never hurt anyone.

Remember to avoid Casing a landing and not fixing it up. You may have paid your £5 but trail etiquette costs nothing.

Nearest Bike/Hire shop
Michael's Cycles (T01234 6352937) are in Bedford; they carry some mountain bike brands and will be able to repair most mountain bike problems.

Local accommodation
Try the Embankment Hotel in Bedford (T01234 248920) situated

JASON WAIN

on the banks of the river Ouse and overlooking the Victorian suspension bridge. Also try De Pary's Guest House (T01234 261982) with an area for bikes and just a couple of minutes' walk from the town centre.

Eating There are some snacks on site, or for great Italian food try Villa Rosa (T01234 269259) in Bedford. The local Dew Drop Inn (T01525 840096) has pub grub.

More info
chicksandsbikepark.co.uk.

> **Lowdown**

Locals do
Warm up on the tabletops and smaller 6 pack jumps before moving onto the bigger sets.

Ride the bombholes – a network of short trails through a series of interconnected bomb holes.

Locals don't
Ride without paying the fee for the day – it keeps this site running.

Pros
Progressive venue, riders can learn a lot each time they visit.

Cons
Limited variation for non-freeriders.

No uplift.

BEN WAIN/JAB-RIDE.CO.UK

↘12 Crowborough – The Bull Track

XC DH FR N

Train station Crowborough/Brighton
Nearest city London
Sat Nav N/A

JASON WAIN

Location The Bull Track is just to the east side of Crowborough, a town around 10 km southwest of Royal Tunbridge Wells. From Tunbridge Wells, take the A267 south towards Heathfield. At Mark Cross (about 5 km down this road), take a left onto Catt's Hill in the direction of Rotherfield onto the B2100. Head down this road keeping to the right in Rotherfield (stay on the B2100), and keep going until you go under the railway tracks as you enter Crowborough. Take the second road on the left after this crossing, then through a water-splash and over a railway bridge, then next right. The Bull Track is on the right. Unauthorised riders run the possibility of having everyone banned, so please call Alvar for permission on T07789 372352.

Facilities The Bull Track often holds race days; otherwise the opening hours for summer should be weekends 1000-1800, weekdays 1800 until dark. There are often hot and cold drinks on site, but only when vans arrive. Otherwise, nearby Crowborough has shops and amenities.

Overview This is a purpose-built DH and freeride area, which regularly holds races and is one of the thriving North Downs mountain biking scene's regular haunts. There is plenty of northshore here, some good jumps and obstacles to ride, and a bit of DH.

Terrain There's plenty of singletrack, with lots of wood scattered around to help out on the boggy sections.

XC There's not a lot here for the XC rider, although some loops on the DH track would be testing!

Downhill The DH track is mostly grassland, and not as technical as those found elsewhere, but it is still fun to ride and the site of many races. There are plenty of Youtube postings of the trail online.

Freeride/DJs There are three main freeride trails, some pretty impressive northshore (with a 15 ft drop), a load of doubles and gaps, and some lines for less experienced riders. Highly recommended.

Conditions The singletrack here is prone to mud, but the problem areas have been worked on. Rideable in most conditions.

ⓘ **More info** jab-ride.co.uk has info and a forum for those who regularly ride and race at The Bull Track, while mudtrail.co.uk has tonnes of info on the local Surrey and North Downs mountain biking scene.

BEN WAIN/JAB-RIDE.CO.UK

↘13 Crow Trails

DJ

Train station Meldreth
Nearest city Cambridge
Sat Nav SG8 6DF

CHRIS MORAN

Location Crow Trails are in Royston, a village around 12 km south of Cambridge on the A10. From the A10, exit for Royston south on the Royston Road, and head about 300 m towards town. Pass Bury Lane on your left, and the trails are immediately in the copse of trees on the right-hand or south – side of the road. Park in Bury Lane.

Facilities Royston has shops and amenities and is a further 200 m down the road.

Overview These are some half-decent DJs with a couple of good lines and some sizeable gaps. Not for beginners.

Conditions This is a copse of trees which are rarely used by the public. Drainage is a problem so expect it to be muddy after rain.

↘14 Danbury Common

DH FR DJ

Train station Hatfield Peverel/ Chelmsford
Nearest city London
Sat Nav CM3 4NN

Location Danbury Common is around 6 km to the east of Chelmsford in Essex. From the M25 exit junction 28 heading towards Chelmsford on the A12. Exit the A12 at junction 18 and head east along the A414 (Main Road) for 3 km to Danbury. In the village, turn right into Copt Hill, and drive another 100 m. To your left will be a track heading into the forest. Park and follow this track on your bike. The Common comprises of all the land to the south.

Facilities Danbury has plenty of shops, pubs and amenities.

Overview This is a cool area for those who like a bit of dirt jumping, some short but technical DH trails, and natural freeriding. There's the main section that splits into separate trails. There's also a freeride area known as 'The Canyon' with plenty of drops, etc. Definitely not worth a long journey, but for those who are in the area, it's well worth checking out. Local riders are friendly and should be able to tell you when build days are on.

Conditions This is forested dirt jumping and natural trail riding with some added, man-made obstacles to compliment the trails, but fairly low budget.

RACHEL BESANT

Local riders
Ben Wain

Bike Giant STP Zero and Norco Atomic
Local spot Private trails, I build more than I ride these days!
Club member The Bull Track, helped a bit with Bedgebury too.
Age 24
Type of rider Prefer full on Downhill and shore. Ride all types though!

Where's the one place you'd recommend above all, for those coming to the southeast?

BW It would have to be Chicksands for the scale of the park and build quality of the trails. It doesn't have 'real' Downhill or XC but it's a great day out any time of year.

Where has the best XC?

BW Last one I enjoyed was Friston Forest. There are some excellent trails around the North Downs too.

Where is the best Downhill?

BW They're all quite short around here, best commercial spot would be PORC (best to go on a race weekend when a track's marked out). There are a few decent secret trails but can't say much about those! Aston Hill is also well worth a look.

The best dirt jumps?

BW Again I would rate Chicksands for excellent build quality. Wisley's good but has limited access! If you want less steep stuff (more full suss friendly) then The Bull Track's your call.

If you were to take a family out – say a cousin who's visiting with his kids – where would you head?

BW It would probably be Bedgebury if you've got the cash to spend (expensive parking!); the two grades of trails cross over at various points so you can sample a bit of both and see who likes what.

What secret stashes do you know about?

BW There's a quite few around that I can't really mention. There are some nice natural drops and rock lines around Tunbridge Wells – worth a look if you're in the area!

If you were a huge fan of cake and wanted to find the best trail with a foodie pit stop, where would it be?

BW Leith Hill and surroundings have some good bike-friendly stop offs. I have been recommended to try Stephan Langton Inn at some point!

Where – if anywhere – outside of your area do you often visit with your bike?

BW I have visited the French/Swiss Alps a few times and love it there. The atmosphere and everything is spot on. Am considering maybe Italy next!

Which websites have the best info on your local area?

BW jab-ride.co.uk for what's happening in the area and photos etc or moredirt.co.uk or Mudtrail.co.uk for general info on spots.

Which is the best shop to head to if you're in the southeast?

BW My personal favorite is Wildside in Tunbridge Wells.

Devils Drop DJs

XC DJ

Train station Hayes
Nearest city London
Sat Nav BR4 9HZ

Location These DJs are on the north edge of West Wickham Common, around 3 km to the east of Farnborough. From the M25, take junction 4 and head towards central London on the A21 past Farnborough. This the Croydon Road, and West Wickham Common is to the north (on the right heading from Farnborough). Park at the Croydon Road/West Common Road entrance and ride through.

Facilities Hayes – on the north side of the wooded common – has plenty of shops and amenities.

Overview There's some XC riding to be had around the common, and at the north end there are some low-budget dirt jumps that contain a few gaps and tables. Not worth a huge detour, but for those in the area it's worth checking out.

Conditions The common can get boggy in the winter, but otherwise it's a fairly decent stretch of wooded area, with some open patches of grass here and there.

Devils Dyke DH and XC

XC DH

Train station Brighton
Nearest city Brighton and Hove
Sat Nav BN1 8YJ

Location Devils Dyke lies 2 miles north of Brighton town centre, and has its own exit sign off the A27. Park at the Devils Dyke Inn. Two hundred before, on the way in you'll pass some of the fantastic DH tracks through the valley to the right of the road – impossible to miss. From the pub, DH routes go off in all directions, with the best being down towards Steyning.

Facilities The Dyke Inn is a pretty average pub considering its stunning location, but does serve food and drinks. The nearest bike shop would be Baker Street Bikes (bakerstbikes.co.uk) or Evans Cycles (evanscycles.com) in nearby Brighton.

Overview DD is the name given to the end of the road pub, and the views from the top stretch to London to the north, the Isle of White to the west and Eastbourne to the east. The whole area is criss-crossed by paths that are part of the South Downs Way, and the area near the pub teems with walkers, kite-flyers, parapenters and outdoor types. Head out in any direction and the crowds clear. The XC is fantastic due to the views, and ranges from easy to fairly challenging, mainly owing to the variety of routes and the potential distances for those looking to do long stretches through quaint sussex villages. Plenty of one-way routes exist (taking the train out to Hassocks and riding back to Brighton is a popular 12-mile run). Not to be confused with the Devils Dyke DJs in Surrey.

Conditions Most routes are singletrack or bridleways and tend to be gravelly and exposed, so avoid in high wind. Mud is a frequent problem.

ⓘ **More info** Check out the Brighton local scene at brightonmtb.org or mtbdiary.co.uk.

CHRIS MORAN

CHRIS MORAN

↘17 Devils Dyke Nonsuch DJs

DJ

Train station Stoneleigh/Cheam/Ewell/Ewell East

Nearest city London

Sat Nav KT17 2DE

Location Devils Dyke DJs are just to the southwest edge of Nonsuch Park, between Cheam and Ewell and near Epsom. From the M25 exit at junction 8 and head north towards central London on the A24. From central London head south to Ewell on the A24. At Ewell, the A24 goes directly past Nonsuch Park. Enter the park, and head to the southwest entrance. One hundred along the park perimeter road there's an entrance into the woods. The DJs are inside here.

Facilities Ewell town centre (200 m away) has plenty of shops and amenities.

Overview These are some of the best DJs in the greater London area, with tight transitions, short ready-times, and good sections. There are some huge gaps, and reinforced landings. Not for beginners. The local BMX riders share them with mountain bikers but respect and helping to build is strongly recommended. Nearby Track 40 in Banstead welcome DH (though small) diversion.

Conditions These are clay jumps with logs to reinforce the landings, all set in a tight copse of public trees.

↘18 Donkey Island DJs

DJ

Train station Shepperton/Upper Halliford/Sunbury

Nearest city London

Sat Nav KT12 2JB

Location Sunbury-on-Thames is just to the south of the M3 inside the M25. From the M3 exit at junction 1, and head south in the direction of Sunbury-on-Thames on Green Street. Turn right after 300 m onto Nursery Road, then left on the A244 Upper Halliford Road for 3 km. Cross the river, and turn left into Hepworth Way on the A350 towards West Molesey. After 1 km turn right into Waterside Drive, and go all the way to the end. Then ride along the water's edge, cross the bridge onto Donkey Island, and go left into the copse.

Facilities Sunbury – just over the river – has plenty of shops and amenities, but the nearest town is Walton-on-Thames.

Overview There's a ditch with berms, drops and some DJs. Not worth a long journey but for those in the area this is worth a look.

Conditions This is a small, wooded area with fairly decent drainage but still prone to bouts of mud after heavy rain.

CHRIS MORAN

↘19 Esher Shore

FR DJ N XC DH F

Train station Claygate/Hinchley Wood/Esher or Hersham

Nearest city London

Sat Nav KT10 8AN

Opening times 1000-1800 Monday to Saturday (until dusk during winter), and 1100-1600 on Sundays and Bank Holidays. £10 yearly membership is mandatory and then it's £5 per day session

Location Esher Shore is on the southern edge of Sandown Park Racecourse, in the town of Esher in Surrey. From the M25 leave at junction 10 and head towards London on the A3. After 4 km take the A244 north towards Esher. In Esher, take the Esher Green road, which turns into More Lane. Take the first right and Esher Shore is signed from there.

Facilities Esher shore is perhaps the UK's only dedicated northshore park. The park is only three acres but the trails weave back and forth and the low speed nature of the northshore obstacles mean that every last inch of ground is utilised in this unique development. The trails are graded blue or red with the blue lines aimed at encouraging beginners into riding the northshore obstacles, whereas the red lines are increasingly technical.

XC There is no XC at Esher, but it can be an interesting diversion from the norm to spend a day riding the intricate and well-made wooden trails here.

Downhill There is no DH at Esher and the nature of the obstacles isn't suited to big DH bikes.

Freeride For those that like northshore and/or trials-type skills riding, there is plenty here to keep you going all day, with lots of varied lines and new stunts being built all the time. Currently there are 4 km of freeride trails with elevated bridges, skinny beams,

BEN WAIN/JAB-RIDE.CO.UK

BEN WAIN/JAB-RIDE.CO.UK

> Lowdown

Locals do
All help out with the construction and development of the park.

Locals don't
Ride the DJs in the wet – you would be asking for trouble. The northshore has chicken wire though.

Pros
Unique, well-worked park in the UK.

Cons
Like marmite, depending on whether northshore is your thing or not, you'll either love it or hate it.

tight turns, rams, berms and drops. The website does give a great pictorial breakdown of the trails at eshershore.com/shore_park.htm.

Easy Start out on the blue-marked northshore. Riders with some previous mountain bike knowledge will progress easily. There is so much here that it is definitely a case of building up slowly to make sure you have mastered what you're riding before moving onto something much bigger.

Hard There are plenty of hard lines to try for the more advanced rider – head for the red-marked runs.

Not to miss The best northshore riding within the M25, possibly in the south of the UK.

Remember to avoid Travelling here in less than perfect weather conditions. Call before you leave.

Nearest Bike/Hire shop Freeborn Bikes (T01372 476969) found in Esher have a good range of stock and a good workshop. They also sponsor the Esher shore park.

Local accommodation
Pine Tree Cottage (T020 8398 8848) and Lilac Cottage (T020 8398 7546) are both found in Esher and offer reasonabl- priced B&B accommodation.

Eating The Conservatory Restaurant (T01372 470957) can be found on Winterdown Road and provides a great getaway to enjoy a social meal.

ⓘ **More info** Freeborn Bike shop at Esher Shore – T01372 476969 or check out the website, eshershore.com.

BEN WAIN/JAB-RIDE.CO.UK

↘20 Epping Forest

Train station Chingford (train)/ Loughton (tube)
Nearest city London
Sat Nav E4 7QL

CHRIS MORAN

Location Epping Forest is the largest open and wooded area within the M25. From central London head for the M11 in the direction of Cambridge. From the motorway, exit at junction 5 and head in the direction of Loughton. Take a left at Loughton onto the A121 towards Buckhurst Hill. After 2 km take a right on Manor Road, then a right onto the A104 Epping New Road, then an almost immediate left into Ranger's Road (the A1069). This is the forest boundary road. Head down here for 1 km then take a right onto Bury Road. Park at the West Essex Golf Club.

Facilities There are plenty of shops and amenities at Chingford, just to the south, as well as a dedicated Chingford Information Centre which has a trail map available.

Overview The forest and open land are ye-olde common land, and very popular with a variety of forest and countryside users, and there is a huge amount of fire-road and bridleways criss-crossing the area. Fortunately, for those who like their riding uncongested, there is also a large amount of singletrack to be had too. Hit the area on a weekend and you'll see plenty of riders (you can join in on a ride by checking out the link below). Or simply meander your way around this gentle XC venue, taking one of the many diverse routes that you come across.

Conditions Mud is particularly a problem here due to the clay base which prevents proper drainage. Avoid in mid winter.

ⓘ **More info** There's a great local scene here who have banded together to form a fee-free club that anyone can join in with, epping-forest-mbc.co.uk.

↘21 Friston Forest

XC FR N

Train station Polegate/Hampden Park
Nearest city Brighton and Hove
Sat Nav BN26 5QF

Location Friston Forest is to the north west of Eastbourne. From the M25 exit at junction 6 and take the A25 all the way south towards Eastbourne. Keep heading into the town centre on the A2270, then turn westwards towards Beachy Head/Newhaven on the A259. Just after the village of Friston – itself around 2 km from Eastbourne – turn north on the B2105 Jevington Road and follow this road for around 1 km. Friston Forest is signed to the left of this road. Alternatively, there is a car park behind the Seven Sisters Country Park off the A259 between Seaford and East Dean.

Facilities The forest is deep countryside, but nearby Friston has shops and amenities, while Jevington – just to the north of the forest – is home to the legendary Hungry Monk restaurant, where the Banoffi Pie was invented!

Overview This is one of the most popular sites for the southeast coast dwellers of Brighton and Eastbourne, and is a very popular horse-riding destination. Maintained by the Forestry Commission, there are several waymarked trails throughout the forest, with plenty for the adventurous XC rider and families alike.

Terrain Loads of both unofficial and waymarked singletrack, as well as lots of bridleways.

XC There's a 7-mile loop known as Butchers Trudge which starts in Butchershole. Most routes are well signed, and a range of difficulties although serious riders might be left wanting. The scenery, and that of nearby Seven Sisters and Beachy Head, is utterly British, with fantastic forest land opening out into rolling hills and huge, chalk cliffs against a sea backdrop.

Downhill There are some short sections of DH but nothing serious.

Freeride There's a strong local scene who build armoured bridges, jumps, drops and some random northshore-style wood around the forest.

Conditions The XC routes are hard-packed chalk and flint singletrack so work in most weather conditions.

ⓘ **More info** Local bike shop Cuckmere Cycle Company in Seven Sisters have a wealth of knowledge on the Forest while mudtrail.co.uk/where-to-ride.php has a page on Friston.

ISOBEL CAMERON/FORESTRY COMMISSION

CHRIS MORAN

ISOBEL CAMERON/FORESTRY COMMISSION

↘22 Fearnley DJs

DJ

Train station Cookham
Nearest city Reading/London
Sat Nav SL6 9TW

Location Fearnley DJs are between Maidenhead and Marlow. From Maidenhead (junction 9 on the M4), head north on the A308 Furze Platt Road towards Marlow. 3 km from the centre of Marlow, take a right onto Winter Hill Road towards Cookham Dean. After 500 m, the DJs are in the woods on your left.

Facilities There is a shop on the brilliantly named Golden Ball Lane a few hundred metres south of the trails.

Overview These are pretty low-budget trails which can be in various states of decline or strength based on how much the local scene is prepared to dig. Not worth a huge journey but possibly good for those living in Maidenhead, Marlow or surrounds if you fancy some freeride practice.

Conditions These woods are little used, so expect them to be muddy and unkept.

↘23 Gunnersbury DJs

DJ

Train station Kew Bridge (rail), Acton Town (tube)
Nearest city London
Sat Nav W3 8LQ

Location These DJs are just north of the M4 in Gunnersbury Park, Brentford. Leave the M4 at junction 2 and head north on Lionel Road North, then take a right (east on Pope's Lane – around the top edge park), then park at the Gunnersbury Park Museum. The DJs are in the southwest corner of the park, just after the lake.

Facilities The museum has a café, and there are plenty of shops and amenities in nearby Brentford.

Overview This is a small area of DJs with a few small lines and one section which might appeal to average riders. Local riders regularly shape and if you do turn up to ride they would definitely appreciate some help in maintaining the jumps.

Conditions Good solid dirt to work with in a secluded corner of private land.

↘24 Harrow Skatepark and DJs

FR DJ

Train station Harrow and Wealdstone
Nearest city London
Sat Nav HA3 5BD

Location As the name would suggest, these two (separate) places are both in Harrow. From Harrow town centre, head north on the A409 Station Road for 1 km just passing Harrow and Wealdstone Underground and train station. Take a right at the next roundabout and the skatepark is well signed off to the right of this road, being about 200 m straight in front of you. To find the DJs, head back to the roundabout, turn right then take the next left onto Canning Road. Carry straight on this road (it turns into Headstone Drive, then Headstone Gardens) for 1 km then take a right into Pinner View. The DJs are around 200 m up this road, just behind the copse of trees on your left.

Facilities Headstone Gardens has shops and amenities.

Overview Harrow is one of the only 1970s concrete wave skateparks left in the UK, and has a strong skate, BMX and mountain bike scene. The DJs are high-quality with plenty of lines ranging from small to fairly big. The scene here is also large, so be prepared to dig if you wish to ride. Worth a visit for locals or those in this general area.

Conditions The skatepark is well drained and the DJs are well maintained, but as always, avoid in bad weather and always fix any cased landings.

ⓘ **More info** Harrow Skatepark has its own wikipedia page at en.wikipedia.org/wiki/Harrow_Skate_Park and website at harrowskatepark.co.uk.

↘25 Hayes Hawks BMX Track

DJ

Train station Hayes and Harlington
Nearest city London
Sat Nav UB3 4NN

Location Hayes Hawks BMX track is in Hayex, around 2 km directly north of Heathrow Airport. From the M4, exit at junction 3 and head north into Hayes on the A312, then at the first roundabout take the left exit (N Hyde Road – the A437) and carry on for 1.5 km, crossing the railway bridge. Hayes Hawks is about 400 m after the railway bridge on the right.

Overview This is an old-school BMX track that is well maintained and good for some freeride and dirt jumping practice for those learning or progressing. These aren't classic DJs but whoops, berms and doubles. Not worth a long journey but for locals it could be worth checking out.

Conditions This area is actually prone to flooding, so obviously avoid if it's been raining.

ⓘ **More info** Hayes Hawks have their own club, hawksbmx.co.uk.

↘26 Highgate DJs

DJ

Train station Upper Holloway (train), Highgate (tube)
Nearest city London
Sat Nav N6 4JH

Location This is a little site just next to the Highgate tube station in North London. From the tube station (which is on the A1 Archway Road), head southeast towards central London. Turn left after 200 m into Hillsborough and park where you can. The DJs are in the little copse on the corner of Archway and Hillsborough.

Facilities Archway Road is full of shops and amenities.

Overview This isn't the biggest set-up in the world, but for those in central and north London dirt jumping spots are hard to come by and this one is a locally-maintained, semi-legal area for BMXers and mountain bikers. All are welcome and there's a small community of riders who try to organize build days, etc.

Conditions This is central London parkland. Expect nearby Queens Wood to be busy with dog walkers but this area should remain fairly undisturbed.

ⓘ **More info** Find the local trailbuilders via Facebook by searching for 'Wall'.

↘27 Highwoods DJs

DJ

Train station Bexhill-on-Sea
Nearest city Brighton and Hove
Sat Nav TN39 5HE

Location Highwoods are on the north west outskirts of Bexhill on the south coast, around 15 km east from Eastbourne. Coming onto Bexhill from the A259 coastal road, head through town and turn north on the A269 Ninfield Road.

CHRIS MORAN

Take a left in Sidley on Turkey Road, and head 4 km westwards (passing Highwoods Golf Club on your left). Slow down as you cross Peartree Lane, and 100 m after there's a pathway heading into the woods on your left (there's usually an 'eggs for sale' sign on the farm entrance opposite. The DJs are in this clearing.

Facilities Bexhill is the best place to get supplies – this is pretty open country.

Overview These DJs were originally built in the BMX hayday of the 1980s, but they have survived and they do now home a decent dirt jumping scene for those who wish to keep their freeride skills up. The line runs slightly downhill to keep your speed up. The perfect learner/intermediate jumps if you find Sidley Woods are too advanced.

Conditions This is a small clearing in the forest that can be prone to bogging and mud.

↘28 Holmes Place DJs

XC DH

Train station Farnborough/Fleet
Nearest city London
Sat Nav GU14 0NY

Location Holmes Place DJs are in Southwood to the west of Farnborough, just to the south of the M3 in Surrey. Exit the motorway at junction 4a heading south on the A327. After 1 km take a left at the roundabout and head over the bridge to the next roundabout. Take a left here, and head towards Southwood with the common on your right. Park where you can and head directly south into the woods.

Facilities Nearby Southwood has plenty of shops and amenities.

Overview This is a locals' dirt jump are with three sets – a four- pack, a medium-sized 12 pack, and a rhythm section with plenty of speed-building pumps etc. There's a decent local scene with both BMXers and mountain bikers. Not worth a long journey but for those in the area it might be worth improving a few skills on the jumps. Please respect the work and effort that have gone into building them.

Conditions This is a classic, local woods set-up which is popular with dog walkers. Expect it to be very muddy in winter and after heavy rain.

ⓘ **More info** The local riders have their own Bebo page bebo.com/HPsauce2007.

↘29 Ipswich BMX Track

BMX DJ

Train station Derby Road
Nearest city Ipswich
Sat Nav IP3 0RG

Location Ipswich BMX track is in a park to the southeast of the Suffolk city. From the city centre, take the A1156 Fore Street eastwards, in the direction of Warren Heath. After 1 km, take a right into Nacton Road, then fork right again into Clapgate Lane. After 500 m, you'll come to Landseer Park on your right – the BMX track is in here.

Facilities There are shops and facilities surrounding Landseer Park.

Overview The UK's oldest BMX track is averagely maintained, and still holds a few thrills for those looking to improve their bike handling skills before heading to some more serious DJs or DH trails.

Conditions The track has drainage, but still gets muddy in bad conditions and is on open parkland in a city suburb.

ⓘ **More info** Ipswich BMX club has its own website, ipswichbmx.co.uk.

↘30 Kuoni Trails

DJ

Train station Dorking Deepdene
Nearest city London
Sat Nav RH4 1SY

Location Kuoni Trails are to the east side of Dorking in Surrey. From the M25, exit at Leatherhead (junction 9), and head south towards Dorking on the A24. As you pass next to Dorking, on Deepdene Avenue, turn left into South Drive and park, or carry on for 200 m and turn or left into a lay-by. The DJs are just in the woods to your left.

Facilities Dorking has plenty of shops and amenities.

Overview There are two lines at Kuoni – the hard and the easy. The easy line is perfect for those with a little skill who wish to improve, while the hard line is definitely for more experienced riders, but won't be too testing for those who can take lines at places like Devils Dyke Nonsuch DJs.

Conditions These are clay-soil DJs built in the forest. Avoid when muddy.

ⓘ **More info** Invasion Cycles run regular trips to Kuoni and know the area well, invasioncycles.co.uk.

↘31 Leith Hill

XC DH DJ

Train station Gomshall
Nearest city London
Sat Nav RH5 6JH

Location Leith Hill DJs are almost part of the Redlands and Surrey North Downs mountain biking scene, and to be found just to the west of the Redlands/Leith Hill XC and DH trails. From the A24 head south from Dorking and take a right at Beare Green onto the A29 towards Ockley. Turn right at Ockley

BEN WAIN/JAB-RIDE.CO.UK

onto the B2126 and carry on for 1.5 km, then turn right into Abinger Road heading to Leith Hill. Carry through the village and the road turns into Leith Hill Road. Carry on straight on for 1 km and park where Sheephouse Lane splits off to the right. Just to the southeast of this junction is a quarry.

Facilities Leith Hill has a shop, but for supplies stock up in Dorking before you arrive.

Overview Leith HIll is fairly steep, and there are some DH trails over to the east of the hill. This side however is for freeriders, with some drops, wallrides and DJs available. Worth a look in if you've come to ride Redlands.

Conditions This is chalky, flinty land, common to the North Downs, and drains well but best avoided after heavy rain.

ⓘ **More info** mudtrail.co.uk is a website dedicated to riders looking for XC, freeride and DH challenges in the North Downs and has a page dedicated to Leith Hill.

↘32 Limpsfield DJs

XC DH

Train station Oxted/Hurst Green
Nearest city London
Sat Nav RH8 0EB

Location Limpsfield DJs are just to the south of the M25 next to the town of Oxted, Kent. Leave the motorway at junction 6 and head south on the A22, then take a right at the first roundabout and head down the A25 towards Oxted, 3 km away. Pass through Oxted, and cross the train tracks and carry on for 1 km. Just before Limpsfield Common, turn right into Wolf's Road, then right again after 400 m as the road forks. Park soon after and head north into the woods. The jumps are in this copse.

Facilities Hurst Green and Oxted have plenty of shops and amenities.

Overview These are some low-budget dirt jumps that are effectively the remnants of an unofficial BMX track built in the 1980s. Surprisingly, they are still maintained by local riders and although not worth a long journey, they are fun enough and offer some good riding and tests for beginners and intermediates.

Conditions This area is wooded common land and popular with dog walkers etc. Nearby Limpsfield Common has a few XC trails and some open land.

↘33 Look Out Gulley

XC DH DJ

Train station Bagshot/Ascot
Nearest city London
Sat Nav SL5 8AY

Location Look Out Gulley is around 2 km north west from Bagshot, at junction 3 of the M3, Surrey. From the M3, take the exit and head north towards Easthampstead on the A322. Park opposite the Berkshire Golf Club and head directly west into the forest.

Facilities The nearest decent pub and shops are in Bagshot. This area is largely unpopulated, although popular with horse-riders and dog walkers.

Overview There are XC trails looping all over these woods, with some short but interesting downhill to be had, while in the middle is Look Out Gulley, a popular freeride spot with drops, some DJs and gaps. Most of it is natural, with a little bit of building starting to make an appearance.

Conditions These woods are prone to boggy conditions during winter, so avoid after rainfall.

CHRIS MORAN

↘34 M3 DJs

XC DJ

Train station Camberley/Bagshot
Nearest city Reading/London
Sat Nav GU15 1PJ (for Sovereign Drive)

Location As the name would suggest, the M3 DJs are just on the north side of the motorway around 1 km west from Bagshot at junction 3. To get there, exit at junction 3, head towards Bagshot and carry on for 1 km until you can turn left onto the A30 London road in the direction of Camberly. Head down this road for 2 km then turn left into the B3015 (The Maultway). Head down here and park before you cross the M3. Head northeast into this grassland (there's an entrance opposite Sovereign Drive), and the DJs are just next to the motorway, around 500 m ride away.

Facilities Camberly has corner shops and amenities.

Overview This is a low-budget area of DJs with a few small lines and one section which might appeal to average riders. Not hugely worth a journey but fine for locals to explore. Plus the local area offers some half decent XC rambling, although the presence of the motorway isn't good for views, etc.

Conditions There is little here to hold off the bad weather, so only take a journey if it's bright outside and has been for a while.

↘35 Mereworth Woods

XC DH

Train station Borough Green & Wrotham
Nearest city London
Sat Nav ME18 5JY

Location Mereworth Woods are around 12 km northeast of Tonbridge. From the M25 exit at junction 4 and head towards Tonbridge on the A228 for 2 km until you reach Mereworth village. Take a right here Beech Road, and go to the end T junction. Mereworth Woods are just opposite this T junction.

Facilities Nearby Mereworth has shops and amenities.

Overview MOD-owned Mereworth Woods contains a collection of trails that local riders have slowly added features to in order to create some short but feature-full DH trails. There are a few jumps, drops and berms, and it's all pretty low budget, but worth a look if you're in the area. There is a good local scene and the riders are starting to band together and improve the trails with armoured bridges etc, and there is a DJ area and possible northshore on the cards too.

Conditions This is all singletrack through forest. Avoid when muddy.

↘36 Mousehold Trails

XC DJ

Train station Norwich
Nearest city Norwich
Sat Nav NR7 8HB

Location Mousehold Trails are just on the northeast suburbs of Norwich. From the A11 heading into Norwich take the A47 ringroad around to the south towards Keswick. Turn left onto the A1042 after 7 km and carry on for 5 km. After Thorpe St Andrew this road turns into Mousehold Lane. Take a left into Plaford Road and head into the woods. The DJs are in a clearing near the centre.

Facilities Nearby Sprowston has plenty of shops and amenities.

Overview There's some XC riding in this fairly large expanse to the north of Norwich town centre, but the main reason to come here would be the DJs built in the middle of the woods. Popular with BMXers and mountain bikers alike, there are several lines ranging from beginner to fairly hard. Not worth a huge journey but something to check out for those in the area.

Conditions This is suburban woodland described as a heath, but there's plenty of tree cover and a good scene on the well-made jumps.

ⓘ **More info** Some local riders have a Bebo page, bebo.com/mtbnorfolk.

↘37 Nature Jumps and Gog Magog XC

XC DJ

Train station Shelford (Cambs)
Nearest city Cambridge
Sat Nav CB1 7AU

Location This is a dirt jumping and XC rambling area just to the south of Cambridge. From the city centre, take the A1307 (Hills Road) south towards Haverhill. Pass Addenbrooke's Hospital on your right and after 1 km, take a left at the roundabout into Cherry Hinton Road. The nature reserve is to the right of this road and can be accessed either from the roundabout, from Cherry Hinton Road or from Worts Causeway (off C Hinton Road). Gog Magog (a range of low chalk hills) are to the south of this area, after the golf course.

Facilities Nearby Cambridge is chock full of shops and amenities.

Overview The dirt jumps in the nature reserve are easy to spot, especially in busy periods when there are other riders around. Not especially large, they offer some fun practice for budding freestylers and freeriders, while the Gog Magog hills offer a few easily accessed kilometres of unofficial singletrack and bridleway riding for XC fans with gentle climbs and mellow descents. This isn't a waymarked area, but has a good scene – see the website below to meet fellow riders.

ADRIAN TAYLOR

ADRIAN TAYLOR

Above: Adrian and Claire Taylor on an XC mission.

Conditions The DJs are in an area prone to bogging, while the chalk hills drain well but are lethal in the rain.

ⓘ **More info** The Cambridge Mountain Bike Group regularly organize exploratory expeditions in their locale, cammtb.co.uk.

38 PORC (Penshurst Off Road Club) aka Viceroy's Wood

Train station Ashurst/Cowden
Nearest city London
Sat Nav TN11 8EP
Opening times 0900-1800 and costs £4.00 per day

BEN WAIN/JAB-RIDE.CO.UK

JASON WAIN

Location PORC (the Penshurst Off Road Club), has recently been renamed Viceroy's Wood and can be found next to the village of Penshurst in Kent. From the M25 exit at junction 5 and head towards Tonbridge on the A21. At Tonbridge, take the A26 south, and after around 1 km turn off to the right towards Penshurst on the B2176 Penshurst Road. At the village turn left onto the B2188 Fordcombe Road, and carry on for 1 km then turn right into Grove Road. Go 1 km down this road and PORC is signposted off to the left.

Facilities The riding area known as PORC has been renamed Viceroy's Wood for 2009, with a new 'Shimla' visitor centre featuring a café, showers, massage area and stunning views of the woodland from this eco building. Penshurst is an historic English village where you can expect to see thatched roofs and quaint old cottages nestled around the old town hall and church. Its location also lends itself to serve much of London, and yet the contrast from the nation's capital to this sleepy village couldn't be greater. The riding area – while relatively small – manages to cram a lot in to maximise the space. It is one of the original bike venues in the UK and has been the venue for historic DH races before the real hills were discovered and courses became a lot more technical. That said, it is still a great place to spend a day honing the bike handling skills on the range of short courses and features and remains at the forefront of UK mountain biking.

Downhill There are a number of short DH routes at PORC/Viceroys which will keep you busy for a day; being a small hill it means the runs are short but that has the advantage of the push back to the top being far easier than some venues.

XC If you went purely with the intention of trail riding you would be very disappointed as although there are some marked out XC trails, the area is very small and you would soon exhaust what is on offer. However, with an open mind you can mix it up with the other DH and freeride tracks as none of them are too steep for a XC bike, and you'll have a good time. That said, the perimeter ride is 3.5 miles long, and perfect for all-comers, including families.

Freeride There are a few freeride gaps, a fun 4X track and a quarry area full of DJs, which makes for a fantastic day out for freeriders/ freestylers out there.

Not to miss The DJs are top class.

Remember to avoid
Not checking out the view from

the Shimla centre. Apparently it's the 'Best in Kent'.

Nearest Bike/Hire shop Nearby Tunbridge Wells has a large cycle dealer called Wildside (T01892 527069) who stock just about everything you could need.

Local accommodation Manor Court Farm B&B (T01892 740279) and Well Place Farmhouse B&B (T01892 870894) both offer comfortable country accommodation in the village.

Eating The Spotted Dog (T01892 870253) serves great food using locally sourced products in Penshurst, while the new Shimla Café should be up and running by the time you read this. Expect much organic produce!

ⓘ **More info** PORC – T01892 870136, or check out the new Viceroy's Wood website at viceroyswood.co.uk. Alternatively, Mud Trail has a page dedicated to the area at mudtrail.co.uk/where-to-ride.php.

> Lowdown

Locals do
Have quite rounded bike skills due to the riding here.

Locals don't
Ride here in the wet – jumps are no fun unless they're dry.

Pros
Good on a hardtail or a suspension bike.

Cons
Dirt jumps aren't very well maintained.

BEN WAIN/JAB-RIDE.CO.UK

↘39 Normandy Hill DH

XC DH

Train station Ash
Nearest city Reading/London
Sat Nav GU12 6DL

Location Normandy Hill is located between Farnborough, Aldershot and Guildford. From the M3 exit at junction 4 and head south on the A331 towards Ash, around 7 km away. At Ash, turn left into the A323 heading for Normandy/Henley Park. After 2 km take a left onto Pinewood Road, then park in Upper Pinewood Road and ride into the woods to the north. The DH trails are around 300 m to the northeast.

Facilities Nearby Ash has plenty of shops and amenities.

Overview This is a locally-built series of DH tracks with some pretty good jumps and step downs along the way. They aren't the longest trails in the world, but probably better than you might expect for this part of the world and definitely flow well. At the end of the DH trails are some DJs, and the area is also criss-crossed with some half-decent singletrack for those who like to mix a bit of XC riding into the day.

Conditions There is little here to hold off the bad weather, so only take a journey if it's bright outside and has been for a while.

↘40 Peaslake

XC DH

Train station Gomshall
Nearest city London
Sat Nav GU5 9RR

Location Peaslake is a beautiful village on the Surrey/Sussex border. From the M25, exit at junction 9 and head south through Leatherhead following signs for the A24 Dorking. At Dorking turn right onto the A25 Guildford Road, and carry on for 7 km to the village of Abinger Hammer. Turn south on the B2126, then take the second right into Rad Lane which leads to Peaslake village. Park at The Hurtwood Inn, on the corner of Walking Bottom and Peaslake Lane.

Facilities Peaslake village has a couple of shops and the Hurtwood Inn pub.

Overview Head up Walking Bottom and take the first left. This parking area gives access to a network of XC routes in some spectacular forest (home to the Germanic battle scenes in the film Gladiator), which summits out with views over the south and north downs. There are a few short but sweet DH tracks to be found up Radnor Road from the village centre. Expect to see plenty of riders who are by-and-large very friendly and only happy to show their trails off.

Conditions Most routes are singletrack or bridleways and tend to be shared with dog walkers etc.

ⓘ **More info** Surrey Hills All Terrain Mountain Bike Tours website, mountain-bike-guiding.co.uk/ is the best place for local knowledge.

CHRIS MORAN

↘41 Peckham BMX Track, and Burgess Park BMX

FR

Train station South Bermondsey/ Queens Road Peckham
Nearest city London
Sat Nav SE15 1RT

Location Peckham BMX Track is in Peckham, SE London just off the A2 Old Kent Road. From central London head out on the A2 from the Elephant and Castle. After 1.5 km, turn right onto Peckham Park Road, then first left into Green Hundred Road. After 200 m, the BMX track is visible in the small parkland area to your left.

Facilities Peckham is full of shops and amenities.

Overview This is a small BMX track with three lines of triples, doubles and some table tops. As with most BMX tracks, it's not worth a long journey, but for those looking to start out on trails and DJs, some practice might be found here. Burgess Park, a kilometre to the north west (turn right off the Old Kent Road onto Albany Road if heading back to Elephant and Castle), has another BMX track.

Conditions This is a small clearing of land in a densely built-up area of London.

ⓘ **More info** Peckham BMX track has its own website and club membership – peckhambmx.co.uk.

CHRIS MORAN

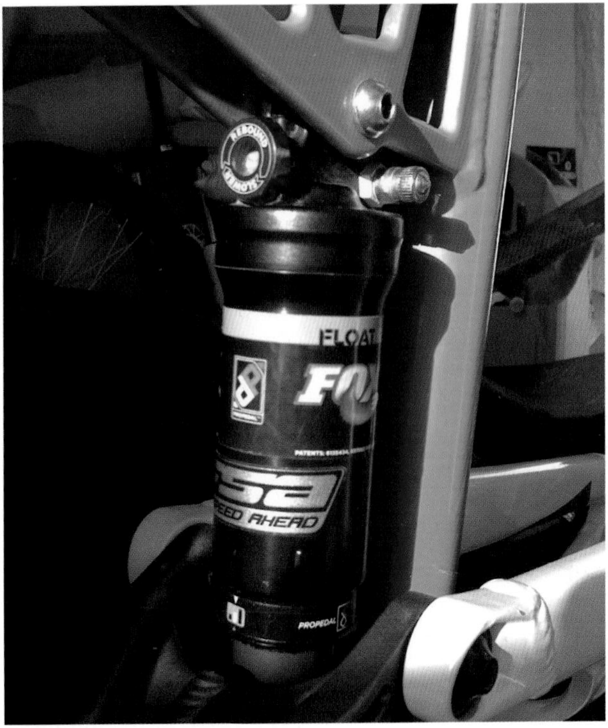

↘42 Rayleigh

DJ

Train station Rayleigh
Nearest city London
Sat Nav SS6 8UP

Location Rayleigh is at the north west edge of Southend-on-Sea in Essex. From the M25 exit at junction 29 and head down the A127 towards Southend. After around 15 km Rayleigh is signed to the left on the A129. Take this exit and carry along High Road to the centre of Rayleigh, then after 750 m turn right onto Eastwood Road, the A1015. Carry on for 2 km and take a left into Lancaster Road. The DJs are at the end of this road where it bends off to the left and changes its name to Grove Road. Park and head off to the right into the woods.

Facilities Rayleigh is full of shops and local amenities.

Overview This is a local DJ spot with some good lines consisting of tables, gaps and a six-pack. Not worth a huge detour but recommended for local riders to check out.

Conditions Forested DJs which work only in dry conditions.

↘43 Redlands

XC DH

Train station Gomshall
Nearest city London
Sat Nav RH5 6JH

BEN WAIN/AB-RIDE.CO.UK

Location Redlands Trails are to the west of Dorking near the village of Wotton in Surrey. From the M25 exit at junction 9 heading south through Leatherhead and aiming for the A24 in the direction of Dorking. At Dorking follow signs for the A25 in the direction of Guildford. After 2 km, you'll hit Wotton; take a left here down Sheephouse Lane, followed by another left after 400 m into Wolvens Lane. The parking area for Redlands is around 500 m up here on the left.

Facilities Nearby Westcott or Wotton have small shops and a few amenities; otherwise, take supplies in from Dorking.

Overview This is a huge expanse of mixed-owned land, and a brilliant example of what groups of mountain bikers can achieve when they form a club and treat the land – and its owners – with due respect. There are tens of purpose-built trails here, criss-crossing the area using either fire-roads, bridleways, or – increasingly as so – mountain bike-specific singletrack.

Terrain This is gentle, hilly country, covered in large, carniferous forest. Some of the area is English Heritage, some privately owned, and most managed in one way or another. Avoid the budding trees or any closed areas, and only build in conjunction with the Redlands riders club.

XC There are several XC loops in the forest, from easy blue runs to more difficult reds, all waymarked and clearly signed as to whether they're bike, walker or horse paths. Summer Lightening, BKB, Golden Birdies and Reservoir Dogs are four of the best.

Downhill There are some short sections of DH around but this is no place for serious DH riders. Nearby Leith Hill has a DH section named 'Deliverance' that is renowned, and has a few drops and rootsy sections, but not worth a long journey.

Dirt jumps Again, there are some great features to ride, but no specific DJs or freeride area. But those on a full-suspension bike will find roots, banks and jumps to hit.

Conditions The XC routes are hard-packed dirt singletrack. The area is very popular with walkers and horse-riders, and is also home to several residents in cottages etc, but well known as a mountain biking centre so expect to see plenty of bikes.

ⓘ **More info** There are loads of great local riders, who regularly get together and help maintain the Redlands area through either redlandstrails.org or the blog site (which contains several videos of the trials) redlands.typepad.com or mudtrail.co.uk/where-to-ride.php, which has a page on Redlands and nearby Leith Hill.

↘44 Shoreham DJs

DJ

Train station Shoreham by Sea
Nearest city Brighton and Hove
Sat Nav N/A

Location Shoreham DJs are in Shoreham-by-Sea, just to the west of Brighton. From the A27 head west from Brighton in the direction of Chichester. Exit, taking the A283 heading towards Shoreham and head south towards the sea. Take a right at the mini roundabout, then turn right and cross the estuary inlet where the road turns into the A259 Brighton Road (heading away from Brighton). As soon as you've crossed the water, take the first right (although it is an illegal turning – head to the roundabout and double back to do it legally). The DJs are at the end of this road.

Facilities Shoreham has plenty of shops and facilities and is just on the other side of the bridge.

Overview These are council-owned but well-maintained DJs covering around a football-pitch worth of trails that criss-cross and are filled with gaps, berms, hips, doubles and drops. It used to be Shoreham's Adur BMX track but has been turned into DJs recently. Possibly worth a visit if you're in the area and love freeriding or dirt jumping; otherwise not worth a journey.

Conditions The ground here dries fairly quickly, but still avoid if it's been raining heavily.

ⓘ **More info** The Brighton local scene has a website at brightonmtb.org.

↘45 Shorne Wood Country Park and DJs

XC

Train station Higham/Sole Street/Cuxton
Nearest city London
Sat Nav DA12 3HX

Location Shorne Wood Country Park and its DJ brother are just to the east of Rochester, Kent. From the M25, exit at junction 2 onto the A2 heading to Rochester. After 10 km, exit the A2 in the direction of Gravesend east (the exit after Singlewell). Turn right and head back over the A2, and the road follows the A2 in parallel until a roundabout 1 km along. Here carry straight on to Brewers Road (direction Shorne); after 500 m Shore Country Park is on the left.

Facilities SWCP has a new visitor centre (an eco construction), with plenty of facilities including a café, toilets, etc.

Overview This is primarily a walkers' and horse-riding destination, but the local mountain bike scene has recognised it as a fantastic XC area. Unfortunately, bikes are officially 'banned' but with care and work that is likely to change and no-one seems to uphold the law. The trails are as expected in this slightly undulating area of Medway – no strenuous DH or horrendous climbs – and mostly naturally-beaten in singletrack. Just to the north on Brewers Road are a series of DJs ranging from easy to medium gaps and tables.

Conditions Avoid if muddy as they tend to wood chip the area for the horse-riders.

ⓘ **More info** kentdowns.org.uk/map_details.asp?siteID=53.

CHRIS MORAN

↘46 Sidley Woods

DJ

Train station Bexhill-on-Sea
Nearest city Brighton and Hove
Sat Nav TN39 5BY

Location Sidley Woods are in Bexhill-on-Sea on the south coast. Coming into town from the north on the A269 (Ninfield Road), take a left into Sidley Street, then a right onto Preston Road. The trails are in the woods at the end of this road, so park in the cul-de-sac and head into the woods (next to the Lovett's Wood sign), and the DJs are right there.

Facilities Sidley Street has plenty of shops and supplies.

Overview These are some competition standard BMX-built trails, so arrive with plenty of respect and help to build or repair any casings or damage you might cause. They are high-level trails, though there are some easier lines if you look for them.

Conditions There is little here to hold off the bad weather, so only take a journey if it's bright outside and has been for a while.

ⓘ **More info** The Source BMX Crew (who run a shop in Hastings) are the people to contact: T01424 460943, sourcebmx.co.uk

↘47 Slindon Quarry

XC DJ

Train station Arundel/Barnham
Nearest city Brighton and Hove
Sat Nav BN18 0LT

Location Slindon Quarry DJs are just off the A27 between Chichester and Brighton. From Chichester, heading east on the A27, drive for around 10 km from Chichester until you hit the village of Fontwell. Here take the A29 (Fairmile Bottom road) in the direction of Pulborough. Go down this road for about 1 km and take the second right into Shellbridge Road (the B2132), then after the houses on the left (around 300 m), park up and ride into the quarry entrance, which is barrier-ed off with steel cable. See the pic as to what the entrance looks like.

CHRIS MORAN

Facilities Fontwell has a corner shop for immediate supplies.

Overview Slindon Quarry is a relatively remote patch of land (although the A27 is just to the south), where local riders have built plenty of drops, berms, doubles, gaps and table tops, and the surrounding area has plenty of unofficial trails for the adventurous XC rider to explore. This is prime South Downs territory, and the area is criss-crossed with plenty of fire-road, single and double track, and has the Cocking Mountain Bike Route 16-mile all weather loop. See website below. Please note that this is private land (and is used for 4X4 and motocross riding) so ride with caution and obey any requests from the landowner.

Conditions The surrounding area can be prone to buddy sections and the quarry itself is used as a 4x4 training area, so the area is very, very muddy after heavy rain.

ⓘ **More info** violetdesigns.co.uk/cocking_mountain_bike_route.htm has plenty of info on XC loops and the South Downs Way.

CHRIS MORAN

↘48 Swinley Forest

Train station Bagshot/Ascot/ Martins Heron

Nearest city London/Reading

Sat Nav SL5 8AY

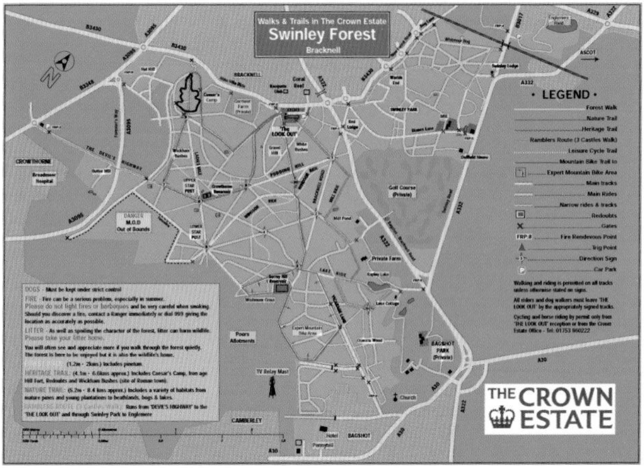

Location Swinley Forest is a tract of Crown Estate between Bagshot and Bracknell, just off the M3 and next door to the Berkshire Golf Club. From the M3 exit at junction 3 and head north past Bagshot on the A322. Swinley Forest is around 2.5 km up this road to the right. Turn off at the first roundabout heading up the A332 and the entrance is 150 m on the right. Follow signs for The Look Out, or The Coral Reef Water World just opposite.

Facilities The Forest is home to The Look Out Discovery Centre (shortened to 'The Look Out'), which houses a café, ranger office, toilets and various facilities. The Wellington Trek Bike Hire (based at the The Look Out) have full-suspension bikes for hire, and the price includes the day permit.

Overview Swinley Forest is part of the greater Windsor Forest, and as such is owned and managed by the Crown Estate. Its 2600 acres of mostly pine woodland is open to riders and there are several waymarked routes for XC riders to follow. The Expert Area is unmarked, but simple to keep on track. You'll need a permit to ride (£2 per day, or an annual pass £18) for insurance purposes.

Terrain There's plenty of purpose-maintained singletrack, built by local fitness and competition organizers Gorrick, as well as local mountain bike club Berks on Bikes. The area is also popular with a range of outdoor users, and although mountain biking is popular, the area is in constant review as to whether this will remain. The locals ask for all riders to respect the areas that are designated bird sanctuaries. There's plenty to ride and it's well kept so it's not a bad deal.

XC There are several XC loops around the forest, although there is also a large proportion that is off-limits to riders. See the trails map either online at gorrcik.com/swinley/map.php or you can buy a trails map from The Look Out for 50p. The Full Nine Yards trail is perhaps the best of the bunch for the all-round rider.

Downhill There are some short sections of DH, but this is predominantly XC and freeride terrain.

Dirt jumps There is a designated area named The Jump Gulley which is well worth a visit, but otherwise pure dirt jumpers are advised to head elsewhere.

Conditions The XC routes are hard-packed, man-made and purpose-maintained dirt singletrack. The area is popular with walkers but well known as a mountain biking centre so expect to see plenty of bikes.

ⓘ **More info** gorrick.co.uk/swinley/index.php.

49 Sloughbottom Park

BMX DJ

Train station Norwich
Nearest city Norwich
Sat Nav NR6 5BB

Location Sloughbottom Park is a competition standard BMX track in northwest Norwich, East Anglia. Coming from the south on the A11, take a left at Daniels Road (the A140) heading north and follow signs for the Sweet Briar Road Industrial Park, then turn right onto Hellesdon Hall Road, and park up on the right next to the football fields. The BMX track is at the south end of the fields.

Facilities Norwich is full of shops and amenities, and there are facilities at Sloughborough Park.

Overview This is another classic, old BMX track with plenty of whoops, berms, doubles and tabletops. Perfect practice for those looking to up their game on jumps. Merlins Trails (a local secret spot) have incredible dirt jumps that are not for beginners. Most riders around here cut their teeth on the BMX track first.

Conditions Avoid after rain but this drains well so it shouldn't be too long after a shower before it's dry.

ⓘ **More info** Norwich BMX track is home to the Norwich Flyers BMX website, norwichbmx.co.uk. In addition, find other dirt jumpers at the Norwich Riders Bebo page bebo.com/NorwichRiders.

50 Teddington DJs

XC DJ

Train station Teddington/ Strawberry Hill
Nearest city London
Sat Nav TW10 7YJ

Location Teddington DJs are on the other side of the river from Teddington in SW London. From Richmond take the A307 south towards Ham. In Ham town centre, turn right into Ham Common, then carry on straight down Lock road. At the T junction turn left, then right onto Dukes Avenue and after 100 m take a left into Locksmeade Road and park up. The DJs are just another 100 m along Riverside Drive; take a left into the common land and head to the waterside on the fire-road.

Facilities Lock Road and nearby Ham has corner shops and amenities.

Overview These are small-ish DJs in the corner of a large expanse of common land next to the water. Don't expect too much, but if you're in the area this is a fun playground with some XC riding to be had around the parkland and some decent freeriding practice on the few lines through the DJs. The park also has some drops and is small enough to explore thoroughly in a few hours. But this is practice only, not worth a journey. The local riders head to Esher or Swinley.

Conditions The jumps are fairly well made and the soil packs well. Please fix any bad landings.

CHRIS MORAN

↘51 Thetford Forest

Train station Brandon
Nearest city Cambridge/Norwich
Sat Nav IP27 0TJ

Location Thetford Forest is just to the north of Thetford town, East Anglia. From the M25 take the A11 towards Norwich. Thetford is around 45 km down the A11. At Thetford take the B1107 north (Thetford Road), towards Brandon. The forest is around 2 km down this road and the public parking is signposted off to the right.

Facilities Thetford is home to the High Lodge Forest Centre, which houses a Go Ape rope access playground, Bike Art cycle hire and bike shop (T01842 810090 – they also sell trail maps for £1), a café, and plenty of amenities such as bathrooms, education centres, etc. Nearby Baker's Oven is a great stop for snacks.

Overview One thing that can be said with certainty about East Anglia is that it's pretty flat, and Thetford is no exception. The trails do make the most of the terrain, however, by providing fast-flowing routes that keep momentum high. When dry and hard-packed the trails actually run very fast and are best suited to hardtails; when it's wet the trails can cut up and run slower.

Terrain There's plenty of singletrack, and four designated routes from family to expert.

XC A great XC area, the forest regularly hosts a round of the national XC race series and the lack of any big hills or descents means that any loop around this forest can be ridden hard and fast. There are four official waymarked routes from green through to blue, red and black. The green and blue are really only of any appeal to young children and leisure cyclists. The red and black routes offer more typical singletrack riding and these can be complimented by the host of unmarked tracks and trails that make up the bulk of the riding for the race courses. Expect swooping singletrack that snakes its way through the forest over whoops and in and out of bombholes.

Downhill and Freeride Forget it!

Conditions The XC routes are hard-packed dirt singletrack. The area is very popular with walkers but well known as a mountain biking centre so expect to see plenty of bikes.

ⓘ **More info** Thetford has its own series of races, the Dusk Till Dawn XC challenges, thetfordmtbracing.com, and the Forestry Commission website has loads of great info on the forest and trails, forestry.gov.uk.

CORKSCREW1082

CORKSCREW1082

CORKSCREW1082

52 Tilgate Forest and St Leonards Forest

XC

Train station Horsham
Nearest city Brighton/London
Sat Nav RH13 6EH (for the Forester's Arms pub)

Location St Leonards Forest and Tilgate are located between Crawley and Horsham, in the North Downs area of Sussex. For St Leonards, park at the Forester's Arms pub. From the M23 carry on down the A23 (the same motorway really), and take the Handcross exit onto the B2110 heading towards Horsham. After 5 km you'll hit a T junction. Turn right onto the A281 and after another 5 km turn right into St Leonards Road. The pub is around 50 m along and to the left. To ride in the woods, carry on up St Leonards Road, and take a right into Hammerpond Road. The forest is on your left.

Facilities The pub has everything you should need, or nearby Horsham is a large town with plenty of shops and amenities.

CHRIS MORAN

Overview This is classic, old-school route-finding XC at its best. St Leonards is chock full of bridleways, fantastic singletrack, fire-roads and open land, and with a flint, chalky base it's pretty good year round. There are no waymarkers, and there's no map available, but there are tens of km's worth of riding to be had and the local scene is relatively small so you're unlikely to find traffic.

Conditions Flint and chalk so is still rideable after some rain, although can have unbelievably slippy sections!

ⓘ **More info** Check out the Brighton local scene who take regular trips to the woods – mtb-nomads.blogspot.com or brightonmtb.org; mudtrail.co.uk/where-to-ride.php has a page on Tilgate too.

53 Track 40

XC DH FR

Train station Banstead
Nearest city London
Sat Nav SM7 3RA

Location Track 40 is a small area of DJs and tiny DH trails next to Banstead Downs Golf Course. From central London head south towards Brighton on the A23 through Brixton. Continue through Croyden, and at Purley take a right onto Foxley Lane (the A2022) heading to Banstead. At the next roundabout, take the right exit (the B2218 Sutton Lane) and head up here for 500 m, then turn right into Freedown Lane and park. Banstead

CHRIS MORAN

Downs are just on the other side of Sutton Lane. Head directly west into the downs, and cross the railway tracks using the bridge. The DH trails are just on the other side of this crossing.

Facilities Banstead has plenty of shops and local amenities.

Overview Banstead Down has some easy XC riding, and on the Track 40 side of the common you'll find a few DJs and some fun riding for those local to the area. Not worth a journey but for everyone local it's a winner.

Conditions Works well in most conditions, and drains well, but still avoid after heavy rain.

ⓘ **More info** The Muddy Moles are a collection of Surrey Riders who have links to the area, muddymoles.org.uk.

↘54 Tring Park

XC DH DJ

Train station Tring
Nearest city London
Sat Nav HP23 6FF

Location Tring Park is around 10 km west from Hemel Hempstead on the A41. Heading north on the A41 from the M25 (exit 20), turn off just before Tring in the direction of Wiggington. Just after the exit, carry along Fox Road for 400 m and then park up. Tring Park is to the right hand side of this road.

Facilities Wiggington is a quaint village a few hundred metres further down the road with some shops and amenities.

Overview There have previously been DJs in this wood, and they sparodically appear and dissappear. The DH trails are easy to find, and short but fairly feature-full, although a stronger local scene would create better terrain. That said, the XC is fantastic, and part of the Central Chilterns Cycleway – a network of singletrack, bridleways, canal paths and colour-coded paths for families and intermediate riders.

↘55 Warley DJs

DJ

Train station Brentwood
Nearest city London
Sat Nav CM13 3DP

Location Warley DJs are just to the south of Brentwood in Essex. From the M25 exit at junction 29 heading east on the A127 towards Basildon. After 300 m, turn off left on the B186 Great Warley Street towards Great Warley. Go through the village, and carry on Warley Road for 400 m before turning right onto Warley Gap. Keep on this road for another 400 m and the DJs are just to the right, off the road in the trees and behind the Brentwood Go Karting Centre.

Facilities The nearby Karting centre has supplies and there are plenty of shops in Warley and Brentwood.

Overview This is a pretty cool set up with loads of BMX and mountain bike riders constantly adding to the impressive DJs. There are small gaps to learn, then craters, drops, big gaps, tables and a six-pack.

Conditions Solidly built DJs with some carpet on top of solidified dirt. Avoid in the rain as usual.

↘56 Whiteways

XC

Train station Arundel/Barnham
Nearest city Brighton and Hove
Sat Nav N/A

Location Whiteways is the local name for this area of the South Downs Way, an incredible network of bridleway, singletrack and walkers' paths that stretch for over 130 km from Winchester to Eastbourne. Whiteways Car Park is located just next to the roundabout where the A29 meets the A284, around 6 km north of Arundel. From the A27, head north from Arundel on the A284 (London Road), and park just after the first roundabout on the left.

Facilities This car park is a popular start for XC riders because of Hikers Café, which has hot food and drinks and some toilets to the south side. Arundel has plenty of shops and nearby Houghton (which can be incorporated into some XC loops) has some shops and amenities.

Overview The South Downs Way is a fantastically beautiful stretch of singletrack and bridleway that is perfect for the rambling XC rider who wants to get out into the country and see spectacular views. There are some challenging rides, but you'll have to head off into the forest to discover them (or hook up with local riders), while the designated and waymarked trails are more likely to be fairly simple. The amount of routes here and the distances available are incalculable, but many riders cite the route from here to Devils Dyke in Brighton as being a bit of a classic.

Conditions This is chalky, flinty and sometimes muddy, but generally good year round if it's not been raining too much.

ⓘ **More info** Check out the local Arundel/Brighton local scene on brightonmtb.org or mtbdiary.co.uk, while the South Downs Way has its own page at nationaltrail.co.uk.

↘57 Wild Park

XC DH DJ

Train station Moulsecoomb/Falmer
Nearest city Brighton and Hove
Sat Nav BN1 9JQ (for Barcombe Road)

Location Wild Park is to the northeast of Brighton where the A270 Lewes Road meets the A27. From the A23 coming into Brighton from the north, turn onto the A27 in the direction of Lewes. Leave at the second exit, and follow signs back on to the A27 going the other way towards the University (unfortunately you can't exit the A27 in this direction heading towards Brighton, hence the detour). This exit is the A270 Lewes Road; head down here for 400 m and Wild Park is on the right. Park just opposite in Barcombe road (running parallel with the A270 Lewes Road).

Facilities Brighton has plenty of shops and amenities and is just down the road. Nearby Moulscomb has corner shops and supplies.

Overview Wild Park is home to the local DH and freeride mountain bike scene. There are some pretty spectacular views of the city and over the University. The trails are short, but feature-full and well loved by the local riders. Not worth a long journey but for those in the area it's a fun day out.

Conditions Like most places on the southeast coast, this is chalky and flinty and can be prone to mud through the winter months.

ⓘ **More info** The local Brighton scene at brightonmtb.org.

↘58 Willen Lake BMX Track

DJ

Train station Milton Keynes
Nearest city London
Sat Nav MK15 0YA

Location Willen Lake is in the north suburbs of Milton Keynes, just next to the M1. From the motorway, exit at junction 14 and take the A509 in the direction of Milton Keynes. Turn right at the first roundabout into Portway, then right again at the next into Tongwell Street. The BMX track is about 500 m down this road on the right.

Facilities The town of Willen is a few hundred metres further up Tongwell Street and has plenty of shops and amenities.

BEN WAIN/JAB-RIDE.CO.UK

Overview This is another classic 80s-style BMX track, and great for those wishing to get into dirt jumping but are too intimidated by straight DJs with near-vertical take-offs. The track has a drop in, and some decent berms, doubles, gaps and tabletops.

Conditions The track is a mixture of clay-shale, in open grassland next to a lake.

ⓘ **More info** The Willen Lake track has its own website mkbmx.com.

CHRIS MORAN

↘59 Wisley Trails

DJ

Train station West Byfleet/Byfleet and New Haw
Nearest city London
Sat Nav GU23 6QD

Location Wisley Trails are just off the M25 near Woking and just next to the village of Wisley. Exit the motorway at junction 10 and head south on the A3 Portsmouth Road. The trails are 200 m on the right, next to Wisley Common. It's not possible to park on the A3, so take the next right (Wisley Lane), and park up there and ride through.

Facilities Wisley (200 m up Wisley Lane) has shops and amenities.

Overview Wisley Trails are high-skill level DJs shaped mostly by BMXers with huge gaps, tables and short preparations. Riders need to pay an annual fee to ride there, contact Gareth on gbmx666@hotmail.com or go to his website for more details (see below). Wisley played host to the 2007 King of Dirt comp.

Conditions Hard-packed soil trails in the forest with some carpet take-offs.

ⓘ **More info** Check out the local scene through digitalbmx.com.

CHRIS MORAN

↘60 Woburn Sands

XC DH FR DJ N WW

Train station Aspley Guise/Bow Brickhill

Nearest city Milton Keynes

Sat Nav MK17 8DE (for the Old Stables Guest House)

Opening times The trails are open 24/7, 365 days a year, and there's a £10 annual fee payable if you see the ranger. The land belongs to the Duke of Bedford and welcome to all comers but there are some rules (easy ones - see the website) and respect is asked from visitors

Location Woburn Sands Trails make up the fantastic trio of riding just 40 km north of Greater London (with Aston Hill and Chicksands being the other two). Woburn is just to the east of Milton Keynes and right next to the M1. Leave this motorway at junction 14 and head towards Wavendon on the A5130. From there follow signs for Woburn Sands on the same road, go through the village (passing the garage on your left) and straight over both mini roundabouts. Pass the Fir Tree pub on the left, and head up the hill for about 500 m. Park on the grass verge to the right – the gate is the entrance to the trails.

Facilities No facilities on site, but nearby Woburn has shops and amenities. Ever since the Quarry closed years ago, the Woburn locals have used Old Wavendon Heath at Woburn Sands for walking and horse-riding; in the last decade mountain bikers have found the dry, sandy soils perfect for season-round riding. It actually works better throughout winter when the ground is firmer.

XC Again, this is Freeride/DJ terrain really, but there are plenty of XC trails ranging from 3 km laps to 20 km. With a sandy base, the area can get slow in the summer.

Downhill Although there are DH trails, this is essentially a dirt jumper's paradise, heavily weighted towards the freeriders. There are five DH trails, though none more than 30 seconds long. That said, they are packed full of features.

Freeride A freeride haven, this area has tonnes of DJs, constantly re-shaped by the high-standard local riders. Expect some serious gaps and fantastic tables, as well as plenty of unusual features and some half decent northshore (although the ground is so perfect for building that the locals tend to use this material). There's also an area of 'Drops' which have been extensively added to over the years and are now RedBull Rampage-style daredevil drops.

Easy Start out on the beginner jumps – there is so much here that it is definitely a case of building up slowly to make sure you have mastered what you're riding now before moving onto something much bigger.

> Lowdown

Locals do

Ride amazingly well.

Mix things up with the odd DH line.

Locals don't

Mind the ludicrously cheap annual fee.

Leave litter in the woods.

Pros

One of UK's top dirt jump facilities.

Friendly atmosphere, rides well in winter.

Cons

Not many immediate facilities.

Short DH.

Hard This is a virtually unlimited spot for the advanced jumper.

Not to miss The DJs – first class.

Remember to avoid In periods of hot weather. The sand gets mushy.

Nearest Bike/Hire shop Try Phil Corley Cycles in Milton Keynes, philcorleycycles.co.uk.

Local accommodation The Old Stables Guest House is a cheap B&B in Woodleys Farm, Bow Brickhill Road in Woburn Sands, T01908 281340.

ⓘ **More info** Woburn Sands has its own website at woburntrails.co.uk.

CHRIS MORAN

The Midlands

- Overview 108
- Bringewood 110
- Brackley DH 111
- Cauldwell Woods DJs 111
- Cannock Chase 112
- Cheshire Ghost Rides BMX Track 114
- Deeping BMX 114
- Eastridge Woods 115
- Hopton Castle 116
- Keele Woods & DJs 118
- Leamington Spa 4X Track & DJs 118
- Ribbesford DH 119
- Perry Park BMX 120
- Rutland Water Cycle Way 120
- Sherwood Pines Forest 121
- Swithland Woods 122
- Tiny BMX Track 123

Hopton Castle's last uphill push before one of the best DH tracks in the UK. [CHRIS MORAN]

The Midlands

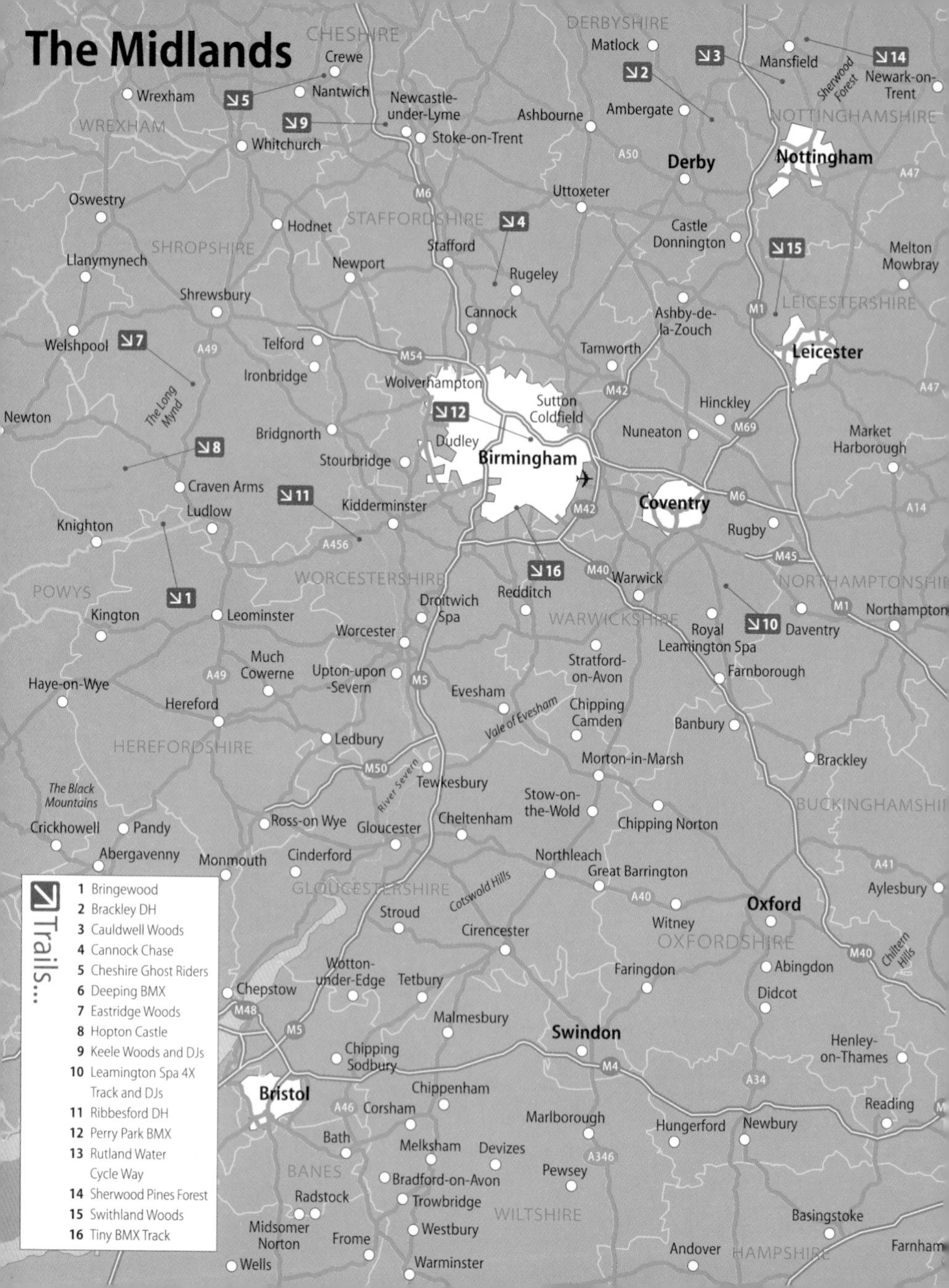

Skegness
Stickford
LINCOLNSHIRE
Sibsey
Wells-next-the-Sea
Cromer
Sleaford
Boston
Grantham
Donnington
Sandringham
Fakenham
A1
A15
Spalding
A17
King's Lynn
13
6
UTLAND
Stamford
Wisbech
Norwich
Great Yarmouth
Swaffham
NORFOLK
Dakham
Peterborough
Newton Flotman
Lowestoft
Mundford
Corby
A11
A140
Chatteris
A1(M)
Thetford
Ely
Huntingdon
Stretham
CAMBRIDGESHIRE
Wellingborough
A1
A14
Bury St Edmonds
A12
SUFFOLK
Eltisley
Cambridge
Newmarket
Bedford
Long Melford
Newport Pagnell
Elstow
Ipswich
Saffron Walden
BEDFORDSHIRE
Letchworth
Woburn
M11
Stevenage
Colchester
Leighton Buzzard
Luton
Bishop's Stortford
Braintree
A1(M)
HERTFORDSHIRE
ESSEX
Clacton-on-Sea
M1
Welwyn Garden City
Harlow
Hemel Hempstead
St Albans
Chelmsford
Epping
Southminster Peninsula
Motorway
High Wycombe
M25
Brentwood
A Road
Watford
B Road
Basildon
Airports
Maidenhead
Ferries
Slough
LONDON
Southend-on-Sea
Gravesend
Windsor
Rochester
Gillingham
Isle of Sheppey
Margate
Whitstable
Bracknell
Ramsgate
M3
Faversham
Woking
M2
Canterbury
M26
Epsom
SURREY
Sevenoaks
Maidstone
M20
KENT
N
10 km
10 miles
Guildford
Reigate
Redhill
Godalming

The Midlands area, home to Birmingham – the UK's second biggest city – has some fantastic riding. Few riders from outside the counties of Herefordshire, Shropshire, Worcs Warwickshire, Northants, Cambridgeshire, Suffolk, Norfolk, Staffs and Leicestershire would think of the area first when planning their next riding trip, choosing instead to head either further north to Scotland, or out west to Wales, but many would be advised to think about the Midlands as a destination in its own right. After all, the trails here are often empty and the infrastructure is incredible: Hopton Castle is one of the best DH venues in the country, and a place where World Champions are often seen in training. And while the area is home to some dense population pockets, there are some surprisingly picturesque areas, even in the middle of sprawling, urban areas. Cannock Chase, a 26-square mile plot of forest land just just to the north of Birmingham, nestles nicely between Rugeley and Cannock itself and is quite a place. Many would think of it as an interesting park, perhaps with a trail or two. In fact it is one of the coolest trail centres in the UK, and has a huge weekend following, drawing in riders from all over the region. Meanwhile, Sherwood Pines is in the process of re-inventing itself as a full-on freeride centre, complete with 4X track, northshore set up, dirt jumps and lots of cool XC to ride

Local scene

There's definitely something in the water in the Midlands. The area has a huge mountain bike population, but is happy enough to stay relatively under the radar. Most head to one of the three major centres at the weekends – Cannock, Sherwood or Hopton, but there are several stand alone sites that are equally worth travelling for. Marc Beaumont's work at Eastridge has resulted in a brilliant all-round set up, while families will love the scenic Rutland Water Way, especially if it's their first time together on bikes. With plenty of places to stop for a cup of tea and some cake, as well as two dedicated bike shops, you couldn't ask for more! We've decided to include the very popular Peak District area in the North section, though very clearly there is good riding to the south of this area that is probably covered by Midlands riders. Apologies to local riders in advance if their allegiances are with their fellow Midlanders.

Hubs

The main three areas here would be Hopton, which has had a loyal DH following for over a decade, Sherwood Pines, which has major plans to become one of the UK's best trail centres, and the fantastically surprising Cannock Chase, which is actually a huge, beautiful forest with some of the best riding facilities in England. If you want to get involved with the Midland's riding scene, then head to one of these trail centres, or check out the websites listed on the inside back cover pages.

Above: Leamington's dirt jumps.
Opposite page: Leamington Spa first corner.

JONATHAN CHEETHAM

JONATHAN CHEETHAM

❺ Best rides in The Midlands

The Midlands has a lot to offer its local riders, as well as those who are up for an adventurous trip to the heart of the UK. Here are five of its best attributes:

❶ Cannock Chase, page 112

The Chase is the number one spot in the Midlands, featuring the epic Follow the Dog trail, some great downhill and northshore, a brilliant visitor centre and fantastic bike shop in Swinnerton Cycles. And we didn't even mention the cake in the café.

❷ Hopton Castle, page 116

For those that like their downhill tracks empty, feature-full and set in stunning scenery, book yourself on to one of Pierce Cycle's uplift days at the Castle.

❸ Rutland Water Cycle Way, page 120

With no less than five brilliant cafés and two bike hire shops, the family loop around Rutland Lake is one of the most picturesque – and fun – days out a family can have.

❹ Sherwood Pines, page 121

Sherwood Pines is definitely setting itself up as a rival to Cannock Chase, with some brilliant XC and family routes, and also for the freeriders out there, with all manner of bike parks in different stages of construction.

❺ Leamington Spa 4X, page 118

Who'd have thought that Leamington Spa would be home to one of the best 4X tracks in the country? Get your speedy, jump-filled kicks, all with a lovely view over the cathedral.

↘1 Bringewood

DH ↗

Train station Ludlow
Nearest city Birmingham
Sat Nav SY8 2HU (for the Downton Estate)

Location Bringewood DH tracks are to be found deep in the Shropshire countyside, around 8 km west from Ludlow. From Ludlow, head to the south side of the river and take Whitcliffe Road signposted towards Wigmore, then after 1.5 km take a left at the hairpin into Lower Wood Road which is signposted 'No through road'. Bringewood us just up this road. When leaving, follow the Downton Estate one way exit system.

Facilities There isn't a great deal at Bringewood itself, but nearby Downton on the Rock is a beautiful estate with the award winning Jolly Frog restaurant, and is where the recent Kiera Knightley and James McVoy film *Atonement* was filmed.

Overview This is full-on DH territory, all set in some remote, beautiful countryside. The DH track has been used for National Champs and features some pretty hefty road gaps, rock sections and some off-camber drops in dense forest. Definitely not for beginners. Pearce Cycles in nearby Ludlow run uplifts here and at Hopton Castle, so check their site or shop for dates and availability.

Conditions This is pretty remote countryside, where phone reception is patchy at best. You're only a few kilometres from Ludlow, but it'll take a while to get there so don't ride on your own.

ⓘ **More info** Pearce Cycles in Ludlow organize plenty of events and uplifts and are the place to head before you go to Bringewood, either online or in person, pearcecycles.co.uk, T01584 879288.

↘2 Brackley DH

XC DH FR

Train station Duffield
Nearest city Derby
Sat Nav DE21 5AU

Location Brackley DH trails are about 10 km north of Derby. From the M1 exit at junction 26 and head westwards on the A610 towards Eastwood. From there take the A608 in the direction of Heanor, carry on through the village and stay on the road for around 5 km until you see a sign off to the right to Horsley Lodge Golf Club on Woodside Road. Take that, then a left into Cloves Hill, and follow the road for around 1 km (through Brackley Gate) until it changes name to Moor Lane. The trails are just to the south (left) of this road, around 600 m after Brackley Gate.

Facilities Brackley Gate has a shop for supplies.

Overview This is a low-budget DH trail area built by local riders. The trails are short, not especially steep, but are packed with features and hold enough for local freeriders and DH riders to keep an interest. Expect plenty of large drops and jumps. The woods also have some unofficial singletrack for XC riders though the forest is quite dense.

Conditions This is a tract of unmanaged forest land which isn't very popular. It isn't waymarked so only go if you're happy and confident in doing some exploration.

ANDY HEADING

↘3 Cauldwell Woods DJs

XC DJ

Train station Mansfield/Sutton Parkway
Nearest city Nottingham
Sat Nav NG18 5BP

Location Cauldwell Woods are just on the south edge of the town of Mansfield, Nottinghamshire. From the M1exit at junction 28 and head towards Mansfield on the A38. After 4 km, take a right onto the A617 heading towards Rainworth/Newark-on-Trent. After about 1 km you'll see Couldwell Woods on your left. Carry on, exit at the next junction, head north towards Mansfield on the A60 (Nottingham Road), and then take the first left and back towards the woods on Cauldwell Road. Park where Cauldwell Road crosses Derby Road (the next crossroads), and head north west into the woods at any available singletrack entrance.

Facilities Head back up Cauldwell Road for the nearest shops and facilities.

Overview These woods are a popular local site for some XC, being criss-crossed with plenty of tracks and hidden trails. Near the middle are some rudimentary DJs that include two lines, both graded somewhere between beginner and intermediate. This isn't a site worth a journey, but for local riders who want to improve their freeride skills, or to start dirt jumping, this is the place to head.

↘4 Cannock Chase

Train station Rugeley Trent Valley
Nearest city Wolverhampton
Sat Nav WS15 2UQ
Opening times 365 days a year and all for free. Just turn up and ride

CHRIS MORAN

CHRIS MORAN

Location Cannock Chase is an Area of Outstanding Natural Beauty located between Cannock and Rugeley, both to the north of the M6 Toll Road. There are a couple of starting points for the trails, but whatever you do, head first to the Birches Valley Forest Centre. Leave the M6 at junction 11 taking the A460 towards Cannock, then Rugeley. At Hednesfield, take a left into Station Road (just after Chase Car Sales), signposted to Pye/Stafford. Then take the first right after 50 m, and go around 3 km along this road until the crossroads (ignore the visitor centre on the right). Take a right at the crossroads onto Birches Road, and the Birches Heath Visitor Centre (home to Swinnerton Cycles) is about 1 km down this road on the right.

Facilities Cannock lends its name to the famous chase – 26 sq miles designated as an Area of Outstanding Natural Beauty that includes an array of important and unusual wildlife and some 600 year-old woodland. The Chase has many kilometres of classic woodland riding and has become a hub for the Midlands mountain bike scene, being only a short drive from a number of big cities. Today, the trail network consists of a number of official and many unofficial trails to meet demand.

XC The main Cannock trail is the 'Follow The Dog' trail which is graded red and purpose-built XC territory. A second route was completed late in 2008 to add to the existing one and in addition there are many kilometres of unmarked, classic, traditional singletrack that keep riders coming back here. There are also a number of leisure green-graded trails which follow flat lowland routes for gentler, more family-oriented rides.

Downhill There are two official DH tracks at the site of Stile Cop: one fully machine-built and graded red, the other a more natural hand-built affair with more roots and features to challenge riders and graded black. We're not talking big hills or long tracks here, but there is still plenty to ride, especially when you take in the many unofficial runs.

Freeride Freeride is pretty much limited to sessioning the DH trails and blasting around the singletracks. Riders looking to be the next Darren Berrecloth should probably look elsewhere.

Easy Start out on the beginner jumps, there is so much here that it is definitely a case of building up slowly to make sure you have mastered what you're riding now before moving onto something much bigger.

Hard There are plenty of hard lines to try for the more advanced jumper. The only limitation in a place like this is your imagination!

Not to miss The fantastic singletrack. It's the reason to visit.

Remember to avoid Travelling a huge distance to try this out if it's DH you're after. It's good, but you might be better heading further west into Shropshire.

Nearest bike/hire shop Swinnerton Cycles Forest Centre

is the local bike shop and hire, T01889 575170, bikechase.co.uk and there are bike maps available from the Birches Valley Forest Visitor Centre.

Local accommodation Try the Oak Farm Hotel (T0870 4784319) located close to the M6, or for budget accommodation the Premier Inn (T0871 7162718).

Eating The Birches Valley Forest visitor centre has a café that provides hot and cold drinks and snacks. Being a reasonably sized town Cannock offers everything from fast food through to world foods and restaurants.

ⓘ **More info** Cannock Chase has a riders association which is run in conjunction with the Forestry Commission, chasetrails.co.uk.

> Lowdown

Locals do

Run their tyres quite firm to cut into the fresher loamy sections.

Get involved with building the trails as well as riding them.

Locals don't

Leave their bikes unattended. While not a crime hotspot, this is an area between plenty of towns and cities.

Pros

Great riding within easy reach of plenty of people. Good family riding and novice/intermediate mountain bike area.

Lots of good unmarked singletrack, great for weekend stop-over.

Cons

Hills not big enough for downhill purist.

Not enough riding to sustain a week's break.

CHRIS MORAN

CHRIS MORAN

CHRIS MORAN

CHRIS MORAN

N5 Cheshire Ghost Riders BMX Track

4X DJ

Train station Crewe
Nearest city Birmingham
Sat Nav CW2 8AB

Location Cheshire Ghost Rider's Track is in Tipkinder Park, in the middle of Crewe, Cheshire. From the M6 exit at junction 16 and head into Crew on the A500. At the first roundabout take the A5020, go straight on at the next two roundabouts and then left at the third onto Nantwich Road (the A534) and past Crewe Railway Station. After 300 m, take a right into Mill Street, and at the end a left onto Dunwoody Way. Take another left onto Wistason Road which turns into Victoria Avenue. Tipkinder Park is about 500 m up this road on the left.

Facilities Victoria Avenue has shops for immediate supplies.

Overview This is one of the oldest BMX sites in the UK and in January 2009 was completely renovated to improve the shape, drainage and surface. It's floodlit until 2200 on certain days and has CCTV protection and a very organized club regularly racing there.

Conditions This is a well-maintained site, with a surface on the BMX track that's been designed to drain well.

ⓘ **More info** Cheshire Ghost Riders have a site at cheshireghostriders.blogspot.com.

N6 Deeping BMX

4X DJ

Train station Peterborough
Nearest city Leicester
Sat Nav PE6 8HT

Location Market Deeping is a small town around 10 km north of Peterborough. From the A1(M), carry on north as it changes to the A1 at Peterborough, then turn off at Stamford in the direction of Market Deeping on the A16. Turn onto the Stamford Road (the B1525) in the direction of Market Deeping town centre, then onto the High Street. Take a left off this road onto Godsey Lane, and around 300 m down this road you'll see the common on your left. The BMX track is to the southeast corner of this land.

Facilities This track is in the heart of Market Deeping, which has plenty of shops and facilities.

Overview An old BMX track that, as of early 2009, has had a complete make-over into a 4X and BMX venue. Expect a competition-level course with a drop-in start and doubles, gaps and tabletops.

Conditions The purpose-built track has a concrete drop-in and is well drained but still to be avoided in the wet.

ⓘ **More info** The track's club Deeping Dragos have their own website at deepingdragons.co.uk, while the local Deeping mountain bike scene has a Bebo page at bebo.com/DeepingTrack.

JONATHAN CHEETHAM

↘7 Eastridge Woods

DH FR

Train station Shrewsbury
Nearest city Wolverhampton
Sat Nav SY5 0DF

Location Eastridge Woods are around 10 km to the southwest of Shrewsbury, deep in the Shropshire countryside. From Shrewsbury, take the A488 towards Minsterley, then take a left into Callow Lane in the direction of Habberley. Carry all the way down this road to the T junction, then take a right, then a right at the fork and the first turning on the right up the narrow lane towards the entrance to the wood and car park.

Facilities There is parking, but little else at the wood.

Overview As part of The Marches, Eastridge Woods are a spectacularly remote and beautiful part of the world, but with the help of DH champ Marc Beaumont (who trains in the area) have recently had a load of incredible, waymarked trails built in the forest. There is now a 2.5-km blue trail, a 5-km yellow route, and a 7-km brown trail, which offer the best XC in the area. However, most riers come here because there are two brilliant DH tracks, with plenty of serious gaps, roots, and switchbacks, and the reason Marc is so good.

Conditions This is forest land maintained by the Forestry Commission, and well maintained. The tracks are waymarked and all-weather but still best avoided after periods of bad weather.

DAVID BAGNALL/FORESTRY COMMISSION

ⓘ **More info** The Forestry Commission site forestry.co.uk has loads of info on Eastridge Woods.

DAVID BAGNALL/FORESTRY COMMISSION

↘8 Hopton Castle

Train station Craven Arms
Nearest city Birmingham
Sat Nav N/A (though Shropshire Hills Discovery Centre, where maps of the area are available, is SY7 9RS)
Opening times The trails are open 365 days a year, but it is worth noting that Hopton Wood is a working forest and areas can be closed due to forest operations

Location Hopton is an area of Forestry Commission land to the west of Hopton Castle, itself around 10 km to the west of the town of Craven Arms, on the Shropshire/Mid Wales border. From the east, head in on the A49 from either Shrewsbury or Hereford, turn off at Craven Arms onto the B4368 and follow this road for 6 km, then turn south onto the B4367 heading to Hopton Heath and again off to the right after 2 km heading towards Hopton Castle. The riding area is difficult to find but around 1 km past the turn off to the Castle. Call in at Pearce Cycles in Ludlow for more detailed directions, or at the Secret Hills Discovery Centre in Craven Arms for a waterproof trails map (£1).

Facilities There's not much at Hopton Castle save for Pearce Cycle's Land Rover and bike trailer (and only on certain days). You're pretty far from civilisation here so take supplies from Craven Arms. The trails in Hopton Woods are varied, from gentle and smooth family trails to the highly technical DH courses. The riding is all enclosed in this plantation wood so its conifer trees-a-plenty and as a result the more technical trails are strewn with roots and stumps. With three XC trails and three DH routes, the wood is a fun place to ride that can cater for beginners through to experts. The ground bakes hard in the summer but can be quite greasy when wet.

XC The routes around Hopton are well waymarked and offer some short, flat rides for novices and kids through to the Hopton Wood Red Trail – a XC loop with some tough climbs and switchbacks. Experienced XC riders will enjoy the more challenging black DH trails here too as the gradient allows XC bikes to be comfortably ridden on the downhills.

Downhill The downhills at Hopton are known for their tight turns and having loads of roots. It's a great place to perfect your bike handling and is regularly used by some of England's best riders as a training ground. The hill is not very steep so it is quite easy to section the trails here.

CHRIS MORAN

Freeride There are no specific trails for freeriders but the downhill routes do contain various small jumps and interesting sections so those who like to be in the air will find something to ride.

Easy Make the most of the singletrack – head out on the Amber trail. If you clear that without any problems, take the more technical and physical red trail for a second loop.

Hard There are three DH routes that can all be ridden by the competent XC rider, so from the

CHRIS MORAN

top of the hill take each one in turn and spin back up the access road. The hill may not be massive but three runs and climbs of this will tire anyone.

Not to miss The uplift days.

Remember to avoid Heading there when the Forestry Commission are felling – the trails will be closed. Call the ranger first (see below for details).

Nearest Bike/Hire shop Fort Royal Mountain Bikes are found in Craven Arms (T01588 673500) and are well stocked with expert staff so will be able to provide for most XC and DH bikes. Otherwise Pearce Cycles in Ludlow is the place to head.

Local accommodation Take in Stokesay Castle during your stay at the Castle View B&B (T01588 673712). Also offering B&B accommodation is Hopton House (T01547 530885).

Eating The Craven Arms Hotel (T01588 672888) offers a biker Brunch on Saturdays and also a daily carvery. The Engine and Tender Inn (T01588 660275) serve traditional home-cooked food.

ⓘ **More info** Pearce Cycles, pearcecycles.co.uk, T01584 879288, and the Forestry Commission, forestry.gov.uk.

> **Lowdown**

Locals do
Take advantage of Pearce Cycle's uplift days. You can get 10 good descents in a day and improve immeasurably.

Locals don't
Ride without a phone – a slam here is a long way from help.

Pros
One of England's best downhill venues.

Uplift (on certain days).

Cons
Very rooty, and hence slippy on bad weather days or after periods of rain.

CHRIS MORAN

↘9 Keele Woods and DJs

XC DH DJ

Train station Stoke on Trent
Nearest city Birmingham
Sat Nav ST5 5BG

CHRIS MORAN

Location Two locations here – the small woods to the north of Keele University (known locally as Keele Woods, home to the DJs), and Springpool Wood, south of the Uni, which has the XC riding. From the M6 exit at junction 15 and at the first roundabout turn left on the Clayton Road (A519), carry on up this road for 3 km (straight over both roundabouts), then straight again at the crossroads onto the A525 heading towards Keele University. Carry on up this road for another 3 km, and Keele Woods are just to the north side (the right) of the road, just after the University turn off to the left. Park at the Uni. Springpool Wood is directly to the south, where the University land meets the M6.

Facilities Keele University is next door to both these locations and has a host of bars, shops and amenities.

Overview The DJs are suitable for beginners to intermediates but certainly not worth a long journey. But for local or Uni riders this is a half-decent practice area. Springpool Wood is home to some very tame DH trails and some pleasant XC singletrack, but again, not worth a long journey.

Conditions Both woods are beautiful areas of relatively wild land, and popular with some dog walkers and flower hunters, but rarely used.

↘10 Leamington Spa 4X Track and DJs

4X DJ

Train station Leamington Spa
Nearest city Coventry
Sat Nav CV32 7UA

Location Leamington Spa 4X and DJs are to the northeast of the city with the same name. From the M4 exit at junction 15 and head in the direction of Warwick on the A429. Head through Warwick and take the A445 towards Leamington Spa. After crossing the river, take a right onto the B4099 Warwick New Road heading into Leamington town centre. After 300 m, take a left into Warwick Place and then sixth left into Clarendon Place. Take the first right here into Clarendon Avenue, which turns into Leicester Street after 500 m, and the 4X track is just to the right in the fields as Leicester Road bends to the left.

Facilities The leisure centre nearby is the closest place to get supplies, although Leamington is full of shops and amenities.

Overview This is an old BMX track that has three great corners and a variety of whoops, berms, tables and doubles. It has a stoney, hardened surface so is good for most weather, and a full-time club that regularly builds and repairs their pride and joy. Next door is a fantastic dirt jumping site with enough trails to satisfy beginners through to pro riders. Definitely worth a visit if you're nearby and fancy improving your jumping and speed skiils.

Conditions This is a well-maintained site, with a surface on the BMX track that's been designed to drain well, and the DJs are well made.

ⓘ **More info** Check out the brilliant Leamington Spa 4X and DJs website at rls4x.com.

JONATHAN CHEETHAM

↘11 Ribbesford DH

XC DH MM

Train station Kidderminster
Nearest city Birmingham
Sat Nav N/A

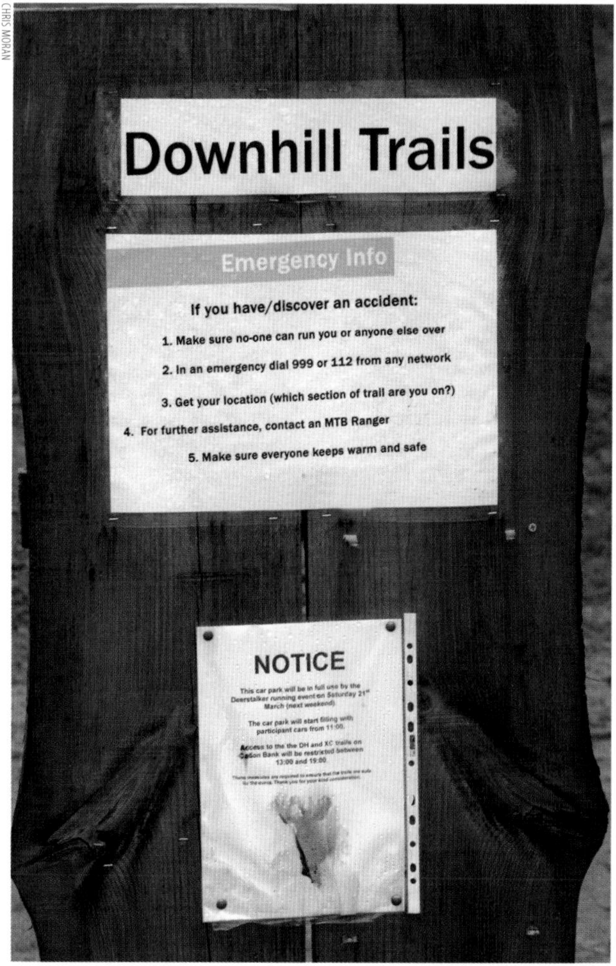

CHRIS MORAN

Location Ribbesford is around 5 km to the west of Kidderminster. From the M5, leave at junction 3 and head towards Kidderminster on the A456. Pass directly through Kidderminster, following directions for Tenbury Wells. As you pass Bewdley on your right, look for the B4194 crossing the road. Don't take that road, but take the second left (Heightington Road). Head up here for 300 m and Ribbesford DH is on the left.

Facilities Bewdley is the nearest town with shops and supplies.

Overview Ribbesford DH Mountain Bike Trails are divided into three sections: the black, the green and the red run. All have plenty of interesting features and lots of roots, jumps, bomb holes, tabletops, reinforcements and purpose-built gaps. Each varies in difficulty, and although there is plenty to test advanced riders, they might be better advised to head to Hopton or Bringewood if they're in this part of the world. For learners or intermediates, this is a fantastic DH place.

Conditions This is an area of beautiful forest with plenty of exposed roots and a clay soil that packs well and is perfect for sustaining the many jumps down this DH trail.

ⓘ **More info** Ribbesford has a Downhill Riders Club with full trail listings, angelfire.com/psy/ribsriders/My Web Sites/riders.htm.

12 Perry Park BMX

4X DJ

Train station Perry Barr/Hamstead
Nearest city Birmingham
Sat Nav B42 2LB

Location Perry Park is around 4 km to the north of Birmingham town centre, and just on the south side of the M6 (not the toll). From the motorway, exit at junction 7 and head south on the A34 towards Birmingham centre. After 2 km Perry Park is well signed on the left of the road. Park by turning left after the allotments into Church Road and then left again into Perry Park's car parking area.

Facilities The leisure centre nearby is the closest place to get supplies, although Leamington is full of shops and amenities.

Overview This is another old-school BMX track that has had a lot of support in turning it into a 4X and BMX track for the 21st century. Currently there's not a great deal to tempt riders on a long journey, with two loops of average to small jumps, but it is in a secluded spot (albeit next to the M6), and has fantastic potential.

Conditions This is a track built in open fields in the corner of a popular, large park with plenty of copses and woods.

13 Rutland Water Cycle Way

XC

Train station Oakham
Nearest city Leicester
Sat Nav LE15 8BL

GEORGE GATE/FORESTRY COMMISSION

Location Rutland Water is the largest man-made lake in Europe, and to the east of Oakham, which is between Leicester and Peterborough. From the A1(M) heading north, head for Peterborough and carry on past the city on the A1 in the direction of Stamford. Here turn left into the A606 and after 6 km take a left at Whitwell into Bull Brig Lane, signposted Rutland Water.

Facilities Around Rutland Water there are five separate cafés and two bike shops – one at Normanton and the other at Whitwell – and there is official parking at both the north and south park entrances.

Overview Rutland's riding is essentially family/novice XC, offering great views, some lovely singletrack and bridleway (all waymarked), and the chance to go round the entire 3,100 acres of lake in a 40 km loop (although families might wish to stop at one of the many rest areas or pubs and head

CHRIS MORAN

back for a shorter ride). There are several places to park around the lake, and for the more adventurous there are suggested harder XC distances in the vicinity, specifically Leicester to Oakham (see website below).

Conditions This is an all-weather surface, but is still prone to some muddy areas in heavy conditions.

ⓘ **More info** Try Rutland Cycling on rutlandcycling.co.uk (T01780 460705).

14 Sherwood Pines Forest

Train station Mansfield/Mansfield Woodhouse

Nearest city Nottingham

Sat Nav NG21 9JL

ISOBEL CAMERON/FORESTRY COMMISSION

Location The Sherwood Pines Forest Park Visitor Centre is around 6 km to the northeast of Mansfield, Nottinghamshire. Exit the M1 at junction 28 and follow the A38 into – and through – Mansfield. Turn left onto the A60 in the town centre, heading out of the town and into Mansfield Woodhouse, and right at the traffic lights onto the A6075 signposted to Edwinstowe. Go down here for around 5 km then turn right at double mini island in the direction of Clipstone. In the village, turn left at the T junction onto the B6030 and Sherwood Pines forest is on your right after 700 m, well signed from here.

Facilities The SPFPVC is a newly-built visitor centre with Go Ape (high rope adventure park), cycle shop and hire, café, toilets and a forest classroom. It's open from 0800 until dusk, and charges a small fee for parking.

Overview This is a fantastic set-up for families and XC lovers of all abilities, with a great set of dirt jumps as well as a Bike Park currently under construction. There are also plans in place to create a northshore park and to add some high-end XC technical trails to the existing singletrack network. Well worth a visit.

Terrain Sherwood Pines Forest has over 50 km of unofficial singletrack, plus the above-mentioned, purpose-built areas.

XC For families and those looking for gentle terrain, there are four waymarked trails: the Green and the Blue Routes a newer Green Route and the Adventure Trail. All have varying degrees of technicalities to challenge younger or less skilled riders and all are purpose-built and all-weather surfaced. There are plenty of rest areas and shortcuts. For more hardcore riders, the Kitchener Trail, a 6-km technical loop, should hold some challenges, and there's a Skills Loop being planned.

Downhill There are some short sections of DH on the Kitchener Trail, but nothing any serious downhiller would travel for.

Dirtjumps/Freeride There are three lines through the DJs: a beginner pack with five tables, an intermediate line with five sets of tables and gaps, and an eight-step rhythm section of gaps for higher standard riders. The northshore area may be up and running by summer 2009.

Conditions The routes have all been built with all-season conditions in mind (with limestone coverings), but still expect to find some mud and boggy conditions in the middle of the forest.

ⓘ **More info** Sherwood Pine Cycles has a wealth of info on the area at sherwoodpinescycles.co.uk, while the Forestry Commission has dedicated a page to Sherwood at forestry.gov.uk.

↘15 Swithland Woods

XC

Train station Loughborough/ Leicester

Nearest city Leicester

Sat Nav LE12 8TN

Location Swithland Woods are part of the ancient Charnwood Forest near Newton Linford, Leicestershire. From the M1 exit junction 22 and head towards Leicester on the A50. After 2 km, take a left into Markfield Lane in the direction of Newton Linford. At Newton, turn left onto Main Street and head north in the direction of Lingdale Golf Club. After 2 km, take a right onto Roecliffe Road. Swithland Woods are to the left of this road after 1 km. Park at the Bradgate Road parking (before you hit Cropston Village), and head north into the woods.

CHRIS MORAN

Facilities There is parking, but little else at the Bradgate Road entrance. Cropston has a few shops and a pub.

Overview This is a beautiful XC site with plenty of public-access bridleways and unofficial singletracks that criss-cross the woods. There is an old quarry that has been filled in (with an inscription carved into the wall), and some fantastically picturesque views to discover. None of the riding is particularly hard, but due to the area being relatively wild and unmarked, novices and those without wayfinding skills are advised to head elsewhere.

Conditions This is forest land maintained by The National Forest, and is a popular horse-riding venue. Expect well-kept bridleways and fire-roads, but the singletrack can be relatively muddy after rain.

ⓘ **More info** There's no specific bike section of the website but The National Forest is nationalforest.org.

↘16 Tiny BMX Track

4X DJ

Train station Bournville
Nearest city Birmingham
Sat Nav B30 2RY

Location Tiny BMX Track is between Stirchley and Kings Heath, around 3 km to the south of Birmingham town centre. From the M5 exit at junction 4 and head towards Birmingham town centre on the A38. After 4 km take a right onto the Bunbury Road at Northfield, then a left after 1.5 km on the A441 Pershore Road heading to Stirchley/Selly Oak. After 1 km take a right into the A4040 (Fordhouse Lane), and after 500 m take a left (just before the railway bridge) into Pineapple Road, then immediately left again into Hazelwell Fordrough. Take the second right (Edwin Road) off Hazelwell and Tiny BMX is in the copse of woods to the right of this road after 80 m.

Facilities There are some shops on Hazelwell road and Stirchley has plenty of amenities.

Overview This is an 80s BMX track that has never been well maintained but still hosts a decent local scene. As one might imagine from its name, it's not the biggest place in the world, but it has a few jumps and a surprising wall ride/berm, and is a good place to start for budding dirt jumpers.

Conditions Tiny drains well but is still best avoided after rainfall.

JONATHAN CHEETHAM

The North

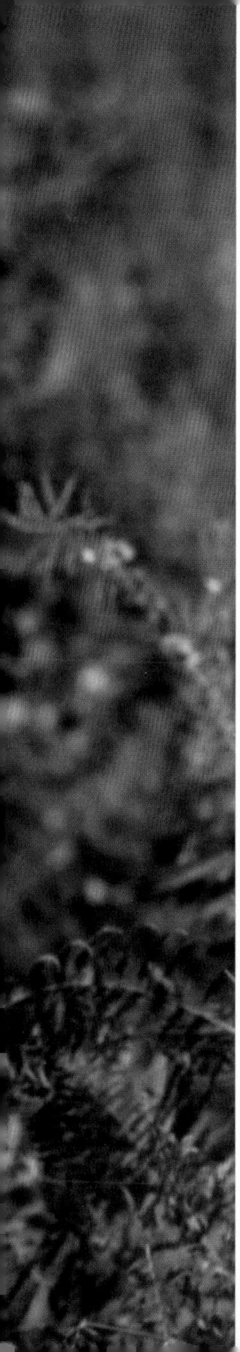

↘ Overview 128
↘ Carlton Bank DH & XC 130
↘ Broomley Trails (DJs) 131
↘ Calverley Woods 131
↘ Chesterfield BMX/ 4X Track 131
↘ Chevin Forest Park 132
↘ Chester-le-Street spots 133
↘ Chopwell 134
↘ Delamere Forest 135
↘ Dalby Forest 136
↘ Devils Cascade DJs 138
↘ Elland Park Wood 139
↘ Gosforth Park DJs 139
↘ Gisburn Forest 140
↘ Greaseborough Trails 141
↘ Great Ayton Quarry DJs 141
↘ Greenway DJs 142
↘ Guisborough Forest 142
↘ Hartlepool 4X 143
↘ Hookstone Woods DJs 143
↘ Local rider, John Storey 144
↘ Hamsterley Forest 146
↘ Hulme Park DJs 148
↘ Hurstwood Trails 148
↘ Ilkley Moor 149
↘ Iron Bridge DJs 149
↘ Kielder Water & Forest Park 150
↘ Ladybower Reservoir 152
↘ Lee Mill Quarry AKA The Adrenaline Gateway 153
↘ Little Switzerland 154
↘ Longridge Fell 154
↘ Lyme Park 154
↘ Manchester Road DJs 155
↘ Meltham Skills Trails 155
↘ Midgley Woods 155
↘ Park Bridge 4X 156
↘ Ramsden Lane DH 156
↘ Roman Lakes Leisure Park 156
↘ Scratchmere Scar Freeride Bike Park 157
↘ Silton Forest DH 158
↘ Setmurthy DH Trails & Cockermouth XC 159
↘ Stainburn 160
↘ Sticks Norden 162
↘ Storthes Hall DH 162
↘ Temple Newsam 163
↘ TNF Grizedale 164
↘ Wassenden DH 166
↘ Wiswell Wood 166
↘ Woodbank DJs 167
↘ Whinlatter Forest 168
↘ Wooler 4X & surrounding area 169
↘ Yeadon BMX Track 169

Delamere Forest in the Spring. Perfect for wheelies through the fauna. [CHRIS MORAN]

The North

Glasgow
Motherwell
M74
SOUTH LANARKSHIRE
West Linton
Oxton
A68
Duns
Berwick-upon-Twe
Lanark
Coldstream
Strathaven
Kilmarnock
Melrose
Kelso
49
Glenbarr
Brodick
Arran
Troon
Prestwick
Ayr
Muirkirk
Symington
Yarrow
Selkirk
Blackwaterfoot
SCOTLAND
Campbeltown
Abbington
SCOTTISH BORDERS
Jedburgh
Ettrick
Maybole
Patna
Cumnock
A76
Hawick
A68
Alnwic
Turnberry
A77
Sanqhuar
Cheviot Hills
Beattock
Rothbury
Girvan
Thornhill
25
Otterburn
SOUTH AYRSHIRE
DUMFRIES & GALLOWAY
Langholm
Locherbie
New Galloway
Corsock
Dumfries
M74
NORTHUMBERLAN
Newtown Stewart
Castle Douglas
Gretna
Bardon Mill
Chollerfor
Brampton
A69
Stranraer
A75
Haltwhistle
2
Carlisle
Kirkcudbright
Alston
7
37
Conse
Port William
Drummore
Maryport
Penrith
DURHAM
39
Cockermouth
Bishc
Auckla
Appleby-in-Westmoreland
Workington
20
48
Whitehaven
CUMBRIA
A66
Bowes
Lake District
Ambleside
A595
M6
Ravenstonedale
Windermere
Coniston
Ravenglass
Kendal
44
Bainbridge
NORTH YORKSH
Isle of Man
A590
Kirkby Lonsdale
Ulverston
Kettlewell
Ingleton
Barrow-
Settle
23
13
Lancaster
M6
5
A65
29
LANCASHIRE
Skipton
Fleetwood
Clitheroe
22
3
16
46
Burnley
Brad
Blackpool
M55
31
Preston
Blackburn
33
27
11
Southport
Chorley
41
M66
42
Ha
M6
M61
Rochdale
Hudder
Irish Sea
Wigan
Bolton
34
Formby
M58
Oldham
21
Manchester
Liverpool
Warrington
M62
45
M60
Stockport
Holyhead
Llandudno
Prestatyn
36
Rhyl
M53
Anglesey
Ellesmere Port
M56
30
Bux
Bangor
Macclesfield
CONWY
A55
Chester
A34
Northwich
Llanrwst
FLINTSHIRE
A51
CHESHIRE
10
24
8
A49
M6
47
Betws-y-Coed
DENBIGHSHIRE
Nantwich
Stoke-on-Tren
Rhyd
Glan Conwy
A5
A483
Ashbour
Porthmadog
Whitchurch
A494
Llangollen
GWYNEDD
A53
N
WALES
St Martin's Ellesmere
Hodnet
STAFFORDSHIRE
Llanbedr
A49
Newport
Stafford
20 km
20 miles
Mallwyd
Shrewsbury
Telford
Rug
A458
Birmingham

Trails...

1 Carlton Bank DH and XC
2 Broomley Trails
3 Calverly Woods
4 Chesterfield BMX/4X Track
5 Chevin Forest Park
6 Chester-le-Street spots
7 Chopwell
8 Delamere Forest
9 Dalby Forest
10 Devils Cascade DJs
11 Elland Park Wood
12 Gosforth Park DJs
13 Gisburn Forest
14 Greaseborough Trails
15 Great Ayton Quarry DJs
16 Greenway DJs
17 Guisborough Forest
18 Hartlepool 4X
19 Hookstone Woods
20 Hamsterley Forest
21 Hulme Park DJs
22 Hustwood Trails
23 Ilkley Moor
24 Iron Bridge DJs
25 Kielder Water & Forest Park
26 Ladybower Reservoir
27 Lee Mill Quarry
28 Little Switzerland
29 Longridge Fell
30 Lyme Park
31 Manchester Road DJs
32 Meltham Skills Trails
33 Midgley Woods
34 Park Bridge 4X
35 Ramsden Lane DH
36 Roman Lakes Leisure Park
37 Scratchmere Scar Freeride Bike Park
38 Silton Forest DH
39 Setmurthy DH Trails and Cockermouth XC
40 Stainburn
41 Sticks Norden
42 Storthes Hall DH
43 Temple Newsam
44 TNF Grizedale
45 Wassenden DH
46 Wiswell Wood
47 Woodbank DJs
48 Whinlatter Forest
49 Wooler 4X
50 Yeadon BMX Track

The North is a multi-faceted area, multi-geographical area. How to combine an area that includes the between-city riding spots of Manchester, Leeds, Sheffield, Bradford and Halifax, whilst also covering the absolute beauty of five of the UK's best national parks: The Lake District, Peak District, Yorkshire Dales, Yorkshire Moors and Northumberland and Kielder Forests? It's a big ask, but we've collated the counties of Northumberland, Tyne and Wear, Durham, Cumbria, North Yorkshire, East Riding of Yorkshire, West Yorkshire, Lancashire, Merseyside, Greater Manchester, South Yorkshire and Cheshire to fit all the trail centres and spots in.

An area so big is naturally very diverse. We would imagine that many of the places mentioned in this chapter are for local riders only. Visitors to the region are probably drawn by the incredible riding to be found in the Lake District. But there is so much more to the North than the Lakes. Northumberland has to rate as one of the most unspoilt counties in the whole of the UK. To ride around Kielder, where one can pop over the border into Scotland, is one of the coolest routes in the whole of the British Isles. The forests of the northeast are absolute world-class centres, with Hamsterley and Chopwell being on any serious UK riders''must see' lists. And if you fancy some old-school, self uplift DH skills, then the moors of Yorkshire and the Peak District are your number one places to visit.

Local scene

There's a very strong freeride and downhill presence in the northeast, with many a long-travel machine hitting up the 4X track and DH areas of Hamsterley each weekend. In fact, jump and race-ready riders from Newcastle, Sunderland, Durham and Middlesborough are spoilt for choice, with Kielder and Chopwell right on their doorstep. Leeds is littered with cool little venues, and if you're into dirt jumping, a move to Stockport would reap huge rewards. Visitors should check out the websites listed at the back of this book as the North boasts some of the most welcoming, organized and cool clubs in the country and a directory of their websites and contact details is listed.

Hubs

As one would expect, the national parks of the North hold the majority of the XC riding, but there are incredible, stand-alone spots literally everywhere. Riding hubs would include the diverse terrain to be found around Leeds, Bradford and Halifax, while the Lancashire areas around Blackburn, Clitheroe, Burnley and Rawtenstall are definitely on the up (especially with the proposed Adrenaline Gateway development – the north's own 7Stanes-esque, purpose-built area). Meanwhile there's the ever-present Dalby Forest, featuring one of the UK's best bike parks, and of course, the brilliant spots in the Lake District, including the Whinlatter trail and the completely rejuvenated Grizedale centre, which would stand out even if they were in the Alps.

Below left: Dalby Forest's incredible bike park.
Below right: A Keilder Forest rock garden.
Opposite page: Hamsterley Forest's 4X in full flow.

Northern England Overview

ISOBEL CAMERON/FORESTRY COMMISSION

❺ Best rides in The North

Hit the North and you're not going home disappointed. Here are five of the best spots:

❶ **Delamere Forest, page 135**

With a newly re-vamped visitor centre, some brilliant DJs, incredible XC and a very family-friendly area, Delamere is an unexpected gem in the Cheshire countryside.

❷ **Roman Lakes, page 156**

This is one of the most perfect set-ups for families (as long as you've got your own bikes), with kilometres of waymarked routes around beautiful canal paths and gentle forest rides. All in a lakeside setting.

❸ **TNF Grizedale, page 164**

There aren't many spots like this in the UK – a stunning setting, beautiful village, and a completely new visitor set up for 2009 means the famous North Face Trail is set to be one of the North's most popular for years to come.

❹ **Dalby Forest, page 136**

It's been at the forefront of UK riding for years, with something for every style of rider – and the park just keeps getting better and better. It's a way out from anywhere really, but well worth the journey.

❺ **Hamsterley, page 146**

For those in the northeast, Hamsterley Chopwell and Kielder Forest offer some rich riding with full visitor facilities, but it's Hamsterley that gets my vote for having literally the best of every type of riding in one spot. And the cafés, visitor centre, bike hire and pubs make it exemplary.

↘1 Carlton Bank DH and XC

XC DH

Train station Northallerton/Thirsk
Nearest city Middlesbrough
Sat Nav TS9 7LQ

Location Carlton Bank is on the western edge of the North Yorkshire Moors, around 20 km direction to the south of Middlesbrough. From the A1, exit at junction 49 and take the A168 to Thirsk, then the A19 in the direction of Ingleby Arncliffe, then take a right onto the A172 (east). Turn off at Carlton and follow the road through the village. Head up the road on to the plateau. There is a car park at the Lord Stones Café, which is just next to the trails.

Facilities The Lord Stones Café (T01642 778227) is one of the best cafés in the UK, with home-cooked meals and a license to serve pints. It is cheap and very bike friendly with toilets and washing facilities and is very popular with outdoor users.

Overview Carlton Bank Downhill has been a competition venue over the years, and the surrounding area has some impressive singletrack XC riding. The area is very popular with all outdoor users, from hangliders landing next to the Lord Stones Café, to fell walkers on the trails and horse-riders on the bridleways. But there is enough room for all and the surrounds are incredibly picturesque.

Terrain This is open moorland which can be very uninviting in bad weather, especially if it's windy. The area is also prone to harsh mud, and several races have had to be cancelled, but hit it on a good day and it's as good as riding gets.

XC There are an untold number of unofficial and un-waymarked routes that criss cross the moors from the Lord Stones Café starting point, but the area is more famous for its downhill course, that starts at the top of the trig point above the café.

Downhill Carlton Bank is a famous downhill course with a fairly flat, pedally top section with a decent-sized jump, then a ridgeline run which turns into a technical, rocky descent later on. There are plenty of drops, and jumps down the course, and good riders should be able to get down in under 2 minutes (it's around 1300 m long). The area has a lot of potential, and there are an increasing number of riders heading there (and the landowner seems keen to have mountain bikers in the area), so expect more DH and XC routes to pop up in the near future. The track was originally a Singletraction enterprise, but is now looked after by the local scene.

Dirt Jumps/Freeride There are no specific northshore, dirt jumps or freeride areas, but there has been a lot of work put into the DH track, which also houses some pretty sizable jumps. If you like being in the air, you'll find something to ride here.

Conditions This is a popular outdoor area, so expect to see lots of other outdoor types. Can be boggy, so avoid after rain, and expect to see some incredible views over the moors.

ⓘ **More info** The North East Freeriders are generally the people behind the building work – join in via nefreeriders.co.uk, while Carlton Bank DH also has its own Facebook page (search for 'Carlton Bank Downhill').

JOHN STOREY/NEFREERIDERS.CO.UK

N2 Broomley Trails DJs

DJ

Train station Stocksfield
Nearest city Newcastle-upon-Tyne
Sat Nav N/A

Location Broomley Trails are DJs located near the town of Stocksfield, itself around 15 km to the west of Newcastle-upon-Tyne. From Newcastle, take the A695 from the A1 ringroad, heading in the direction of Hexham. After passing through Stocksfield, carry on for another 1 km – passing the turn-off for the B6309 on your left – and take the next left after that, signposted towards Broomley. The DJs are on the left, around 250 m you pass under the train tracks.

Facilities There are no facilities at the DJs, though Stocksfield has a few shops for supplies and is only around 1 km ride away.

Overview This is a low-budget DJ spot built in some woods and features a few lines with a decent selection of jumps from some small, beginner lines to a couple of good sized gaps and rhythm sections. Not worth a long journey, but for those nearby who want to practise their handling skills, or start dirt jumping, this is a great spot.

Conditions The DJs are well built, but this is a remote spot and is prone to serious mud after rain. Please don't ride the jumps when they're wet.

N3 Calverly Woods

XC DH

Train station Baildon/Horsforth or New Pudsey
Nearest city Bradford/Leeds
Sat Nav BD17

Location Calverly Woods are around 6 km northeast of Bradford and 10 km to the north west of Leeds, just outside the town of Calverly which is 3 km east of Shipley. From the M62 take the M606 towards Bradford, then exit at the end of the motorway onto the A6177 ringroad around Bradford heading anti-clockwise towards Laisterdyke. Turn right off the ring road onto the A658 in the direction of Yeadon, and after 4 km take a right off this road into Parkin Lane (just after you cross a river). Head down this road and re-cross the same river into Calverly Cutting. The woods are at the end of this lane.

Facilities Apperly, back over the bridge, has a shop and pub (the Stansfield Arms) for supplies.

Overview This is a completely natural wooded area with purpose-built trails; however there are a couple of DH trails descending the woods and there's some half-decent XC to be had. It's a fairly popular spot for local Leeds and Bradford riders.

Conditions This is ancient woodland. Cycling is permitted but please don't build or add to the trails.

ⓘ **More info** For all Leeds mountain biking info, MTB Leeds is the place to head, mtbleeds.co.uk.

N4 Chesterfield BMX/4X Track

4X DJ

Train station Chesterfield
Nearest city Sheffield
Sat Nav S43 1DQ

Location Chesterfield BMX is next door to Ringwood Hall, between the towns of Hollingwood and Brimington and around 2.5 km northeast from Chesterfield. From the M1 exit at junction 30 and head towards Chesterfield on the A619 Chesterfield Road. After 4 km Ringwood Hall is signposted on your left. The BMX track is just before the Hall turn off.

Facilities Hollingwood is a small village but it has plenty of shops and amenities.

Overview This is an old BMX track that has had a revamp in recent years and is perfect for those looking to get some experience before heading out to more serious DJs or to take their jumping skills to the DH trails. It's also wide enough to have some 4X races on, and welcomes all riders. There's a drop in, lots of jumps (though rollable), and three brilliant berms, including one wall ride. The track has been recently upgraded to National Standard.

Conditions This is a well-maintained track with concrete and chalk surface. Drains well and is in a lovely park.

ⓘ **More info** Chesterfield BMX club has its own site at chesterfieldbmx.co.uk.

↘5 Chevin Forest Park

XC DH

Train station Menston
Nearest city Leeds/Bradford
Sat Nav LS21 3JL

CHRIS MORAN

Location Chevin Forest Park is just to the south of the village of Otley, itself around 12 km northeast of Bradford, and 15 km north west of Leeds. From Leeds, head towards Skipton on the A660. After 15 km Otley is on the right. Exit left here onto East Chevin Road, then Birdcage Walk, then Johnny Lane, following signs for Chevin Forest Park. The car park is at the end of this road.

Facilities There's nothing at the Park (save for The White House, which is for pre-booked groups only), though Otley is full of shops and amenities.

Overview Chevin Forest Park has plenty of gentle XC and DH trails, suitable for all riders from families and beginners through to good intermediates. There are no official waymarked trails (though Leeds Council has been making noises about putting some official runs in since the success of Temple Newsam). Most are easy to find though, and there are usually plenty of riders around the park to ask.

Conditions This is a popular site for all fans of woodland and well-kept gardens. Please ride with care and be respectful of the other (often elderly) park visitors.

ⓘ **More info** Chevin Park Forest has its own website, though no specific details of the trails are mentioned, chevinforest.co.uk.

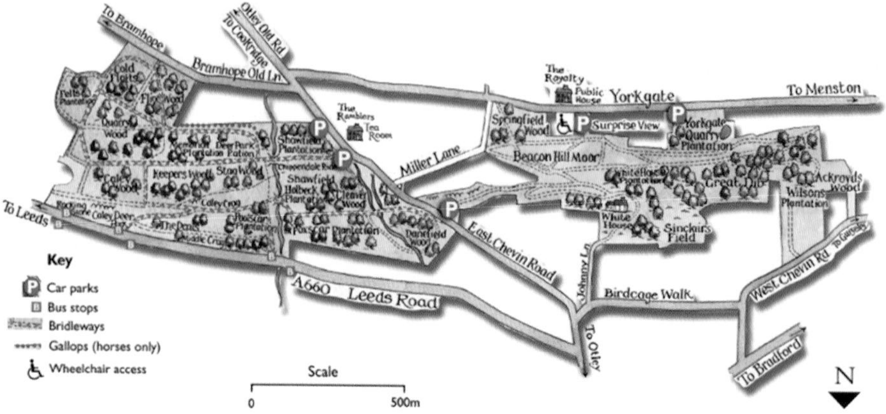

↘6 Chester-le-Street spots

DH DJ

Train station Chester-le-Street
Nearest city Sunderland
Sat Nav Various, see below

Location Chester-le-Street is around 10 km to the west of Sunderland, just off the A1(M). From the motorway exit at junction 63 and take the A167 into the town.

Facilities Chester-le-Street is a large town with plenty of shops and amenities. The riding spots are never more than a few minutes from supplies, though those heading to Old Mine Pits should take some food and drink with them.

Overview Chester-le-Street has a couple of great riding spots, with the western edge of town being fringed with some cool DH tracks, and some good DJs to the south of town. For those in either Newcastle or Sunderland, or in the northeast in general, it's worth a look in, though others from further afield might wish to bypass and head straight to the bigger trail areas, such as Hamsterly, Chopwell or Kielder. The spots are: **Doctors Downhill** off Waldridge Lane (sat nav postcode: DH2 3RY), **New Road downhill and dirt jumps** off Warkworth Drive (DH2 3TW), **Fox Wood dirt jumps** (200 m east of where the A167 meets the trainline to the south of town), and the best of the bunch – **Old Mine Pits**, a dirt jumping, freeride and downhill spot to the west of Waldridge and just to the north of Fleece Terrace. From Waldridge, head towards Edmondsley and turn to the right halfway down.

Terrain These are various terrains, with the Old Mine being a mixture of forest land and open quarry freeriding area, while the other DH spots are short, forested runs and the dirt jumps are being located in a copse of trees next to the main road.

XC There is plenty of XC riding to be had surrounding Old Mine Pits, but this is a spot for downhill bikers or for those who like to get in the air.

Downhill Old Mine Pits is the place to head, though Doctors has some short, technical riding and has the beginnings of some northshore riding.

Dirt Jumps/Freeride The local riders here have worked hard to make sure that at each spot there are plenty of obstacles to mess around on.

Conditions The XC routes are hard-packed dirt singletrack. The area is popular with walkers but well known as a mountain biking centre so expect to see plenty of bikes.

ⓘ **More info** Tyne Road Club have a mountain bike division who regularly ride over to Chester-le-Street, tynerc.co.uk.

JOHN STOREY/NEFREERIDERS.CO.UK

↘7 Chopwell

Train station Blaydon/Wylam
Nearest city Newcastle-Upon-Tyne
Sat Nav NE39 1LT

Location Chopwell Woodland Park is around 10 km southwest from the centre of Newcastle Upon Tyne. From the A1(M) exit at junction 65 and take the A1 Newcastle ringroad west towards Whickham. After 8 km, take the A694 south towards Rowlands Gill, then take a right onto the B6315. Carry on up this road for 3 km to High Spen, where the entrance to the park is signposted off to the left just before Garesfield Golf Club.

Facilities Chopwell Wood has a car park and toilets, but there are no refreshments or supplies to be found at the trails. Take supplies with you. The nearest shops are in High Spen.

Overview Chopwell Wood is a 360 hectare Forestry Commission site that has four purpose-built trails designed and built by the North East Freeride Association (NEFA), and The Chopwell Mafia. While there are no facilities on site, the trails offer something for everyone, from families and novices to expert riders.

Terrain These are short but fun and intensive trails that will interest and challenge XC and novice freeriders with the technical and fast singletrack.

XC The Festival Cycle Trail is a green-graded, waymarked 2.5-km loop along the old railway line and through the picturesque Derwent Valley, and is perfect for families and novices. The Outside Line is a blue-graded 5.8-km XC loop through the forest with great views and some gentle riding.

The Powerline Trail is a 3.5-km red-graded loop that was the main attraction for years (the site has had building work since 2001), taking in the river Derwent, the overhead powerlines (hence the name), and packs a technical punch with plenty of built features to ride, while the High Voltage Trail is a short 300-m loop that has some very technical, black-graded riding and is the most recent trail in the area.

Downhill There is no specific DH trail here, but the Powerline Trail has plenty of short descents that are good for DH practice.

Dirt Jumps/Freeride There are no specific areas for freeriders or dirt jumpers, but the shortness of the other trails means they are packed full of features such as northshore bridges, drops, jumps and berms. Those who like to get in the air will definitely find something to ride.

Conditions This is forest land and open to all so please be aware of other users and be respectful of the amount of work that has gone into the trails.

ⓘ **More info** The Forestry Commission site has a page on Chopwell, forestry.gov.uk, while visitnortheastengland.com/mtb has a load of info on the trails, or go direct to the builders by clicking on nefa.co.uk.

JOHN MCFARLANE/FORESTRY COMMISSION

↘8 Delamere Forest

XC DH FR DJ

Train station Delamere/Cuddington
Nearest city Manchester
Sat Nav CW8 2JD

Location Delamere Forest Park is a tract of Forestry Commission land 12 km to the northeast of Chester and 18 km southwest from Manchester. Take the B5125 north out of Delamere – itself on the A54, and the forest is well marked with plenty of parking along the quiet roads and plentiful access points.

Facilities There is a newly-built Linmere visitor centre for the forest, complete with bike-wash area, which can be accessed by the Delamere railway station (although most mountain bikers arrive by car), and the excellent Delamere Forest Café (delamerecafe.com), which serves food and has wifi internet. The nearest bike shops are either Royles in Wilmslow (royles.biz), or The Edge Cycle Works in Chester (theedgecycleworks.com), although Tracs UK are on site and offer bike hire, sales and guiding if pre-booked (T07949 088477, tracs-uk.co.uk).

Overview It's the largest woodland area (9.5 sq km) in Cheshire, with some great XC trails, a brilliant DJ area and some short but interesting downhill. There's a designated 'Skills Area' with a 4X course, the DJs, and some DH which includes some chutes and road gaps.

CHRIS MORAN

CHRIS MORAN

Terrain There's plenty of unofficial singletrack, but the majority of the routes here are fire-road.

XC There's a 12 km loop around the forest which takes in the Skills Area and includes plenty of interesting sections such as drops and well-trodden singletrack.

Downhill There are some short sections of DH in the Skills Area, and a longer course named Old Pale nearer to the Visitor Centre.

Dirtjumps There are several lines through the jumps ranging from medium to difficult with tabletops, gaps and doubles. Beginners will struggle with the size and speed of the jumps, while super-pros may find them fun but un-testing. Generally speaking though, the DJ lines are of a high standard, well packed and well maintained.

Conditions The XC routes are hard-packed dirt singletrack. The area is popular with walkers but well known as a mountain biking centre so expect to see plenty of bikes.

ⓘ **More info** Linmere Visitor Centre has its own page on the Forestry website at forestry.gov.uk.

↘9 Dalby Forest

XC DH FR 4X N

Train station Malton

Nearest city York

Sat Nav YO1 2JN or the Visitor Centre on YO18 7LT

Opening times The Visitor Centre is open from 0930 until 1630 every day, while the trails are open 24/7, though check with the Forestry Commission website as they often close the XC routes for maintenance or during bad weather. Entry into the forest by bike is free but £7 for a car

TONY BARTHOLOMEW/FORESTRY COMMISSION

Location Dalby Forest is a Forestry Commission site in the North Yorkshire Moors near Pickering, around 15 km to the west of Scarborough. From the M1 exit at junction 49 and take the A168 in the direction of Thirsk, then turn onto to the A170 in the direction of Scarborough. After Pickering, and in the small village of Thornton-le-Dale, take a left at the village square and take the road going North, following signs for Dalby Forest Visitor Centre.

Facilities/Overview Dalby Forest is one of the northeast's best mountain biking spots, with everything from family riding through to hardcore DH trails, plus bike hire and on-site accommodation and amenities. Being another Singletraction site (like Stainburn and Guisborough Forest), the work here is first class with solid dirt jumps, sturdy northshore, purpose-built XC trails and some good downhill. It is popular with riders from as far as Leeds and Manchester, and has a host of facilities in the Visitor Centre from The Purple Mountain Bike Centre & Café (purplemountain.co.uk), which has Yeti hire gear, a bike wash and all the spares you'll need, to another Go Ape facility, and further café and bike hire facilities at nearby Dalby Courtyard. There's also the Tree Tops Restaurant at the Dalby Forest Visitor Centre and shops, maps, toilets and bike wash available on site.

XC There are some fantastic XC routes at Dalby, including two

TONY BARTHOLOMEW/FORESTRY COMMISSION

grade green Family Trails (The Ellersway Family Cycle Route – a 3-km easy loop from the Visitor Centre, and the Adderstone Cycle Trail, a 10-km loop that is slightly higher ground but still built for fun and easy riding). There's the Blue Trail, a 14-km upgrade for those who fancy a gentle but challenging loop through the forest; the Dalby Forest Red Trail, 27 km of feature-full riding with plenty of climbing and technical riding; while the Black Trail is a 10.4-km waymarked loop with plenty of off-camber riding and northshore style additions to make the trail as interesting as possible. Much of the loops have been reinforced and laid with gravel to make them all-weather trails, and all feature brilliant, flowing singletrack, jumps, rock sections, and enough differences through the seasons to keep even the most technical rider on their toes. Well worth a visit. In addition, the Visitor Centre can be used as a launchpad for hundreds of kilometres of unofficial XC singletrack into the North Yorkshire Moors.

JOHN STOREY/NEFREERIDERS.CO.UK

Downhill The new DOA Downhill trail at Dalby has been built by the guys at Singletraction and Team DOA, and is an on-going project with plenty of features and obstacles built into the trail near Crosscliffe. It's not the longest DH in the world, but has been carefully planned for maximum entertainment.

Freeride There's a 3 acre, purpose-built bike park at the disused quarry in Dixon's Hollow, with a brilliant, competition standard 4X track, some great DJs (that would suit beginner to intermediate), loads of northshore and testing riding, and some freeride obstacles to mess around on. This is one of the major attractions to the forest, and includes a corkscrew, some skinny logs and inventive obstacles, though it can be slippy in the wrong conditions.

Easy There are some good lines through the Bike Park that learners will love.

Hard The Black Route isn't the hardest in the world but definitely a challenge for most riders.

Not to miss The Bike Park brings 'em in from miles around.

Remember to avoid Turning up when one of the waymarked runs is closed. Check online first.

> Lowdown

☺ Locals do
Ride to a super-high standard.

Ride most trails on offer.

☹ Locals don't
Really come from here! Lots of the riders here have travelled long distances.

Worry about paying the steep car park charge. The forest is worth it.

✔ Pros
One of the UK's top mountain bike facilities.

Great chilled, friendly atmosphere.

✖ Cons
No uplift available for the DH trail.

Spread out.

Nearest Bike/Hire shop
Purple Mountain Bike, on site, purplemountain.co.uk.

Local accommodation
The Warrington guest house in Thornton Le Dale (T01751 475028) or for some luxury living in the forest, why not hire one of the wooden cabins set in stunning locations in nearby Cropton, call Forest Holidays on (T01751 417510).

Eating The Tree Tops Restaurant or the Purple Café are the places to head, otherwise try the Brandysnap Bistro (T01751 474732) restaurant in Thornton Le Dale, one of the prettiest villages in Yorkshire.

ⓘ **More info** Dalby Forest has several pages on the Forestry Commission site, forestry.gov.uk, while there is a load of info on the Singletraction site, singletraction.org.uk.

↘10 Devils Cascade DJs

DJ

Train station Poynton
Nearest city Stockport/Manchester
Sat Nav SK12 1HE

Location Devils Cascade DJs are around 300 m to the north of Poynton Railway Station, itself around 3 km to the south of Stockport near Manchester. There are several ways in to Poynton, but from the M56 exit at junction 6 and take the A538 Wilmslow Road past Manchester Airport towards Wilmslow. Turn right onto the A34 Handforth Bypass then after 300 m a left onto the A538 Prestbury Road. After another 300 m take a left onto the A5102 Adlington Road then after 5 km take a right at the roundabout onto the A5149. Poynton is 1 km up this road and the railway station is clearly signed on the left. The next road on the left is Hazelbadge Road, and at the top of this road is a field with the DJs. Please close the gate as there is livestock.

Facilities Poynton has plenty of shops and amenities on hand.

Overview This is two sets of DJs, one for learning and one fairly large, with some more tabletops and random jumps scattered around in the fields surrounding this area. Poynton is a very popular venue for dirt jumping, and there are lots of BMXers around who have built numerous sites in the area, some secret, some not so. Ask around and you're likely to find many more spots, but Devils Cascade is a well-known spot and a good place to start.

Conditions This is open grassland belonging to the farm next door. Please respect the farmer's wishes and leave the site as you found it for other riders to carry on enjoying.

ⓘ **More info** Poynton has a fantastic and varied mountain bike scene. The FlapJackers are a bunch of local riders that can be found at flapjackers.blogspot.com.

CHRIS MORAN

↘11 Elland Park Wood

XC DH

Train station Halifax/Sowerby
Nearest city Bradford/Leeds
Sat Nav HX5 9HZ

Location Elland Park Wood is to the north of the town of Elland, itself halfway between Halifax and Huddersfield. From the M62 exit at junction 24 and take the A629 in the direction of Halifax. After 3 km, exit this dual carriageway signed for Elland, and take the B6114 Elland Riorges Link towards Elland. At the first roundabout take a right onto Huddersfield Road, then after 500 m take a right over the bridge, then a right onto Park Road. After another 500 m the entrance to Elland Park Crematorium is on your left. Go through here and access the park to the rear. The DH trails are to the east end of the park in the wooded area.

Facilities Park Road, which rings the park, has plenty of shops and facilities, plus there are some good pubs, such as the Collier's Arms on the canal just opposite the entrance of the crematorium.

Overview This is a great spot for those just getting into the sport, although none of the trails here are waymarked so you'll have to either use your natural navigational instincts or chat to some of the local riders and find some of the trail starts. There are a few gentle DH trails here, as well as plenty of XC and freeriding to be had in both the wooded and open areas of the park. The crematorium puts many off riding here but no-one seems to mind, though there is also access further down the canal should you prefer. Again, talk to local riders to get the lowdown and there should be plenty around.

CHRIS MORAN

Conditions This is a large expanse of park which is popular with walkers and dog owners but due to the nature of its size you're unlikely to meet many people if you head off following the singletracks into the woods.

ⓘ **More info** The Bracken Way Bikers Club is the local Elland mountain biking hub, though primarily for XC riders. They meet regularly to ride and have a website at bwbclub.co.uk.

↘12 Gosforth Park DJs

FR DJ

Train station Regent Centre (metro)
Nearest city Newcastle-upon-Tyne
Sat Nav NE3 5HN

Location Gosforth Park DJs are in the grounds of the Newcastle Marriot Gosforth Park, itself in the northern Newcastle suburb of North Gosforth. From the A1 exit at North Gosforth onto Rotary Way (the A1056). At the next roundabout turn south on the B1318, then after 100 m turn into the hotel entrance on the left. Go through the Marriot carpark, turn left and go up the dirt track, then over the metal bridge.

Facilities Gosforth Park is full of shops and supplies are easy to come by. This is an inner-city area.

Overview Gosforth Park is a relatively well-kept DJs site which is popular with BMXers and mountain bikers, and consists of a small area of woods within the Marriot complex that have had lots of interconnecting lines built. Not worth a long journey, and there are better secret DJs in Newcastle, but good to get into the local scene and worth a visit for those nearby.

Conditions This is a well-known area and the jumps can be trashed easily, but they do go through periods of being good and having lots of maintenance.

ⓘ **More info** To find more north eastern dirt jumps try mtbnortheast.ning.com.

↘13 Gisburn Forest

XC DH FR

Train station Long Preston
Nearest city Bradford/Leeds
Sat Nav BD23 4SQ (for the centre of Tosside)

Location Gisburn Forest is on the southwest corner of the Yorkshire Dales, around 15 km north of Clitheroe and 4 km to the west of the village of Long Preston. From the M65 exit at junction 13 and take the A682 north in the direction of Gisburn, then Long Preston, then turn off to the left on the B6478 heading towards Slaidburn. At the village of Tosside, take a right onto Bailey Lane and Gisburn Forest is at the top of the hill overlooking Stocks Reservoir.

Facilities There isn't anything at the forest aside from two car parks. The nearby village of Tosside has the Dog and Partridge Pub and a shop for supplies, but you're best bringing in your own if you need food and drink whilst riding. The pub has a power washer and is very bike friendly owing to a large client base from the forest! Cycle hire available from Cycle Bowland (see website below).

Overview Gisburn Forest, inside the beautiful Forest of Bowland, is an area of reknown for the northwest mountain biking community, with plenty of DH and XC riding to be had in the surrounding hills and woods. Recently, in conjunction with the Forestry Commission and Lancashire Council, the area has been upgraded with £180,000 worth of trails being installed as part of the 'Adrenaline Gateway Project' which has turned the Lancashire Pennines into an outdoor activity area. There have also been plans for Rowan Sorrell's Back On Track to install some additional purpose-built trails in Gisburn Forest. Currently there are 3 waymarked XC routes and plenty of unofficial DH and XC singletrack over the area.

Terrain There's plenty of singletrack, but the majority of the routes here are fire-road.

XC There are three XC waymarked loops (though most local riders prefer to go the opposite way around the loops), offering short bursts of feature-full terrain from 7- to 12-km loops.

Downhill From the top of the hill there is one obvious DH trail which is well maintained and has re-inforced drops and jumps, while throughout the forest there are plenty of hidden DH trails. Though short, they are enough for the large local mountain biking scene.

Dirt Jumps/Freeride There is nothing specific for freeriders here, though the disused quarry sees lots of drop and DJ action. Plenty of jumps and features on the XC and DH trails should keep most satisfied. If the plans go ahead, the area may turn into a full trail centre, though that seems a long way off at the present time.

Conditions This is Forestry Commission land that is still in full working order. Expect well worn tracks and mostly fire-road to ride on, though there is plenty of hidden singletrack to explore. Most of it is in a natural state, so parts become largely unridable after heavy rain. There are man-made tracks, natural tracks, woodland and a quarry.

ⓘ **More info** Build days are every second Sunday or Saturday, contact Martin.Charlesworth@lancashire.gov.uk to get involved in helping to shape the area, or go to adrenaline-gateway.co.uk to get more on the whole Adrenaline Gateway area. Try Cycle Bowland in Settle (cyclebowland.com) for bike hire, maps and more info.

↘14 Greasborough Trails

4X DJ

Train station Rotherham/Sheffield
Nearest city Sheffield
Sat Nav S61 4QH

Location Greasborough Trails are just to the south of Greasborough, which is around 2 km to the north of Rotherham town centre. From the M1 exit at junction 34 and head east towards Rotherham on Meadow Bank Road (the A6109), then take a right onto the New Wortley Road (A629) towards Rotherham town centre. At the next roundabout, take the first exit into Greasborough Street and go 1 km up this road to the roundabout where the B6375 heads off to the right. Turn left here into Ginhouse Lane, then ride back up Car Hill (straight on at the roundabout up the hill), then turn left into the first gap in the fence. The Trails are in a field around 50 m down the hill. If you carry on up the hill and hit the recycling centre on the left, you've gone too far.

Facilities Rotherham town centre has plenty of shops and amenities and is a short ride away. Fosters Cycles on Thames Street in Rotherham (just opposite the B&Q centre), helped build the trails so call in.

Overview These are a set of old trails originally built by Tom Martin, that are now constantly being updated and shaped by the local riders, led by Mark Nixon. There are currently over 10 sets, with everything from 5 to 15 ft gaps. Friendly outsiders are welcome.

Conditions This is open land with great views over Rotherham. The site drains well (it's on a hill), but still avoid after heavy weather.

ⓘ **More info** Check out nixonthecreator.spaces.live.com, or email marknixon@blueyonder.co.uk if you wish to get involved with helping to maintain the trails.

↘15 Great Ayton Quarry DJs

XC FR DJ

Train station Great Ayton
Nearest city Middlesbrough
Sat Nav TS9 6EY (to Roseberry Crescent)

Location Great Ayton is on the northwestern edge of the North Yorkshire Moors and around 10 km southeast of Middlesbrough. The quarry (actually called Roseberry Quarry, but known locally as Ayton Quarry), is to the northeast of the town. From the A1 coming from the south, exit at junction 49 heading to Thirsk on the A168, then north towards Middlesbrough on the A19 with the North Yorkshire Moors on your right. At Ingleby Arncliffe, take the A172 to Stokesly, then the A173 to Great Ayton. Head through town and take the next right after Roseberry Crescent (the last of the houses in Ayton). After crossing the railway line, park up and ride up the road to the quarry at the top of the lane.

Facilities There's nothing up at the quarry, but there are plenty of shops and amenities in nearby Great Ayton.

Overview Roseberry Quarry has two fantastic attributes: the first is that it has brilliant access to the amazing XC riding that the North Yorkshire Moors has to offer. But most people come to ride here for the brilliant DJs and freeride area that the quarry houses. It's been built mostly by the local mountain biking scene, and is perfect for everyone, from beginners through to good riders looking for some practice. There are tens of lines scattered around the quarry, with plenty of drops, gaps, doubles, rhythm sections, step-ups and more. Well worth a visit for those nearby as it's a large site with a lot of variety.

Conditions This is a well-maintained site, with lots of jumps that are always being added to. The ground is apparently fine-ground dolomite which is superb for DJ building and drains very well. Park at the main road or Roseberry Crescent if the access road is busy (lots of people use this road to get to the Moors).

ⓘ **More info** Trail Blasters are the people to contact about the quarry, trailblasters.co.uk.

↘16 Greenway DJs

DJ

Train station Bradford or Halifax
Nearest city Bradford
Sat Nav BD19 3LB (for Bradford Road)

Location Greenway DJs are on a piece of common land between the M62 motorway and the A58, just to the north west of Cleckheaton and around 5 km south of Bradford. From the M62, exit at junction 26 (don't get onto to the M606 heading to Bradford, though this is the direction you'll be heading). Instead, exit the M62, go around the exit roundabout and get off at the second exit – Bradford Road, heading in the direction of Bradford. Turn immediately to your left (the turning is virtually on the roundabout), and park up. Follow this lane along with the barn on your left (and the A58 parallel on your left), until you hit the bridge crossing the A58. Go over this, and the DJs are in the woods on your left, between the A58 and the M62.

Facilities The nearest facilities are in Cleckheaton – carry on to the bridge over the M62 which goes straight into Cleckheaton.

Overview There are several fairly decent jumps here with a good local scene who look after their trails. Definitely not for beginners, though they're not the biggest trails in the world either. Worth a look if you're in the area but otherwise don't make a long journey.

Conditions This is woodland between major roads that is rarely used by others because of its proximity to motorways etc. Expect to see other riders there.

↘17 Guisborough Forest

XC DH

Train station Gypsey Lane or Nunthorpe
Nearest city Middlesbrough
Sat Nav TS14 8HD

Location Guisborough Forest is a tract of land on the north western tip of the North Yorkshire Moors, around 7 km to the east of Middlesbrough. From the A1(M), exit at junction 57 onto the A66(M), which turns into the A66 in the direction of Middlesbrough. Follow this road almost to Middlesbrough town centre, but take a right onto the A19, heading south towards Thirsk. After 2 km take a left on the A174 towards Nunthorpe, then a right off the A174 onto the A172. Carry on this road for 2 km, then take the A1043, and then the A171 towards Guisborough. Just before you hit town, take a right onto the A173 and the Guisborough Forest and Walkway Visitor Centre is signposted off this road, after around 250 m on your left.

Facilities The Visitor Centre has toilets, but for full shops and supplies you'll have to go to Guisborough, another 2 km along the A171.

Overview Guisborough Forest is another Singletraction site with two main XC routes – the Blue Route and Black Route. The Blue is around 6 km in length, waymarked and suitable for learners and families who can already ride, while the Black Route is a 12-km harder course for intermediate/advanced riders. There is also a fair amount of unofficial singetrack, shale riding and some fantastic, technical descents dotted around the area, and it's fairly popular with the local riding scene (check out trailblasters.co.uk for more routes and maps). This area might not be worth a very long journey but for those nearby or in the northeast, it's high on the list of places to visit.

JOHN SOTREY/NEFREERIDERS.CO.UK

JOHN SOTREY/NEFREERIDERS.CO.UK

Conditions Anything Singletraction do is worth a visit. They show a high level of care and attention to detail and work closely with the Forestry Commission. This is forest land with open areas, all waymarked and any problem areas have had work done for drainage and support. But still avoid after bad weather.

ⓘ **More info** The Forestry Commission has a Guisborough Forest page at forestry.gov.uk, while this is another Singletraction-built area so join in at singletraction.org.uk. Also worth checking is the brilliant North Yorkshire site trailblasters.co.uk. Finally, this is the official training ground of the North East Freeriders and their website contains a wealth of info on the area as well as how to get involved with their club, Team NEFR – nefreeriders.co.uk.

N18 Hartlepool 4X

4X DJ BMX

Train station Hartlepool
Nearest city Middlesbrough
Sat Nav TS25 4LL

Location Hartlepool is around 10 km north of Middlesbrough. From the A1(M), exit at junction 60 and take the A689 towards Hartlepool. Pass the Greatham turn-off and go through two sets of traffic lights and at the third set take a left signposted Summerhill. At the next set of lights, next to The Fens pub, take a right onto Catcote Road through town. Keep following signs for Summerhill, turning left off Catcote towards the Summerhill Visitor Centre. The BMX track is next door and part of the centre's amenities.

Facilities Summerhill Visitor Centre is a council-run initiative with lots of facilities including car parking, toilets, changing rooms, lockers and drinks machines. There is also a rope course, a climbing centre and fitness loop.

Overview This is a fantastic BMX and 4X track that has been cut into the hill with a unique design put together by 4X designer Phil Saxena. There are six straights and loads of berms, jumps, tabletops and gaps. Well worth a visit if you're nearby or a fan of 4X riding.

Conditions This is a purpose-built site which drains well and has been designed to work in all weathers.

ⓘ **More info**
Hartlepool BMX has a club website at northeastbmx.co.uk.

N19 Hookstone Woods DJs

DJ

Train station Hornbeam Park
Nearest city Harrowgate/Leeds
Sat Nav HG2 8PN

Location Hookestone Woods are to the east of Harrogate, Yorkshire. From the A1(M), exit at junction 47 and head towards Knaresborough/Harrogate on the A59. After 2.5 km take the A658 south towards Follifoot, then a right onto the A661 heading towards Harrogate town centre. After 2 km take a left into Hookstone Drive, then another left into Hookstone Wood Road. Near the end of the road, turn right into Hookstone Woods and the dirt jumps are 200 m to the west of this point.

Facilities Hookstone Woods is an area of outstanding natural beauty – being part of the ancient Knaresborough Forest – and very popular with the inhabitants of Harrogate, but this is a natural area and there are no on-site facilities.

Overview Hookstone DJs are the fruits of the local riders' hard work and although small, are well kept and a good place for beginners and intermediate riders to get into freestyle and freeriding. Not worth a huge journey, as there are only a few jumps on offer, but for those in the area they are well worth a visit.

Conditions This is public forest, though you probably won't see many people at the jumps themselves. Avoid after rain as the area is prone to serious mud and please don't ride the jumps when they're soft.

Local riders
John Storey

Bike Intense Socom & Giante Trance x3
Local spot Guisborough
Club member Manager of Team NEFR
Age 27
Type of rider Downhill Racer

Where's the one place you'd recommend above all, for those coming to the north?

JS It's got to be Hamsterley Forest – purpose built facility with many different types of tracks for all abilities. There are long or short XC routes, a beginner's skills loop and the expert-level DH Courses and 4X.

Where has the best XC?

JS That would have to be Hamsterley. You can combine different routes together to create your own way. The black route is my favourite and is the most technically challenging trail, with steep technical climbs, smooth flowing singletrack and some superb rooty, rocky descents. It's got some great natural riding that will challenge even the best cross country bikers.

Where is the best Downhill?

JS Again that'd be Hamsterley Forest with its purpose-built DH facility, featuring numerous tracks with loads of variety. The fast flat out top sections are full of big jumps and sweet berms. Depending on which bottom section you ride the course gets very steep, rocky, rooty and technical and also includes a number of drops and jumps. It's notorious for its rock gardens on the lower sections of the course.

The best dirt jumps?

JS Great Ayton quarry is by far the best Dirt Jump spot in the north, famous for its huge 6 pack. People come from all over the country to ride these jumps. The jumps have been continually modified by generations of local riders and it's bmx and 26-inch wheel friendly! They even shot a section of Earthed DVD series at these Dirt Jumps.

If you were to take a family out – say a cousin who's visiting with his kids – where would you head?

JS The best place for a family ride would have to be Dalby Forest. There are many different family rides to choose from, varying in length and skill level. The facilities at Dalby are also excellent, with loads of parking, toilet and changing facilities, café's and good cycle route signs. The whole forest is very clean and tidy and there's a lovely, friendly atmosphere about the place.

What secret stashes do you know about?

JS Ha ha!! I must admit I do know of quite a few! Guisborough woods, my local training ground is littered with secret trails all over the forest. Steep shale descents and technical short DH tracks are scattered throughout the forest, but you really do need local knowledge to find them. I also know of one or two other secret spots around the Hamsterley area and also at Innerleithen and Glentress in Scotland!

If you were a huge fan of cake and wanted to find the best trail with a foodie pit stop, where would it be?

JS The best foodie pit stop would have to be Castleton Tea rooms. It's a small café in the North Yorkshire village of Castleton. It's lovely little spot and is very popular amongst the XC community. The XC riding around the area is superb! Close to hand you have the North Yorkshire Moors and Guisborough Forest. But to be Honest I much prefer a bag of crisps and a pint after a ride!!!

Where – if anywhere – outside of your area do you often visit with your bike?

JS Innerleithen in Scotland!! It's a great DH venue that regularly holds races for the SDA and NPS series. There are so many different DH trails up there I would be here all day trying to list them. It's one of my all time favourite tracks to ride. Fast, flat out, steep and technical… you name it, it's got it!!

OLIVER COATS

Which websites have the best info on your local area?

JS The best websites for local riding information would have to be my own team website, Team NEFR (nefreeriders.co.uk) and Trailblasters (trailblasters.co.uk). Team NEFR Website is geared more towards the DH and Freeride aspect of the sport with regular information and updates on local DH race series as well as national races, product reviews and race reports. The site also has a number of videos featuring races from around the country as well as the local area. It has a very popular forum where riders log on to organize rides and meet up with each other and find out about the local mountain bike community. Trailblasters on the other hand is geared toward the more general aspect of riding and XC across Guisborough and the North Yorkshire moors. The site has lots of videos made by local riders, which give an insight into the trails, technical descents and superb singletrack that are on offer in Guisborough woods and surrounding North Yorkshire moors. Between the two websites I think we pretty much have the north of England covered for local information.

Which is the best shop to head to if you're in the North?

JS The best bike shop to head to would have to be Peddlers in Redcar. Peddlers have a great selection of bikes and equipment ranging from kids bikes and BMX, right through to full on DH Bikes. Greg Winspeare the owner actually rides for Team NEFR and my thanks have to go to Greg for all his help and support for Team NEFR.

↘20 Hamsterley Forest

Train station Bishop Aukland

Nearest city Newcastle-upon-Tyne

Sat Nav DL13 3NL

Opening times You can ride the XC trails at any time, although the 4X and DH trails cannot be ridden without a membership fee (to cover insurance costs); a day pass permit for the DH and 4X costs £5.

Location Hamsterley Forest is around 5 km west of Bishop Auckland, 10 km southwest from Durham, 25 km southwest of Newcastle Upon Tyne, and 20 km north west of Middlesbrough. From the A1(M), exit at junction 60 and head along the A689 in the direction of Bishop Auckland. Turn left onto the A688, then after 4 km after take a right onto the A68 at West Aukland. The Hamsterley Forest Visitor Centre is signed from here, but just in case, go up this road for 5 km then take a left onto Saunders Avenue, signposted for Hamsterley. Just after Hamsterley take a right into Bedburn Road signed to Bedburn, then straight through the village, across the stream, then left onto Redford Lane. Follow this road for 3 km to the Forest Lodge at the end. There's a £3 fee to enter and park.

Facilities/Overview This is one of the North's best mountain bike centres. It's a simple set-up with all the gravity trails (DH, 4X, duel and DJs) located together on one side of the hill, and the XC trails running out into the forest where green, blue, red and black graded trails await all riders. The easier trails are surfaced and skimmed for smooth riding, while the red and black trails contain more natural terrain which is made up of plenty of roots and can be quite slick when wet. The site is incredibly popular, and constantly evolving, so expect each visit to have new, evermore interesting terrain to ride.

GARY EWING

XC There are green and blue family and beginner trails, and red and black trails for the more experienced riders, so whatever the age and ability, there will be something that works for all. There's also the Trailquest Course – a map-reading (on bikes) area with the emphasis on finding checkpoints. This will take you right out to the corners of the forest on easy-going tracks and also boasts a skills loop for rider development. Finally there is the Grove Link Cycle Trail for families, which meanders gently along the Bedburn Valley.

Downhill Hamsterley is one of the only venues offering official downhill trails in the north of England. There is one main run with plenty of split sections offering different styles from rock gardens to technical singletrack, wide open berms and jumps. There is usually a good scene on weekends and holidays with plenty of local riders sessioning the track.

Freeride With a duel track, a 4X track and a set of DJs, Hamsterley has enough to keep most riders who like to get airborne busy. The 4X trail is of a national standard, having hosted several rounds of the NPS 4X series and some say is second only to Fort William's impressive set-up. There's also a new 'Loop Mountain Bike Skills Area', with wood and stone northshore and testing obstacles.

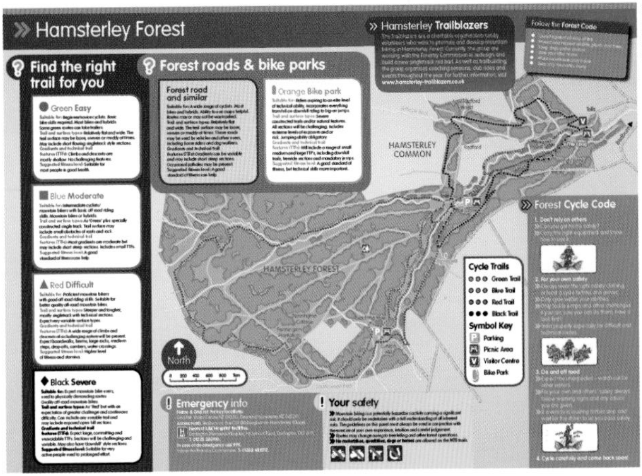

GARY EWING

Easy The trail quest is a non-technical ride to get groups out into the forest, but if you are looking for some real riding it's not until the red route that you will find singletrack, and at 12 km it's a fairly easy ride if you take your time. Brush up your skills on 'the loop' – a one-mile skills training loop with plenty of features to learn the basics.

Hard XC riders should head out on the red loop and after a quick break follow it up with the shorter but more technical black loop. For the freeriders and downhillers there are plenty of challenges on the hill, be it cleaning the rock garden or root sections on the downhill or putting together the rhythm sections on the 4X.

Not to miss Coming here at least once in your riding career!

Remember to avoid The old NPS Downhill track which is quite flat. It does make a great XC route though.

Nearest Bike/Hire shop Wood N Wheels is a small shop based on site at Hamsterley (T01388 488222) and offers cycle hire and repairs for many brands.

Local accommodation For B&B close to the forest try the Dale End (T01388 488091) in Hamsterley, or Mayland Farm Cottage (T01388 718237). In Durham try the Kings Lodge Hotel (T0191 370 9977).

Eating Snacks and meals are available at the Hamsterley Forest Visitor Centre during opening hours. Two local pubs offering meals to hungry bikers near the trails are the Cross Keys (T01388 488457) in Hamsterley and the Moorecock Inn (T01833 650395) in Egglestone.

ⓘ **More info** hamsterley-trailblazers.co.uk has a wealth of info on the trails, trail maps (and stats) and is the place to head to gain membership to the area, while descendhamsterley.co.uk has details of the uplift days and race events taking place. Both are worth a good look around. The Forestry Commission website also has a page on the Visitor Centre at forestry.gov.uk and finally, visitnotheastengland.co.uk/mtb is a great source of info for all sites around the northeast.

> Lowdown

Locals do

Get involved with the trail building in the forest too.

Reap the benefits of the above!

Locals don't

Dodge out of buying a day permit on the downhill or 4X – you'll ruin it for everyone else.

Pros

Hamsterley can offer something for most riders.

A good club and scene at the trails.

Cons

Hills rather than mountains.

Can be quite muddy on the unsurfaced trails in winter.

21 Hulme Park DJs

DJ

Train station Deansgate
Nearest city Manchester
Sat Nav M15 6HE

Location Hulme Park is just to the south of Manchester City Centre. From the M62 follow signs all the way into Manchester City Centre, which will lead you to exiting at junction 3 of the M602. From here, go round the roundabout, don't get on the Mancunian Way (the overhead motorway that starts here), but take the B5218 exit (Chorlton Road) and head down here for 200 m before turning right into Jackson Crescent, then left into Birchvale Close. The dirt jumps are at the end in Hulme Park.

Facilities Hulme Park is a redevelopment area with plenty of shops and amenities.

Overview This is a DJ specific site built in conjunction with Manchester Council and the BMX group M15 after the demolition of a BMX site nearby. It's a 600 sq m area and houses plenty of lines from beginner to expert. Many shy away from coming here with expensive bikes as this is a notorious inner-city park, but incidents have been rare and there is a thriving riding scene, though many BMXs.

Conditions This is an inner-city, purpose-built BMX and DJ venue with good drainage.

ⓘ **More info** Manchester City Council has a website with a Hulme Park page manchester.gov.uk.

22 Hustwood Trails

XC DH FR

Train station Hebden Bridge/Mytholmroyd
Nearest city Bradford
Sat Nav HX7 7AZ

Location Hurstwood Trails are in the moors between Burnley, Halifax and Bradford. From the M65 exit at Burnley and take the A646 towards Hebden Bridge/Halifax. At Hebden Bridge, turn north towards Heptonstall on the Heptonstall Road, then Smithwell Lane, Slack Road and Widdop Road (all the same road which changes name), all of which are signed towards Nelson. After 5 km, park at Widdop Reservoir and cross the dam to the start of the trails.

Facilities There's nothing up at the trails, but Hebdon Bridge is a beautiful town with plenty of quirky cafés and full of shops and amenities.

Overview This is a brilliant, natural area full of XC trails with some

RICHARD NORGATE

interesting downhill sections, plenty of jumps and drops, all set in some spectacular countryside with beautiful views across the numerous lakes and reservoirs, including Widdup and Gorple Reservoirs. As part of the Pennine Way, it can be popular with walkers, but there is enough space on the trails here for everyone.

Conditions This is open-land singletrack and shared bridelways for miles around, with stone walls, reservoirs and small copses over the rolling hills. A lovely XC day out for those nearby.

↘23 Ilkley Moor

XC DH FR

Train station Ilkley or Ben Rhydding
Nearest city Bradford
Sat Nav LS29 8RX (for Escape Mountain Biking in Ilkley)

Location Ilkley is a small village on the road between Leeds and Skipton and around 12 km north of Bradford. From Leeds, take the A660 out of the city centre towards Skipton. After 15 km, after passing through Otley and Burley-in-Wharfdale, you'll come to Ilkley. The trails are on the moor, directly overlooking the town to the south.

Facilities Ilkley is a picturesque village with plenty of facilities and amenities and is a gateway to the moors, which are popular with all sorts of outdoor types.

Overview Ilkley Moor is an enormous expanse of the Yorkshire Dales, criss-crossed with fire-road, bridleway and fantastic singletrack. There is everything here from incredible XC riding to the most technical and steep downhill. None of it is waymarked, and many of the routes are popular with walkers and other fell users, but everyone from families to good riders should be able to find a decent line or two.

Conditions This is open moorland with plenty of shaley and gravelly singletrack owing to the large amount of limestone to be found in the area.

ⓘ **More info** The Leeds MTB club has info on Ilkley, mtbleeds.co.uk, and Escape Mountain Biking are a small outfit offering guiding and tuition services, based in Ilkley.

↘24 Iron Bridge DJs

XC DH DJ

Train station Rose Hill (Marple Railway Station), or Romily
Nearest city Stockport/Manchester
Sat Nav SK6 7EJ (for the Hare and Hounds pub on the south side of the river)

Location From the M60 exit at junction 27 and take the A626 St Marys Way into Stockport. After 600 m take a left onto Hall Street (still the A626) and carry on down this road for 2 km to Marple. At Marple, take a left into the A627 Dooley Lane and carry on for 600 m, then just as the road crosses the river, take a left into Mill Lane. Follow the lane with your bike then take a left between the horse fields, and the Iron Bridge is at the bottom of the hill with the DJs in front.

Facilities Nearby Marple has plenty of facilities and the Hare and Hounds is a good after-ride stop.

Overview Iron Bridge DJs are another Goyt Valley spot (similar to Woodbank, and nearby Devils Cascade DJs) that the locals regularly ride. There are a couple of sets, each with some gaps, tables and hips, not for complete beignners, but there's something for most to ride here. On the hill next to the bridge there are a few freeride obstacles and a DH trail, or head up the Goyt Valley for some XC riding. A good little spot but not worth a long journey, though could be worth a look in if you're visiting Roman Lakes Leisure Park.

Conditions This is picturesque farm and common land with some copses of trees overlooking the villages of Marple and Poynton.

↘25 Kielder Water & Forest Park

XC DH FR N

Train station Gretna Green

Nearest city Carlisle

Sat Nav NE48 1HX

Opening times The trails are open 365 days a year, day and night. The only closures are due to forest operations and status of the trails are posted on the websites visitkielder.com and forestry.gov.uk. All trails are free, though there is a £3 parking fee at the Visitor Centre

CHRIS MORAN

Location Kielder Water and Forest Park is on the western edge of the Northumberland National Park. From the M6 exit at junction 44 just north of Carlisle and head towards Longtown on the A7. Pass through the Scotland/ England border, and then take a right onto the B6357 towards Canobie, go through the village, and keep on the B6357 for around 20 km until you hit Saughtree, where Kielder Water, and Forest Park and Kielder Castle Forest Park Visitor Centre are clearly signed to the right. Follow this road and park at the Visitor Centre at the end of the road, after about 10 km down the road.

Facilities/Overview The Kielder Castle Forest Park Visitor Centre is an old Georgian abode, the former hunting lodge of the Duke of Northumberland that has since been transformed into a Visitor Centre with bike shop, café, parking, toilets and a maze! Plus there's lots of info on the castle and the walking and riding trails in the area. Kielder Water is the largest man-made lake in northern Europe, and can be popular with other users, but it's a big enough area to have your own space. There are nine purpose-built trails here, ranging from family rides through to black-graded runs and skills loops, that should appeal to the hardiest of riders.

XC The Castle Wood Skills Loop has been designed to check your level of riding so you can choose which of the routes suits your riding; the Lakeside Way Trail is a green-graded, novice or family route that takes in 14 km of beautiful countryside; the Castle Hill Trail is a blue-graded, 11-km loop; the Village Connection Trail is 14 km of blue-graded XC; the Borderline Trail is 9 km of blue-graded, easy riding down an old railway line along the Scottish border; Deadwater Trails is a 16-km red-graded loop taking in the lake; The Cross Border Trail is a 48-km red-graded loop into Scotland and back; the Kielder to Calvert Trail is a red-graded 21-km loop; the Humble Loop is graded red and 12-km in length; the Up and Over Trail is a black-graded trail over Deadwater Fell and was designed by world-cup competitor Gary Forrest. All are waymarked and packed with features suitable for their gradings.

Downhill There are sections of some of the more difficult trails that have technical descents, but there are no specific DH trails here, though you could loop the Up and Over trail for the best thrills.

Freeride There's no specific freeriding here, but plenty of jumps and some northshore based on the Up and Over and Deadwood Trails.

Terrain At 250 sq miles, Kielder Water and Forest Park is England's largest forest, and also includes the country's largest blanket bog, which gives you an idea of the going underfoot. All the trails in the forest have had to be constructed from imported aggregate so that riders don't sink into the soft ground.

Easy The Skills Loop has been designed to work out your level of riding, with green, blue, red and black-graded obstacles to try out, but the Lakeside Way is the easiest route in the forest.

Hard The Up and Over trail peaks out at 1900 ft. A good bit of downhill but a gruelling ride up.

Not to miss A slice of cake after riding in The Duke's Pantry.

Remember to avoid Taking on a huge route without trying one of the smaller loops first.

Nearest Bike/Hire shop
The Bike Place in Kielder, T01434 250457, or try The Bike Place in Newcastle (T01654 700411) who also do bike hire.

Local accommodation
In Kielder Water and Forest Park Twenty Seven B&B (T01434 250366) is the only hotel, but there's a youth hostel and a camping and caravanning site as well as luxury lodges at Leaplish Waterside Park and Calvert Trust Kielder. There is a variety of accommodation in the local area – go to visitkielder.com for information.

Eating The Anglers Arms (T01434 250072) in Kielder Village serves hot meals, while The Duke's Pantry Tearoom at the Kielder Castle Visitor Centre is also open on weekends and busy periods. Other visitor centres in the Park include Tower Knowe Visitor Centre and Leaplish Waterside Park, both of which provide food.

ⓘ **More info** Kielder Water and Forest Park, T01434 220616, visitkielder.com. The Forestry Commission website also has a page on forestry.gov.uk, Visit North East England has a page on Kielder Water & Forest Park with a breakdown of most of the trails, visitnortheastengland.com, while North East has info on build days and local riders; the organized Kielder Trail Reavers are the people behind most of the trails and can be found at kieldertrailreavers.org.uk.

> **Lowdown**
>
> **Locals do**
> Loop back up the forest road to ride the final descent of the Deadwater again.
>
> **Locals don't**
> Ride off the marked trails as the ground is soft and easily damaged by bikes.
>
> **Pros**
> Huge forest with plenty of trails, perfect for all levels.
>
> **Cons**
> Unofficial, unmarked XC trails can be boggy.

PHILIPPA CLARK/NORTHUMBRIAN WATER

↘26 Ladybower Reservoir

XC DH ● ● ● ● ●

Train station Glossop
Nearest city Manchester/Sheffield
Sat Nav S33 0AQ (for the Visitor Centre)

CHRIS MORAN

Location Ladybower Reservoir is on the north side of, and right next to, the Snake Pass (the A57), which connects Manchester to Sheffield. From either city, follow the A57 and roughly midway between the two there is a well-signed turn-off for Ladybower; follow signs for the Derwent Visitor Centre Car Park exit for the most facilities.

Facilities There is a newly-built Upper Derwent Visitor Centre, which has a café, museum (for the Dambusters who practised on Ladybower), parking (£3 for the day, £1 per hour), bike wash and toilets. Park before the centre and it's free. The centre also houses a bike shop with half-day rentals for £11 and full day for £14.

Overview This is a fantastic gateway to some of the Peak District's best XC routes. The sheer amount of available riding is staggering, with the whole of the Peaks – theoretically – at your disposal. There are short loops so you can stay relatively close to the Visitor Centre's amenities, or there are plenty of long-haul missions to be had incorporating some of the UK's most picturesque villages and spectacular moorland and lake views. Highly recommended for those who like their riding very rambling-esque.

Terrain The peak district is mostly open moorland, but hidden in the valleys are plenty of woodland areas and secret copses. These are often referred to as short, sharp routes, but the truth is that there is every type of XC riding to be had here.

XC Where to start? Perhaps the Short Circuit or Ladybower Classic above Ladybower and Derwent are for those who want to test their limits cautiously: leave the Visitor Centre and loop around Derwent Dam and Ladybower, up over Cutthroat Bridge and climb up the moorland before a long descent back to your starting point – 11 km with gentle climbs. But the possibility of endless riding is here, taking in Edale, Castleton, Mam Tor and the popular Jacob's Ladder. There are also local routes Mardy Bum (17 km), Pain for Pleasure (17 km) and the well-named Rawhide, a 35-km beast with technical DH as well as gruelling climbs. There are plenty of specific Peak District XC guides (perhaps the best being Dark Peak Mountain Biking: True Grit Trails, and White Peak Mountain Biking: The Pure Trails, which cover the north and south Peak District XC routes respectively), and serious local riders would be well advised to invest in one. Others can simply route find and ask other riders on the climbs – there's plenty to search out for yourself.

Downhill There are no purpose-built DH trails, but there are plenty of technical descents on many of the XC routes that will completely satisfy DH riders.

Dirt jumps/Freeride This is predominantly a XC area, but those on full-rig freeride bikes will undoubtedly find things to ride.

ⓘ **More info**
peakdistrictonline.co.uk has plenty of advice for mountain bikers, peakdistrict.org has info on the various visitor centres dotted around, the mentioned guide books can be bought through amazon.co.uk, and mountainbikerides.co.uk is the best source for local riders to discover more routes and meet each other.

↘27 Lee Mill Quarry (aka The Adrenaline Gateway)

XC DH FR

Train station Rochdale

Nearest city Manchester

Sat Nav OL12 8XG (from the south, heading from Rochdale). OL13 0BB (heading from the north and parking at Future's Park)

CHRIS MORAN

Location Lee Mill Quarry is a disused quarry around 10 km north of Rochdale on the A671. From Rochdale take the A671 in the direction of Bacup. After the village of Whitworth, turn off the road left into Tong Lane, then a right onto Back Lane (with Cowm Reservoir on your right), then High Barn Lane. At the end of this road the access road for Lee Mill Quarry starts. Follow this dirt track to the quarry, around 600 m further uphill. Alternatively, coming in from Rawtenstall to the north west, take the A681 to Stacksteads and follow signs for Future's Park. Park there and the quarry is behind (to the south).

Facilities There is nothing up at the quarry, but Whitworth is a small village with shops and some amenities, as is Stackstead. The quarry is part of the Adrenaline Gateway project, and over the coming years Lancashire Council aims to convert the area into a 7Stanes or Coed Y Brenin style centre for mountain biking, so facilities should be forthcoming.

Overview This is an old quarry which has been appropriated by the local riding scene for some years. There are plenty of lovely XC trails heading off into the nearby moors, and there are lots of drops, berms and jumps scattered around, some threaded together to make some half-decent DH trails. The area is also very popular with Trials Bikes, as the large quarried stone make for perfect hopping obstacles. Since 2008 the area has undergone a huge redevelopment (though it is in phases) and had two new routes added, both designed and built by trail builder Dafydd Davis and local contractors Terra Firma. Over the coming years, Lancashire Council hopes to turn this site into a world-class mountain biking site, so keep your eye on the progress from now on!

Terrain There's plenty of unofficial singletrack, but it's mostly rocky riding around here.

XC There are currently two main XC loops – a 4.5-km red route (2 km uphill, 2 km downhill – some gruelling climbs and decent descents), and a 1-km severe black loop which is for experts only (and body armour is advised); there is also a skills area with drops, jumps and tests of balance on the natural rock etc...

Downhill There are some short sections of DH around the quarry and the red route has a decent couple of sections for those looking to practise their downhill.

Dirt jumps/Freeride In addition to the natural terrain which has plenty of technical riding (drops mostly), there is a purpose-built Trials Bike area designed by one of the UK's top trials riders, Ali Clarkson. Over the coming years, expect there to be more facilities for freeriders and those who prefer to be in the air.

Conditions This is a stone quarry with fields and moorland surrounding it. There are plenty of small lakes and reservoirs and the views can be quite breathtaking. The surface is naturally very rocky, though the red is fine. The black run is for those with body armour as a fall could cause damage.

ⓘ **More info** To read more about the proposal for the Adrenaline Gateway, head to adrenaline-gateway.co.uk.

↘28 Little Switzerland

XC DH

Train station Ferriby

Nearest city Hull

Sat Nav HU13 0LN

Location Little Switzerland is the name given to an area of the Humber Bridge Country Park, which is next door to the mighty Humber Bridge in Hull. From the M62 exit at the end of the motorway onto the A63 in the direction of Hull. Head into the town centre and the A63 takes you right to the bridge, where the entrance to the Humber Bridge Country Park is clearly signed.

Facilities There are plenty of places to stop and get a bite to eat in the Country Park, including the fantastic Mrs B's Woodland Café.

Overview Little Switzerland is the name given to the chalky-edged cliffs in the Humber Bridge Country Park, which house a couple of interesting trails for local riders. Not worth a huge journey, but the old quarry has some jumps, there are some short but interesting DH trails (though more XC oriented), and there is access to a whole host of XC routes by way of the Yorkshire Wolds Way, which passes directly through the park and underneath the bridge. This is always a good backdrop to a quick ride.

Conditions This is chalk surface, so very slippery when wet – avoid after recent rain and through the winter.

ⓘ **More info** The Yorkshire Wolds Way has a page on the site nationaltrail.co.uk.

↘29 Longridge Fell

XC DH

Train station Preston/Pleasington/Blackburn

Nearest city Preston

Sat Nav PR3 2TY (for Longridge Golf Course)

Location Longridge Fell is a popular outdoor venue around 6 km northeast of Preston and 10 km to the north west of Blackburn. From the M6 exit at junction 31a and head in the opposite direction to Preston, following signs instead to Longridge on the B6243. In Longridge, go all the way through the village to the T junction, then take a right onto Kestor Lane, then a left onto Higher Road, then at the fork take the right into Forty Acre Lane and follow this road to the top of the hill, passing the golf course on your left. The start of the trails is around 5 km from Longridge.

Facilities There isn't much up at the fell, but Longridge has plenty of shops and amenities.

Overview This is the local hub for Preston and Blackburn, and is an open spot with a few DH trails with some jumps, drops and berms. There's also plenty of unofficial singletrack and bridleway to explore, and it's suitable for complete beginners through to half-decent riders who want to get some practice in. Not worth a huge journey but great for those in the area. This is predominantly natural terrain, with rocks, roots and drops, although the local riders have reinforced one or two areas.

Conditions This is open moorland with some copses along the way; avoid in high winds and it can become a real bog in the winter months.

↘30 Lyme Park

XC FR

Train station Disley

Nearest city Stockport/Manchester

Sat Nav SK12 2NR

Location Lyme Park starts around 5 km to the southeast of Stockport and 7 km to the northeast of Macclesfield. From the M60 Manchester ringroad, exit at junction 1, heading south through Stockport on the A6 Buxton Road. Around 3 km after the village of Hazel Grove and High Lane, you'll see signs off to the right indicating Lyme Park's entrance.

Facilities Lyme Park is home to a very popular mansion house (seen in 1995's *Pride and Prejudice*), which has a museum, visitor centre and café. There are plenty of facilities in the park, from ice cream vendors to toilets and showers. There's an entrance fee of around £5 per car including parking, though prices change through the season and are reduced if you tour the house and gardens.

Overview This is a popular XC venue, with plenty of trails that head out into the fabulous park with its historic woods and well-maintained gardens. As of winter 08/09 there have been conflicts of interest and bikers might lose out (some complain of the park rangers not wishing them to ride), but there is a cycling link on the National Trust's website, so with respectful riding the park may well come to the conclusion that having mountain bikers is a good thing. Please ride carefully. Some of the routes are technical, but there are other areas (the cycle path from Pott Shrigley to Lyme Park for example), that are suitable for all, including families.

Conditions This is National Trust land, with varying terrain from cycle paths to bridleways, unofficial singletrack and park roads. Avoid in wet weather as it gets very boggy.

ⓘ **More info** Check out nationaltrust.org.uk.

N31 Manchester Road DJs

DJ

Train station Accrington
Nearest city Blackburn
Sat Nav BB5 2PQ (100 m to the southeast of the DJs)

Location Manchester Road DJs are just to the south of Accrington, a town between Blackburn and Burnley. From the M65 exit at junction 7 and take the A6185 Dunkenhalgh Way towards Accrington. Carry on towards the town centre (the road changes to the A679) then the A680), and head south on Abbey Street (the A680 main road through town) until that road changes name to Manchester Road. After 1 km from the centre of Accrington, there's a break in houses on either side of the road, with woods on your left, and a park on your right. The DJs are in the woods to the left.

Facilities Accrington is a large town with plenty of shops and amenities.

Overview These are some DJs built by local BMXers and mountain bike crew. Worth a look if you live or ride nearby but otherwise not worth a long journey as it's a relatively small area, though packed with plenty of decent-sized jumps.

Conditions This is a soil clearing in some public woods. Avoid after rainfall.

N32 Meltham Skills Trails

XC FR

Train station Brockholes/Slaithwaite
Nearest city Huddersfield
Sat Nav HD9 4HL

Location Meltham Skills Trails are just to the east of the town of Meltham – just on the northeast edge of the Peak District – and around 6 km to the southwest of Huddersfield. From Huddersfield take the A616 south to Armitage Bridge, then take a right onto the B6108 (Meltham Road) towards Meltham. Just before you enter the town, take a left into Meltham Mills Road, then another left onto Knowle Lane. After 250 m the trails are just to the south (right) of the road, in the woods that lead to Meltham Mills Reservoir.

Facilities This is an area of forest land next to the town of Meltham. There are no facilities in the woods, but Meltham has plenty of shops and amenities.

Overview Hidden in the woods here are some nice freeride obstacles, drops and jumps, though this isn't a classic DJ run with flowing lines. Definitely one for locals who are in the area rather than those looking to make a journey, but could be combined with a trip to some of the other north Peak District rides as there's also plenty of unofficial XC riding to be had in the woods around Meltham Mills Reservoir.

Conditions This is forest land on the edge of the Peaks, and is prone to being boggy throughout the winter; it is a popular spot for fell runners and walkers.

N33 Midgley Woods

DH FR

Train station Mytholmroyd
Nearest city Bradford
Sat Nav HX7 5LR

Location Midgley Woods are to the northeast of Mytholmroyd, around 5 km to the west of Halifax centre. From the M62, exit at junction 24 and take the A629 north in the direction of Halifax. After 4 km turn left into the A646 (Dryclough Lane) and follow this road for 6 km in the direction of Mytholmroyd. At the town of Mytholmroyd, take a right into Midgley Road, and after 1.5 km Midgley Woods are on the right, just after Brearley Lane.

Facilities There's nothing up at the woods but Mytholmroyd has plenty of shops and facilities.

Overview Midgley Woods are a low-budget freeride and downhill spot, with local riders practising their jump skills on some tabletops, gaps, drops and berms that have been shaped here. Definitely not worth a long journey but for those in Halifax or nearby that want to get some mild dirt jumping on the go, it might be worth a look in. There are more trails planned, but this is an unofficial spot and you'll have to meet with the local riders to get involved in any potential building work.

Conditions This is sparsely wooded land with soil jumps and little work gone into the trails but plenty of natural drops and drop ins to get speed.

34 Park Bridge 4X

DH 4X

Train station Hollinwood/Ashton-under-Lyne
Nearest city Oldham
Sat Nav N/A

Location Park Bridge (also known as Bankfield Clough) is around 2 km south of Oldham, just next to the village of Bardsley. From the M60 (Manchester ring road), exit at junction 22 and take the A6104 (Hollins Road) eastwards. At the next T junction, take a right onto the A627 Ashton Road south towards Bardsley, and after 1 km take a left onto Park Bridge Road. Park after 1 km on the left and follow the red-topped posts from the wooden bridge on Park Bridge Road. Head to the top of the hill for the start of the 4X.

Facilities This is a disused hill with no facilities on site, but nearby Bardsley has plenty of facilities and amenities.

Overview This is a fantastic set-up with a gravity-assisted downhill 4X track that was cut into the forested hill by the local mountain bike scene. The track is steep, wide, and has doubles, drops and a large final step-up jump. Everything is rollable but good intermediate riders will undoubtedly get the best from the track. Definitely worth a journey for local riders.

Conditions This is a clay-based track which doesn't drain particularly well so avoid after heavy rain.

ⓘ **More info** The people who built the track made a video which is on Youtube at youtube.com/watch?v=miNmx04TJG8.

35 Ramsden Lane DH

DH

Train station Brockholes
Nearest city Huddersfield
Sat Nav N/A

Location Ramsden Lane is 2 km to the southwest of Holmfirth, itself 6 km south of Huddersfield, and just on the edge of the Peak District. From Huddersfield, head south on the A616 towards Honley, then the A6024 to Homfirth, then carry on towards Holmbridge. Just after Holmbridge village, turn off onto Dobb Topp Road following signs for Brownhill Reservoir on Brownhill Lane. Carry on for 1 km with the reservoir on your right, then turn left into Ramsden Lane, and after 600 m the DH trail is on the left at the top of the hill.

Facilities The reservoir doesn't have a visitor centre like many of the other lakes in the Peak District, but nearby Holmbridge has plenty of shops and facilities.

Overview This is a low-budget downhill track that starts at the top of the hill and finishes at the house near the bottom. It's very rocky with plenty of shale, and can be popular with walkers. Popular with local riders due to the ability to uplift if you've got a car.

Conditions Very rocky in sections – especially the middle – but essentially this is open field land with beautiful views over Brownhill and Ramsden Reservoir.

36 Roman Lakes Leisure Park

XC

Train station Marple Central or Rose Hill
Nearest city Stockport/Manchester
Sat Nav SK6 7HB

Location From the M60 exit at junction 27 (Stockport) and follow the A626, signposted Marple. In Marple go straight on at the first traffic lights – where the A626 goes left – and up the hill through the middle of Marple on the B6101. At the top of the hill, cross the

PETE FULLER/ROMANLAKES.CO.UK

canal and the road turns sharp right, but bear left on Oldknow Road and then cross Arkwright Road onto Faywood Drive. This becomes Lakes Road which leads to Roman Lakes Leisure Park.

Facilities The are plenty of facilities at the park, including a café, free car parking, toilets, picnic area and a boules area! This is primarily a walking and nature reserve, with plenty of bird watchers and horse-riding on the go, but it is also a specific mountain bike centre, and families are very welcome.

Overview There are 12 waymarked trails from 8-40 km loops surrounding the park with family routes that follow bridleways and canal paths, and more serious XC routes can be found by riding over Mellor Moor, New Mills and Hayfield. There is a route map and brochure called Mountain Bike Rides Around Roman Lakes which costs £1 from the café, written by Pete Fuller. The book has detailed descriptions of the trails, as well as maps and pictures of strategic sections on the routes, and is indispensable for all riders. For those looking for a more serious XC challenge, Roman Lakes offers a 100 km loop start and finish around the Peak District, see the website page romanlakes.co.uk/mountain_biking.htm for more info. The park opens at 0800 and closes at dusk.

Conditions This is a selection of singletrack, bridleway, canal path and fire-road (possibly some tarmac). Mostly waymarked but some longer routes need navigation.

ⓘ **More info** Check out romanlakes.co.uk as the park often hosts demo days and is a popular bike-testing venue.

↘37 Scratchmere Scar Freeride Bike Park

XC DH FR

Train station Lazonby and Kirkoswald
Nearest city Newcastle-upon-Tyne
Sat Nav CA11 9PF

Location Scratchmere is just on the eastern side of the Lake District, next to the M6 and halfway between Penrith and Carlisle in Cumbria. From the M6 exit at junction 41 and take the B5305 towards Plumpton (not to Hutton in the Forest). At the next roundabout, take the first left (the A6) towards Plumpton, then turn off to the right at Plumpton onto the B6413 towards Lazonby. 1 km down this road, turn off to the right and Scratchmere is at the top of the road.

Facilities There is little at Scratchmere Scar at the moment (Feb 2009), but the company has plans to turn this area into one of the UK's premier DH and freeride areas, so expect that to change over the summer of 09. Uplift charge is £15 per day when running.

Overview Scratchmere Scar Freeride Bike Park is one of a new bunch of purpose-built areas for riding, offering a regular (weekend) uplift service, which puts riders on one of the three DH trails. There are also plans to build a 4X track, a freeride area, northshore, a foam pit, slopestyle park and some purpose-built XC trails in the surrounding beautiful countryside. However, right now, there are simply three DH trails, and the uplift service runs, but throughout winter 08/09 it hasn't been as smooth as expected.

Terrain This is beautiful forest land on the edge of the Lake District. Very remote, so expect to only see other riders, which makes for a great atmosphere.

XC There are some hidden XC routes, and more purpose-built singletrack is planned, but currently this area is DH specific so any XC you find would be a bonus.

Downhill There are three tracks in operation, each offering some serious DH terrain of big drops, huge jumps, and some technical upper forest sections. In general, each track starts through dense, steep forest, and mellows out in gradient and tree density, but increases in speed and the size of the jumps. Plenty of off-camber and technical riding, as you would expect from a purpose-built centre.

Dirt jumps/Freeride Despite the name, there isn't that much to ride as of going to print, but that is set to change. Some have complained that the centre has boasted too much too soon, though with time all of the proposed tracks may materialise. Best to give this one time and check the website. If that's working, and the pictures show some freeride obstacles to ride, then go.

Conditions This is dense forest which can become very muddy, though many of the problem areas have been reinforced and had bridges spanning the mud.

ⓘ **More info** Check out the website cumbriabikeparks.co.uk.

↘38 Silton Forest DH

XC DH

Train station Northallerton
Nearest city Middlesbrough
Sat Nav YO7 2JZ (to the Gold Cup Inn)

Location Silton Forest is on the eastern edge of the North Yorkshire Moors, almost halfway between Harrogate and Middlesbrough. From the A1(M), exit at junction 49 and take the A168 north towards Thirsk, then the A19 towards Middlesbrough. Around 5 km north of Thirsk take a right onto Leake Lane in the village of Leake, heading in the direction of Nether Silton. Carry on up this lane for 2 km, then take a right onto West Lane towards Nether Silton, then a left after the village into Kirtk Ings Lane, then a right into Skirt Bank/ Moor Lane and head to the top where the forest car park awaits. From the car park, ride up the fire-road to the crossroads, then go left.

Facilities There's nothing up at the forest but the Gold Cup Inn is a great after-ride spot!

Overview This is a tract of Forestry Commission land which is prone to change due to the working nature of the forest. However, there are generally two DH trails, both a mixture of natural and man-made obstacles, and both opening out and getting faster nearer the bottom. There's plenty of unofficial singletrack in the surrounding area, and lots of good jumps, but most of it is rollable and suitable for learners and intermediates too.

Conditions This is a Forestry Commission site in an Area of Outstanding Natural Beauty. The trails are mostly natural, so avoid after heavy rainfall as they become almost unrideable.

ⓘ **More info** Silton Forest has its own page on the Forestry Commission site forestry.gov.uk, or for riding buddies check out mtbleeds.co.uk.

JOHN STOREY/NEFREERIDERS.CO.UK

↘39 Setmurthy DH Trails and Cockermouth XC

XC DH

Train station Maryport
Nearest city Newcastle-upon-Tyne
Sat Nav CA13 9HA

CHRIS MORAN

Location Cockermouth and Setmurthy are two towns (Cockermouth the bigger of the two) on the north west edge of the Lake District, Cumbria. From the M6, exit at junction 40 next to Penrith, then head west on the A66 to Kewick, then Cockermouth. To get to the XC and DH trails, head out of Cockermouth eastwards on Main Street in the centre of town. This road turns into Castlegate, then Castlegate Drive which is a country road heading towards Setmurthy. Carry on for 3 km down this road. The DH trails are on the hill to your left and there are three access roads that turn left into the hill between Cockermouth and Setmurthy, each with good access to the XC riding.

Facilities There is nothing up at the trails, but Cockermouth is a popular town on the edge of the touristy Lake District, with plenty of shops and facilities including two good bike shops.

Overview Cockermouth and Setmurthy are two nearby towns with a joint XC and downhill region. There is a big mountain biking scene in the area, so expect to see other riders. None of the trails are waymarked, and the area is a low-budget scene that doesn't advertise its existence to all. That said, there have been years of investment put in by the local riders, with plenty of re-inforced areas and flowing lines etched out of the brilliant local terrain. Don't expect this to be a fully-catered-for site, but the are plenty of fantsatic trails to ride.

Terrain There's plenty of unofficial singletrack, loads of bridleways and fire-roads and tricky rock sections.

XC There are several loops of around 10-15 km with great climbs and perfect descents for those who love rooty, flowing singletrack. As before, none of the area is marked (though that may change soon), but exploring and discovering is part of the charm of this area.

Downhill Closer to Setmurthy there are a couple of brilliant DH trails. The locals call it Minileithen because it rides like the Innerleithen Trail in Scotland, with loads of flowing berms, rock gardens, jumps and hefty drops. Not for beginners.

Dirt jumps/Freeride
There is plenty here for good freeriders to enjoy, though nothing specifically built for simply jumping. Northshore has been put in at Setmurthy, but Forestry Commission wrangles mean its future is far from certain.

Conditions This is Forestry Commission land with dense forest and some beautiful open spaces which is definitely to be avoided after rain.

ⓘ **More info** 4Play Cycles have maps to the trails and organize build days if you want to get involved, T01900 823377, 4playcycles.net, while there's a 'Save the Northshore' petition at setmurthy.zoomshare.com/2.shtml and finally the Setmurthy Downhillers have a Bebo page at bebo.com/setmurthy.

↘40 Stainburn

XC DH

Train station Burley-in-Wharfdale

Nearest city Manchester

Sat Nav N/A

Opening times The trails are open 24/7, 365 days a year and are free to use, though you can join Singletraction as a member for a small fee to help the upkeep of the site or to get involved with building days

Location Stainburn is an area of Forestry Commission land roughly midway between Shipley and Harrogate in Yorkshire. It is around 18 km north of Leeds. From Leeds, take the A660 north from the city centre in the direction of Otley/Skipton. Turn right at the A658 towards Harrogate, after 300 m turn left on to the B6161 towards Leathley and Farnley. Follow this road for 1.5 km, then turn left at a small lodge just after a humped back bridge towards Farnley. Follow this road for 2.5 km to Farnley Village, then take the first right onto the B6451. Follow this road for 3 km through Farnley, past the farm and down to Lindley Wood Reservoir. Stay on this road and Stainburn car park is 500 m after the reservoir on the left as you go round a sweeping left hand-bend.

TIM SELLORS

Facilities/Overview Singletraction (the people behind Stainburn, Wharncliffe, Guisborough, Silton and Dalby) have worked with the Forestry Commission to produce a fantastic site, and Stainburn Forest's trails have been built with care and attention to the forest, with one purpose-built trail and several natural routes, all waymarked. This is a great place for serious riders to head, though it should cater for all tastes (though families and complete beginners may wish to try elsewhere first). There is plenty of XC riding elsewhere in the forest, and there is a constant stream of trail additions and improvements being made. Well worth a journey.

XC This is a predominantly XC trail centre, though they are very downhill oriented. There are three waymarked trails, including the Warren Boulder Trail, a purpose-built and man-made, obstacle-strewn route of around 4 km that is packed with features and has had an enormous amount of work poured into it; there are also the Norwood Edge trails, featuring a Black Route and a Gold Route, both of which have aimed to stay more natural than the Warren Boulder Trail. All three have been gaining an increasing reputation as some of the best built and most challenging out there. It's definitely a case of quality over quantity but that just adds to the fun of the riding here as it encourages riders to try moves over and over again to clean sections as they don't have to worry about the 50 km that they still have to ride!

Downhill There are plenty of short DH sections on the XC routes, but the new Descent Line Trail is the latest addition to Stainburn, and is a short, but action packed route with rocks, roots, berms and jumps.

Freeride There are no specific areas for freeriders, though the Warren Boulder Trail should have enough features for those who like to be in the air, and there are some northshore-esque bridges and reinforcements.

Easy Try the Black Route and cut out at waymark 12 to loop back. It'll loop you back to the start quicker and give you an indication as to whether you want to try the whole route.

Hard The Warren Boulder Trail is a must.

Not to miss The Warren Boulder Trail should be on every rider's wishlist.

Remember to avoid Heading there after recent rainfall. It's not worth it.

Nearest Bike/Hire shop Boneshackers Bike Shop in Harrogate sponsor the trails, boneshakersbikes.co.uk.

Local accommodation Dowgill House in Otley is a Georgian House with fantastic rooms, T01943 850836, dowgillhouse.co.uk.

Eating There are no facilities at the site, and the nearest supplies are at Otley, some 2 km riding away. Take supplies with you.

ⓘ **More info** Stainburn has been built by Singletraction, the group behind Dalby Park and Silton Forest. Check out their site at singletraction.org.uk or check out the Facebook 'I Dig Stainburn' page.

> **Lowdown**

Locals do

Become members of Singletraction and get involved with dig days.

Take food and drink with them.

Locals don't

Build anything illegally.

Worry too much about meeting other forest users. There aren't many people out here.

Pros

One of the UK's most feature-full sites.

Great atmosphere.

Cons

In the middle of nowhere with no facilities.

Constant building and evolving. Which can also be a plus!

TIM SELLORS

41 Sticks Norden

XC DH FR

Train station Rochdale
Nearest city Rochdale
Sat Nav OL12 7TD

Location Sticks Norden is a small venue on the moors between Rochdale and Ramsbottom. From the south, take the M66 past Bury and exit at Edenfield, taking the A680 between Ramsbottom to Rochadale. Just before you hit the outskirts of Rochdale, turn north (left) onto Greenbooth Road, signposted towards Tenterhouse Mill. The trails are just on the other side of the reservoir (called Doctor Dam) from the road.

Facilities Nearby Rochdale has plenty of shops and facilities but there is nothing up at the trails.

Overview This is the local riding spot, with plenty of building going on to help create a fantastic mountain biking area. There's not a huge amount of vertical drop, but enough to have a couple of DH tracks, and the area is best enjoyed on a freeride bike with plenty of drops, jumps and berms to ride and practise skills on. Again, not worth a huge journey, but great for local riders to test out their skills.

Conditions The Sticks Norden area is forest land, but there are plenty of XC trails fanning out onto the moors to the north and past several reservoirs in the area. Avoid if it's been raining as they are unrideable.

42 Storthes Hall DH

DH FR

Train station Stocksmoor
Nearest city Huddersfield
Sat Nav HD8 0WN

Location Storthes Hall DH track is around 5 km to the southeast of Huddersfield. From the centre of Huddersfield take the A629 eastwards through Tandem, and on to Highburton. Just after Highburton, you'll see Boothroyd Wood on your right. Take the next right (Thunder Bridge Lane), which is around 1 km after Highburton, then the next right (Grange Lane), and follow the road as it turns into Wood Lane. Park after 300 m, and go through the gap in the wall to your right, down the path and past the field to the start of the downhill.

CHRIS MORAN

Facilities Storthes Hall is a popular student accommodation venue, so there are plenty of good pubs and shops nearby.

Overview This is an unofficial site which is pretty low budget but still has plenty of features including some pretty big jumps, drops and berms on the three downhill tracks. All are short, but technically difficult, and definitely not for novice riders.

Conditions Some of the jumps have been reinforced with logs, but there is otherwise little addition to the natural terrain here, which is steep forest land.

↘43 Temple Newsam

DH FR 4X

Train station Cross Gates
Nearest city Leeds
Sat Nav LS15 0LN for Templenewsham Road, the bottom of the trails

Location Temple Newsam is the name given to an historic estate on the east edge of Leeds. The trails in Temple Newsam are more aptly described as being south of Coulton, in Avenue Wood. From the M1, exit at junction 46, and take a left at the first roundabout onto the A63. Go straight at the first roundabout but at the next, take the second exit left (Selby Road, the A63 still), and follow this road until the first lights then take a left onto Colton Road. Go down here, straight over the mini roundabout, then right at the fork, and carry on for 600 m. There's a turning to the right with a gravel car park at the end. This is the start of the trails.

Facilities There are plenty of facilities back at Selby Road or at the bottom of the trails. This is an inner-city area so there are shops everywhere.

Overview MTB Leeds and Leeds City Council joined forces in 2004/2005 to build this fantastic downhill area that is perfect for beginners and good riders alike. Not strictly a DH trail, it is wide enough to be used as 4X and has jumps and log drops (though all rollable), berms and a very flowing, gravelly surface. For those that like XC, the track is loopable by riding back to the top. Definitely worth a look in if you're in the area, and for those wishing to learn; it's also one of the main haunts for the local riders, though it can be a little rough at the wrong time as it's not the best area in Leeds.

Conditions This is a purpose-built trail with a sandy, gravelly base which drains really well. It's not strictly singletrack (though there is some around), but more like a downhill fire-road with jumps.

ⓘ **More info** For all Leeds mountain biking info, MTB Leeds is the place to head and they have a great website at mtbleeds.co.uk.

CHRIS MORAN

↘44 TNF Grizedale

Train station Windermere
Nearest city Preston
Sat Nav LA22 OQJ
Opening times 1000-1630

CHRIS MORAN

CHRIS MORAN

CHRIS MORAN

Location The Northface Trail is part of an incredible set up at the Grizedale Visitor Centre, slap bang in the middle of the Lake District. From the M6 exit at junction 36 and take the A590 towards Kendle, then the A591 towards Windermere, then Ambleside, and turn off here on the A593 in the direction of Coniston, then take the B5286 towards Hawkshead. Go through the village and at the T junction pick up the brown signs towards Grizedale, which is around 3 km over the hill from Hawkshead. You can park at either the Moor Top car park, or carry on to the Grizedale Visitor Centre, just off this road on the right.

Facilities/Overview As you might expect from the name, the trail at Grizedale has been heavily backed by The North Face, along with some investment from the Forestry Commission. It is a perfect example of the increasing popularity of mountain biking and the heavy investment it is beginning to attract. There is a new Grizedale Visitor Centre (which should open in spring 2009), which is a multi-million pound venture featuring a bike shop, rental, visitor centre with café, restaurant, bike wash and plenty of helpful information and maps available. The main trail here is The North Face Trail, and plenty of work has gone into the building of this, but there is plenty of room to expand here and make the area as good as one of the 7Stanes sites.

XC The North Face trail is the main one here – a fun, 16-km red-graded run (though some of that is an optional loop), which has plenty of wood to ride over, as well as some fun uphill sections that disguise the ascent. However, the singletrack straight from the Visitor Centre lulls you into a false sense of security – much of the route is fire-road, and far too much considering it's the flagship route here. That said, it's a great run when you get off the roads.

Downhill There are no specific DH tracks here, though the end section of the North Face Trail is quite good fun and you can self uplift by driving to the Moor Top car park.

Freeride No freeride.

Easy The entire trail is relatively straightforward, but the Great Escape section should be brilliant for groups of differing abilities. You'll find fire-road for the kids and some trickier singletrack for the little ones.

Hard You'll enjoy Under The Boardwalk; the two long sections have narrow line for the confident and a fun 360 loop.

Not to miss The boardwalk sections.

Remember to avoid If you're extremely experienced you might find it frustrating.

> Lowdown

☻ Locals do

Throw in a detour to make it a bit more challenging. Check the map and some of the bridleways.

Gun down the singletrack sections.

☹ Locals don't

Jump - it could do with more kickers.

✔ Pros

Great family run out.

Incredible infrastructure with the new Visitor Centre set up.

✖ Cons

Experienced riders might find it too easy.

Almost half the route is forest road, and there's no specific DH track.

Nearest Bike/Hire shop
Grizedale Mountain Bikes are based at the new visitor centre, and have a full range of hire bikes including full-suspension models from Scott, Kona, Rocky Mountain and more (grizedalemountainbikes.co.uk, T01229 860 369).

Local accommodation
The Grizedale Lodge B&B (T01539 436532) is next door to the Visitor Centre, while the Forestry Commission website has a PDF of fantastic, affordable accommodation in the area.

Eating There is a state of the art café at the visitor centre, plus supplies can be bought in the shop.

ⓘ **More info** Try forestry.gov.uk/thenorthfacetrail, or call the visitor centre on T01229 860010. The Northern Munkies, a local bike club, has a brilliant section on the NFT at northernmunkies.co.uk .

CHRIS MORAN

↘45 Wassenden DH

XC DH

Train station Brockholes/Slaithwaite
Nearest city Huddersfield
Sat Nav HD9 4EU

Location Wassenden DH is in the north of the Peak District, halfway between Holmfirth and Saddleworth on the Holmfirth Road. From either east or west, take the A635 through the Peak District. Midway through, take the small road to the north (Wassenden Head Road) signposted to Meltham, and after 200 m turn off to the left for the start of the downhill trail.

Facilities This is in the middle of the Peaks, with no facilities nearby so bring your own or carry on up Wassenden Head Road and get supplies from Meltham. There are shops at the finish line in Marsden.

Overview This is a fantastic singletrack ride all the way down to Marsden in the north, a journey of about 5 km through spectacular and empty moorland (Wassenden Moor) and passing Wassenden and Butterley Reservoir. You can uplift using a car but you'll need someone to pick you up from Marsden, a loop of around 8 km by car.

Conditions This is open moorland so expect it to be almost unrideable after heavy rain. There are some rocky sections – it's not too steep overall – and there is a large possibility of meeting fell-walkers nearer the reservoirs as this is part of the popular Kirklees Way. Otherwise it's a fantastic day out and a few laps of this will make most riders' days.

↘46 Wiswell Wood

XC DH

Train station Whalley
Nearest city Blackburn
Sat Nav BB7 9DR

Location Wiswell Wood is to the northeast of the village of Whalley, around 4 km south of Clitheroe and 8 km to the northeast of Blackburn. From the M65 exit at junction 7 and follow the A680 to Clayton le Moors, then north towards Whalley. At the end of the A680, you'll come to the junction where that road meets with the Burnley Road (the A671); here, turn left onto the A671, then immediately right into Portfield Lane – almost as if you were going straight across the junction – and then another right onto Clerk Hill Road. Head up here for 500 m and Wiswell Wood starts at the copse of trees just off

FORESTRY COMMISSION

the road on the left. Park at the old schoolhouse and head for the red phone box for the start of the trails.

Facilities There's not a great deal up at the woods and fields, but nearby Whalley has plenty of shops and facilities. Take supplies with you.

Overview There are two fantastic downhill tracks here, and even though they are short (compared to their Welsh and Scottish counterparts), there are enough features such as rock gardens, purpose-built gaps and drops next to the dry-stone walls down the trail to keep the local riders happy. This is a very popular mountain biking area, so expect to see lots of other riders who should be happy to share the secret XC trails that criss cross the fields around the area if downhill isn't your thing. There are the beginnings of north shore being built and many of the heavily eroded areas have been reinforced. Help with building the trails is always appreciated.

Conditions This is a popular and large spot out in the open offering the chance to drop into some dense woods, though felling often changes the area and the trails without warning. Avoid in high winds or after heavy rain.

ⓘ **More info** The Woollybacks Mountain Bike Club regularly ride at Wiswell Wood, and have a page dedicated to the site (with maps and advice etc) at thewoollybacks.co.uk.

↘47 Woodbank DJs

XC DJ

Train station Bredbury/Stockport
Nearest city Stockport/Manchester
Sat Nav SK1 4JR

Location Woodbank Memorial Park and Vernon Park are next door to each other in the village of Offerton, on the east edge of Stockport. From the M60 Manchester ringroad, exit at junction 27 and take St Mary's Way (the A626) south for 500 m. At the next major junction take a left onto Spring Gardens, then left immediately into Turncroft Lane. Go to the end of this lane, and the entrance to the park is in front of you as the road bends sharply to the right.

Facilities Vernon Park and Woodbank Memorial Park are well-kept Victorian parks with a museum and extensive gardens. There are cafés and facilities at the main gates and houses but the DJs are unofficial so there are no facilities on site.

Overview There are some impressive, though unofficial DJs at both Vernon Park and Woodbank Memorial, though you'll have to meet up with local riders to find their exact location (or you could ride around – Vernon isn't a huge park), and many local riders here combine a day messing on the jumps with a leisurely stroll down the river Goyt (Woodbank turns into riverside countryside to the southeast). Perfect for some gentle XC riding.

Conditions This is well-maintained park land with areas of outstanding natural and cultivated gardens and fauna. There are no specific riding areas in the parks, but it is tolerated.

ⓘ **More info** Stockport Council's website has a page for both parks, stockport.gov.uk.

CHRIS MORAN

↘48 Whinlatter Forest

Train station Windermere/Workington
Nearest city Carlisle
Sat Nav CA12 5TW

Location Another fantastic Forestry Commission initiative in the Lake District, the Whinlatter Forest Park sits on the B5292, just outside Keswick. From the M6 exit at junction 40 and head towards Keswick on the A66. Carry through the town of Keswick in the direction of Cockermouth, and at the village of Braithwaite turn on to the B5292 Whinlatter Pass. Head along here and turn off at the Forestry Commission car park.

Facilities There's a visitor centre, toilets and the Cyclewise Whinlatter shop (T01768 778711) on site, stocking clothing as well as offering bike hire facilities and courses. The Siskins Café is open from 1000 till 1700 in the summer and 1000 to 1600 in the winter, offering great home-cooked food. There's also a Go Ape! facility for you to monkey around on.

Overview This well-run centre is the longest purpose-built trail in the Lakes, with a 9-km South Loop and a 10-km North Loop to choose from, both graded red.

Terrain Whinlatter Forest boasts beautiful, steep slopes with commanding views over Bassesnthwaite Lake. The going is fantastic, purpose-built singletrack that works in all weathers thanks to a shale surfacing and reinforced areas over any potentially boggy ground.

XC There are plenty of unofficial routes spreading out in every direction here, but the main route is the Altura Trail, a 16-km loop that leaves the new visitor centre and takes riders on a scenic and energetic tour of the forest featuring berms, jumps, tabletops and plenty of rock features. It's more picturesque than sister trail TNF at Grizedale, having better views over the lakes, and packs in more singletrack compared to TNF's forest road, and yet is less popular. Well worth a look in for intermediate riders who wish to get the full Lake District experience in a neat package.

Downhill The last section features a swift downhill that adventurous beginner to intermediates will love.

Dirt jumps/Freeride Both loops have jumps, berms and some more technical sections but there are no specific dirt sculptures for freeriders.

Conditions Predominantly hard-packed singletrack, with some stony and gravel sections. Walkers and horse-riders are asked not to use the trail so it's pretty much ours alone!

ⓘ **More info** forestry.gov.uk/forestry/infd-79yfhn.

CYCLEWISETRAINING

FORESTRY COMMISSION

N49 Wooler 4X

XC DH N 4X

Train station Cathill
Nearest city Newcastle-upon-Tyne/ Edinburgh
Sat Nav NE71 6QP

Location Wooler 4X is a national standard 4X venue at the north end of the Northumberland National Park and near the border with Scotland. From the south, approach Wooler on the A1 from Newcastle, then take a left just after Warenford on the B6348 heading to Wooler. From the north, take the A68 from Edinburgh and turn off at Saint Boswells on the A699 to Kelso, then the A698 Coldstream, then the A697 south to Wooler. In town, head for the Haugh Head Garage, 1.5 km south of Wooler on the A697, which is the hub for the 4X venue and also hires and sells bikes.

Facilities Haugh Head Garage is a petrol station and bike shop in one, and the place to head to buy a ticket for the 4X venue (which is around 600 m to the northeast of the garage, off Brewery Road, but closed to the public unless pre-paid). The garage has plenty of supplies, but there's nothing up at the 4X course.

Overview This is a 4X course that has had plenty of national standard competitions held on its banks, and there are plenty of other jumps, gaps, tabletops and some northshore up at the same venue, all built by the enthusiastic and hard-working Cheviot Hill Riders (aka Team CHR). You can pay per visit to the 4X course, of pay a yearly membership fee. Helmets are obligatory.

Terrain The 4X track is a purpose-built surfaced track dug into the side of a hill which drains well.

XC Thrunton Woods is the local XC spot. Call in to Haugh Head Garage for details or check the website for stats and directions.

Downhill Wooler Common has a DH track (signposted at the top 'Technical Steep Downhill Track'); start at the common and go through two gates to the top of the hill, and also Wyndy Gyle is a popular DH trail in the area.

Dirt jumps/Freeride The 4X track has plenty of jumps, and the DH trails in the area are worthy of a look in for those who like to get in the air.

Conditions The 4X track is all-weather, while the other spots around Wooler are a mixture of average to poor drainage areas, culminating in what the CHR riders call Slymefoot Slidings on Wyndy Gyle, a boggy and slippy downhill (hence the name).

ⓘ **More info** Cheviot Hill Riders have a brilliant website with all the info on their favourite local haunts at team-chr.co.uk.

N50 Yeadon BMX track

XC DH

Train station Guiseley
Nearest city Bradford/Leeds
Sat Nav LS19 7UR

Location Yeadon BMX track is at the north west end of the Leeds Bradford Airport in Yeadon, itself around 5 km northeast of Bradford, and 9 km north west of Leeds. From Bradford take the A658 to Yeadon, following signs for the airport. Take a left in Yeadon (if you go under the runway tunnel you've gone too far!), onto High Street, then a right onto Cemetary Road. The BMX track is just after the lake (Yeadon Tarn), on your right.

Facilities Yeadon is a small town with plenty of shops and amenities and a short ride away.

Overview This is a brilliant, chalky BMX track with loads of berms and jumps to get some good dirt jumping or freeride practice on, and a popular spot for the local Leeds/Bradford scene. Not worth a huge journey, but worth a look in for nearby riders and perfect for those learning as everything is rollable.

Conditions This is a chalky, sandy base which drains quickly so can be used soon after rainfall. It's a flat area so not perfect for 4X but fun to practise on.

ⓘ **More info** For all Leeds mountain biking info, MTB Leeds is the place to head, mtbleeds.co.uk.

Wales

↘ Overview 174
↘ Afan Forest Park 176
↘ Abercarn 178
↘ Aberhafesp Woods & DH 179
↘ Caerphilly DJs 179
↘ Brechfa 180
↘ Betws Y Coed (Snowdonia East) 182
↘ Clarach DH 183
↘ Clyne Woods 183
↘ Coed Llandegla 184
↘ Coed Trallwm 186
↘ Top riding tips, Josh Bryceland 187
↘ Coed Y Brenin (Snowdonia West) 188
↘ Cwm Rhaeadr 190
↘ Cwmcarn 192
↘ Foel Gasnach DH 194
↘ Gethin Woods 195
↘ Gwydwr Forest 196
↘ Kilvey Hill 197
↘ Henblas/Caersws nr Newton 198
↘ Llantrisant Woods DH 198
↘ Llanwrtyd Wells 199
↘ Maindy Road BMX Track 200
↘ Moelfre 200
↘ Mountain Ash DH 201
↘ Ponciau Banks 201
↘ Machynlleth 202
↘ Nant yr Arian 204
↘ Rheola DH Trail 206
↘ Rudry DJs 206
↘ Sandjumps 206
↘ Snowdonia National Park 207
↘ Wentwood DH 208
↘ Local riders, Rowan Sorrell 209

Nant yr Arian's switchbacks have incredible views.
[FORESTRY COMMISSION]

Wales

Trails…

1. Afan Forest Park
2. Abercarn
3. Aberhafesp Woods and DH
4. Caerphilly DJs
5. Brechfa
6. Betws Y Coed (Snowdonia East)
7. Clarach DH
8. Clyne Woods
9. Coed Llandegla
10. Coed Trallwm
11. Coed Y Brenin (Snowdonia West)
12. Cwm Rhaeadr
13. Cwmcarn
14. Foel Gasnach DH
15. Gethin Woods
16. Gwydwr Forest
17. Kilvey Hill
18. Henblas/Caersws
19. Llantrisant Woods DH
20. Llanwrtyd Wells
21. Maindy Road BMX Track
22. Moelfre
23. Mountain Ash DH
24. Ponciau Banks
25. Machynlleth
26. Nant Yr Arian
27. Rheola DH Trail
28. Rudry DJs
29. Sandjumps
30. Snowdonia National Park
31. Wentwood DH

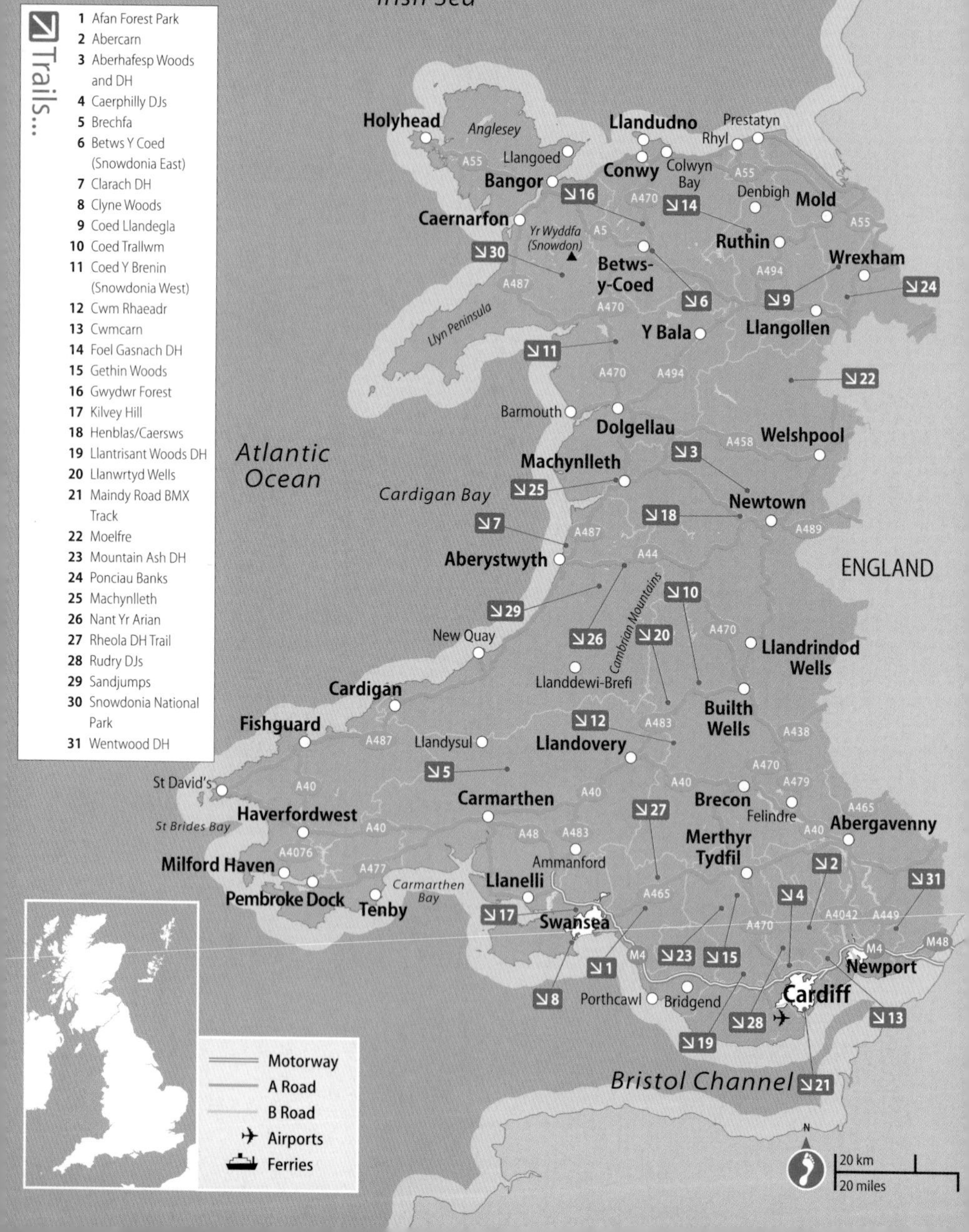

Wales is largely responsible for being the place that kick-started the trail centre experience in the UK. The original centres of north Wales have shaped how and where we ride today. Not that it was ever a case of age before beauty; the original centres sparkle in the shadows of the Snowdonia National Parks Mountains and still cut it today. Add to this the many new centres have opened over the years throughout Wales and what you get is a strong scene as diverse in its riding styles as it is in its landscapes.

The craggy, rocky and rugged beauty of the north combine with the strong industrial past of the south to make an interesting tour of what, in real terms, is a relatively small country. Luckily for us it is has a big heart and lots to offer the mountain biker.

Culturally, visitors can learn about the heavy industrial past that typifies many regions, and even go down a former working mine at the Big Pit, Blaenafon Torfaen. It is also a pleasure to hear the most widely used Celtic language, Welsh, spoken by the natives and also visit the many beautiful beaches along the Pembrokeshire coast.

As a mountain bike destination Wales seems to serve two distinct markets – the day trippers from the many nearby English towns and cities and those on long weekend or week breaks who tend to base themselves around one or two centres. Look slightly beyond this and you will find a country that offers a great variety of terrain across the different disciplines of biking, from the family holiday to the thrill-seeking downhillers. Wales has got it covered.

Local scene

It might be a bit of overkill to say that mountain biking has saved the Welsh tourism industry, but the sport is definitely bringing in a new generation of visitors to this spectacular corner of the world. From Snowdonia in the north to the Welsh borders, down to the remote, incredibly picturesque valleys in the south, Wales is absolutely choc full with world-class riding spots. And the Welsh know it. Some of the best trail-builders are from this area, the riding scene here is super-strong, and with every passing year the trails get more varied, more interesting and the maps grow larger. Long may it continue.

MUDDYMOLES.CO.UK

CHRIS MORAN

Top: Winning in Afan!
Above: The Severn Bridge – gateway to the good stuff.
Previous page: Caerphilly DJs in action. [FORESTRY COMMISSION]

ISOBEL CAMERON/FORESTRY COMMISSION

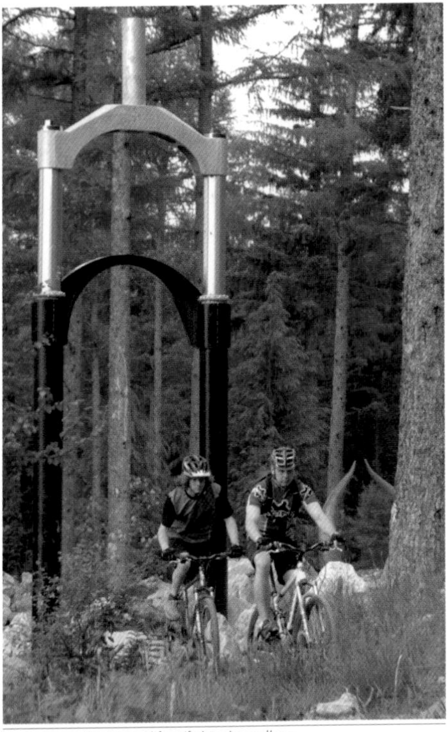

Coed y Brenin. Always good for a 'fork in the road' gag.

Hubs

There are spots of fantastic rides all over the country, but broadly speaking, the XC areas in Snowdonia have the most heritage (Coed y Brenin is widely hailed as the first purpose-built UK trail centre), and with the addition of Machynlleth in the south and Gwydyr Forest and Betws y Coed to the northeast of the National Park, the riding here is still first class. Meanwhile, there are plenty of stand-alone spots such as Moelfre, Aberhafesp and Brechfa, as well as the incredible riding to be found near the seaside resort of Aberystwyth (the Sandjumps trails are a sights to behold). But it's the south Wales spots of Cwmcarn and Afan that now pull in the majority of outside riders to the country. Why? Because they could compete with any trail centre in the world for views, facilities, variety, XC riding, and, in Cwmcarn, downhill tracks.

⑤ Best rides in Wales

Wales has a wealth of world-class riding spots, and virtually every one mentioned in the following chapter is worthy of a long journey. But we reckon the following should comprise your 'must visit' list:

❶ Cwmcarn, page 192

With a new £5 million visitor centre, a permanent uplift (the fantastically-named Cwmdown bus), a freshly installed freeride park for spring 2009, and some spectacular south Wales scenery, this place is a total winner. Add in sausage, eggs, chips and beans post ride (all for £3), and you're looking at heaven.

❷ Afan Forest, page 176

Afan boasts not one but two brilliant visitor centres, some of the best, flowing singletrack in the whole of the UK, and what can only be described as 'magical' forest. We rate this as our favourite spot in Britain.

❸ Coed y Brenin (Snowdonia West), page 188

The trails have been re-named recently, but this is still the 'home' of UK mountain biking. Take a trip to where it all began at the very first purpose-built riding centre, just on the edge of the spectacular Snowdonia National Park.

❹ Aberystwyth, pages 183, 204, 206

Who'd have thought that a holiday town on the west coast would have such fantastic riding nearby? With Clarach Downhill, the impressive Sandjumps DJs and Nant yr Arian on tap, this town makes a great weekend stop.

❺ Coed Llandegla, page 184

For riders in the northwest, Coed Llandegla represents one of the great new generation of trail centres, with brilliant freeriding, family and XC facilities on site.

↘1 Afan Forest Park

Train station Maesteg

Nearest city Swansea

Sat Nav SA13 3HG

Opening times The trails are open 365 days a year, day and night. The only closures are due to forest operations and details are posted on the website mbwales.com. All trails are free although there is a car park fee currently of £2.60

CHRIS MORAN

Location Afan and Glyncorrwg are around 15 km to the northeast of Swansea. From the M4 exit at junction 40 and take the A4107 Afan Valley Road north. The visitor centre is brown-signposted from the motorway (though make sure you take a left at the first roundabout), but if you're worried about getting lost, go 8 km along the A4107 then turn off at Cymer, heading north on Sunnyside Terrace torwards Glyncorrwg. From the A4107 there are signs for Afan Forest Park from Cymer follow Glyncorrwg Mountain Bike Centre.

Facilities/Overview Afan Forest Park is affectionately known as 'Little Switzerland' and it offers two visitor centres and start/finish points at Afan Argoed and Glyncorrwg. The former is better suited to the day tripper with Glyncorrwg taking on the flagship role. With six trails (Rheilffordd, The Wall, White's Level, Skyline, W2 and the Penhydd Trail) and more all-weather singletrack than any of the other Welsh mountain bike centres, this is a must-do for any keen trail rider. The forest block is also one of Wales's largest and the trails really do get you into the thick of it. The trails are of a similar style – flowing singletrack – but it is a great riding venue for all bikers as there are as many thrills on the way down as there are views on the climb up. Now with a stunning visitor centre and a bike-friendly attitude, a stable mineral soil (that holds up well in all weathers) along with plenty of smaller irregular pieces of rock combined with the exposed roots, this is one of the UK's best sites.

XC The trails are predominantly aimed at the trail-riding XC rider, with long climbs and contouring flowing descents. Inexperienced riders should start with the short blue trail and longer Penhydd route out of the Afan Argoed centre. Technically proficient riders will love the speed they can achieve on The Wall and the Whites level trails. For those looking for a more tranquil, scenic experience, the skyline trail at 46 km is the longest and has long forest road stretches linking singletrack sections where the great vistas can be taken in.

Downhill Glyncorrwg does not at present offer any DH specific trails, although many of the descents built into the four trails offer plenty of challenges for the average rider and many riders quote the final descent of the wall as their favourite. There are future plans to construct a permanent DH course in Glyncorrwg so contact the centre for the latest information.

Freeride Glyncorrwg does not have any specific freeride trails, although the black run and energy section on the Whytes level trail both contain various jumps, berms and small drops to session. Looking around the hills of the valley there are huge glacial boulders stranded on the hillsides which the skilful and imaginative can put to good use.

Easy Starting from Afon Argoed, take on the brand new blue beginner trails and with their modular sections you can build up your skill and confidence. After lunch take a steady ride around the 22-km Penhydd trail.

Hard Starting at either centre the W2 trail is a challenge, linking both the Wall and the Whytes level trail; you will ride some 43 km, which take in all the best sections of singletrack in the valley. Whichever way you ride it you will have a café at the halfway point and somewhere to have a cup of tea and recall your tales after.

Not to miss The Wall final descent should be done by all who visit the forest park. And another thing – it is possible to uplift the wall final descent using your own vehicle on the public road.

Remember to avoid The long forest road ride along the old railway at the start of the wall – tag onto someone who knows the shortcut!

Nearest Bike/Hire shop Skyline cycles (T01639 850011) are based at both centres; they are very well stocked with excellent mechanics. Both shops also hire bikes as well as Afan Valley Bike Hire.

Local accommodation
There are a number of bike-friendly B&Bs in the area perfect for individuals and small groups, as well as camping and caravan spots with electric hook up available at the Glyncorrwg Mountain Bike centre. If you're travelling in a group of four or more try out the superb log cabins at Bryn Bettws, (T01639 642040) situated on the side of the Wall trail.

Eating Both visitor centres offer food although the bike-friendly sized meals in the Drop Off café are not to be missed. The nearest supermarket is in Port Talbot so best to stock up before you drive up the valley.

ⓘ **More info** Afan Argoed Centre (T01639 850864), Glyncorrwg Centre (T01639 851900 or mbwales.com). There are also bike maps available for £2.50 at the visitor centres.

> Lowdown

☻ Locals do
Ride the fun bits on the Whytes level before cutting across to the skyline descent.

Have regular evening rides and night rides through the winter.

Relax in the Drop Off café afterwards.

☹ Locals don't
Always ride the trails the way they are waymarked – they find their own routes around the forest.

Ride when it's chucking it down.

✔ Pros
The trails will give most riders a wide grin.

All-weather riding surface.

Very friendly atmosphere at the centres and on the trails.

✖ Cons
Won't satisfy the diehard downhillers or freeriders due to lack of uplift and stunts (though Cwmcarn isn't too far away).

Can be quite exposed when the weather closes in.

MATT ADDISON/MUDDYMOLES.CO.UK

CHRIS MORAN

CHRIS MORAN

↘2 Abercarn

XC DH

Train station Risca
Nearest city Cardiff
Sat Nav NP11 7EU (roughly)

Location Abercarn is next door to Cwmcarn, around 9 km north of Newport, S Wales. From the M4 exit at junction 28, heading north on A467 past Risca and Crosskeys towards Abercarn. Park in the village where you can.

Facilities Snacks and meals are available at the Cwm Carn Forest Visitor Centre during opening hours (see the Cwmcarn Page). Evening meals are available in local pubs and restaurants; try the Cross Keys pub.

Overview This downhill track is overshadowed by its big brother (and neighbour) Cwmcarn, but the all-weather course here is perfect for those who like their trails a bit more low budget and loose. There's also some great XC to be found by heading out on the many kilometres of singletrack that criss-cross the woods here or jumping on the comp circuit by checking out Dragon Downhill. Many local riders here like to hit the Twrch Trail of Cwmcarn and then head off into Abercarn's unofficial singletrack.

Conditions This is an all-weather site that has been cut through the hill, with plenty of switchbacks etc, into the brilliant Welsh forest.

ⓘ **More info** dragondownhill.co.uk.

DANNY MILNER

DANNY MILNER

N3 Aberhafesp Woods and DH

XC DH

Train station Caersws
Nearest city Welshpool/Shrewsbury
Sat Nav SY16 3HT (for Aberhafesp village centre)

Location Aberhafesp Woods are around 3 km north west of Newtown, itself between Welshpool and Aberystwyth in mid-Wales. From Shrewsbury, take the A458 to Welshpool, then the A483 to Newtown. Head north through the town, then take a left onto Milford Road (the B4568) to Aberhafesp. To get to the woods, carry on through the village and after 600 m take a right, then first right, then first right again and the woods are at the top of this hill.

Facilities Aberhafesp has a few shops and a pub.

Overview While nearby Henblas Downhill is a popular venue for the comp scene, Aberhavesp is a more mellow venue with plenty of XC to be had in the singletrack throughout the woods, while there are a few DH trails that the locals have added to and strengthened over the years.

Conditions This is very remote land with staggering views and unpopulated paths.

N4 Caerphilly DJs

FR DJ

Train station Aber
Nearest city Cardiff
Sat Nav CF83 1LB

Location Caerphilly DJs are in the east of the town of Caerphilly, which is itself around 5 km to the north of Cardiff. From the M4, exit at junction 32 heading north on the A470 to Pontypridd. After 3 km, take the A468 to Caerphilly town centre. Head through the centre of town on Nantgarw Road, then take a right onto Castle Street (you'll have to loop around the Castle), then after 200 m take a left onto Van Road. Head down here, past the Goodrich Pub, go straight on at the roundabout and after 1 km the Coed Parc y Van Forestry Car Park is on the left. The DJs are around 200 m up a dirt track to the right (then right again) off the car park.

Facilities The Goodrich Pub does a mean bit of grub, otherwise central Caerphilly has plenty of shops and facilities.

Overview This is a public-access DJ site that is very popular with the local mountain bike scene. There are numerous lines through the area, with plenty of gaps, tables, rhythm sections and enough jumps to satisfy everyone from absolute beginners all the way through to decent dirt jumpers. Some of the bowls are tight, and the preparation times super-quick, but there are also easy lines for those wishing to progress. Well worth a visit for those in the area. There is talk of moving this site to Cwmcarn though, and murmurs of the jumps being bulldozed as a result. Litter is a frequent problem and hasn't helped the DJs' cause.

Conditions This is a well-maintained site, with a clay hard-packed base all set in an open clearing of forestry commission land. A great set-up. Please don't ride them when they're wet, and be sure to fix any damage.

ⓘ **More info** Dragon Downhill, dragondownhill.co.uk.

CHRIS MORAN

↘5 Brechfa

Train station Llandovery

Nearest city Swansea

Sat Nav SA32 7SN

Opening times The trails are open 365 days a year, day and night. the only closures are due to forest operations and details are posted on the website mtbwales.com

ISOBEL CAMERON/FORESTRY COMMISSION

Location Brechfa is the name given to the open countryside near the town of Abergorlech between the towns of Carmarthen, Lampeter and Llandeilo, around 30 km north of Swansea and to the west of the Brecon Beacons. From the M4 head all the way to the end of the motorway (junction 49), where it turns into the A48. Keep on this road for around 10 km, then exit onto the B4310 heading towards the National Botanic Garden and Nantgaredig; continue on this road to Brechfa (a total journey of around 12 km). Abergorlech is another 6 km along this road with the Forestry Commission Car Park clearly signed to the left.

Facilities/Overview This is essentially one of Wales's best mountain bike venues – the XC/DH trails at Brechfa have caused quite a stir in both their design and construction, traversing through stunning mixed woodland of oak, beech and conifer; the routes are fast and flowing and sure to bring a grin to any rider from the novice to the experts. The Gorlech red route will challenge the experienced cyclist and peak adrenaline levels while the green and blue Derwen trails starting at Brwrgwm car park are gentler, but still flow amazingly well and are great for novice mountain bikers. Brechfa is a shale area and the trails have been built using this shale mixed with the soils to give a really smooth, hard and fast trail surface that never gets muddy.

XC Brechfa is a fantastic area for XC riding; the waymarked trails take you through this stunning forest and there are plenty more trails away from the waymarkers to find and explore further afield. Brechfa is a different style of trail to its Welsh counterparts, with a much smoother trail surface and more obvious descents with features to maintain flow.

Downhill There are no official downhill trails in Brechfa forest but the descents on the blue and red trails, especially the final descent of the red, have earned a popular following among the DH crowd due to their speed, features and flow.

Freeride No specific freeride course, though obstacles have been designed into the XC trails such as tabletops, step up jumps, natural wallrides and northshore obstacles. The additions make these trails fun for all to ride.

Easy Start out on the green Derwen trail and head for the blue extension loop. This is still within the easy skills level, so continue out on this, following the blue waymarkers. The blue descent back down to the green trail is one of the best in the forest.

Hard Starting in Bwrgwm it is possible to follow the black trail out from the car park and link it into the red route before returning back

NICK BAYLISS

> **Lowdown**

☻ Locals do
Link the red and blue loops by riding across the top of the hill.

Ride most of the more challenging optional sections on the trail.

Always take in the blue descent as part of their rides.

☹ Locals don't
Hang about – the style of trail and the multiple climbs soon develop fitness, skill and speed.

✔ Pros
Pretty, quiet part of rural Wales with some of the best riding out there.

Best beginner green and blue trails for novices and kids that contain real mountain biking singletrack.

✖ Cons
Limited facilities on site.

The shale can be slippery when it's very wet.

following the black waymarkers. This will however be one big ride, around 45 km with five climbs. Anyone completing this will be feeling it for days to come, but it takes in all the best sections and has some amazing views.

Not to miss The food (well earned) at the Black Lion!

Remember to avoid Heading too far out on your first visit! You're a long way from help.

Nearest Bike/Hire shop There is no bike shop in the Brechfa forest area so make sure you bring spare tubes etc. The nearest shop with a good range of stock for repairing high-end bikes is Summit Cycles in Aberstwyth (T01970 626061).

Local accommodation There are a few B&Bs but try local bike enthusiasts Carl and Ivy at Bike Brechfa (T01558 685811), who can accommodate you and guide you around Brechfa's hidden corners.

Eating You'll do well to beat the food in the Black Lion (T01558 685271) in Abergorlech where the red Gorlech trail starts.

ⓘ **More info** Aberystwyth Tourist Info (T01970 612125, mtbwales.com) and bikebrechfa.co.uk

ISOBEL CAMERON/FORESTRY COMMISSION

NICK BAYLISS

↘6 Betws Y Coed (Snowdonia East)

Train station Betws y Coed
Nearest city Chester
Sat Nav LL24 0AE for the visitor centre

Location Betws Y Coed is a popular, touristy village (often called the Outdoor Capital of Wales) on the northeast edge of the Snowdonia National Park and is the park's official gateway. From the west, coming in on either the A5 from Shrewsbury or the A55 from Chester, turn onto the A470 which heads directly to Betws Y Coed.

Facilities There is a newly-built Snowdonia National Park Visitor Centre which is the gateway to the national park and well signed from Betws Y Coed town centre. It has a café and all amenities you could wish for. However, where the trails start (at the forestry car park), there are few facilities, so take your supplies on the short ride from Betws town.

Overview Betws Y Coed is a beautiful alpinesque village, much of which was built in Victorian times. It is also the principal village of the 800 sq mile Snowdonia National Park and situated where the River Conwy meets its three tributaries flowing from the west – the Llugwy, the Lledr and the Machno. Surrounded by mountains with cascading waterfalls, hill-top lakes, river pools and ancient bridges, it is clear to see why Betws is such a popular destination. With all this rugged beauty and terrain it wasn't long before bikers caught on and started riding in the area, and the Forestry Commission developed purpose-built trails first at Gwydwr Forest to the north, then later in the Penmachno and Mynydd Cribau trails.

Terrain The trails here are located in some of the most beautiful forest in the UK. It has everything from technical riding through to gentle meanders, though some would say this is quite an old-school place to ride, which is often a plus!

XC The Mynydd Cribau and Penmachno routes (either 19- or 32-km loops) includes an honesty box at the start. The trails are built and maintained by a local bike club and have fantastic features, flowing lines and armoured bridges in some of the most stunning scenery in the country. They are two of the newest additions to the Welsh XC trails and both highly regarded. It's worth noting that the trail was built as part of a community funded scheme to help regenerate poor areas so riders should make an effort to spend some money in the Village of Penmachno itself. The outreaching possibilities of Snowdonia national park are only limited by one's imagination and fitness. The geology in this region is ancient, with some of the oldest rocks in the world found here; again this translates well into the

SNOWDONIA-GUIDES.CO.UK

trails, with many rocky sections that make for great singletrack.

Downhill There is no specific DH track here, but head north into Gwydwr Forest and you'll find plenty of unofficial trails.

Dirt Jumps/Freeride Apart from the challenge of some of the hidden downhills, which are very technical, Betws Y Coed does not offer the freerider any features.

Conditions The XC routes are hard-packed dirt singletrack. The area is popular with walkers but well known as a mountain biking centre so expect to see plenty of bikes.

ⓘ **More info** Betws Y Coed Tourist Information Centre, T01690 710426, website mbwales.com or betws-y-coed.co.uk.

↘7 Clarach DH

XC DH FR

Train station Aberystwyth

Nearest city Aberystwyth

Sat Nav SA43 3LN (to Cardigan Bay Holiday Park)

Location Clarach is just to the south of Cardigan Bay Holiday Park, a huge expanse of caravans on the coast around 1 km north of Aberystwyth, mid Wales. Heading into Aberystwyth from the west, you'll be arriving on the A44. Just before you arrive at the town centre, take the A487 back out of town in the direction of Machynlleth, then after 800 m take a left onto the B4572. After 1 km the Cardigan Bay Caravan Park is signposted off to the left. Head down here, park at the site, and head into the woods to the south of the caravans.

Facilities Cardigan Bay Holiday Park has plenty of facilities and amenities, though perhaps a little inflated in price. Aberystwyth is a short ride away and full of shops and students!

Overview Clarach is yet another string to the impressive Aberystwyth bow. This is a DH site with a few short, but feature-full trails through the woods. The views over the bay are beautiful, and there is plenty of XC riding and some decent drops, jumps and flowing lines for the freeriders. Add in Nant yr Arian nearby, plus the impressive Sandjumps (not to mention Machynlleth up the road), and there's plenty of first-class riding to be had in this old seaside resort. Plus it's a very happening town with a lively university.

Conditions This is forest land next to the sea, with spaced trees and great soil for building features. Plenty of chicken lines or decent jumps for the brave, including a road gap.

ⓘ **More info** Aberystwyth local riders the Chainslappers Crew have built most of the trails. Help with the next push by going to freewebs.com/chainslappers/aberridingspots.htm.

↘8 Clyne Woods

XC DH FR

Train station Swansea

Nearest city Swansea

Sat Nav SA3 5AS

Location Clyne Woods are to the southwest of Swansea, just to the north of the Mumbles. From the M4, exit at junction 47 and head south towards Swansea centre on the A483. After 4 km take a right onto the A4216, heading to Cockett and Black Pill. After 2 km, take a right into the coastal road (Mumbles Road, the A4067) and head towards Black Pill. Just after the Shell Garage on your right, follow the brown bike sign off to the right and park at either Clyne Valley Country Park (here at sea level), or climb up Derwen Fawr Road, then take a left onto Ynys Newydd Road (signed to the recycling centre), and take a left just before into the higher Clyne Woods car park (though this is locked at night).

Facilities The sea level Clyne Valley Country Park has some hot and cold snacks available, and nearby Black Pill is the place to head for shops and amenities.

Overview You probably wouldn't travel that far to session Clyne Woods, but for local Swansea riders, this makes a welcome change to other, bigger trail centres nearby, and features some impressive DJs, the beginnings of some northshore, a load of freeride drops and bombholes, and some feature-full (if not short) DH trails. All set in some spectacular scenery.

Conditions Can be muddy through the winter months, but otherwise drains fairly well, and is a mixture of woodland and cleared, DJ area with solid, buildable land. Be sure to fix any casings on the DJs.

ⓘ **More info** The MTB Pigs is a Swansea-based mountain biking club whose website contains info about Clyne and other local XC routes, mtbpigs.co.uk.

CHRIS MORAN

↘9 Coed Llandegla

Train station Wrexham General/ Wrexham Central

Nearest city Chester/Wrexham

Sat Nav LL11 3AA

Opening times The trails are open 365 days a year and technically you can ride them any time. The café and bike shop have varied opening times from Tuesday through to Sunday but are closed on Mondays. All trails are free although there is an all-day car park fee currently of £2.50

Location Coed Llandegla Forest is located on the A525, 10 km west of Wrexham. From the north west take the A483 south from Chester towards Wrexham then take the A525 west, signposted towards Ruthin. From the Ruthin area take the A525 east towards Wrexham. Coed Llandegla Forest is signed from the road.

Facilities/Overview This is a fantastic set up with four well-maintained XC trails featuring plenty of technical riding with a green, blue, red and black trail to test all abilities. There's a fantastic visitor centre with the One Planet Café, bike shop and workshop for all your mechanical, thirsty and hungry needs. This is a hugely popular site due to its proximity to Chester and some of the North West cities, and is a very well-maintained – predominantly XC – site. Perfect for families too or for those who simply want to have a lovely meander in the forest.

XC All four trails at Llandegla are suitable for the XC rider as even the most technical black sections can be rolled through safely at a moderate speed. The trails range from short family loops of 5 km to the black loop at 21 km with a blue novice (12 km) trail and red intermediate (18 km) slotting in between.

Downhill In keeping with most of the Welsh trail centres, Llandegla does not offer any specific DH runs, but it does have plenty to keep the DH rider entertained. Used by many pro riders to have a fun blast while keeping the fitness levels up, Llandegla throws berms, tabletops and plenty of whoops that will keep you manualling and jumping through the fun black sections. Not suited to long travel DH bikes though.

Freeride For the aspiring freerider looking to develop his jumping skills, the black runs at Llandegla are perfect as they have various jumps of different sizes to learn and progress on. There are no big obstacles though so more skilled riders will not be challenged, but for the majority there is plenty of fun to be had. Dirt jumpers and pure freeriders looking for drops might like to take a trip back towards Wrexham, where Bwlchgwyn Quarry (just off the road, in the town of Bwlchgwyn) has some decent terrain.

ONE PLANET ADVENTURE

Easy Follow the novice (blue) trail around the loop and back to the centre. Too easy? Take the intermediate (red) loop as well after lunch.

Hard Take the black route. Each black section is a loop branching off the intermediate trail, so if you enjoy it, loop back around and hit the section again. You'll soon find you're running low on energy but the fun will keep you going back to the centre.

Not to miss Those pumpy, swoopy black sections.

Remember to avoid Not contributing – please pay the parking fee (it helps fund the trail upkeep).

Nearest Bike/Hire shop The One Planet bike shop (T01978 751656) at the Llandegla visitor centre stocks many parts and accessories and you can hire one of the Kona bikes from them there. Elsewhere there is a good shop in Chester, The Edge Cycleworks (T01244 399888), which stocks a wide range of brands.

Local accommodation
There is no accommodation on the Llandegla site itself, but nearby Wrexham and Chester offer a wide range of accommodation from B&B to hotels. In Wrexham try the Scandinavian self-catering cottages of Three Tops County Leisure (T01352 770648), and also the Windings (T01978 720503) for B&B. In Chester there is an abundance of good accommodation; try the Comfort Inn (T01244 327542) for reasonable prices or look at the range of accommodation at visitchester.com.

Eating The One Planet café in the log-cabin style visitor centre is the place to eat when you're hitting the trails. Run by enthusiastic bikers, they know exactly what you need.

ⓘ **More info** One Planet Centre (T01978 751656), Chester tourist info (T01244 402111), Wrexham tourist info (T01978 292015), website coedllandegla.com.

> Lowdown

Locals do
Session the black bits.

Learn to manual over the wooden northshore bridge.

Socialise at the centre.

Locals don't
Always ride the trails the way they are way marked – they find their own shortcuts to their favourite bits.

Try and out-jump local builder Jason Rennie (he set the world long jump record here at 134 ft!).

Pros
The trails are enjoyable to all.

Very relaxed vibe.

Cons
You will have to stay elsewhere and commute.

Some doubletrack can be quite boring for the more experienced.

ONE PLANET ADVENTURE

10 Coed Trallwm

Train station Llanwrtyd
Nearest city Cardiff
Sat Nav LD5 4TS

Location Coed Trallwm is around 6 km north of Llanwrtyd Wells, in the heart of Wales. From the Llanwrtyd, take the A483 north west out of town in the direction of Treflys. Here, just before you cross the river into the village take a left on the road signposted to Abergwesyn. Five kilometres up this road the Coed Trallwm Mountain Bike Centre is clearly signed on the right.

Facilities The mountain bike centre has a café with log-burning stove, plus there are several delightful, self-catering cottages available to rent. Open 1200 to 1600 through winter. Cost: £2 for the day. For those not wishing to overnight, there are showers and a bike wash facility.

Overview This is a privately-owned area with some fantastic singletrack for riders of all abilities (although there are no complete beginner trails), plus some fantastic facilities and incredibly beautiful cottages available for those looking for a weekend – or longer – retreat. There are three waymarked trails: the Blue, a 4-km gentle loop with 95-m climb and descent; the Red, a 5-km, 140-m hike; and the Black, a 5-km, 155-m tough climb with some spectacular views at the top. The trails are well made and packed full of features, and the area is a great stopoff for the fantastic riding in nearby Llanwrtyd Wells and the varied and natural Elan Valley singletrack. There is also more unofficial riding above and around the Trallwm site but not waymarked.

Conditions This is a well-maintained site, but still quite raw so it can be muddy in the winter.

ⓘ **More info** Call the Coed Trallwm Visitor Centre on T01591 610546, coedtrallwm.co.uk.

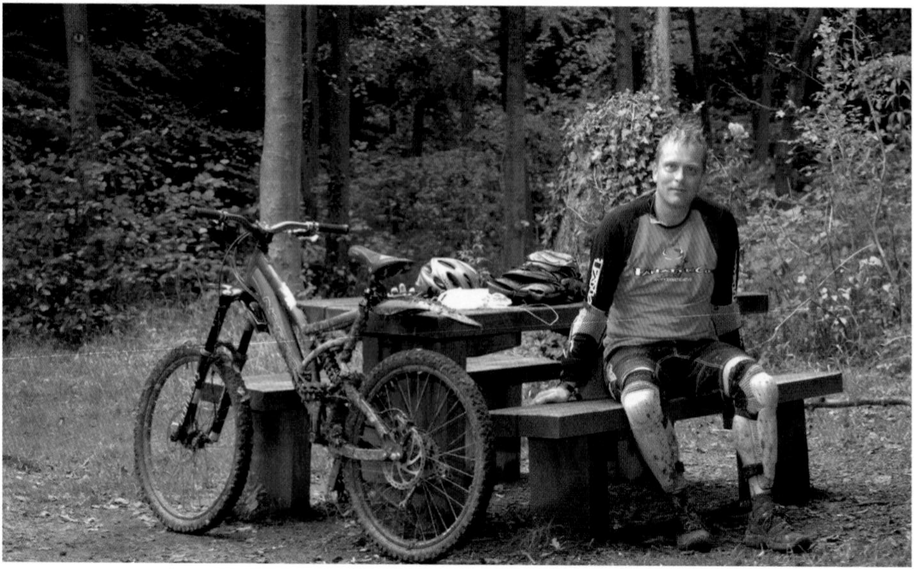

FORESTRY COMMISSION

Top riding tips
Josh Bryceland

Josh Bryceland is the 2007 and 2008 UCI World Cup Downhill Jr Champion and sponsored by Santa Cruz, The Syndicate, and Nike 6.0. Here are his 5 tips for better riding and five spots to try them out on…

JOSH KNOX

❶ Drops
Most people lean back heavily. They lift the forks up and hope to land on the back wheel. Really though you want to soak up the drop, so if it's about a foot, you try and push the bike into the floor. Ride towards the drop, get over the back wheel and compress into the bike before you've left the ground. As you leave, extend your legs and arms and push the bike into the floor as quick as you can. If it's a bigger drop, compress before the drop like before, then stay in that position with the bike and push the bike to meet the floor. Best place to learn them? I reckon a really good place to try them out is at the skills training centre at Fort William. They've got really good drops of all size.

❷ Cornering
Common mistakes are probably where you don't commit or if you brake while you're in the turn. I reckon it's best if you do all the braking before the corner, then just lean in to it, commit, and look as far out of the turn as possible. If you look at the middle of the corner, you're not committing to the turn as much as if your look all the way to the end. Try it, it really works! A place that has good corners is Llandegla in Wales. There's a cross country trail with loads of berms all the way round it that's amazing to lean into and bank it.

❸ Jumps
In downhill, the most common mistake is when people just launch off a booter and just pull up on the bars. What you want to do is look for a jump, roll at it a few times, judge the speed and let the jump do the work. Try and land with both wheels at the same time, keep you eye on the landing and try and get your wheels parallel to the landing. I never use my brakes when I'm in the air, but I always have, finger on each brake lever at all times. Cwmcarn is perfect for practicing 'cos there's a track with some cool small jumps at the top and they get bigger as you go down.

❹ Braking
A common mistake is people just locking up the back wheel because they're only using one brake. Remember you should have two levers, and the front brake works just as much if not more than the back brake. So you want to use both evenly. Also try braking as hard and as late as possible. If you just use your back brake you'll simply skid as you come into the corner, if you use both you'll be more in control. A good place to try this out - where there are loads of steep sections – is Hamsterly 'cos it's pretty steep at the bottom so it's all about being good on your brakes.

❺ Save energy and keep focused
A lot of people burn themselves out 'cos they can't save their energy on longer routes like at Fort William. Any downhill course over two minutes long – unless you're incredibly fit – you can't ride the top sections and push on it. If you're riding a really long course, and you're peddling, remember to breathe a really deep breath, and save some energy at the bottom because you won't make up on a short peddling section what you lose if you're tired and bouncing off roots and rocks and getting messed up in the trees. Have a sit down on an easier section, and take some deep breaths. If it's smooth give your hands a quick shake and get back into it! A good place to try this out? Try Fort William's DH track – it's really long, and is proper knackering.

↘11 Coed Y Brenin (Snowdonia West)

Train station Talsarnau

Nearest city Welshpool

Sat Nav LL41 4YA

Opening times The trails are open 365 days a year, day and night. The only closures are due to forest operations and details are posted on the website mbwales.com. All trails are free although there is a small car park fee

FORESTRY COMMISSION WALES

FORESTRY COMMISSION WALES

Location Coed Y Brenin is right in the heart of the Snowdonia National Park. From the M6 take the M54 past Telford, then the A5 around Shrewsbury and then the A458 through Welshpool. Head for Dolgellau and at the village turn north onto the A470 where, after 7 km, there's a well-signed right into the Coed Y Brenin Visitor Centre.

Facilities/Overview For many years this was the UK's flagship trail centre, and the trails at Coed Y Brenin have led to the evolution of many new venues across the country. Its name means 'forest of the kings' – an apt moniker for this large block of forestry containing over 21,000 acres. The area is a rugged former volcanic region with many mineral deposits that have been mined for years. For those interested, there is a geology trail from the fantastic new multi-million pound Visitor Centre. For the biker though this means there is an incredibly hard-wearing, rocky surface to rip through the forest on. The trails hug beautiful, river-carved valleys with technical rock features and climb out over untamed mountain tops. Mountain biking is huge in Coed Y Brenin and the whole region has really taken to the development of the bike centre and its trails. When you add the drama of southern Snowdonia's mountain views and the very real possibility of seeing the magnificent red kites circling overhead, it makes for a great day in the saddle. Although many of the trails have been recently re-named, many insist on calling the trails by their old names. So you don't get too confused on the hill, the Red Bull trail is now known as the Tarw (Welsh for bull), the MBR route remains and the old Karrimor trail is now affectionately known as The Beast!

XC Coed Y Brenin is the original British XC trail centre and as such is an XC rider's mecca. There are six trails in total: The Beast, a 38 km gruelling hike; The MBR Trail at 18 km; Dragon's Back (the old Karrimor Trail) at 31 km; The Tarw Trail (Red Bull Trail) at 20 km; the red-graded Temptiwr Trail at 9 km (giving a great short loop to test out whether the longer trails are within your grasp); the new 'Yr Afon' trail suiting family and novice riders and the red-graded 'Temptiwr'.

With one green-graded trail, three red trails and two graded black, there is something here right across the board for every XC rider. Remember the trails are rocky and contain small drop offs, but any regular mountain biker will relish the challenge.

Downhill Coed Y brenin does not have any DH courses or trails that are suited to downhill bikes as there is no uplift and the trails are all built with gentle gradients. Downhillers often ride here on trail or XC bikes though as the terrain offers some technical challenges and the loops offer a good day's riding away from the downhill bike.

Freeride Although Coed y Brenin does list a dual slalom course among its assets, it's not really up to modern-day expectations. Built a long time ago and without input from expert riders, it wouldn't be worth a long trip. It is now just utilised by XC riders on their way out or back from longer rides. Unless you're a budding freerider who simply wants a good day's aerobic exercise, then Coed Y Brenin is not really for you.

Easy If you consider yourself a novice either hit the family trail 'Yr Afon' or the red-graded 'Temptiwr'. Experienced riders looking for an easier day should ride the MBR trail, which at 18 km long won't leave you too tired.

Hard The only really physically challenging route is the black trail 'The Beast': at 38 km long and with a ride time of between 3-6 hrs depending on fitness, it will leave you ready for some coffee and cake back at the café.

Not to miss The chance to ride on an all-weather surface stone path! They're fantastic.

Remember to avoid Heading out on the longer rides without a spare tube and pump – it's a long walk back.

Nearest Bike/Hire shop Beics Brenin will be your best call for spares, repairs and bike hire (T01341 440728).

Local accommodation There are a number of places to stay in Dolgellau such as the Ty Seren B&B (T0131 423407), or for a self-catering cottage try the Isfryn House (T01229 583761). If you want to stay closer to the trails you can cycle to them easily from the Ferndale (T01341 440247) which can accommodate up to 24 people and is bike friendly and reasonably priced.

Eating On site there is a café, 'Bwyd y Brenin', that serves good food to hungry bikers and can keep your energy levels topped up. In Dolgellau, try Y Sospan (T01341 423174), once the town courthouse and jail where now you can get all-day food. The Callanish Restaurant (T01341 422008) is a popular choice, as is Frankies (T01341 423948) fish and chip bar

ⓘ **More info** Coed Y Brenin Visitor Centre (T01341 440742), Dolgellau Tourist info (T01341 422888) or try mbwales.com.

FORESTRY COMMISSION WALES

> Lowdown

Locals do

Ride the rocks very well.

Layer up in winter, as it can be cold on the hill tops.

Locals don't

Ride much else other than XC.

Use super lightweight tyres – they will tear and puncture.

Pros

Unique stone pitching throughout the trails, interesting to ride and weatherproof.

Stunning new Visitor Centre to start and finish your rides.

Area is very bike friendly.

Cons

Won't satisfy the diehard downhillers or freeriders due to lack of uplift and features.

↘12 Cwm Rhaeadr

Train station Sugar Loaf/Llanwrtyd
Nearest city Cardiff
Sat Nav SA20 0SR

Location Located about 40 miles north of Swansea, fair smack in the middle of South Wales. Follow signs for Cilycwm from the A482 or A483 (near Llandovery). Once in Cilycwm village, continue northwards towards Llyn Brianne Reservoir until signs for Cwm Rhaiadr can be seen.

Facilities An excellent new, predominantly XC trail purpose-built by local master trail builder and pro rider Rowan Sorrell. The red-graded trail is around 7 km in length and climbs up to great views of the Tywi Valley, before dropping back down through the Douglas Fir forest. Apart from the great trail, there is not much on offer in terms infrastructure.

Overview While only a relatively small area of Forestry Commission land, the trails have been designed by mountain bikers for mountain bikers. Great forest, excellent technical sections and it has something for everyone. Also usually uncrowded, especially during the week.

Terrain Steeper and mostly singletrack with technical section with variable surface types.

XC Tabletops, berms and drops all come into play on this XC loop; however, importantly it has been designed by Rowan as an all abilities trail. Thus even beginners can roll over all the obstacles, while experts can go as hard as their talent allows. The trail starts and finishes in a small forestry car park; from there it's a long gentle climb up the forest road until you reach the singletrack which steepens and switches back up the steep hillside. This takes you to the highest point and the views out over the valley and waterfall are stunning. From here there is an option to leave the waymarked trail and follow the bridleway out onto the Mynydd Mallaen for a much longer ride. Sticking with the main trail it's a fun blast all the way back to the car park with berms, jumps, bombholes and loose shale. Whilst in the area it is worth riding some of the natural trails up at Llyn Brianne.

Downhill There are some short sections of DH in the descent, but no set DH trail.

Dirt Jumps/Freeride While there is no set-aside jump and park area, there are several lines through the trail that incorporate tabletops, medium steps and drops.

Conditions The XC routes are hard-packed dirt singletrack designed specifically for mountain biking and usually in very good condition.

ⓘ **More info** Cwm Rhaeadr has its own website on the Forestry Commission website forestry.gov.uk, while mbwales.com is always the place to head.

CHRIS MORAN

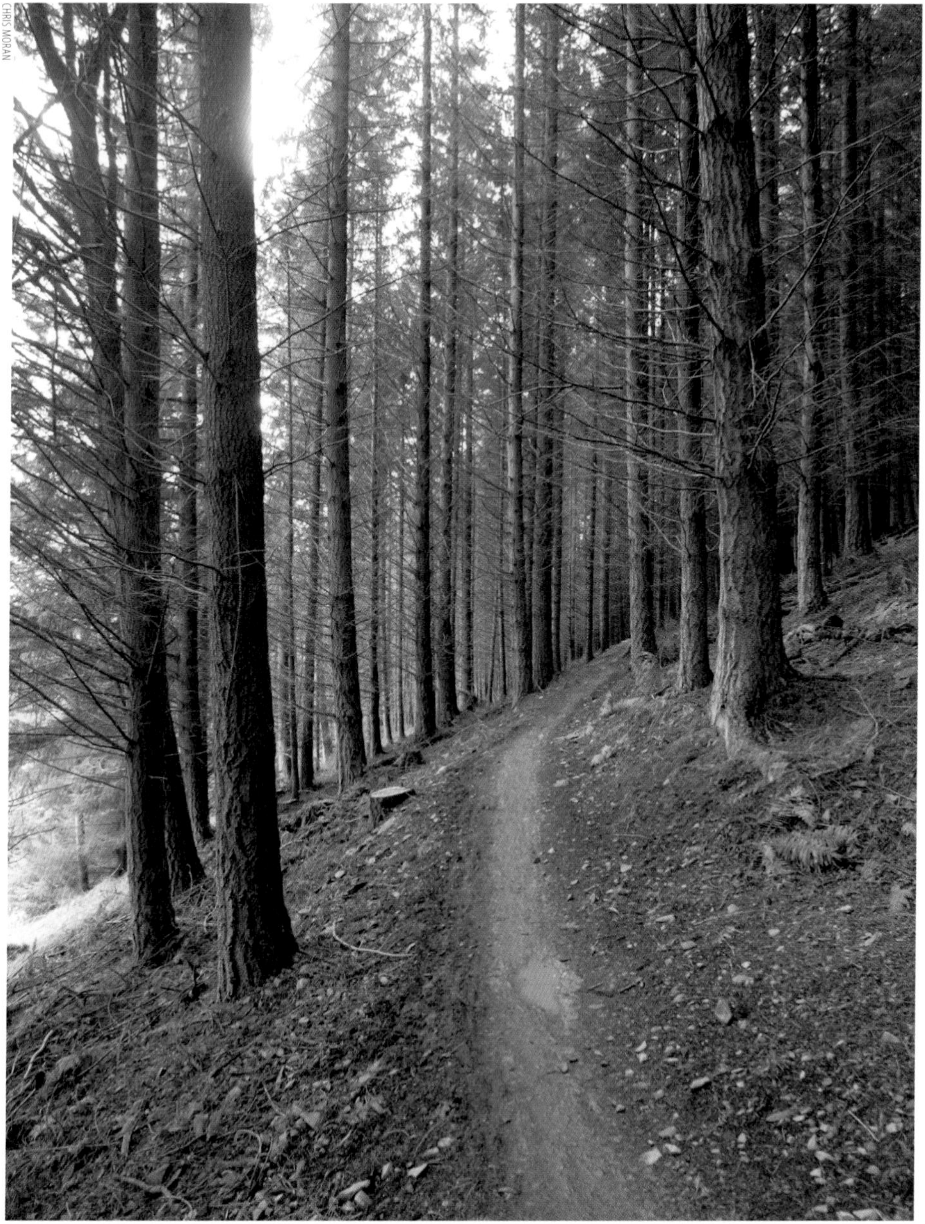
CHRIS MORAN

↘13 Cwmcarn

Train station Risca

Nearest city Newport

Sat Nav NP11 7EU

Opening times The trails are open 365 days a year, day and night. The only closures are due to forest operations and details are posted on the website mbwales.com. All trails are free. Uplift pass £22-£25 per day

CHRIS MORAN

Location Cwmcarn is a small town around 8 km to the north west of Newport in South Wales. From the M4 exit at junction 28, heading north on A467 past Risca and Crosskeys towards Abercarn. The Cwmcarn Visitor Centre is found by following the brown Forest Drive signs off to the right.

Facilities/Overview Cwmcarn Forest drive is a pretty little valley tucked away from the terraced housing below it and it is up here that you will find the excellent trails that either cling to its contours or dissect them, diving down steeply to the valley floor. However, with perhaps the most efficient uplift service currently operating in the UK, you'll be able to make the most out of your time on this hill. The terrain here is made up of steep sided valleys while the soil is excellent – loamy and buff on the lesser known local trials and super hardpacked on the main routes, ensuring it drains very well and making Cwmcarn a great place to get out on the bike when the weather isn't so kind.

XC With just one waymarked XC trail you'd think the offer is limited here, but as good as the Twrch trail is, explore a little further afield and the riding is epic in every direction. The Twrch trail is suited to those with some previous off-road experience and high level of fitness as the climb is quite tough.

Downhill The Y Mynydd Mojo DH track at Cwmcarn is one of extremes; super fast and with some big lines as well as the availability of smaller easier jumps. One fact is constant though: everything is rollable. At 1.9 km, it's probably not suited to the total beginner, but anyone with some previous DH experience will get plenty of thrills out of this course. Either ride up the Twrch to the start or use the Cwndown uplift service for plenty of runs.

Freeride Cwmcarn has a small freeride area with some drops, tabletops and a superb curved wallride/corkscrew. Many freeriders will be found sessioning the bottom section of the DH course, perfecting their jumping skills. It's just at the top of the Twrch Trail.

Easy For complete novices and young children make use of the Brecon-Monmouth canal which is perfect for gentle rides. Riders with off-road experience should take in the Twrch trail.

Hard Head out on the Twrch trail climbing up to the highest point, then cut up onto the open hill and moorland. Here you can extend your ride as far as your body and mind will allow before finishing your loop back down to the forest drive.

Not to miss Cwmcarn boasts probably the best uplift service currently running in the UK. Cwmdown can transport up to 40 riders on a weekend. A full day ticket is between £22-£25 and you can expect anything up to 13 runs! On-line booking at cwmdown.co.uk.

Remember to avoid Accidentally hitting the infamous quarry jump on the DH course.

Nearest Bike/Hire shop There is a small shop in the Visitor Centre carrying basic spares to keep you on the hill. For more urgent repairs and hire see Martin Ashfield Cycles in Risca and for specialist parts see Sunset MTB or Don Skene Cycles in Cardiff.

Local accommodation
For B&B try the bike-friendly Coed Mamgu Guest House (T01495 270657) situated in the village

at the foot of the forest drive. The forest drive has a campsite with electrical hook up. For those looking for a more cosmopolitan stay, nearby Cardiff and Newport offer plenty of accommodation for all budgets.

Eating Snacks and meals are available at the Cwm Carn Forest Visitor Centre during opening hours. Evening meals are available in local pubs and restaurants; try the Cross Keys for simple bar meals or Vittorio's (T01633 840261) in Newport for a good restaurant meal. Morrisons is the nearest supermarket, is situated on the A469 between Newport and Cwmcarn.

ⓘ **More info** Cwmcarn Forest Drive (T01633 850864), Taxi (T01633 614615), website mbwales.com.

› Lowdown

☺ Locals do

Have lots of secret trails – you'll never find them all!

Use the Cwmdown uplift service to get the most out of their days and get some extra descents in.

Ride to a high standard.

☹ Locals don't

Always park at the centre; many incorporate the centre's trails into longer rides, parking elsewhere.

✓ Pros

A centre that offers all kinds of riding, XC/DH/FR

A great local riding scene with lots of trails.

✗ Cons

You'll wish you had three bikes.

Theft of bikes and bike gear can be a problem from the car park.

FORESTRY COMMISSION WALES

CHRIS MORAN

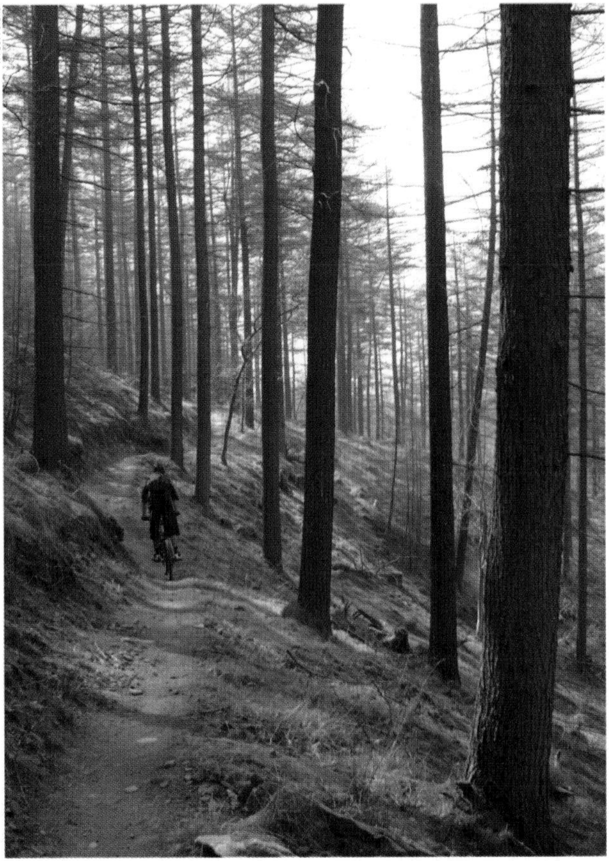

↘14 Foel Gasnach DH

DH FR 4X

Train station Colwyn Bay
Nearest city Chester
Sat Nav LL15 2DN (Cyffylliog)

Location Foel Gasnach is a remote downhill area around 10 km west of Ruthin, deep in the Welsh hills to the east of the Snowdonia National Park. From the west head from Chester on the A55 or from Shrewsbury on the A5 and turn off towards Ruthin on the A494 (from either north or south). At Ruthin, head north on the A525 in the direction of Denbigh, and then after 1.5 km turn off to the left, heading towards Bontuchel first, then Cyffylliog. At Cyffylliog, take the second left heading southwest, and carry on down this road for 2 km, then take the first right at the crossroads just after the red phone box. Stay on this road and take the first left after a large turn-around.

CHRIS MORAN

Facilities Cyffylliog has a small shop and the Red Lion Pub, but the DH tracks are out in the middle of nowhere. When race days are on there is often some supplies and facilities; otherwise bring your own.

Overview This is one of Wales's best downhill sites and is built in conjunction with the Forestry Commission as well as a hard-core team of local riders. Plenty is planned for this venue so expect it to keep getting more popular. Fantastic due to the ability to do self-uplifts (as long as you have a vehicle and a spare driver!) and loved by more advanced riders. Definitely not for beginners due to large drops, big gaps and the presence of danger at every turn.

Terrain There's plenty of unofficial singletrack (including the DH trail), but the majority of the routes here are fire-road if you want to do some exploring.

XC There is XC riding to be had in area, but this is hardcore DH territory so expect to see mostly full suspension rigs.

Downhill There are four downhill trails here, each one with a 100 m vertical drop and demanding a very technical few minutes of your life with steep sections, big jumps and even bigger drops. Foel Gasnach was formed after the loss of the infamous 'Scouse' track in Nannarch. In general the trails are rooty and can be pretty slick in the wet. It is possible to do a lot of runs in a day here and there is a good local scene. The track (and club) are run along with the Forestry Commission and have plenty of comps on through the summer and autumn. There's a pro standard 4X in planning too.

Freeride Freeriders might enjoy the large drops and impressive gaps here. There's a DJ spot in the pipeline for summer '09.

Conditions The downhill here is largely in Forestry Commission land, very remote, and very prone to bad conditions after rain. However, there has been a huge amount of time invested in bridging problem areas and making the tracks weather-worthy, but still best avoided after periods of rain.

ⓘ **More info** foeldhriders.com has all the info you might need, including news on track advancements and races.

↘15 Gethin Woods

XC DH

Train station Pentre-Bach
Nearest city Cardiff
Sat Nav CF48 1HJ (roughly)

CHRIS MORAN

Location Gethin Woods are located just next to the town of Abercanaid, around 2 km south of Merthyr Tydfil. From the M4 exit at junction 32 and head north towards Merthyr Tydfil on the A470. After 15 km you'll come to a roundabout where the A4060 heads off to the right towards Pentrebach. Instead of taking this exit, take the fire-road exit to the left (the first exit), into the Forestry Commission area brown-signed as Gethin Woods. Turn right here and park in a choice of elevated car parks, or go left to self-uplift on the forest fire road.

Facilities Nearby Abercanaid has shops and amenities as well as the Pentre-Bach Railway Station.

Overview Although surrounded by some world-class DH, Gethin can hold its own. There's only one DH trail, but it's got some incredible switch backs at the top, a brilliant rock garden near the bottom and some big gaps to deal with. There's also a whole heap of unofficial single track to be had in the surrounding area, so those on a freeride set up or full suspension XC bike will have a blast. Nearby Mountain Ash is worth a visit too.

Conditions There are some expert mountain bikers round these parts, and they often add to the trail with some purpose building. Drains well but still best avoided in winter.

ⓘ **More info**
dragondownhill.co.uk have uplift days when there's a comp on.

CHRIS MORAN

↘16 Gwydwr Forest

XC DH FR N

Train station Betwys y Coed
Nearest city Chester
Sat Nav LL26 0LB for Llanrwst town centre

Location Gwydyr Forest is around 1 km to the southwest of the town of Llanrwst on the northeast edge of the Snowdonia National Park. From the west, coming in on either the A5 from Shrewsbury or the A55 from Chester, turn onto the A470, which heads directly to Llanrwst. Once in town, head over the river and towards the national park on the B5106 (clearly signed to Snowdonia), then as you near Gwydyr Castle turn left up a minor road into the forest and take the first forest road on your left. The Marin Trail is clearly waymarked from here, and parking is available at Nant Cottage, the start of the trail.

ISOBEL CAMERON/FORESTRY COMMISSION

Facilities Head back to Llanrwst for supplies or into nearby Betws y Coed for their fantastic mountain bike and forest visitor centre.

Overview Gwydyr Forest is home to one fantastic waymarked XC route – the Marin Gwydyr Trail, as well as a whole host of unofficial singletrack routes, fire-roads, bridleways and some secret downhill trails. In addition, some of the loops take in the Betws Y Coed area, and the two mountain bike centres are inter-twined and an absolute must for lovers of beautiful XC riding.

Terrain There's plenty of unofficial and waymarked singletrack, but also a fair bit of fire-road and bridleway.

XC The Marin Gwydyr Trail is a 25-km loop with a 450 m climb/descent that has some technical and rocky riding with stunning views and was one of the first purpose-built trails in the country. The trail contains a lot of forest road that won't be to everyone's taste, but the singletrack is very good and a novice cyclist should be able to complete the loop, perhaps walking the odd section, in around 2-4 hrs.

Downhill Gwydwr forest is littered with DH trails from flowing to super steep and technical. It has long been a stomping ground and training place for much of North Wales's Downhill contingent who have developed some pretty crazy runs. It is important to realise that these are not officially recognised, so you will require some local knowledge to find them.

ISOBEL CAMERON/FORESTRY COMMISSION

Dirt Jumps/Freeride Apart from the challenge of some of the hidden downhills, which are very technical, the forest doesn't offer the freerider any features.

Conditions This is a well-maintained route, with plenty of shale and rock that drains well, and is almost an all-weather area.

ⓘ **More info** The Forestry Commission website (forestry.gov.uk) has a page on Gwydyr Forest; try Beics Betws in Betws y Coed, T01690 710766, or the Snowdonia Cycle Hire and Training, Llandudno, North Wales T01492 878771, while Llanrwst has lots of info on its site, llanrwst.net.

↘17 Kilvey Hill

DH FR

Train station Swansea

Nearest city Swansea

Sat Nav SA1 7AP (roughly – it's an access road for the tower, no postcode)

CHRIS MORAN

CHRIS MORAN

Location Kilvey Hill is just to the east from Swansea city centre. From the M4 exit at junction 45 and take the Neath Road (A4067) south towards Swansea. Go straight at every roundabout and pass the stadium on your left; Kilvey Hill is now just on your left (with the transmission tower on the top). From here follow the brown signs for the Marina (first exit on the roundabout just after the stadium, straight on at the next roundabout, second exit at the next, then first left after this roundabout into Pentre-chwyth Road), and take the first right off this road into the Kilvey Hill car park and start of the sculpture trail.

Facilities Swansea is a major city with plenty of amenities and shops.

Overview At 193 m tall this is a fairly decent descent (especially for inner-city riding), and the views from the top are brilliant – Swansea city centre, docks, bay, Neath, Port Talbot, etc… However, it can be popular with other users. Perhaps this is why the trail – while technically a DH trail – has been adapted (largely by the Swansea student riding population) into more of a freeride trail with plenty of jumps and features that'll please those who love to be in the air. Worth checking out Kilvey and Clyne Woods if you're in the area and for local riders this is one of the best city sites in the UK. There is an access road up to the tower (head into Pentrechwyth and take a right up the hill), but it is for 4x4s only, and the gate is often locked.

Conditions The hill drains well although still best avoided after heavy downpours.

ⓘ **More info** Check out the Swansea Mountain Bike Club, mtbpigs.co.uk.

↘18 Henblas/Caersws nr Newton

DH FR

Train station Caersws
Nearest city Welshpool/Shrewsbury
Sat Nav SY17 5JE

Location Henblas is around 8 km to the west of Newtown, itself between Welshpool and Aberystwyth in mid Wales. From Shrewsbury, take the A458 to Welshpool, then the A483 to Newtown, and then the A470 towards Caersws. After 3 km along the same road, you'll hit Pontdolgoch; here pass the B4568 to Llanwnog, but take the next right (just before the train tracks), and then the second right. Henblas is at the top of this hill.

Facilities Pontdolgoch has a pub and a local shop for supplies; otherwise bring your own.

Overview Henblas is a series of three DH trails that make full use of the fantastic natural terrain and have been added to and built up by the local mountain bike scene. There are regular monthly uplifts run by the landowner and the trails are of expert standard (though with some chicken lines), and are home to the Caersws Cup Downhill series. Expect steep, rugged and technically demanding runs. Has an uplift service during the race days.

Conditions A great place to ride, with three DH runs and tons of different sections, on each of which you could make up a different trail every run. The ground always tends to be drier here than surrounding areas; somehow Cearsws seems to have its own microclimate. A super efficient uplift and a good mix of roots, fast trail, jumps and technical sections means it's a great place to spend the day. Uplifts can be organized with the landowner; you will need a group of 15 or more to book the day. To arrange an uplift day call T07977 987755.

ⓘ **More info** The Caersws Cup has its own website at caerswscup.co.uk.

↘19 Llantrisant Woods DH

XC DH

Train station Pontyclun
Nearest city Cardiff
Sat Nav CF72 9XA for Lanelay Road

Location Llantrisant Woods are just to the west of the town of Llantrisant, itself around 10 km north west from Cardiff. From the M4 exit at junction 34 and take the A4119 towards Llantrisant. Take a left at the first roundabout onto the A473, then over the next roundabout (with the McDonalds on it), then take a right at the next roundabout towards Talbot Green on Lanelay Road and immediately take the first left up a dirt track. The Forestry Commission car park is on the left some way up this fire-road.

Facilities Talbot Green and Llantrisant have plenty of shops and facilities but the forest area is a BYO spot.

Overview There are two DH trails in this area of forest, both of which have plenty of armoured sections, good jumps and decent lengths (expect rides of around 3 mins for good riders). The top sections are fantastic singletrack through dense forest, while the mid and lower areas open out into fast, feature-full lines of flowing jumps and fire-road sections. Well worth a visit.

Conditions This is a well-maintained site, with potentially muddy upper sections but well-drained lower, gravelly areas. Lots of roots make it slick in the wet. Best ridden in the dry when the trails are running fast, as the hill is not too steep. Many riders trail ride here and come down the DH routes as part of a longer XC ride.

ⓘ **More info** To get involved with the Llantrisant MTB Club, and to help out building the trails, contact Sean at msoc1976@hotmail.com. Good trail cam action of Llantrisant can be found on Youtube.

↘20 Llanwrtyd Wells

Train station Llanwrtyd
Nearest city Swansea
Sat Nav LD5 4BA

Location Llanwrtyd Wells is a small village in the middle of Wales, around 15 km north of the Brecon Beacons. The town sits on the A483 and can only be reached via this main thoroughfare from either the northeast or the southwest.

Facilities/Overview Llanwrtyd Wells – via the Green Events company – has changed its fame from being a mineral springs resort to the world capital of crazy escapades such as the bog snorkelling world championships, a peculiar but brilliantly entertaining event that has now sprung an off shoot – the bike bog snorkelling event. Those aside, there is plenty to make this town stand out; rolling hills and rugged mountains, spectacular passes and gentle valleys, open pastures and thick forest, trickling streams and, perhaps most interesting, the Mid Wales Beer Festival.

Overview Not so much a Forestry Centre as the other featured Welsh sites as the riding from Llanwrtyd is mostly around the town. Some trails are waymarked and maps can be collected from the town; other routes are not and require a bit of headwork. Nearby Coed Trallwm has three short forest trails and a lovely café (see the Coed Trallwm page). Many riders base themselves in Llanwrtyd then head over to the excellent Elan Valley singletracks. Perhaps the best way to learn the multitude of tracks here is to combine your visit with an event such as the Red Kite Mountain bike bash or the Real Ale Wobble. See the Green Events website for more details, green-events.co.uk.

Terrain Some of the trails around the town tend to be out in the open country and can be quite soft going if it has been very wet.

XC A great place for the purist XC rider as so many of the trails follow old bridleways and paths and it really does have a different feel to the other Welsh trail centres. There's no better way to explore than to book into the Real Ale Wobble. This is held once a year and is a non-competitive event based on having a good time. Half pints of ale are provided at check points and the route is marked out so that hopefully even the most inebriated will find their way home…

Downhill Although there are numerous big hills and mountains around Llanwrtyd Wells, there are no DH trails and no DH scene in the surrounding towns.

Dirt Jumps/Freeride There are no trails or facilities suited to freeriders.

Conditions Some of the trails around the town tend to be out in the open country and can be quite soft going if it has been very wet.

ⓘ **More info** Green Events put on most of the activities, green-events.co.uk; Llanwrytd Wells Visitor Centre (T01591 610666), website mbwales.com.

ANDY LLOYD

S21 Maindy Road BMX Track

4X DJ

Train station Cardiff
Nearest city Cardiff
Sat Nav CF24 4HL

Location Maindy Road is just to the north of Cardiff city centre. From the M4 exit at junction 32 and head into Cardiff on the A470. After 3 km you'll pass through the suburb of Maindy. Turn off left into Maindy Road and the BMX track is immediately on your left, and clearly visible from the road.

Facilities Maindy is a city suburb with plenty of shops and amenities.

Overview This is an old BMX track that has undergone a renovation in recent years with a complete overhaul by the guys at Dragon Downhill in 2005. It's a tight track which you can pump all the way around, either gapping all the jumps or rolling them. Good for those just learning and wanting to perfect their bike handling skills before hitting proper DJs. Blackweir DJs are nearby, but unofficial, so ask at Maindy for directions and local riders should give you directions.

Conditions This is an inner-city site which is half concrete – the drop in and some corners – and half DJs. It drains well but still avoid in the rain.

ⓘ **More info** Check out the cad drawings on dragondownhill.co.uk.

Right: Moelfre local and world champion Rachel Atherton in action.

S22 Moelfre

XC DH FR 4X

Train station Gobowen
Nearest city Oswestry
Sat Nav CV32 7UA

Location Moelfre is an area of oustanding natural beauty around 10 km to the west of Oswestry, just inside the Welsh border. From Shrewsbury (itself off the M6 and M54), head north west towards Oswestry on the A5. At Oswestry, take the B4580 heading for Rhydycroesau on the border with Wales. Carry on a further 5 km on this road and turn to the right, signed Moelfre. There's plenty of XC trails but the downhill should be fairly obvious, being cut into the side of the open fields to the northeast of the village.

Facilities The leisure centre nearby is the closest place to get supplies, although Leamington is full of shops and amenities.

DAN BROWN

Overview This is one of the best DH tracks in the UK, and has helped shape champions Gee, Dan and Rachel Atherton (as well as being home to numerous NPS DH events). The trail is around 3 minutes long for a decent rider, and cuts through open fields where features have been built to accommodate dips, gulleys and jumps. There are plenty of chicken lines, good jumps (including a large drop at the top section) to challenge good riders and the high-speed open fields and natural corners and undulations are fantastic for all levels. There's also a 4X track, and uplift days are frequent (as are camping weekends with uplift included).

Conditions This is open land with no trees, good, fast-draining top layer, and some rocky, gritty sections. Very fast.

ⓘ **More info** borderline-events.co.uk run uplift sessions.

↘23 Mountain Ash DH

XC DH

Train station Merthyr Tydfil
Nearest city Cardiff
Sat Nav CF45 4LJ (roughly)

Location Mountain Ash is a small town on the A470 between Cardiff and Merthyr Tydfil. From the M4 exit at junction 32 and head north on the A470 in the direction of Merthyr Tydfil. Head past Pontypridd, then at the first roundabout take a left on the A4059 heading in the direction of Aberdare/Mountain Ash. After 4 km take a left into the forest access road signposted Lletti Turner Woods. Park at the bottom before the metal access gate (if you want to be sure of being able to exit), or head up the road for 150 m to the car park, from where the trails start.

Facilities Mountain Ash – further up on the A4059 – has shops and amenities, as there are no facilities at the trails.

Overview This is a first-class downhill site, built and maintained by Dragon Downhill. It's a fast DH without many obstacles (though this may change); there is an uplift on competition days or when Dragon Downhill organize one, so check their website. Well worth a journey and especially worth it if you're in the area and want a fast, smooth DH day out. Park on the road at the bottom and then either ride up the forest road to the top or push up the trail to section it bit by bit. This is a working forest though and the trail is subject to closures.

Conditions The top section is rooty, but there are plenty of rocks around and some very slippery slate. This is Forestry Commission land, and rarely used except by other riders.

ⓘ **More info** For organized uplifts see dragondownhill.co.uk.

CHRIS MORAN

↘24 Ponciau Banks

4X DJ

Train station Wrexham
Nearest city Wrexham
Sat Nav LL14 2LA

Location Ponciau Banks BMX Track is in Rhosllanerchrugog, 4 km southwest of Wrexham in Ponciau Banks Park. From the A483 from Wrexham or Oswestry take the turnoff for Rhosllanerchrugog (the B5426), then take a right at Chapel Street and a left on Clarke Street. Ponciau Banks Park is at the end of this road.

Facilities Rhosllanerchrugog is a small town but it has plenty of shops and facilities and the park is right in the town centre.

Overview This is a beautifully sculpted pump track that's great on a mountain bike or a BMX and will polish up those jumping, manualing and pumping skills in no time. Some of the jumps are quite advanced but most people will have a great time riding this track. It's been designed to be ridden in several different styles and directions. Situated about 10 minutes from Llandegla trail centre so can be incorporated into a trip there.

Conditions This is a purpose-built mountain bike and BMX centre built by Dragon Downhill. It's a concrete/tarmac surface and was put in at the end of 2006, so drains well and has modern lines.

ⓘ **More info** dragondownhill.co.uk.

↘25 Machynlleth

Train station Machynlleth
Nearest city Welshpool/Shrewsbury
Sat Nav SY20 8EB
Opening times The trails are open 365 days a year, day and night. The only closures are due to forest operations and details are posted on the website mbwales.com. All trails are free although there is a pay and display car park in Machynlleth centre and an honesty box at the Climax Trail

Location Machynlleth is a town on the southwest edge of the Snowdonia National Park, just a few kilometres inland from the Irish Sea. From the east, head in from Shrewsbury, take the A5 towards Welshpool, then take the A458 towards Machynlleth, all well signposted as they're the biggest towns in the area.

Facilities/Overview The town of Machynlleth is the ancient capital of Wales and is now well known for its Centre for Alternative Technology and the town's eco-friendly slant on modern living. Don't look for major chain stores here – nearly every one the shops and stores on the high streets of Machynlleth, Aberdyfi and Tywyn are owner-occupied traders and businesses. As British towns become more and more like clones of each other, it is a refreshing change walking around Machynlleth. Riding from Machynlleth itself there are three waymarked trails: the Mach 1, 2 and 3. These are suitable for the bikers who enjoy a steadier form of biking, Mach 1 being the shortest at 16 km and Mach 3 being the longest at 30 km. The thrill seekers amongst you will do better to head up the Dyfi valley to the Climax Trail in Dyfi forest. This 16-km loop is packed with fast, sweeping singletrack and the final descent just keeps on flowing.

XC The three Mach trails will get you out into the hills but to truly make the most of the Dyfi valley, go and speak to the guys in the bike shop for some great natural XC riding. The Mach trails (1, 2 and 3) are all waymarked from town, with 1 being southwest from town heading out on the A487 towards Aberystwyth, while Mach 2 and 3 are on the same road in the opposite direction.

Downhill There are no DH specific trails in the area, although on a short travel suspension bike you can have a lot of fun on the Climax trails descents.

Freeride No freeride trails although the 'Eye of the Needle' drop on the Climax Trail would challenge some of the best riders.

> Lowdown

Locals do
Loop back up the forest road to ride the final descent of the climax again.

Have a wealth of natural riding in the Dyfi valley.

Locals don't
Ride when there has been heavy frost – the trail gets very sticky.

Pros
Healthy living, alternative, bike-friendly town.

Cons
Limited without exploration or guide.

ANDY LLOYD

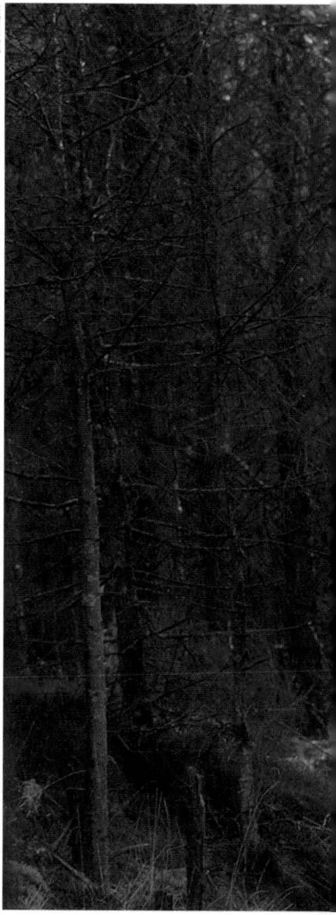

Easy The Mach 1 is a Blue Trail of 16 km with some tarmac sections and some staggering views.

Hard The 30 km Mach 3 is the toughest of the bunch with the most technical DH section in 'The Chute'.

Not to miss The pleasant town with its no-chain policy.

Remember to avoid Trying to open a Starbucks here.

Nearest Bike/Hire shop The Holy Trail Bike Shop in Machynlleth (T01654 700411) will look after you.

Local accommodation There's a range of accommodation available in this popular tourist town. The Dyfi Guest B&B, T01654 702562 is very bike friendly.

Eating There are no big commercial chains, so expect quality local produce and while you'll pay a little more, it's so much better; try the Maengwyn Café (T01654 702126).

ⓘ **More info** Machynlleth Tourist Info (T01654 702401), website dyfimountainbiking.org.uk.

↘26 Nant yr Arian

XC DH FR Kids Camping

Train station Aberystwyth

Nearest city Aberystwyth

Sat Nav SY23 3AD (for Ponterwyd)

Opening times The trails are open 365 days a year, day and night. The only closures are due to forest operations and details are posted on the website mbwales.com. All trails are free, though parking is £1

FORESTRY COMMISSION WALES

Location Nant yr Arian is around 13 km east of Aberystwyth in mid Wales. Assuming you're coming in from the west on the A44, pass through the village of Ponterwyd, then after 2 km take there's a bus-stop (for the 525 bus); directly opposite is the car park entrance for the trails.

Facilities/Overview There is no town at Nant yr Arian forest itself; the only thing staying there are the Red Kites… Aberystwyth is the nearest town at a 15-minute drive away and is a coastal resort surrounded by three hills with a busy student community and some 50 pubs that retains a friendly, community feel. Nant yr Arian forest sits high on the mountains just inland from Aberystwyth, and offers stunning high-level wilderness riding with trails heading out into the epic scenery of the Cambrian Mountains. This is a fantastic area for those who like their riding rugged; just be prepared for everything, from true mountain climbs to river crossings to technical rocky descents.

XC There are three main reasons for coming here – the Pandam Trail, Summit Trail, and Syfydrin Trial – which offer up some true all-mountain riding and run across exposed moorland and through tight, technical singletrack. Pandam is a short (9 km) blue-graded taster trail; Summit is the longer singletrack (16 km) slog, while Syfydrin is the expert and gruelling

FORESTRY COMMISSION WALES

trail at 35 km long. Summit and Syfydrin are both graded red.

Downhill There are no official downhill trails in Nant yr Arian, but call into Summit Cycles in Aberstwyth and they can tell you where the locals have their DH courses.

Freeride There are no specific freeride trails here, but for those who like being in the air, there are certainly some features on the trails that will keep you interested. Also, there's the incredibly impressive Sandjumps DJ spot nearby.

Easy Start on the Pandam area to get your bearings and legs back if it's been a while since you were in the saddle!

Hard There are plenty of hard lines to explore on the Syfydrin trail.

Not to miss The views from the top of the Summit Trail.

Remember to avoid Travelling here in less than perfect weather.

Nearest Bike/Hire shop The excellent Summit Cycles (T01970 626061) are based in Aberystwyth and sponsor the 'Summit trail' at Nant yr Arian.

Local accommodation
The George Barrow Hotel is a mere 1.5km from the visitor centre, and well used to looking after mountain bikers. thegeorgebarrowhotel.co.uk (T01970 890230).

Eating In Aberystwyth, The Honoured Guest (T01970 617617) is the best restaurant but it's a pretty cheap and cheerful place to find food; otherwise, there are limited supplies.

> Lowdown

Locals do
Rip down the 'Mask of Zorro' descent.

Ride in groups.

Locals don't
Ride the Syfydrin trail without appropriate protective gear.

Pros
Varied trail riding and vibrant seaside town.

Cons
Limited facilities for non XC riders.

ⓘ **More info** mbwales.com, aberystwyth-online.co.uk, Summit Cycles has a trails section at summitcycles.co.uk, Aberystwyth has a local riding hub via the Chainslappers Crew at freewebs.com/chainslappers/aberridingspots.htm.

FORESTRY COMMISSION WALES

↘27 Rheola DH Trail

DH

Train station Neath
Nearest city Swansea
Sat Nav SA11 4DU (roughly)

Location Rheola DH is just to the south edge of the Brecon Beacons, around 18 km to the northeast of Swansea. From the M4 exit at junction 43 and head towards Neath on the A465 for 10 km, reaching Blaengwrach and then Glyn Neath. Take the left after the McDonalds onto the B4242 Glyn Neath Road. The entrance is 4 km down this road, on the right opposite a lay-by before the village of Pentreclwydau.

Facilities Glyn Neath or Resolven are the nearest towns with facilities.

Overview Rheola's one DH trail has hosted many rounds of the British National Series and also the National Championships. It is a technical DH course that is overall quite fast but has a few slower, tricky sections. The trail contains lots of bus stops and is quite rough with lots of exposed rock. There are potential uplift days when there are comps on (check the website), otherwise this is a push-up area, well worth a visit for good riders while learners and intermediates might find other trails in the area more rewarding.

Conditions Exposed rock and roots give good riders a challenge. Otherwise this is a beautiful area with few intruders so expect to see few people save for other riders.

ⓘ **More info** dragondownhill.co.uk.

↘28 Rudry DJs

DJ

Train station Aber
Nearest city Cardiff
Sat Nav CF83 3DP

Location Rudry Dirt Jumps are not too far from the fantastic Caerphilly DJs, both around 5 km to the north of Cardiff. From the M4, exit at junction 32 heading north on the A470 to Pontypridd. After 3 km, take the A468 to Caerphilly town centre. Head through the centre of town on Nantgarw Road, then straight on into Bedwas Road (the B4600). After 1 km you'll hit a roundabout; take the last exit (signed to Rudry), then the first left (again signed to Rudry). Head down here for 2 km then turn right off Starbuck Street just after the houses. The DJs are just up this road in the copse of trees to the right.

Facilities Head back to Caerphilly for main supplies, although there is a small shop on Starbuck Street.

Overview These are some low-budget DJs built near the famous Caerphilly public access jumps. They are smaller than Caerphilly and would suit those looking to learn. Definitely worth a visit for those in the area, or for those overwhelmed by Caerphilly.

Conditions A hard-packed base all set in a small clearing of trees. Please don't ride them when they're wet, and be sure to fix any damage.

ⓘ **More info** dragondownhill.co.uk.

↘29 Sandjumps

DJ

Train station Aberystwyth
Nearest city Aberystwyth
Sat Nav SY25 6DN (Miner's Head pub)

Location Sandjumps are on the edge of a disused lead mine 10 km to the southeast of Aberystwyth. Approaching from the west on the A44, head towards Aberystwyth. At Ponterwyd, take the A4120 south. At Devils Bridge take a left onto the B4343. Head down here for 4 km and take a right at the T junction towards Ysbyty Ystwyth. At Pontrhydygroes turn off to the right, then after 500 m take a left (at the stone cottage) heading towards the river. Follow this road to the end. The DJs are on the right.

Facilities There's a pub back in Pontrhydygroes, but this is open land remote from most facilities.

Overview These are some fantastic DJs fashioned from the black sand deposits left by the old lead mine. There are a huge variety of hips, gaps, doubles and drops scattered around the area, perfect for beginners and pro riders. Worth a detour if in the area, or a longer journey for those who love DJs.

Conditions The DJs are made of a black sand deposit, and drain well, but as always, avoid in the rain and please fix any broken landings.

ⓘ **More info** Local riders the Chainslappers Crew have built most of the trails. Help with the next push by going to freewebs.com/chainslappers/aberridingspots.htm.

↘30 Snowdonia National Park

XC DH FR

Train station Llanrwst/Betws y Coed
Nearest city Chester
Sat Nav LL55 4EU (to Pete's Eats, Llanberis)

Location Snowdonia National Park (Parc Cenedlaethol Eryri in Welsh) is a protected parkland area of some 2170 sq km in the north west corner of Wales and contains the country's highest mountain – the 1085-m Mt Snowdon. From the west head in on either the A5 (from Shrewsbury in the south), or from Chester on the A55. Either way, the town to head for is Llanberis, in the north west corner of the park, home to the local mountain bike, climbing and social scene nearest the mountains. Llanberis is on the A4086 between Capel Curig in the west and Caernarfon in the east.

Facilities Snowdonia is an area of outstanding natural beauty, and a hugely popular destination for all lovers of the outdoors. As such, there are plenty of cafés and visitor centres dotted around the immense national park, and each town is a picture-perfect little tourist hub with gift shops and amenities. There's almost too much to cover in one page and certainly too much to go into in any detail.

Overview There is an astounding amount of XC riding to be had in the area, as well as numerous DH tracks, some with the ability to have uplift if you've got a car. You will have to share the area with walkers and other mountain users, and clashes do happen. Please ride with respect. For those looking for purpose-built trail centres, the Coed Y Brenin centre north of Dolgellau is the place to head. See the Coed page in this book. There are other waymarked XC routes too, most notably Gwydyr Forest (featuring the Marin Trail, Myndd Cribau and Penmachno waymarked routes), along with plenty of unofficial singletrack to explore and self-navigate around. Otherwise, for downhill, go to Llanberis and hit some of the biggest mountains in the UK.

Terrain There's plenty of unofficial singletrack, but the majority of the routes here are fire-road, open land, or rambling routes.

XC For true XC riding there are a number of guide books specifically on long routes in the National Park, available at the local bike shop. We suggest Best MTB Trails in Snowdonia, 25 routes for Llanrwst, Betws-Gwydyr, Coed Y Brenin, Llanberis and Conwy Mtn (bike-fax.com).

Downhill The three most popular trails are Moel Cynghorion, Moel Eilio and Snowdon itself. This is one of the most thrilling descents in the UK, with the trail being partly the bridleway back to Llanberis (which can be congested with walkers). It's a very rocky descent with big drops and slate surface in parts (which can cut both tyres and skin!). Locals often push up the Festiniog Railway track – which can take up to 2 hours – but the reward is a 1000-m descent of up to 20 minutes. For a more detailed breakdown of location and expected terrain for all the routes, look on the Pete's Eats website (see below).

Dirt Jumps/Freeride There is no specific or purpose-built northshore or freeride area in the Snowdonia (though there are some armoured bridges on the Mynydd Cribau route), but with such a huge area to cover there is an enormous scope for finding and sessioning some good spots, from road gaps to neolithic northshore to root jumps. Call in to Energy Cycles in Llanberis (T01286 871892) for some local hidden spots! Remember to call into Pete's Eats café too – said by many to be the 'best café in the world' and an incredible source of local mountain biking information.

Conditions Everything from forest land, hidden singletrack through to high-speed open field running.

ⓘ **More info** Perhaps the best source of info on the region is Pete's Eats Café (petes-eats.co.uk), while snowbikers.com run a 'Ride With a Guide' session, taking groups of all levels and abilities on routes they might find suitable.

↘31 Wentwood DH

XC DH FR

Train station Newport
Nearest city Cardiff
Sat Nav N/A

Location Wentwood DH is around 15 km to the northeast of Newport, in South Wales. From the M4 exit at junction 24 and take the A48 in the direction of Chepstow. After 4 km exit to the left in the direction of Parc Seymour. Pass through the village and head out on the north road in the direction of Pen-y-Cae-Mawr. Head 2.5 km up this road, then take a right off the road into the Wentwood Car Park. For more detailed directions email Wentwood through the website address below.

Facilities There are few facilities on site, save for on race days (which are fairly frequent with Dragon Downhill being involved in this part of the world), when some hot and cold drinks and snacks turn up. Otherwise, this is a BYO site. Nearby Parc Seymour has shops and amenities.

Overview This is a fantastic, locally-maintained rider set-up, which is run in conjunction with the Forestry Commission and Dragon Downhill. Wentwood has seen plenty of competitions in its day, and is one of the UK's premier downhill destinations, perfect for intermediate to good riders looking for a new challenge. It's also out of the way, meaning you're unlikely to encounter anyone save for other riders.

Terrain Mostly singletrack, with the DH trail being a mixture of re-inforced bridges, purpose-built jumps, and fantastic rootsy, rocky, natural terrain. The top section is soil, with the bottom area being more rocky.

XC There's plenty of unofficial XC which isn't marked but easily found. With so many natural trails it's a good place for XC and the DH trail complements this set-up. Perfect for any bike really.

Downhill There is one DH trail here, which is approximately 760 m of fantastic riding, with plenty of chicken lines for those who aren't up for hitting the bigger jumps. There's a full description of the track on the Wentwood website (see below), but this is definitely worth a journey to session.

Dirt Jumps/Freeride There are several jumps down the DH track, so those on a freeride set-up will find plenty to occupy their time.

Conditions The XC routes are hard-packed dirt singletrack, while the downhill trail is purpose-built and well maintained. All are on a red clay base which gets very slick in the wet, so as always, avoid after periods of heavy rain.

ⓘ **More info** Wentwood has its own website at wentwooddownhill.co.uk, or the Forestry Commission has a Wentwood page at forestry.gov.uk.

CHRIS MORAN

Local riders
Rowan Sorrell

Bike Orange Blood 224, Alpine 160
Local spot Wentwood, Cwmcarn
Club member Afraid not, there are so many riders in south Wales you don't need clubs.
Age 28
Type of rider Skids and wheelies kind of guy

ANDY LLOYD

Where's the one place you'd recommend above all, for those coming to Wales?

RS Glyncorrwg, good trails and great centre.

Where has the best XC?

RS I'd have to say the Afan Forest park.

Where is the best Downhill?

RS Cwmcarn or Caersws – they're both good fun.

The best dirt jumps?

RS Swansea: the scene is going off there but invite only I'm afraid.

If you were to take a family out – say a cousin who's visiting with his kids – where would you head?

RS Head straight for Brechfa green and blue trails, they'd love it.

What secret stashes do you know about?

RS Plenty – but they are secret…

If you were a huge fan of cake and wanted to find the best trail with a foodie pit stop, where would it be?

RS The Drop Off Café in Glyncorrwg is the place to be.

Where, if anywhere, outside of your area do you often visit with your bike?

RS Redhills in the Forest of Dean.

Which websites have the best info on your local area?

RS If you want people to show you round the trails then try mtb-wales.com.

Which is the best shop to head to if you're in Wales?

RS Skyline cycles in Glyncorrwg – they have good mechanics, loads of stock and they're located bang on the trail head.

Rowan taking on a rock garden.

BUT STILL IT SATISFIES

Southern Scotland

↘ Overview 214
↘ Local riders, Chris Ball 216
↘ Ae Forest (7Stanes) 218
↘ Dalbeattie (7Stanes) 220
↘ Drumlanrig Castle 222
↘ Glentress (7Stanes) 224
↘ Glentrool (7Stanes) 226
↘ Innerleithen (7Stanes) 228
↘ The Jedforest Trails 230
↘ Safety, Steve Ireland 231
↘ Kirroughtree (7Stanes) 232
↘ Mabie (7Stanes) 234
↘ Newcastleton 236

Ae Forest's 'Stane' – halfway round the Omega Man trail, one of the best in Southern Scotland.
[CHRIS MORAN]

Southern Scotland

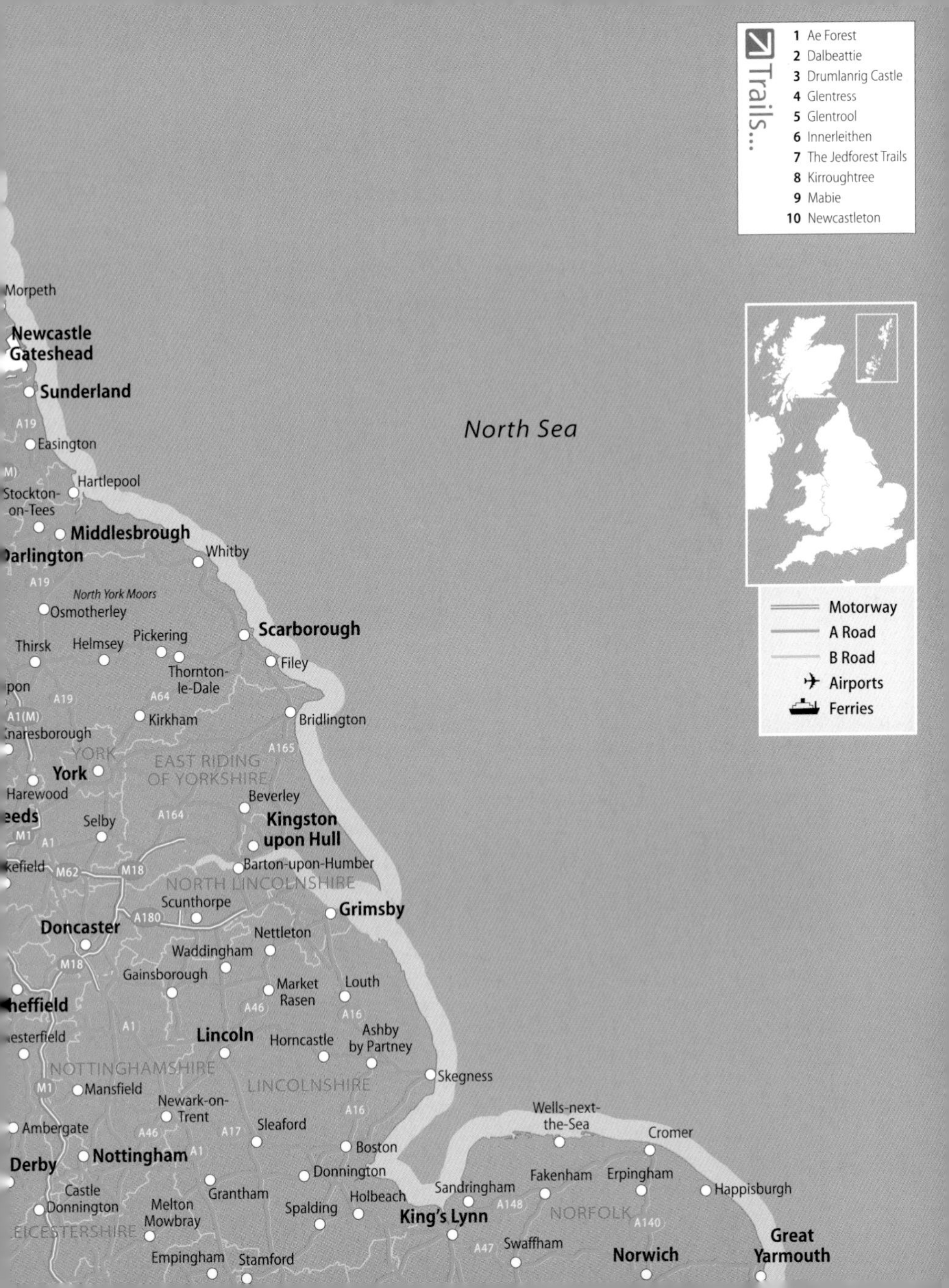
Trails...
1 Ae Forest
2 Dalbeattie
3 Drumlanrig Castle
4 Glentress
5 Glentrool
6 Innerleithen
7 The Jedforest Trails
8 Kirroughtree
9 Mabie
10 Newcastleton
North Sea
Motorway
A Road
B Road
Airports
Ferries
Morpeth
Newcastle
Gateshead
Sunderland
Easington
Hartlepool
Stockton-on-Tees
Middlesbrough
Whitby
North York Moors
Osmotherley
Scarborough
Thirsk
Helmsey
Pickering
Thornton-le-Dale
Filey
Kirkham
Bridlington
York
EAST RIDING OF YORKSHIRE
Harewood
Beverley
Selby
Kingston upon Hull
Barton-upon-Humber
NORTH LINCOLNSHIRE
Scunthorpe
Grimsby
Doncaster
Nettleton
Waddingham
Gainsborough
Market Rasen
Louth
Lincoln
Horncastle
Ashby by Partney
NOTTINGHAMSHIRE
Skegness
Mansfield
LINCOLNSHIRE
Newark-on-Trent
Ambergate
Sleaford
Wells-next-the-Sea
Cromer
Boston
Nottingham
Derby
Donnington
Fakenham
Erpingham
Castle Donnington
Grantham
Sandringham
Happisburgh
Melton Mowbray
Spalding
Holbeach
King's Lynn
NORFOLK
Swaffham
Great Yarmouth
Norwich
Empingham
Stamford
A19
A64
A165
A164
M1
A1
M62
M18
A180
A46
A16
A17
A148
A140
A47

Southern Scotland is of course dominated by the mighty 7 Stanes project – a Forestry Commission initiative that takes in seven purpose-built trail centres all south of Glasgow and Edinburgh. They are perhaps the UK's most visited riding centres, and it's easy to see why: each with its own distinct characteristic, the areas offer fantastic facilities such as cafés, bike shops and visitor centres, absolutely world class trails, jaw-dropping views and careful, thoughtful layouts. Their website – 7stanes.gov.uk – has a wealth of info including videos and maps, and an explanation as to the name (each trail centre features a 'Stane' or sculpture, and they hope you'll try and visit each one to complete your experience). Roughly speaking Ae Forest is the family-friendly but freeride-heavy site, Dalbeattie is perfect for riders who love the rockier side of things, Kirroughtree is another family-friendly area with incredible singletrack, Glentress is the flagship centre, being closest to Edinburgh, and features absolutely everything you could wish for, Glentrool is the perfect introductory 'Stane', Innerleithen is the full downhill set up and just next door to Glentress, Mabie is the place to head if you like northshore, while Newcastleton is the beautiful, empty, gentle giant of the centres. But of course, there are exceptions to these rules, and each centre has lots of diversity.

But southern Scotland has more to offer, and the absolutely stunning Jedburgh Forest (shortened to Jedforest Trails), are for lovers of route-finding, proper old-school mountain biking, with the added bonus that you can ride back to England and join up with some of the Kielder routes. Meanwhile, Drumlanrig Castle is simply out of this world. Its trails are first class, the setting is exactly as one would imagine for a Scottish Castle, and it is where the bicycle was actually invented! All in all, southern Scotland is perhaps the most exciting area in the UK for its diverse range of mountain biking.

Local scene

Scotland's strengths are undoubtedly its bona fide mountains, its tourist infrastructure, and in a few places (Fort William, Glencoe and Innerleithen), permanent uplift operations. The riding scene is growing at an incredible rate, thanks no doubt to both the increase in the number of trail centres and the raised awareness that the Fort William World Cup has brought to Scottish mountain biking. The country has a vast amount of open space in comparison to England and Wales yet its centres are generally located quite conveniently close together, making it possible to tour through the whole country taking in the sights, sounds, culture and trails in an exciting and packed two-week break. Of course if you do have the motivation and nerve to trek across the open land now accessible to mountain bikers, then the possibilities are quite literally endless, but it is not for the inexperienced or unprepared as you can ride for days without seeing a soul in some of the more remote areas of the country.

Hubs

Scotland has a great scene on both social and competitive levels. The hub sites of Innerleithen and Fort William are developing internationally competitive riders; indeed, Innerleithen is home to a Scottish Junior Downhill World Champion, Ruaridh Cunningham. At the trail centres, fed by the central lowlands where most of Scotland's population lives, there are regular meets between riders often organized through the many web forums. The larger centres really encourage a chilled riding experience where you can hang out in their onsite cafés and bike shops. There is both a Scottish Downhill and a Scottish Cross Country race series which are very popular and use the best venues in the country, see sda-races.com and sxc.org.uk. Probably the most extensively used Scottish website is descent-world.co.uk, which is more focused on the downhill side of the sport but the forums are full of trail meets too. There are companies who are making the most of the landscape by offering guiding services off the beaten track (see mountainbiketrax.co.uk) and then there is Dirt School, offering coaching to all abilities of riders, dirtschool.co.uk.

⑩ Best rides in Scotland

For the most varied, wild, and exhilarating rides in the UK, Scotland is the place to head. Below are 10 of the very best centres.

❶ Glentress, page 224

Simply put, Glentress is the most well-rounded trail set up currently operating in the UK. It has every grade of trail from the most family-friendly through to the hardest of hardcore; there's a super-friendly vibe, and a brand-new visitor centre scheduled to open during 2009.

❷ Fort William, page 246

Fort Bill's infamous downhill track constantly wins the rider's vote of 'best run' by world cup downhillers. Add in a brilliant 4X track, some incredible XC riding, and the UK's only gondola uplift, and it's definitely on the must visit list.

❸ Ae Forest, page 218

One of the coolest 7 Stanes set ups features the unbelievable Omega Man trail, a twisting, turning freeride beast which is perfect for a day's excitement.

❹ Drumlanrig Castle, page 222

Rik Allsop has built what can only be described as magical trails. Add in the castle, a cool vibe, some wonderful countryside and perfect terrain, and this is the Afan of the north.

❺ Isle of Arran, page 252

If you want your trails truly, truly empty, with staggering views and beautiful villages to visit, then this easily-accessible isle is the place to head.

❻ Innerleithen, page 228

In terms of downhill riding, Innerleithen offers more varied tracks than Fort William, and for those living in Glasgow and Edinburgh (or south of the border), it's a lot closer than the Highland centre.

❼ Mabie, page 234

If it's northshore that floats your boat, then the Kona Darkside has nearly 4 km of wood to test your nerve, balance and skill. There are beautiful views too, but you'll probably be too focused on the 10 cm-wide sections to notice.

❽ Golspie Highland Wildcat Trails, page 250

The Highland Wildcat Trails up at Golspie have staggering views over the Moray Firth and the North Sea oilrigs, not to mention some incredible flowing trails.

❾ Laggan Wolftrax, page 256

Laggan offers just one trail from each of the possible grades, from super easy to very tricky. While some might think that's not a huge choice, the fact that each run is absolute perfection makes this a fantastic, well-rounded Highland's site.

❿ The Kyle of Sutherland Trails, page 254

It's a long way north, but the fact that you get to stay in a truly wonderful castle (for next to nothing), and get to ride some empty, flowing and beautiful trails will more than make up for the journey.

CHRIS MORAN

CHRIS MORAN

The entire town of Innerleithen is made from bike parts salvaged from the hill.

CHRIS MORAN

Local riders
Chris Ball

Chris Ball spent six years on the UCI Downhill circuit and is a former Scottish national Champ. He now coaches the Scottish youth and junior MTb Teams (leading to Ruaridh Cunningham to a gold at the Junior World Championships) as well as running a public coaching service named 'Dirt School'. See the fantastic dirtschool.co.uk for more info.

You've got friends visiting for just one weekend and they can go anywhere in Scotland. Name the one place you'd definitely have to take them.

CB Scotland is small and compact enough to squeeze more than one trail into a weekend. Based in the Tweed valley, the trails at Glentress and Innerleithen are a must and could both be done in a long day or taken at an easier pace over a couple of days.

Which trail centre or resort has the best party scene or the best after-riding activities?

CB For pubs you want to choose the trails nearest to the bigger towns. You can have a good night in Peebles – not far from Glentress – or Fort William, near Laggan and the Witches Trail. For a bigger night, to Edinburgh, only 25 miles from Glentress and Innerleithen.

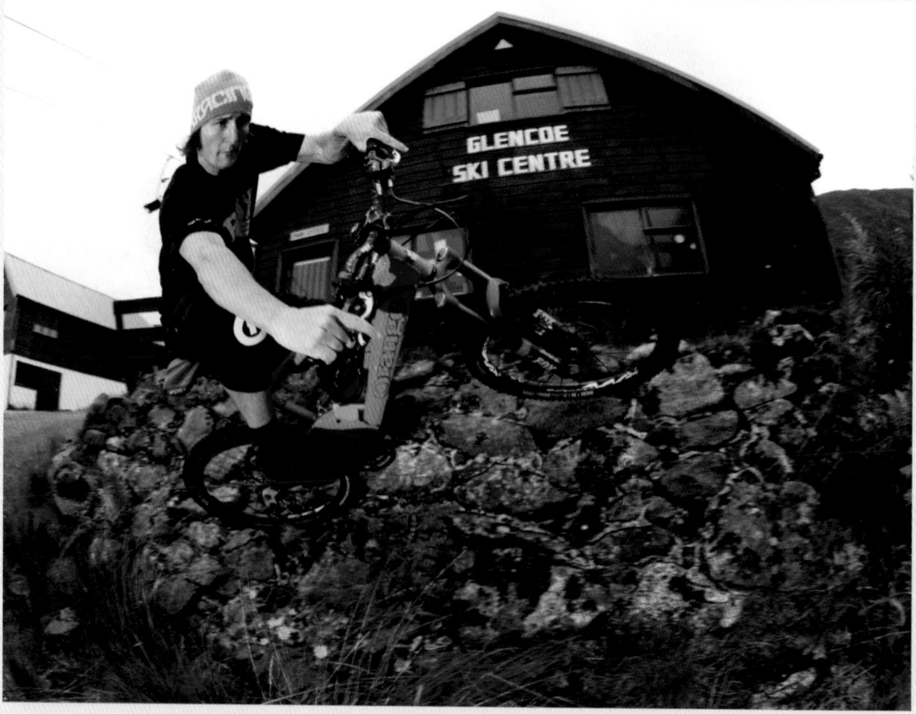

Where did you learn to ride, and where would you send beginners to ride?

CB The great thing about Scotland is its variety. I learnt on the massive roots and rocks of Dunkeld, the flat out fast straights of Fort William and the tight technical forestry of the Tweed Valley.

There are more green and blue routes now than ever before so try the blue at Golspie for sandy trails and great sea views, or Glentress for a huge variety of all levels of trails.

Where's best for mixed ability groups?

CB Some of the larger centres like Mabie, Glentess, Drumlanrig and Laggan have a good mix of trails all near to each other. That way the group can stay together and everyone can enjoy the day. These sites also have cafés so riders wanting a shorter day can relax with a coffee whilst waiting for the others to return from their epic.

Where's the best place for views, sunsets, or just total rustic charm, etc?

CB Without a doubt, the summit of Golspie has to have the best views of any black route in the world. With the vast expanse of the North Sea out in front of you and the rolling green hills of Sutherland to each side, the scenery is incredible. With only the little town of Golspie below and the odd oil rig in the distance, there's nothing to disturb you up there.

In your opinion, which is the best downhill track in Scotland?

CB Fort William boasts the only World Cup track in the UK and gondola uplift too. The five minute plus track sorts the men from the boys and you can ride knowing that the world's best have battled for the elusive rainbow stripes on the very same dirt you're riding on too.

If you had friends visiting and they could only bring one bike – a hard tail – where would you take them?

CB Some of the smoother trails in the south of Scotland would be the best bet. Mabie, Ae forest or Dalbeattie would all make a good day out.

Where would you take kids to learn?

CB The Skills Loops at Glentress or further north at Fort William offer a great way to teach the basics in a safe environment. Glentress's Blue trails also give a great feeling of speed but with very low risk. The flow as the trails sweep through Tweed valley pine forest is unparalleled.

Where's the best place to avoid peddling uphill? Where has the best uplifts? Would you avoid anywhere?

CB Fort William has uplift seven days a week in the comfort of an enclosed gondola but Innerleithen also runs uplift by bus a couple of times a month. Either are a good choice. Avoid using your own transport in Forests like Dunkeld as it has a negative effect on Forestry-run venues trying to grow the sport in a safe and planned manner.

Where's best for total variety?

CB For the best variety, try and road-trip to as many venues as you can. The 7Stanes trail network or Golspie, Learnie and Laggan are all grouped close enough that you'll find a huge variety, all within an hour or so of each other.

↘1 Ae Forest (7Stanes)

Train station Dumfries
Nearest city Glasgow
Sat Nav DG1 1QB
Opening times The trails are open 24/7 365 days a year and are free to ride

Location Ae Forest is around 12 km directly north of Dumfries. From Dumfries, take the A701 towards Moffat and the A74(M). After 10 km there are signs for Ae off to the left. Head through the village and take a right towards the Forestry Commission site (signposted 7Stanes). The new trail head & car park is around 100 m down this road on the left (opposite Ae bike Shop & Café).

Facilities/Overview Ae used to be a one of Scotland's premier downhill spots, and was predominantly for higher standard riders and those who wanted to launch big airs down scary, big downhills. But in recent years there have been family-level trails added, and a XC side to Ae has emerged. The result is one of the most well-rounded trail centres in the 7Stanes portfolio. There is a café & a bike shop (which hires, sells & fixes bikes and equipment, is a Specialized Test Centre, has wireless internet, showers and bike wash), uplift service (on certain days), car parking is free (at the moment) and the café sells beer!

XC The XC routes are new, and fantastic, starting with the green-graded family trail The Ae Valley Trail, a real, singletrack green route that actually gets kids and novice riders out into the forest and away from the tarmac. It's 9 km as a loop, with plenty of stopping points. The blue-graded Larchview Trail is a 13.5-km loop along a similar vein but with some northshore sections and some deeper forest riding. The red-graded Ae Line is named after the A-Line in Whistler, and shares similar attributes – good jumps, fast, technical riding and some good descents (including The Omega Man – see downhill). As 24 km of concentration, it's pretty tiring, but well worth a try. Has

FORESTRY COMMISSION SCOTLAND

been renamed the Ae Line Scottish Power Renewables Trail.

Downhill This is prime DH territory, with the original course having hosted events for the past 10 years. There are two DH tracks, the first being the original Downhill Course, a 1.6 km track with the 22 ft Coffin Jump and some other hefty drops and jumps. Walk it first. If you want to build up to that, there's a second, recently-built course named 'The Shredder',
1 km route on the same hill with less intimidating features. There's also a decent DH section on the red-graded Ae Line named 'The Omega Man', which is the final section and features tables, jumps, drops and gaps (there are several lines to take, depending on how big – or rollable – you want your jumps and drops to be). For uplift days, check withupliftscotland.com or contact Tally on T07709 144299 or tally@ae-up.co.uk (should be around £25 for ten uplifts).

Freeride The Shredder is designed as a freeride trail, albeit with a slant to improving your skills as part of a build up to the full on Downhill Course. There´s also plenty of northshore on the XC trails, and enough jumps to keep the hardiest of freeriders happy.

Easy The green route here is commendable for getting families off the beaten track.

Hard The competitions DH track is pretty fierce, but the Omega Man descent on the Ae Line is one of the best sections of trail in the UK.

Not to miss The Omega Man section of the Ae Line trail. Incredible.

Remember to avoid Trying the Downhill Course without checking out the drops beforehand.

Nearest Bike/Hire shop The Ae Bike Shop is part of the café building which sells and hires a range of bikes for XC and DH as well as having Specialized Demo bikes to test. They also have a dedicated workshop and on site mechanics if your bike gets bashed on the trails or needs a service. T01387 860541.

Local accommodation
Ae Forest Cottages, Gubhill Farm, visitsouthernscotland.com has self-catering cottages.

Eating There's a café at the trail head – the Ae Bike Shop and Café, Ae7.co.uk open from 1000-1600 midweek, 0900-1800 at weekends. The café also opens as a restaurant on certain weekends throughout the year (checkae7.co.uk for details), and is licensed to serve alcohol. Alternatively take supplies, with the nearest village being Ae (the shortest named town in the UK).

ⓘ **More info** The 7Stanes site is 7stanes.gov.uk, the Ae Bike Shop and Café Ae7.co.uk.

Below: The cake is spectacular.
Middle: The bottom of the Omega Man has plenty of options.
Bottom: Smooth, flowing and flull of jumps. Perfect.

CHRIS MORAN

CHRIS MORAN

CHRIS MORAN

> Lowdown

Locals do
Ride downhill to a ludicrously high standard.

Look forward to more trails and infrastructure in the coming years.

Locals don't
Push up the Omega Man – there are always people coming down; use the special push up track to the side.

Pros
Classic downhill.

Tranquil location with few riders during weekdays.

Cons
Uplift infrequent.

↘2 Dalbeattie (7Stanes)

Train station Dumfries
Nearest city Glasgow
Sat Nav DG5 4QU
Opening times The trails are open 24/7/365 days a year and are free to use

Location Dalbeattie is around 20 km southwest from Dumfries, and overlooks the Irish sea and the Lake District beyond. From the A74(M), exit at junction 17 or 18 (Lockerbie), and head west on the A709 towards Dumfries. Carry on into town, then take a left on to Shakespeare Street, then a right onto White Sands, and a left onto Galloway Street crossing the river. Carry on down this road (it turns into the A711 Dalbeattie road), to Dalbeattie, and the 7Stanes trails are signposted as you approach town.

FORESTRY COMMISSION SCOTLAND

Facilities/Overview Dalbeattie has been a granite quarrying area since the 1790s, and the trails here take full advantage of this incredible natural asset with most of the routes being very grippy and all-weather draining. Since its inclusion into the 7Stanes portfolio, the site has broadened its trails to include something for every rider, but to pigeon hole the centre, this is for people who like to ride over tricky rocks, of which there are plenty. Dalbeattie doesn't have a huge vertical drop, so no massive climbs or super-long descents (compared to other centres in Scotland), but still plenty of technical riding, and the infamous 'Slab' rock (read on.). Facility wise, there's not much up at the trails, though there is a bike washing area at the bottom. All the cafés and bike shops are located in Dalbeattie town, 1.5 km to the north of the start of the trails, Richorn car park.

XC For novices there are green and blue trails, the green Ironhash Trail being an 11.5 km loop which used to start on forest road but has recently been upgraded to singletrack in parts. The blue-graded Moyle Hill Trail has again been upgraded from its once forest-road beginnings, and keeps some staggering views over its 14 km of gentle riding. The red-graded Hardrock Trail is 25 km and the original feature here, and includes the infamous 'Slab' – a 14 long boulder which many find incredibly intimidating to ride over. It's steep, riddled with lines, and only the confident rider who leaves the brakes off will pass. The 'Terrible Twins' are a similar feature further down the trail, and even though they're smaller, they are no less able to catch even good riders out (the features are graded black, but can be bypassed so don't increase the trail's overall grading). The trail also features the Rock Don't Roll area of undulating rocks which can be tricky. All the features on the trail are rollable should you not want to try them out though.

Downhill There are no specific DH trails here.

Freeride The new Skills Area is 1.5 km of testing northshore and

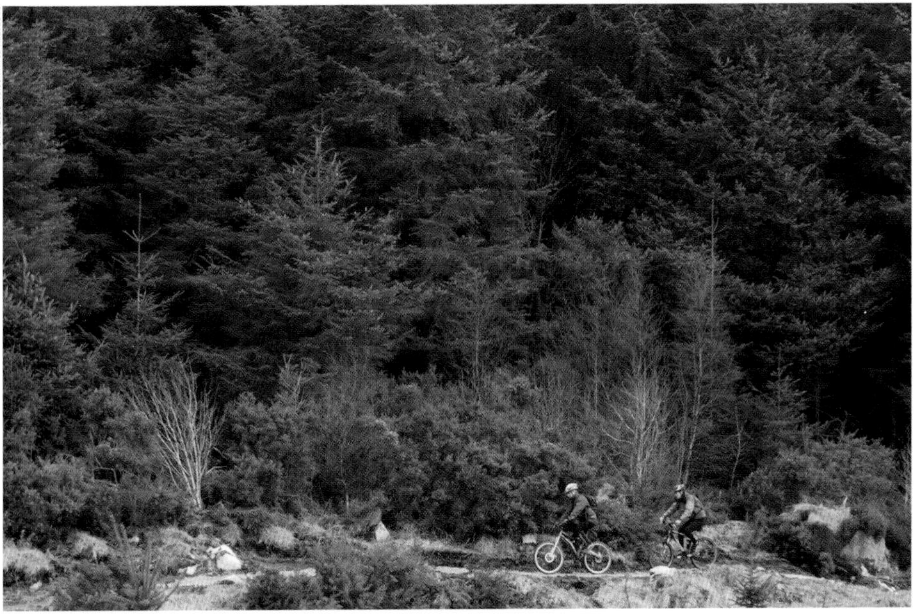

FORESTRY COMMISSION SCOTLAND

feature riding that most freeriders will love, though if it's pure jumps you're after, then other 7Stanes sites might be more in keeping.

Easy The Skills Area is the place to head in order to work out what standard of trail you should be hitting.

Hard The Slab, The Terrible Twins, and Volunteer Ridge are all technically difficult riding, and bravado-testing, bits of trail.

Not to miss The Slab.

Remember to avoid The Slab!

Nearest Bike/Hire shop
MPG Cycles in Dalbeattie (T01556 610659) have bikes for hire, as do Gorsebank near the Dalbeattie trailhead, gorsebank.com, T01556 611634.

Local accommodation
The Bellevue (T01556 611833), a B&B in town or Maidenholm Forge Mill (T01556 611552) for a self-catering cottage.

Eating There are a choice of restaurants and pubs in Dalbeattie, try the Sea Horse T01556 611173.

ⓘ **More info** For info on Dalbeattie try its official page on the 7Stanes site – 7stanes.gov.uk, and to get in touch with the Dalbeattie Hardrock Cycle Club, dalbeattiehardrockchallenge.org.

> Lowdown

Locals do
Meet up on Thursday evenings for group rides (as part of the Dalbeattie Hardrock Cycle Club, dalbeattiehardrockchallenge.org). Visitors are welcome.

Locals don't
Ride too slow. Attack the trail, as speed is your friend over the rocks.

Pros
Plenty of interesting terrain that'll definitely get your rock riding up to scratch.

All-weather trails work in most conditions.

Cons
Has been criticised for using lots of forest road instead of singletrack, but this has been largely tackled over 2008 and is the area the trail builders are constantly upgrading.

↘3 Drumlanrig Castle

Train station Sanquhar/Dumfries

Nearest city Glasgow

Sat Nav DG3 4AG

Opening times The trails are open 24/7 365 days a year. There's a £4 charge for riding which goes into the upkeep of the trails. You won't begrudge paying it

CHRIS MORAN

CHRIS MORAN

Location Drumlanrig Castle is around 20 km north of Dumfries on the A76. From the M74 exit at junction 18 (from the south) or 15 (from the north), head through Dumfries and then north towards Kilmarnock on the A76. Head through the village of Thornhill, around 25 km north of Dumfries and a few kilometres after Drumlanrig Castle is clearly signposted off to the left.

Facilities/Overview In amongst the mightily impressive 7Stanes trail centres, it would be a brave company to challenge their trails. However, Drumlanrig has some incredible advantages: a fantastic castle (which was where the bicycle was invented, and houses a bike museum), and a forward-thinking estate, with plenty of facilities such as tea shops, cafés and restaurants, sustainability workshops, salmon fishing and plenty more besides. And then there are the trails – Rik Allsop has built some of the most natural and flowing singletrack in the UK around the estate, with both complete novices and the most expert of riders in mind. This is one of the best-kept riding centres in the country and has been home to National Point Series competitions since 2002. And if you're done with the trails here, Ae Forest is only 10 km away, while Newcastleton, Mabie, Dalbeattie, Kirroughtree and Glentrool are within 30 km.

XC This is an XC valhalla, with perfect introduction routes in the four green-graded trails: The Policy (a 3 km loop around the castle), Rocking Stone (a 5 km loop through woodlands and around the castle), Low Gardens (an 8 km route past the loch and river), and Burnsands (13 km ride to Burnsands village and back). There are two blue-graded trails: Copycat (a 9-km loop through the forest which incorperates some of the easier riding of the red-graded trail), and Secret Forest (11km of woodland riding). Then there are the two serious routes: the red-graded The Old School, a 20-km loop of classic, flowing singletrack with plenty of roots, drops, jumps and technical sections; and the black-graded Hell's Cauldron – 8-km of testing riding which will push your roots skills to the limit. All routes are waymarked and within the estate grounds, which makes for incredibly pleasant riding, and some routes have uncovered the old estate paths from the victorian era, when the estate employed up to 80 path builders. Time Team eat your heart out.

Downhill There are no specific DH trails at Drumlanrig, but the nature of the trails means downhillers will find something fun to ride and definitely keep their bike skills up to scratch. There is an uplift service (which could indicate a DH trail coming soon?) though it runs infrequently – call Rik on the bike shop number or email on mtbrik@aol.com.

Freeride There are no specific freeride obstacles at Drumlanrig.

Easy Any of the green routes should be perfect for families looking for a perfect riding day out.

Hard There are sections of the red route that will really test your root-riding abilities. If you can handle them, move on to the black run.

Not to miss A visit to the bike museum.

Remember to avoid Pushing your bike uphill to section the downhill bits. The trails are hard enough without having to navigate people on the way down!

Nearest Bike/Hire shop Rik's Bike Shop is on site (T01848 330080, and there's a Rik's page on the site drumlanrig.co.uk) and has a range of hire bikes from baby seats all the way to black trail worthy bikes.

Local accommodation Druidhall Farm has a camping and caravan site in Thornhill, T0870 214 3271; Scaurbridge House is a B&B in Thornhill T0870 214 3547 and Lotus Lodge is a Hostel in Wanlockhead T01659 74544, hostel-scotland.co.uk.

Eating The castle grounds are home to a tea shop and the fantastic Old Stables Snack Bar (which is open through the winter) and hosts a farmers' market every fourth Sunday.

ⓘ **More info** drumlanrig.com is the Estate website and has plenty of pages on the facilities and trails, while scottishmountainbike.com has a wealth of information on the trails and nearby trail centres.

CHRIS MORAN

CHRIS MORAN

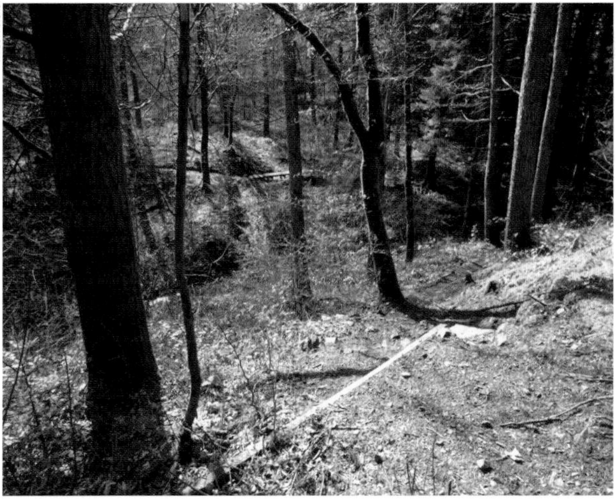

> **Lowdown**

Locals do
Ride when it's wet – the roots are *even more* challenging, and there's a bike powerwash installed (and a shower block for riders) so getting muddy is no problem.

Locals don't
Advertise their trails too much. This is one of the best-kept secrets in the UK.

Pros
Brilliant, natural terrain, with incredible views and infrastructure.

Perfect family or multi-activity day out.

Cons
Could have more high-end trails, and a DH track (though more trails are planned).

4 Glentress (7Stanes)

Train station Carstairs/Edinburgh

Nearest city Edinburgh

Sat Nav EH45 8NB

Opening times Open 24/7 365 days a year, though check the 7Stanes website for closures on specific trails. They are free to ride, though the car park is pay and display (£1 for short stay, £3 for the day, £6 for minibus/van, or £50 for yearly membership). Showers cost £1 for 5 minutes

Location Glentress is 1 km to the east of the town of Peebles, itself around 30 km directly south from Edinburgh. From either Edinburgh or from the south approach the area from the A702 and exit at the A721 towards Blyth Bridge, then take the A72 towards Peebles. Carry on past the town and Glentress is signposted off to the left after 1km.

Facilities/Overview Glentress is often regarded as the best – and most well-rounded – trail centre in the UK. Many stay for weekends or longer breaks in the nearby, bike-friendly town of Peebles, and ride at Glentress and its sister centre Innerleithen. There's a fantastic visitor centre in The Hub Café and Bike Shop, which hires bikes (and nearby Peebles has plenty of hire facilities). The terrain here is perfect for every rider from the novice family through to the best riders in the world, and the area is hugely popular with every level in between. It's a must-visit spot for all riders.

XC For all riders, start at the skills area, which has a variety of features and obstacles you might encounter on the trails (with explanations of what the feature is called, as well as tips on how to ride it written on panels), and should give you a good idea of what level you wish to go for. There's a green-graded 4.5-km route, perfect for families and novices, built in 2007 with the idea of getting riders into the forest as soon as possible. The blue-graded route is a 16-km loop with fast, flowing singletrack that first ascends and finishes with a fantastic, long descent back to the car park. The red-graded run is the classic route, built in 2000 by Pete Laing and added to ever since. See the downhill section above – the Spooky Wood section at the top of the hill is always super-popular. The black route is 29 km of technical singletrack that drains most riders 2/3 of the way round. There are three main sections – Deliverance,

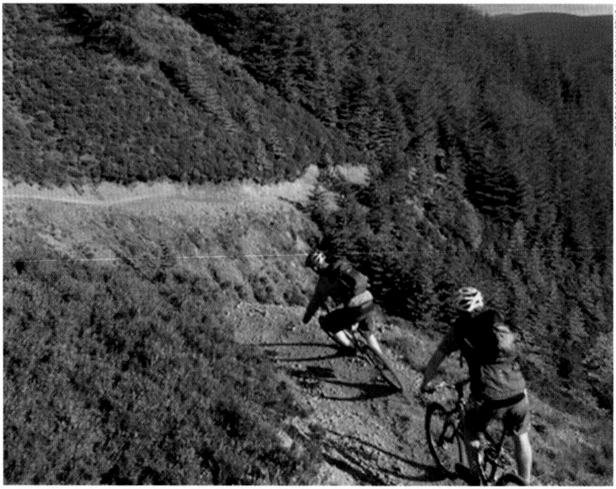

FORESTRY COMMISSION SCOTLAND

> Lowdown

Locals do
Ride at night – there's a regular meeting of night-riding with lights (see the Hub website for details).

Locals don't
Share their shortcuts!

Leave anything behind on the trails.

Pros
Perfect for families, beginners and intermediate riders.

Well managed, plenty of facilities and a great atmosphere.

Cons
Die-hard downhillers will want to head to Innerleithen.

No uplift.

FORESTRY COMMISSION SCOTLAND

CHRIS MORAN

CHRIS MORAN

the Ewok Village (northshore area), and Britney Spears, each with their own individual character and each purpose-built to test and thrill the best riders. Plenty of switchbacks, tough climbs, rock gardens and swooping corners await. All the trails interconnect, so there are bail-out areas, or you can upgrade if you fancy something more difficult along the way.

Downhill While there are no specific DH trails in Glentress, there is plenty of DH-style riding here, especially the second half of the red route, which contains 18 jumps, 17 tables, four rock drops and 12 switchbacks. For pure DH tracks, nearby Innerleithen is the place to head.

Freeride The Freeride Park has plenty of DJ lines, random one-off launches, wallrides and plenty of northshore to test yourself on. You can start off small, and work your way up to the biggest of jumps.

Easy The skills area is incredible for all levels of riders and the tips panels are great for getting some immediate coaching.

Hard The black route is not to be approached light-heartedly.

Not to miss Racing your mates down Spooky Wood is the perfect end to the day.

Remember to avoid Paying for a round of cakes at The Hub Café by coming last!

Nearest Bike/Hire shop The Hub Café and Bike shop has bikes to rent, thehubintheforest.co.uk.

Local accommodation
Crossburn Caravan park in Peebles, T01721 720501, Rosetta Caravan Park in Peebles, T01721 720770, Lyne Farmhouse B&B, T01721 740255 or Melrose Youth Hostel in Melrose, T0870 0041141 are all good bike-friendly places to stay, but Peebles has plenty more and most are used to people coming to ride at Glentress and Innerleithen.

Eating The Hub Café at the bottom of the trails is a classic, with locally-sourced produce and brilliant cakes. The perfect pre- or post-ride grub.

ⓘ **More info** The 7Stanes website is always the place to head for, 7stanes.gov.uk, while a good round up of the routes can be found at cycling.visitscotland.com.

↘5 Glentrool (7Stanes)

Train station Dumfries

Nearest city Glasgow

Sat Nav DG8 6SZ

Opening times The café and Glentrool Visitor Centre (T01671 840302) are open April 13-Oct, 1030-1630pm (1730pm peak season). Trails are open 24/7/365 days a year and are free to ride

FORESTRY COMMISSION SCOTLAND

Location Glentrool forms part of the Galloway Forest and is signposted off the A712 close to the A714, between Newton Stewart and Girvan. The trail head is at Glentrool Visitor Centre, about a mile from the village. The nearest train station is at Barrhill, around 18 km from the trailhead by main road.

Facilities/Overview Of all the 7Stanes areas, Glentrool is the most mellow and suited more for ambling riders who just wish to get into the great outdoors rather than riding their bikes to tackle some technical trails. Boasting excellent great beginner and intermediate trails, Glentrool offers two green runs, mostly root-and-rock free and perfect for the family. They start heading out on short loops of forest road, and return back to the Visitor Centre. The Green Torr, the only blue run, is almost 9 km long, of which 70 per cent is purpose-built singletrack. There is a 218-m vertical ascent and a 2.8-km meandering descent back to the Visitor Centre. Fast and swooping with bermed corners, it is rated as moderate in terms of difficulty and length; however, the off-road smooth surface and long final descent make it easier for less experienced riders. All trails do take in the amazing scenery around the Loch Trool, giving great views of the area known as 'the Highlands of the Lowlands'.

XC Whilst the Green Torr trail itself offers a relatively short XC loop, the 58 km Big Country Route is a waymarked trail using forest roads set in some of Scotland's most spectacular countryside. At nine hours it will be your fitness, rather than your technical ability, that will be tested.

Downhill No specific DH runs here, although the relatively steep descent on the blue run offers plenty of speed and you'll need to know how to use your brakes effectively.

Freeride No freeride facilities available.

Easy The green trail around Pulnagashel Glen at 6 km is the perfect way to start your day and loops back to the Visitor Centre. After that, you will be ready for the other green trail, which is longer at 14 km but offers the same degree of difficulty.

Hard With only one blue run on offer, the Green Torr run is your only option. The beauty of the obstacle-free surface and long descent, however, means that riders who would otherwise not attempt this level of difficulty will be tempted to push themselves.

Not to miss The Burns Stone, at the top of the blue trail, which overlooks Glen Trool and commemorates Robert the Bruce's first victory.

Remember to avoid Travelling here on gusty days – the winds of Galloway Forest are legendary and make riding difficult.

> Lowdown

☺ Locals do
Ride fast down the 2.8 km descent on Green Torr.

☹ Locals don't
Expect miles and miles of technical singletrack.

Party into the night in Glentrool village.

✓ Pros
Amazing scenery.

Excellent trails for families and intermediates.

✗ Cons
Limited trails with only one blue run.

Visitor centre and café closed through all of winter.

Nearest Bike/Hire shop The Breakpad (T01671 401303) is a B&B and bike hire shop in nearby Kirroughtree. Open 1000-1700 each day and public holidays.

Local accommodation Conifers Leisure Park (T08445 433409) has self-catering lodges and camping about six miles from the trails. Waterside Lodges (T01671 840252) in Knowe offers two self-catering lodges about seven miles from Glentrool.

Eating The café located at the Glentrool Visitor Centre is set on the river and has loads of picnic tables. A perfect place then to take in their famous delicacy: a haggis toastie. The village doesn't offer much in terms of eating out, so you might want to get two of those toasties.

ⓘ **More info** cycling.visitscotland.com and 7Stanes (T01387 272440), 7stanes.gov.uk.

FORESTRY COMMISSION SCOTLAND

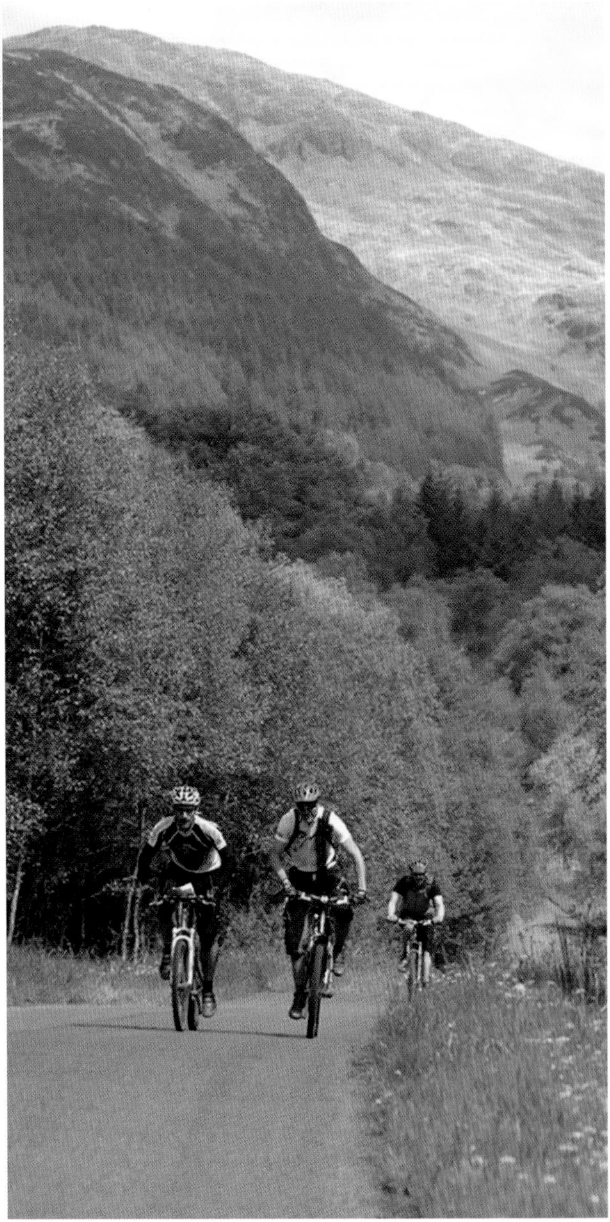

6 Innerleithen (7Stanes)

XC DH FR N

Train station Carstairs/Edinburgh

Nearest city Edinburgh

Sat Nav EH44 6PD

Opening times The trails are open 24/7/365 days a year, and are free, though uplift days cost £30 per rider per day, and there's a charge of £2 for the day for cars (£5 for minibuses/vans) though that money goes into the trail building

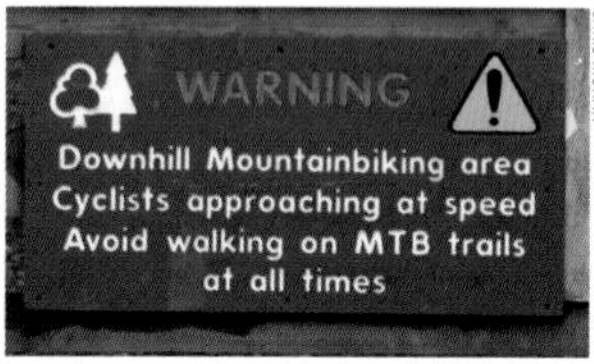

CHRIS MORAN

Location Innerleithen is around 10 km to the east of the town of Peebles, itself around 30 km directly south Edinburgh. From either Edinburgh or the south approach the area from the A702 and exit at the A721 towards Blyth Bridge, then take the A72 towards Peebles. Carry on past the town towards Innerleithen and upon entering the village turn right into Traquair Road (the B709). Follow this road for about 1 km then turn left at the T junction onto the minor road and Innerleithen car park is on the right-hand side. Innerleithen is clearly signposted from Peebles, and the 7Stanes area is signposted as soon as you enter the town.

Facilities/Overview This is another fantastic 7Stanes site, and one originally built for downhill riders, though with the inclusion of the XC route this has changed somewhat. The centre lacks any easy routes, and for a reason – this is tough riding and made for those who know what they're doing. Families and those learning would be better sticking to nearby Glentress. As such, Innerleithen is a quiet, serious mountain biking destination, with good facilities in the village of Innerleithen but little at the trails. The geology here is also perfectly suited for mountain bike trails with an excellent hard, stony soil that drains well, making this a great all-weather venue.

XC The Tarquair XC trail is graded red in some sections and black in other parts, and it is both physically and technically challenging, so is only suited (as the grading suggests) to the more experienced riders. The climb is long, with multiple false summits, but the views are outstanding. The new red-sections give the option of a shorter red graded loop which has opened up the hill to more riders, but the trails are generally a lot quieter than those at nearby Glentress. Those who love natural riding will be spoilt with a plethora of paths on this and the surrounding hills, though none are waymarked so do require some exploration.

Downhill The DH trails on Plora Rig of Innerleithen are infamous in the UK. While there are only four main marked runs it's like a rabbit warren, with so many lines linking different sections. You could easily spend a day on the hill and not hit the same line twice, not that you'd want to as many of the runs are steep and technical and require some learning. On many of the more natural style downhill runs expect plenty of roots and tight turns through the conifer trees, an Innerleithen trademark. The trails all run down to the same finish with the bombhole jump which has seen many of the world's finest racers launching into the finish arena over the years. Uplifts are courtesy of David 'Tally' Tallontine on T07709 144299 (or upliftscotland.com).

Freeride The DH courses are graded orange for freestylers as they contain plenty of jumps, drops, berms and technical riding that'll get you in the air whether you want them to or not. The final descent of the XC (known as Caddon Bank) has some fantastic jumps and really flows, but is best ridden on something other than a DH bike. For those riding long-travel forks, it's best to stay on one of the downhill routes.

Easy There isn't much here that would be classed as easy – for novices there's nearby Glentress. However, perhaps the easiest route down the hill is 'Make or Brake'. Although the trail is made up of multiple jumps, they are all rollable for those that have managed to get this far, and are probably the least technical sections of the hill, if you can keep your wheels on the ground.

Hard If you're looking to downhill all day, book one of the uplift weekends and spend a day mastering the DH tracks, tackling the roots and pinning the turns.

Not to miss A run down Make or Break.

Remember to avoid Heading here if you're unsure of your ability. Go to Glentress first.

Nearest Bike/Hire shop
Alpine bikes (T01896 830880) can be found in the old church in Innerleithen and is well equipped for all the riders using the testing trails in the area.

Local accommodation There are a few hotels and guest houses here, such as the Traquir Arms Hotel (T01896 830229) or for self-catering cottage accommodation try The Bothy (T01896 831227), which is ideal for groups of riders.

Eating While there is little at the trails, Innerleithen has a host of bakeries and cafés. Don't forget to try the award-winning ice cream in the paper shop, and the Traquair House Tea Rooms or Riverbank Restaurant (T01896 831221) for really good post-riding grub.

ⓘ **More info** The 7Stanes website has a wealth of info, 7stanes.gov.uk, while the Visit Scotland site is a great source of knowledge, cycling.visitscotland.com.

> **Lowdown**

Locals do
Rip! Innerleithen has raised some of the world's fastest riders.

Section the downhills; it's a long push from the bottom back to the top.

Locals don't
Hit the jumps when it's windy: Caddon Bank has a wind sock at the top, just to warn you.

Ride without appropriate gear as the top of the black route is way up there.

Pros
Great variety of downhill trails.

Technical riding.

Uplift available on some weekends.

Cons
Not suited to novice or less confident riders.

Uplift only runs some weekends and is often oversubscribed.

IAN LINTON

↘7 The Jedforest Trails

Train station Berwick-upon-Tweed
Nearest city Newcastle-upon-Tyne/ Edinburgh
Sat Nav TD8 6BE

Location Jedforest Trails start from the town of Jedburgh, just on the Scottish Border and around halfway between Newcastle and Edinburgh on the A68. From either north or south take the A68 to Jedburgh and follow signs for the town centre. There's a Town's Car Park with tourist information next door who will be happy to give you a free trail map. All trails start from the centre of town.

Facilities Jedburgh is a picture-perfect borders town with plenty of infrastructure for thirsty and hungry riders, as well as plenty of B&Bs. There are no cafés or snack stops on the trials, but all start and finish in town so you can simply loop back to get some food or take supplies up into the hills with you; there are plans to extend some of the routes to the Harestanes Woodland Centre, which has a café and plenty of facilities, though nothing is waymarked just yet.

Overview Jedburgh is another local community who have taken their tourism industry in-house and formed an association that looks after their surrounding countryside, and have instigated walking, horse-riding and mountain bike trails for the benefit of the local riders and of the local tourist industry as a whole. If the nearby 7Stanes centres are for those looking for mountain bike thrills, then Jedburgh is for people who just want to get out on their bikes and see some beautiful countryside, with plenty of stopping points of interest, and some of the trails being ancient Roman thoroughfares that the Jedburgh community have lovingly restored. This is a very historical area and the town is keen to preserve what assets they have.

Terrain There are plenty of man-made sections on the trails, to keep them flowing and to reinforce boggy sections etc, but essentially these are natural trails that sometimes piggyback on forest roads and even the odd bit of tarmac.

XC There are three main routes on offer here (though the Jedburgh community is looking to expand their network in the coming years): the un-graded (but blue & green likely) Family Trails which consist of the 6.5-km Lanton Loop; a jaunt around Lanton Woods which has been earmarked for work as a bike park; and the Dere Street Dash, which is a forest road and ancient Roman road-aided ascent to Joogilie Brig, followed by a descent on singletrack back to Jedburgh, the whole thing being just over 10 km. The main trail here though is the red-graded Justice Trail, which combines technical riding with great views over the Oxnan and Jed Valleys and the Cheviot Hills in the distance. It is listed as being 40 km, which makes it a huge loop with all manner of singletrack adventures along the way, but in reality there are opt-out points at 5, 10,15, 20 and 30 km so you don't have to do the full trek if you start to get tired. That said, there are plenty of stops along the route should you wish to go the distance, including a castle stop and plenty of stream crossings.

Downhill and freeride There are no specific DH tracks here, and those who like freeride or downhill are best advised to head to nearby Innerleithen or Glentress.

Conditions Being mostly natural riding, there can be a fair amount of mud around during the winter months, and there is a huge horse-riding scene in the area too (though Jedburgh have built separate routes for riders in places), but this merely adds to the natural feel of the trails.

ⓘ **More info** The Jedforest Trails have a great website with all the info you could need on their history, construction and the ethos behind the town, jedforesttrails.org.

Safety
Steve Ireland

Steve Ireland is behind the "Think Safe, Think 7" campaign. Here's how it breaks down:

❶ Before you leave the house

Make sure your bike is well serviced and up to the trails you plan to ride. Make sure you're packing a good quality helmet, gloves, elbow and knee protection. If you're going on an XC route, have all the relevant maps with you, note any diversions or closures when you get to the trail centre, and make sure the route isn't above your fitness and skill level. Carry some first aid kit, and have some way of contacting the emergency services. Don't forget that a whistle is handy for when there's no mobile coverage. The distress signal is six whistle blasts or six torch flashes once every minute.

❷ Expect and anticipate

Dry conditions make tracks dusty and loose, wet conditions lead to mud. Anticipate other track users and beware of vehicles. Take special care at junctions. If you're in a group, always progress at the pace of the slowest member. Stay together.

❸ Here is where I am

Be aware of where you are at all times, use trail or ordnance survey maps and keep be aware of landmarks identified on these. Look out for emergency information posts on some of the more remote routes.

❹ Always stop to help others

Always offer to help someone if they appear lost or in trouble. Having someone to talk to can help a lot.

❺ Protect yourself and others

If you come across an accident don't put yourself or others in danger, assess the situation and immediate area, and warn other users to avoid further accident. Protect yourself and the casualty.

JOSH KNOX

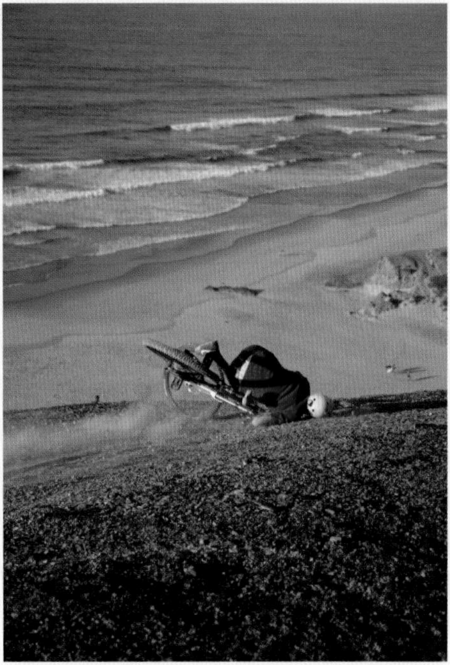

❻ Provide First Aid if you can

Assess the casualty and decide what to do. Remember A.B.C. (Airway, Breathing, Circulation – signs of life, blood loss). Be aware of spinal injuries - never move an injured person if they complain of back or neck injuries. Control any bleeding with pressure and elevation. Make the casualty warm and comfortable and place unconscious casualties in the recovery position if possible.

❼ Yell and tell

Consider options for safe return to trailhead or send for/call for help using 999 or the local emergency number. 911 on a mobile abroad gets you through to the local emergency services. Ask for Police (Mountain Rescue) and THEN Ambulance if not in easy reach of a route suitable for an ambulance If it's not possible to send for or call for help, use the international distress signal to attract attention (again - six whistle blasts/ torch flashes repeated every minute).

↘8 Kirroughtree (7Stanes)

Train station Dumfries
Nearest city Glasgow
Sat Nav DG8 7BE
Opening times The trails are open 24/7/365 days a year and are free to ride, though the car park is pay and display

Location Kirroughtree is around 4 km to the southwest of Newton Stewart, itself some 40 km directly to the west of Dumfries heading towards Stanraer. From the A74(M), exit at junction 17 or 18 (Lockerbie), and head west on the A709 towards Dumfries. Just before town, take the A75 Dumfries ringroad and stay on this road as it heads out west towards Newton Stewart. Turn off the A75 at Palnure – signposted for the Visitor Centre – and follow the road for approx 500 m, then take the left hand fork, again signposted for the Visitor Centre. The road leads into the Visitor Centre car park and the start of the trails.

Facilities/Overview Kirroughtree is a little further out than the other 7Stanes sites, but that generally means its trails are emptier. And what trails! The Galloway Hills are part of the largest tract of forest in the UK, and the site has some spectacular, purpose-built trails that intersect the area. The McMoab area is a must ride for all UK mountain bikers, while the trails themselves have gained a good reputation for their excellent contouring lines and the large granite rock features incorporated in the harder red and black routes. The surfacing used to build the trails makes for a very artificial road-type surface, but the curves and lines make up for this, mixed in with the exposed areas of rock. There's a great Visitor Centre with café and bike shop and everything you could wish for at the end of a day's riding.

XC This is pure XC country, with singletrack straight from the Visitor Centre and very little forest road anywhere on site. The green-graded route (Bargaly Wood) is a 6 km loop around the forest, though does use some minor public roads. Perhaps a better route is the 2 km off-road taster singletrack area. The blue-graded Larg Hill is 10 km of easier trails that mirror the original red-graded run here, and there's nothing to stop you dropping in to try it out. The blue-graded Doon Hill Extension is just that – a 4-km addition to the Larg Hill trail that takes you to a spectacular viewing point. The two major trails here though are The Twister – a red-graded 17-km loop close to singletrack perfection, with lots of flowing sections that join together through varied terrain and are what mountain biking should be – and the Black Craigs route which at 31 km includes the brilliant McMoab area, a large outcrop of grippy granite rocks (hence the name – Moab in the US is considered a haven for mountain biking), that have painted lines indicating the best routes through. This is a serious XC route with plenty of technical riding and tests for those with ability.

Downhill No specific DH trails here.

Freeride There is nothing here specifically for freeriders, though the McMoab area would suit those who love northshore style riding, and there are plenty of jumps and drops around the trails. However, it might be best to head to another

FORESTRY COMMISSION SCOTLAND

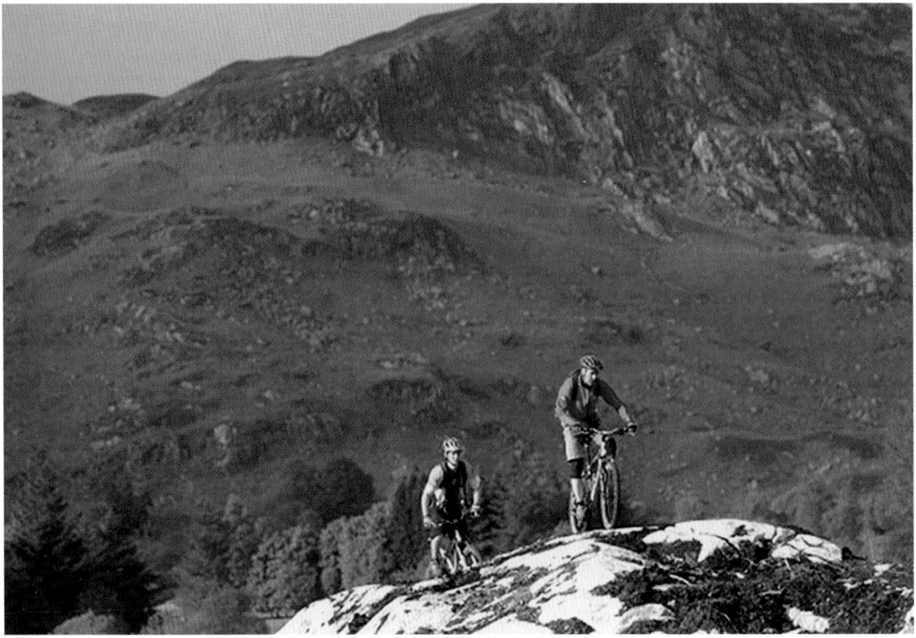

FORESTRY COMMISSION SCOTLAND

trail centre if you're looking for specific bike parks.

Easy The blue routes are relatively easy and pure singletrack.

Hard McMoab is technically demanding, but incredibly rewarding with some unbelievable views and a real feeling of being in the great outdoors.

Not to miss McMoab – one of the coolest trail features in the UK.

Remember to avoid Heading here if you want monumentous vertical drop.

Nearest Bike/Hire shop The Break Pad (thebreakpad.com, T01671 401303) is at Kirroughtree Visitor Centre, where all the trails start. They hire all Trek bikes, from kids to full-suspension rigs and carry out repairs on site.

Local accommodation
The Brake Pad has a B&B at Castle Douglas, (T01556 502693) with full workshop and bikers needs in mind, or Eskdale B&B (T01671 404195) is one of many bike-friendly stays in town.

Eating The Visitor Centre, housing the Brakepad Bike Shop and Kirroughtree Café is the place to head for refreshments. Open daily from 1030 to 1630.

ⓘ **More info** 7stanes.gov.uk.

> Lowdown

Locals do
Know all the routes through McMoab off by hand.

Locals don't
Ride off the marked trails as the ground is soft and easily damaged by bikes.

Pros
Good rock features and sinuous singletrack.

Cons
Not suited to novice or less confident riders.

Not as many thrilling descents as other Scottish sites.

↘9 Mabie (7Stanes)

Train station Dumfries
Nearest city Glasgow
Sat Nav DG2 8HB
Opening times The trails are open 24/7/365 days a year and are free to ride

Location Mabie is around 4 km to the south of Dumfries. From the A74(M), exit at junction 17 or 18 (Lockerbie), and head west on the A709 towards Dumfries. Carry on all the way into town, then take a left onto Shakespeare Street, then a left onto Dockhead, then a right onto Pleasance Avenue and another left onto the A710 New Abbey Road in the direction of New Abbey. After 3 km Mabie 7Stanes is signposted off to the right of this road.

Facilities/Overview Mabie is one of Scotland's original mountain bike centres (opened by John Craven and the Newsround team in the 1980s) and was well known for its fantastic Phoenix Trail long before it became part of the 7Stanes group. With that amalgamation have come good additions to the centre including graded routes for all standards of rider, and the longest northshore run in the UK. Well worth a visit for all standards, though fans of balanced, technical riding will perhaps get the most from the site, and fans of northshore will be in their element.

XC For those who are unsure about off-road riding, the 12 km Purple Trail Lochbank Loop is a mixture of forest road and b-roads around the site. For those wanting to get off-road, there's a skills area with blue- and red-graded obstacles which will give you an indication of what the trails have to offer. The green-graded Big Views Loop is an 8-km family-oriented trail that takes in some gentle climbs and fun descents with picturesque view point stops (hence the name). The blue-graded Woodhead Loop is a 10-km more technical version of the Big Views Loop with brilliant views and some slightly trickier riding, but still largely fun-based. The red-graded Phoenix Trail is the

FORESTRY COMMISSION SCOTLAND

> Lowdown

Locals do
Ride amazingly well, especially on the wood.

Ride at night and on regular evenings organized by the Shed crew.

Locals don't
Ride the northshore clean in one go. It's that tricky.

Go hungry – the food at the Shed is superb.

Pros
Traditional singletrack centre.

Great chilled, friendly atmosphere.

Cons
No specific DH trails.

classic route here, a 17-km loop of natural and manmade singletrack that snakes through the incredible scenery, offering you fantastic views and some flowing, twisting trails with plenty of rootsy sections and good jumps. It's classic old-school riding at its best.

Downhill There are no specific DH trails at Mabie.

Freeride The double black diamond-graded (the toughest grading) Kona darkside is a 3.8-km northshore trail that climbs and contours along the hill over rocks and stumps. It is for experts only and requires excellent balance and trails-like skills to ride the wood, which is as narrow as 10 cm in places, and make the tight turns. There is also a skills park with dirt jumps, and a mini 4X track that has rollable jumps and is a must for all visitors!

Easy The skills area is always worth a quick hit to warm up.

Hard Make no mistake – the Kona Dark Side is full of tricky sections and is nearly 4 km of serious concentration and not to be taken on by novices.

Not to miss At least checking out the Kona Dark Side (even if you don't want to ride it).

Remember to avoid Leaving your gloves on the wood burning stove at the Shed.

Nearest Bike/Hire shop The Shed at Mabie Forest, with kids' bikes, hard-tail and full-suspension bikes for half, full day and 24-hour rentals. See cycle-centre.com, T013872 70275.

Local accommodation
Try the Glencairn Villa (T01387 262467), a B&B in walking distance of the town centre with wireless web connection, or, for a self-catering cottage, the Belmont Stables Cottage (T01387 268032), which has secure bike storage.

Eating The Shed in Mabie Forest is both a fantastic local-produce café (with log burner and home-made food), and also the bike rental centre (see above).

ⓘ **More info** 7stanes.gov.uk.

Below: The Kona Darkside snaking its way over the thistles.
Opposite page: Good uphill sections.

FORESTRY COMMISSION SCOTLAND

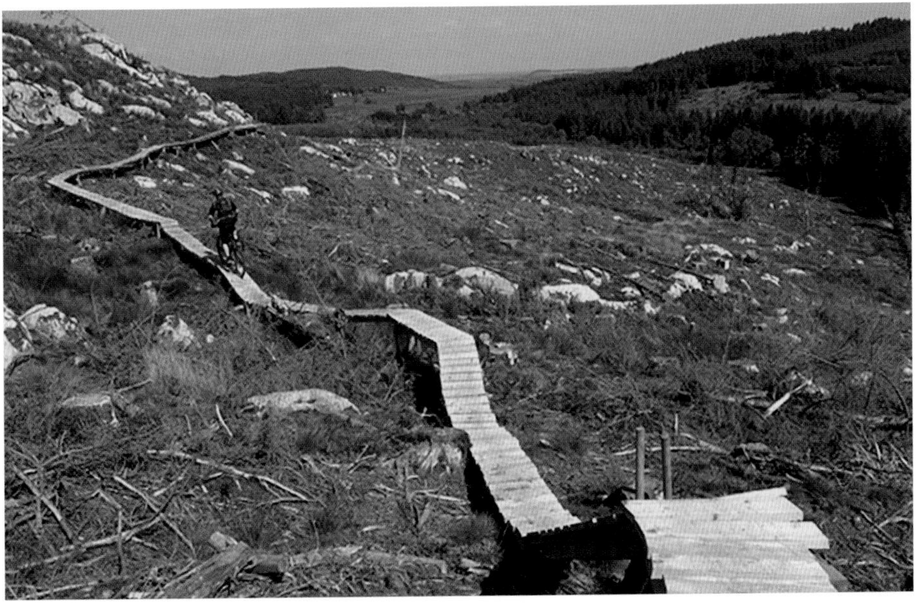

↘10 Newcastleton

Train station Gretna Green
Nearest city Edinburgh
Sat Nav TD9 0TD
Opening times The trails are open 24/7 365 days a year, and are free to ride

Location Newcastleton is just on the north side of the Scotland/England border, around 30 km directly north of Carlisle. Heading from Edinburgh, go south on the A68, then take the A7 towards Harwick, then the B6399 to Newcastleton. For those in England and the south, exit the M6 at junction 44 and head north on the A7 over the border, then take a right into Canonbie and go through the village on the B6357 towards Newcastleton. From the village the 7Stanes site is clearly signposted.

Facilities/Overview This is another of the immensely popular 7Stanes sites, and generally considered the entry-level trail centre, with a good choice of easy routes which don't have huge vertical climbs (or drops) and have been carefully constructed for those getting into riding. That said, it also features a brilliant northshore section and a skills area, plus a decent red route that can be either tackled by riders looking to push themselves, or by good riders looking to get a fast bit of singletrack under their tyres. There aren't a great deal of amenities at the Newcastleton site itself, though the Dykecroft Visitor Centre (the trail head car park), does have toilets and changing facilities and may be in for an overhaul in the near future. However, there are plenty of cafés, restaurants and accommodation back in Newcastleton, a very picturesque borders town.

XC Newcastleton is all about flowing singletrack with two good blue routes and a mildly testing red. To start off though there's the green-graded skills area at the start of the trails, which is perfect for getting to grips with your bike, or for practising a few moves before hitting the trails proper. Then it's onto either of the two blues: the Caddrouns route (a 5.5 km route in which the uphill sections are on forest road, while the descents are feature-full singletrack through the forest, ending with a 2-km ride down with plenty of bridges and swooping berms to try out); or the Linns – an 8-km ride which meanders along the river and up and down through the forest with no real testing climbs. The Red route is an 11-km, beefed up version of Caddrouns, with some technical climbs and fun descents along the way, ending with the final descent of Swarfe Hill that flows so well that many riders will wish to repeat it immediately.

Downhill There are no specific DH tracks here, but the XC loops all feature long sections of downhill riding, though good riders will not be greatly taxed by the terrain.

Freeride There's an orange-graded northshore area which has plenty of challenging rides for the level of mountain biker that Newcastleton attracts. For those that absolutely love their northshore, perhaps Mabie would

Below: Chainless bikes beware.
Opposite page: Hone your northshore skills.

CHRIS MORAN

FORESTRY COMMISSION SCOTLAND

FORESTRY COMMISSION SCOTLAND

be better suited, but this is still a very testing and fun site. Elsewhere, there aren't as many jumps and gaps on the trails as at other sites.

Easy Either of the blue runs are perfect for easing into some genuine singletrack forest riding, but Caddrouns is perhaps better suited for those who might prefer gravity-assisted riding.

Hard Some of the northshore here is genuinely tricky, with skinny rides over decent drops.

Not to miss The Hidden Valley area is packed full of well-thought-out features such as flowing lines, bridges and boardwalks.

Remember to avoid
Getting stuck in The Bog.

Nearest Bike/Hire shop
Harwick Cycle Hire in Harwick, T01450 373352

Local accommodation
The Liddlesdale Hotel (T01387 375255), or the Sorbietrees B&B (T01387 375215), both in Newcastleton, are bike-friendly places to stay.

Eating Head to Newcastleton and try the Olive Tree (T01387 375479) or Ell Deli (T01387 381711).

ⓘ **More info** Check out the official website, 7stanes.gov.uk.

> Lowdown

Locals do
Keep adding to the trails. The Newcastleton Trail Warriors are constantly improving the site.

Ride over to England to loop Keilder Forest if they want a longer XC ride.

Locals don't
Forget to bring supplies.

Have a fully-catered Visitor Centre, but hope that will change soon.

Pros
Brilliant place for novice and intermediate riders to head.

You can ride to England and back!

Cons
Not as challenging for good riders as the other 7Stanes sites.

Not a huge vertical drop – no huge descents or challenging climbs.

Central & Northern Scotland

↘ Overview 241
↘ Aviemore 242
↘ Balnain Bike Park 243
↘ Carron Valley Trails 244
↘ Comrie Croft Bike Trails 245
↘ Fort William 246
↘ Glencoe 248
↘ Golspie Highland Wildcat Trails 250
↘ Isle of Arran 252
↘ Kyle of Sutherland Trails 254
↘ Laggan Wolftrax 254
↘ Learnie Red Rocks 258
↘ Moray Monster Trails 260
↘ Pitfichie Mountain Cycle Trails 262
↘ Pollock Country Park 263
↘ Strathpeffer 264
↘ The Fire Tower Trail 265
↘ The Kelpies Trails 266
↘ Donkey Hill Dirt Track 267
↘ Duchany Woods 267
↘ Dunkeld DH 267
↘ Kirkhill Mountain Bike Park 268
↘ Best Films, Callum Swift 269

[FORESTRY COMMISSION]

Central & Northern Scotland

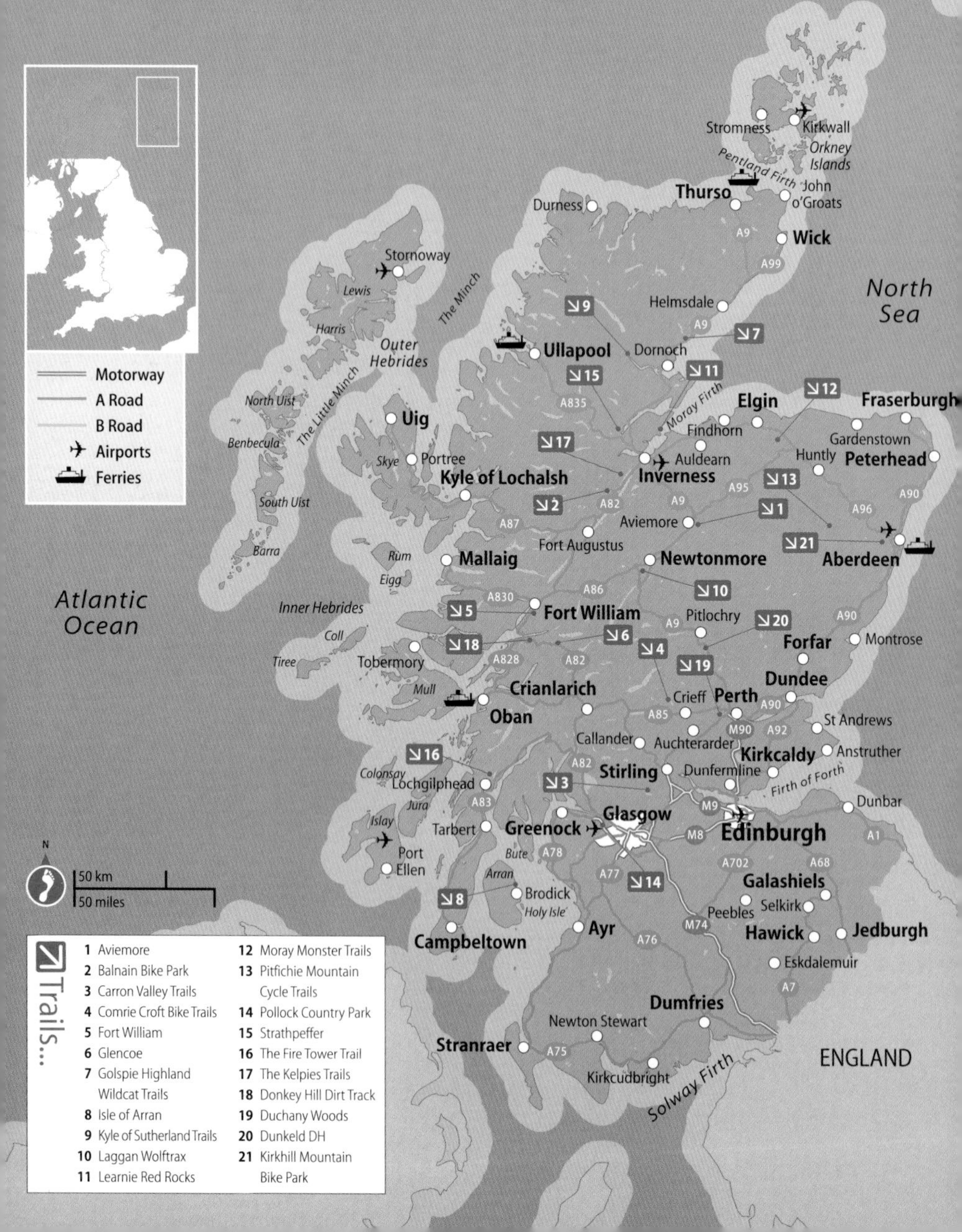

Northern Scotland is home to some of the most outstanding riding in the whole of the British Isles, and if you like your riding empty, scenic, and hardcore, then this is the place to head. The area is of course dominated by the mighty Fort William. It's been home to the UCI World Cup Tour since the early 2000s, and in 2008 played host to the actual World Championships. Featuring the UK's only full-time gondola uplift (much like one might find in the trail centres of Europe such as Les Gets and Schladming), Fort Bill has been at the forefront of UK riding for what seems like an eternity. But this part of the country is also home to other outstanding gems, not least the stunning Kyle of Sutherland Trails, where a stay at Corbisdale Castle Youth Hostel would make any Scottish break an incredible holiday to remember. The sheer amount of man-hours that are going into building trails in this region is staggering, and if centres such as Golspie, Learnie Red Rocks and Kirkhill were to be found in southern or central England, they would dominate the local scene. In this part of the world, they are merely yet another ultra-cool place to visit. Of course if you do get spoilt for choice, and actually over-ride many of the trails here, you could always pop over to the Isle of Arran where another level of super-interesting riding (in even less-populated areas) is underway. If you find that this is too crowded for you, then I'm afraid a one-way ticket to Mongolia with a bike, a shovel and the intention to dig your own trails is the only remedy.

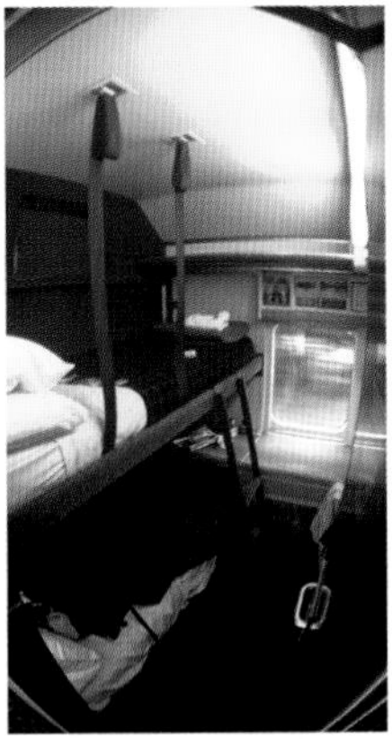

Overview

Most visiting riders come to this part of the world in order to test themselves on the awesome Fort William downhill track. Many would do well to hang around for a while once they're here. The city of Inverness in particular is a real anomaly in terms of how much riding is to be had in ratio to its riding population. Within half an hour of the city limits one can ride at Balnain Bike Park, The Kelpies Trails, Contin Forest and the incredible Learnie Red Rocks on the Black Isle. Go a touch further and Laggan Wolftrax, Aviemore and the incredible, windswept views of Golspie are rideable. A touch further east and the north sea city of Aberdeen is home to Pitfichie and Kirkhill Forest, and the link road between the two cities goes directly past Moray Monster Trails. It might not be an obvious destination, but a trip to the two centres would reap huge benefits, and the staggering quality of the trails would only be matched by how empty they are. A loop back round to Edinburgh and Glasgow via Perth's Dunkeld and Comrie Croft centres would complete a brilliant north Scotland adventure. We suggest getting the sleeper train to Fort Bill and heading east from there. The cabins are brilliant (see the pictures above). For those who riders around Edinburgh and Glasgow who want to try something other than the southern 7 Stanes sites, the Carron Valley Trails is the obvious option, though if you can handle a small journey, a trip to the Fire Tower Trail on the way to Jura will be rewarded by one of the coolest days out ever.

↘1 Aviemore

XC DH

Train station Aviemore
Nearest city Inverness
Sat Nav PH22 1QU (for Glenmore Lodge)

Location Aviemore is on the A9 main trunk road through the highlands between Perth and Inverness. From either city, head along the A9 to the town, then follow signs for Cairngorm Mountain along the B970. Around 7 km from the town heading up the hill to the ski lifts, you'll come to Glenmore Lodge, home to the Scotland National Outdoor Training Centre, which can be used as a starting point for the riding and is home to the Glenmore Lodge Skills MTB Centre.

Facilities Aviemore is in line with Fort William as being one of Scotland's premier outdoor hotspots, with plenty of cafés, outdoor shops and supplies. Glenmore Lodge has a café and dining area, bar, and all sorts of adventurous facilities such as climbing walls, swimming pools and massage areas.

FORESTRY COMMISSION SCOTLAND

Overview Aviemore, and its neighbouring mountain Cairngorm, have been at the forefront of Scotland's winter sports industry for decades, so it is strange that they haven't embraced the mountain bike revolution as much as other centres such as Fort William. The omission is more startling as Aviemore's infrastructure includes numerous ski lifts, arguably the most scenic of the highland peaks, and Scotland's only funicular mountain railway, which would be perfect as a bike uplift. Perhaps this will change in the near future, but currently there is only a skills loop at Glenmore Lodge (though small, and not permanently open to the public – call before heading there), and plenty of natural singletrack on the surrounding hills. None of it is waymarked, nor reinforced or had any trail-building to surface the routes. Cairngorm say this is because they wish to keep the riding here (which is certainly popular), very natural and man-made-trail-free. But others cite the area's mismanagement and laziness behind this rather strange decision. Either way, the riding here is spectacular in its own right (and the town boasts two good bike shops), but it will involve route-finding, and possibly walking over boggy sections or muddy areas if there has been recent rain. If you want to know what riding was like in the highlands 15 years ago, before the advent of purpose-built trail centres and infrastructure to keep riders coming back for more, this is the place to head.

PAULINE SANDERSON/GLENMORELODGE.ORG.UK

Conditions There are no purpose-built trails here, so the weather will determine what the singletrack conditions are.

ⓘ **More info** While there are no waymarked trails, there is still a thriving mountain bike community. To go on organized rides, try Glenmore Lodge's website, glenmorelodge.org.uk, or you could try Bothy Bikes in Aviemore, bothybikes.co.uk, or, lastly, the Cairngorm Mountain Bikers organize weekly rides into the hills and are pushing to bring Aviemore in line with other trail centres, mountainbikers.org.uk.

↘2 Balnain Bike Park

FR N

Train station Inverness
Nearest city Inverness
Sat Nav IV63 6TN (to the Steading Pub, just past Balnain)

Location Balnain Bike Park is near Drumnadrochit, around 25 km to the south of Inverness and on the west bank of Loch Ness. From either the north or south, the access road is the A82 to Drumnadrochit. Here, head along the A831 in the direction of Balnain, around 7 km up the road. Turn left at the Glen Urquhart Forestry Commission sign on the left of the road, and cross the river to the car park. Balnain Bike Park is 200 m along the forest road on the left side of the car park.

Facilities There are no facilities at the trails (apart from some unique 'chill out shelters'), so take supplies with you. The nearest cafés and shops are in Drumnadrochit or the Steading Pub further along the A831. Inverness is the nearest town with a decent bike shop.

Overview The Balnain Bike Park is a unique venture in Scotland, being a freeride paradise for those who love northshore and balance testing riding as well as being in the air. Imagine a skatepark for forest users, with all manner of wooden structures. There are skinny planks to ride, gap jumps, table tops and an incredible amount of northshore, including some imaginative obstacles such as the see-saw and fun box – a freestanding block of wood with transitioned trails leading up to it.

Terrain This is forested land, but the majority of the structures in the park are built from locally-sourced logs and planks. The Forestry Commission – who manage the site – were keen to use local craftsmen to design and build both the trails and the wooden structures that make up the park.

XC The are no specific XC trails here, though there is plenty of unofficial singletrack riding around the area.

Downhill There are no DH tracks at Balnain.

Dirt jumps/Freeride This is pure freeriding, with a smaller skills area that will test your riding and give you an indication as to whether you should then head to the park itself. There's also a trials bike area, with impossibility-defying northshore to conquer. All in all, this is a very advanced place, and though intermediates may improve quickly, it is no place for complete novices.

Conditions This is forest land, which can be exposed in bad weather, though much of the trails have been built with good drainage cover.

ⓘ **More info** Balnain Bike Park has its own page on the Forestry Commission site, forestry.gov.uk.

BEN WAIN

Northshore balance test.

↘3 Carron Valley Trails

Train station Camelon
Nearest city Glasgow
Sat Nav FK6 5JL

Location Carron Valley Trails are next to Carron Bridge, a small village around 10 km to the west of Falkirk and roughly half way between Glasgow and Edinburgh. From Glasgow head out on the M80-A80-M80 towards Stirling, and leave the M80 at junction 5, heading to Denny on the A872. Go through Denny and take the B818 west in the direction of Fintry, and after you pass through Carron Bridge look for a turning to the left around 2 km further along the road. From Edinburgh, head north west on the M9/M9 towards Stirling and then take the M876 to Denny and follow the directions as above.

Facilities There are no facilities at the trails except a car park, which is open from 0730 until 1800 in winter and from 0730 until 2100 in the summer. Food and drinks are available from either Carron Bridge (10 km) or Kilsyth (10 km), so take supplies with you if you want to eat, drink and ride.

Overview Carron Valley Trails have been enormously popular with the Glasgow, Stirling and Edinburgh riders since the early 2000s, and the trails here have been built with year-round riding in mind. There is one waymarked trail – the Red Trail, a 10.5-km loop which branches out here and there and consists of four different styles of riding to suit virtually everyone.

Terrain This is a Forestry Commission Scotland site, which was largely built by the Carron Valley Development Group, who have poured thousands of man-hours in to the area and created some amazing purpose-built trails.

XC The four broad sections of the Red Trail are: Pipe Dream, an uphill singletrack section with drops and snippits of downhill that leads to the beginning of uphill towards Eas Dubh (the Black Waterfall); take a rest at the top before the descent, which includes Kelpie Staircase and the the switchbacks of Birling Boghills. Then comes the swooping lines of the Cannonball Run, and finally The Runway – a feature-packed descent with fun-park style obstacles such as banks, wallrides and tabletops.

Downhill There are plenty of places on the trail that will appeal to downhillers, but there are no specific DH tracks.

Dirt jumps/Freeride Again, there's plenty to keep freeriders happy here, but no specific bike park or northshore areas.

Conditions This is a mixture of forest land with plenty of all-weather surfacing and rock features.

ⓘ **More info** A downloadable map of the region is available from the Forestry Commission site, forestry.gov.uk.

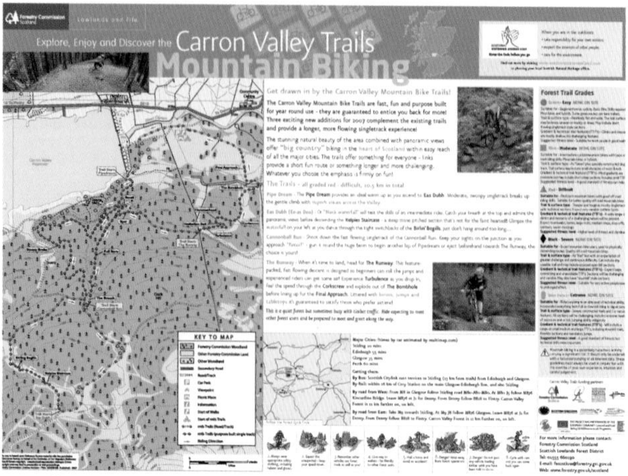

↘4 Comrie Croft Bike Trails

Train station Dunblane/Stirling/Perth or Crainlarich

Nearest city Dundee

Sat Nav PH7 4JZ

Location Comrie Croft Bike Trails are in the private grounds of the Comrie Croft – a four star independent hostel, itself around 25 km west from Perth on the A85. From Perth, simply head west on the A85 and just after the town of Crieff take a right into the hotel grounds. From the south, head north on the M9, then the A9 towards Perth. Take a left onto the A822 towards Crieff, then the A85 towards Crainlarich and the hostel is on the right, off the main road.

Facilities This is an impressive set-up – the Comrie Croft Hostel is a four-star, 70-bed building with communal lounging areas, laundry, drying, games room, café, bike wash and snack stop. There's also a bike shop with Giant bikes available for hire, as well as an eco campsite, toilets, route maps, showers and high-pressure bike wash.

Overview This is another example of great work between local riders and a forward-thinking landowner who has turned this old croft lodging into a brilliant, concentrated mountain bike centre, with fun trails and a great atmosphere. They also organize regular races (the Hairy Coo), and have everything on hand for a good day or weekend out. Perfect for those who can already ride and fancy something more chilled than the 7Stanes areas, or who just want another angle on highland riding. With the eco campsite, the emphasis here is on sustainable tourism and enjoying the countryside.

Terrain This is in the heart of Perthshire, with staggering views, waterfalls and open moorland to explore.

XC There are two ways to ride Comrie: the first is to use the Croft's private trails, which are essentially a 6-km, red-graded loop into the private forest, which weaves up and down, includes a stop at a disused quarry where there's a bike park, and ends with a cool descent back to the centre HQ. The route is almost entirely on purpose-built singletrack (though with some fire-road uphill), and features plenty of cool obstacles along the way. The alternative is to use the Croft as a launchpad into some of the available XC riding in the surrounding hills and Strathearn Valley. There is lots to choose from, with varying degrees of difficulty (for example, you could head to Comrie Village on a green-graded 5-km loop, or do the Loch Tay route – a 35-km expert trail), and Comrie Croft have handily drawn quite cute maps showing each of the tens of routes available.

CHRIS MORAN

CHRIS MORAN

Downhill There are no specific DH tracks here, but the Comrie Croft trail does feature a descent with plenty of obstacles to keep most riders happy.

Dirt jumps/Freeride The disused quarry at the top of the Comrie Croft loop has a bike park which is ever expanding.

Conditions The trails have been built to work in most conditions, though some of the longer, unofficial XC routes pass through areas which may be boggy after heavy weather.

ⓘ **More info** Try the fantastic Comrie Croft official website, comriecroftbikes.co.uk.

↘5 Fort William

Train station Fort William

Nearest city Inverness

Sat Nav PH33 6SW

Opening times The trails are open 24/7 365 days a year and are free to ride. However, the Gondola is open from May through to September, from 1030 to 1600 and costs around £20 for a day ticket (which could equate to around 8-10 runs if you're very good; please check the website for concessions and age/price ranges). Also check the website before leaving as many of the trails are often closed for competitions and/or maintenance

NICK BAYLISS

CHRIS MORAN

Location Fort William is on the banks of Loch Linnie in western Scotland, roughly midway up the country. From any direction, the A82 is the major road into the town. To get to the trails from the centre of town, head northeast on the A82 in the direction of Inverness and follow signs for Aonoch Mor/Nevis Range Gondola after 3 km.

Facilities/Overview Where to start? This is easily the most famous UK mountain bike centre, due to Fort William having hosted world cup races here since 2002 (and the stand-alone World Championships in 2007). It's the UK's only gondola uplift (lots of mini cablecars), and has arguably the best infrastructure, – including a visitor centre, with cafés and restaurants at both the bottom of the hill and at the peak. There are purpose-built DH tracks, an incredible 4X track, world champs-standard XC courses, and hundreds of kilometres of singletrack stretching in every direction over the highlands. Fort William town (affectionately known as Fort Bill), is the self-proclaimed Outdoor Capital of the UK, and filled with outdoor types. Hiring a bike and getting some bike-friendly accommodation is the easiest thing in the world.

XC The main XC trail at Fort William is the Witches Trail – a World Cup, 15-km-long technical route. The route stays on the lower wooded slopes of the hill in the Leanachan Forest, and there are a further 25 miles of trails in the forest ranging from easy, low-level forest tracks and disused railway lines to technical, purpose-built singletrack. The Cour Loup is an 18-km blue-graded loop designed to get riders out into the incredible scenery. The red-graded 10 Under The Ben is a 17-km enduro test with some really tricky sections, specifically at the Nessie descent. The World Champs loop is a classic red-graded 9-km loop with one big uphill and a corresponding DH trail that the UCI World Cup uses as a race route.

Downhill The DH at the Nevis Range is commonly known as simply the Fort William Downhill. It is one of the toughest on the world cup circuit, though it doesn't have many particularly steep sections compared with some courses. However, the combination of the high speeds, big rocks and holes on the upper slopes, and physicality on the bottom of the course make this a real stern test for both riders and bikes. The top of the course is very exposed so can be difficult in very windy conditions. It constantly wins the riders' award for best DH and is for very good riders only. In addition, there is an easier DH track under construction, hopefully open for spring 2009.

Freeride There is a competitions standard (some say the best in the UK) 4X course at the bottom of the gondola, which is perfect for those wishing to get in the air, while at the base station there is a skills area; here you can try out some of the obstacles that you might encounter out on the Witches Trail, or enjoy it in its own right. There is also a dedicated DJ area near the quarry, with three lines ranging from beginner to expert and good progression throughout the sets.

Easy Try the skills area to see what grade of trail you're going to be comfortable on.

Hard The Fort William Downhill is one of the best, and trickiest runs in the world, never mind the UK.

Not to miss In good weather a trip up Ben Nevis, Britain's highest mountain, is a must.

Remember to avoid Taking a run down the DH track without walking it first.

Nearest Bike/Hire shop Off Beat Bikes (offbeatbikes.co.uk) is the specialist bike shop in the town. They have a fully equipped workshop and also hire bikes from both the shop on the high street and also from the Nevis Range building itself.

Local accommodation Unless your stay coincides with the UCI Mountain bike world cup, you're not going to have any problems finding somewhere to stay in Fort William. There are plenty of hotels such as the Cruarchan (T01397 702022) and B&Bs, such as Burntree House (T01397 701735), so you'll be able to find something to suit your needs here.

Eating The Pine Martin Café is at the bottom of the gondola (and has wifi), while the Snowgoose Restaurant is at the summit. In the town there are plenty of take-aways and pubs serving hot meals and restaurants. Situated on the Lochside, Crannog Seafood Restaurant (T01397 705589) is well known for its locally-sourced fish from an area renowned for the quality of its fishing waters. For pub food try the Grog and Gruel (T01397 705078), found on the main street.

ⓘ **More info** The official website is ridefortwilliam.co.uk, while there is a local club that organizes fun comps and regular rides for those in the area, whwheelers.org.

CHRIS MORAN

› Lowdown

Locals do

Section the downhill as it's a very full run.

Float the rock sections.

Locals don't

Goup the the gondola in high winds. The top station is always ten times worse than the car park.

Just ride the Nevis range; check the ride Fort William site for some of the other excellent trails in the area.

Pros

Great facilities and town.

Ride the courses that the world's best battle it out on.

Stunning setting when the weather is good.

Cons

Can have long periods of bad weather.

6 Glencoe

Train station Bridge of Orchy/ Fort William
Nearest city Glasgow
Sat Nav PH49 4HZ

Location Glencoe is another of Scotland's permanent ski resorts, 30 km south of Fort William, on the A82. From either the north or south, take the A82 trunk road between Glasgow and Fort William and the ski centre is clearly signed as you go over the high pass of Rannoch Moor.

Facilities Glencoe is a fully-functioning ski resort in the winter, although there isn't too much in the way of a base lodge. The best neraby facilities are found at the Clachaig Inn (clachaig.com) – a brilliant, traditional pub which also has accommodation and a thriving calendar of events.

ED DAYNES/GLENCOESCOTLAND.COM

Overview Glencoe has two good attributes: a double-black-graded downhill (that some claim is even more difficult than nearby Fort William's track), which is accessed by the appropriately named Access Chairlift (tickets cost around £20 for the day and should get you around 10-15 uplifts), open from April through to October. In addition, there are a wealth of XC routes in the surrounding hills, including a fantastic 7 km descent down to Kinlockleven. The Glencoe area is a satellite of the mighty Fort William mountain bike centre (it is in the same council district of Lochabers) and many of the XC routes around Glencoe are on the Fort William website (ridefortwilliam.co.uk). However, since a management buy-out of the resort at the beginning of 2008, there have been plans to rejuvenate the area and use the ski lifts for mountain biking during the summer months. While there has only been one route put in so far (the downhill track from the Access Chair-lift), the summer of 2009 should see much more work going into the resort and more routes waymarked around the mountain.

Terrain This is some of the steepest terrain in Scotland, and a highland moor mostly bereft of trees from Rannoch Moor upwards. Expect rocky, shaley descents, over granite and heather tracks. However, it is possible to descend past the base at Glencoe and into some lovely forest to the east and west of the ski lifts. It is possibly the most hardcore of all the Scottish resorts, and has a fabulous, outdoor history, much of which is shown in photographs on the walls of the Clachaig Inn. The area has a rugged beauty that is almost unique, even in Scotland, and the incredible colours of the valley have been used in many recent films, including the recent *Harry Potter and the Prisoner of Azkaban*.

Conditions Much of the XC riding at the moment is forest road and even tarmac before descending into singletrack offshoots to various villages. This needs to change before Glencoe can take its rightful place alongside the 7Stanes and Fort William trail centres, and the signs are encouraging that it will.

More info glencoescotland.com has a lot of info on the XC routes around the area, as well as having links to accommodation and plenty of local interest information, while glencoemountain.com is the official website dealing with the chair and button lifts of the resort. The Forestry Commission website has a page on the Glencoe forests, forestry.gov.uk, and Fort William has suggested XC routes as well as nearby bikeparks and other places of riding interest at ridefortwilliam.co.uk.

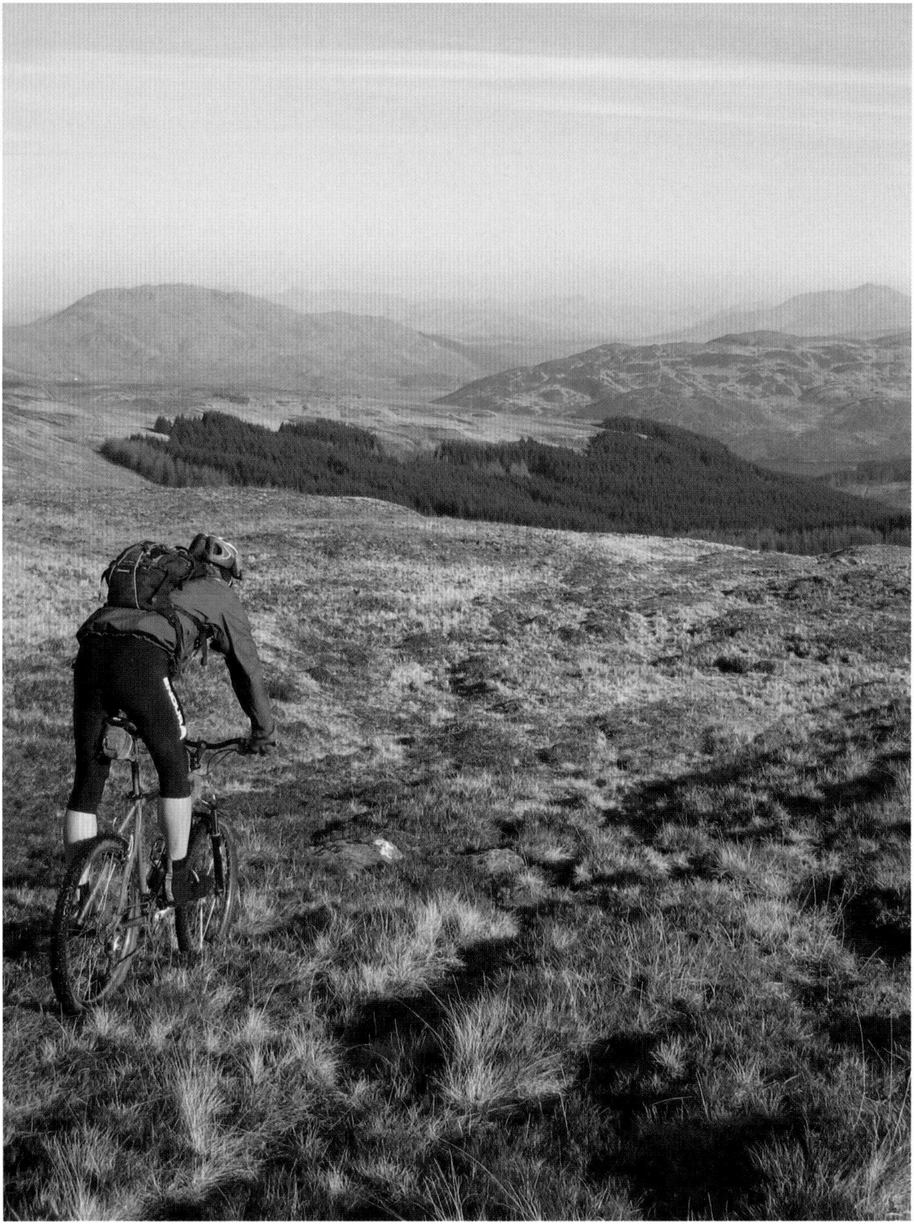

ED DAYNES/GLENCOESCOTLAND.COM

↘7 Golspie Highland Wildcat Trails

XC DH N

Train station Golspie/Dunrobin Castle

Nearest city Inverness

Sat Nav KW10 6TH (for the town car park)

Opening times The trails are open 24/7 365 days a year and are free to ride

Location The Highland Wildcat Trails are the most northern purpose-built trails in the UK, and start and finish in the town of Golspie, roughly 60 km north of Inverness. From Inverness, take the A9 north along the coast, and the road leads directly through Golspie. There are three starts to the trails – the first is from the Town's Car Park and clearly waymarked (though it starts with the red-graded uphill); alternatively you can get back on the A9 heading north out of Golspie and take the first left (signposted for Backies) or second left (Queens Drive, also signposted to Backies), for either of the other two car parks; this will save some uphill climbing (though you'll always have to go and get the car at some point!).

Facilities/Overview Golspie trails have a number of attributes – they are the most northerly purpose-built trails in the UK, they were designed by Pete Laing (the man behind much of Glentress's incredible trails), and they have absolutely jaw-dropping views over the Moray Firth and North Sea, with only the odd castle to disturb your vista. They have also kept things nice and simple – there are three main trails: a blue, a red and a black. All start in Golspie, and climb 367 m to the top of Ben Bhraggie (pronounced Ben Vraggy), and then whizz back to town. There are no facilities on the actual trails, but since they start and finish in town you get to use Golspie's plentiful shops and amenities.

XC The three routes have one thing in common – you'll need to do some proper climbing from Glospie to access all the fun stuff. But this is where the genius of the place comes in. There has been as much care going in to the getting up as the coming down, and with plenty of features to distract you on the ascent, you'll be summiting in no time. This is actually the longest stretch of purpose-built uphill singletrack in Scotland at over 7 km. The Blue Trail is a 6.5-km route from either town (or the sneaky car park higher up the hill), and has views pretty much all the way up and all the way down, while the Red Trial is 7.5 km of rollable jumps, plenty of flowing singletrack and those fabulous views. The Black Trail is basically the same as the red, though when you get to the top of the hill there's an additional loop around the summit with lots of big jumps,

MORVEN MUNRO/SCOTTISHWOODLANDS.CO.UK

MORVEN MUNRO/SCOTTISHWOODLANDS.CO.UK

technical sections and additional climbs and descents. You can also head off towards Dunrobin Castle to access plenty more unofficial singletrack and forest road to meander your way around this stunning, empty countryside too, though these aren't waymarked or part of the official Highland Wildcat trails.

Downhill Although not billed as a DH centre, the loops here are clearly aimed at getting to the top of the hill, then back down again, so downhillers will definitely find something interesting to ride.

Freeride There is no specific bike park of northshore here, but the Black Trail has enough jumps and features to keep most freeriders happy.

Easy The Blue Route is a brilliant bit of riding to keep most novices absolutely enthralled.

Hard The Black Route has shortcuts, but is still a pretty arduous ride, though packed with enough interesting features (and views), to make it a classic.

Not to miss The swooping descents on brilliant, purpose-built track for all abilities.

Remember to avoid Forgetting a camera. The views and riding shots are there for the taking!

Nearest Bike/Hire shop Square Wheels are in Strathpeffer, around 40 km to the south, squarewheels.biz, 01997 421000.

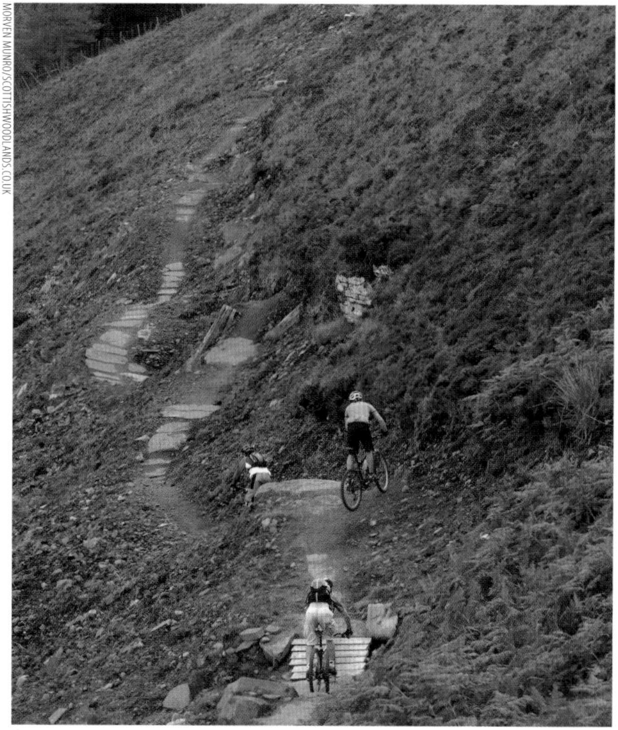

MORVEN MUNRO/SCOTTISHWOODLANDS.CO.UK

Local accommodation
Try the Morayview B&B on Golspie's Main Street, T01408 634429.

Eating Coffee Bothy in Golspie is a bit of a classic local café, as is the Twenty Twenty Café, though for interest try the Theme Tea Rooms in Dunrobin Castle, with a steam-powered Fire Engine from the 1800s in the dining room.

ⓘ **More info** The Highland Wildcat Trails have an official website with downloadable route map, highlandwildcat.com.

> **Lowdown**

Locals do
Stop to admire the view from the Duke of Sutherland monument at the summit.

Take supplies up there.

Locals don't
Go up when it's windy – this is a very exposed place.

Pros
Empty trails, great views, and fantastic singletrack.

All-weather surface (limestone) drains exceptionally quickly.

Cons
Far from most UK towns and cities.

Weather can be bad for days on end.

↘8 Isle of Arran

Train station Ardrossan
Nearest city Glasgow
Sat Nav KA27 8DP (for Brodick centre)

Location The Isle of Arran is the most southerly and accessible island off the West Coast of Scotland and is reached by car-ferry from Ardrossan to the Island's capital, Brodick. Alternatively, there is a summer-only service which runs from Claonaig on Kintyre to Lochranza in the north of the island. You can either take a car over, or simply jump on the ferry with a bike as all the main trails start from Brodick and the island is only 20 km long and 10 km wide, with one main ring road, so finding your way around is incredibly easy.

GERARD TATTERSFIELD

Facilities Brodick is a small fishing village with an imposing castle overlooking the bay and hits most visitors as a stunning, picturesque place that is akin to going back 50 years in time. The rest of the island is similarly picturesque, with many remarking how Arran is a condensed version of Scotland: incredible hills, beautiful lochs and some awe-inspiring views over the sea. There are also some fantastic, old-school B&Bs, village shops and roadside cafés.

Overview There are two reasons why Arran is a brilliant mountain biking destination: the first is that the terrain is so incredibly suited to bike riding, with enormous, empty and ancient mountains rolling down to the sea, and a quiet ring road, which will get you to supplies in the form of a small village within every 3 km; the second is that the Scottish Tourist Board and The Arran Bike Club have both done an outstanding job in promoting the island as a cycling paradise. The ABC have built some brilliant trails already, but are pushing to implement the Arran Trails Project, in which the island's tourist infrastructure is lined up with the outstanding natural terrain to create a 7Stanes-style, island-wide trail network and centre. It's an ambitious project, but considering the trails that are currently on offer, it's likely to be realised.

Terrain The rugged mountains here are some of the oldest in the world. This is serious granite country, with gorged valleys and awesome, empty Glens to match. It is, in a word, unspoiled. These mountains are beautifully complimented by the forests and rugged moorland to the South of Brodick, more ideal mountain bike country.

XC The blue-graded Castle and Trailquest Route is an ABC-venture that starts at Brodick Castle and loops around the castle and surrounding hills, with views back to the mainland and over to the majestic Goatfell and Cairsteal Abhail mountains. The 10-km loop has some gentle sections and is suitable for both serious mountain bikers and adventurous families

GERARD TATTERSFIELD

alike. The Red Trail starts at the Ferry Terminal and heads uphill to Corriegills and the Clauchland Hills Forest, where there's plenty of tough singletrack and stunning views, before the descent on the other side of the hill down to the bay of Lamlash, with its Holy Isle dominating the horizon. The village is quaint, and bustling with cafés and pubs – the perfect mid-ride stop. The loop back takes in the Cnoc Na Dial Hill and descends back into Brodick for a total of 18 km all in. The Black Route uses some of the same trails, but an additional loop into Glencoy and miles of forest singletrack above Lamlash and Whiting Bay makes this an awesome full days' ride at 35 km in length. There are many more routes available, please check on the Arran Bike Club website for more ideas.

Downhill There are no official DH tracks on the island, but the hills here are just under 900 m high, and full of granite-strewn trails, so there's plenty to explore.

Dirt jumps/Freeride Again, there's nothing official built here, but this should change if the planned Arran Trails Project is completed.

Conditions Arran can be exposed in severe weather, but otherwise the island is generally mild and sheltered with palm trees lining the shore and not too many ramblers, horse-riders or dog walkers to contend with.

ⓘ **More info** The Arran Bike Club can be found at arranbikeclub.com, while the official Arran Tourist Board site is visitarran.com.

↘9 Kyle of Sutherland Trails

Train station Inverness
Nearest city Inverness
Sat Nav IV24 3DP

Location The Kyle of Sutherland Trails are actually two trail centres next door to each other, Balblair and Carbisdale, and easily within riding distance of one another. The main hub for the two is the fabulous Carbisdale Castle, perhaps the grandest Youth Hostel in the UK and situated to the west of the Dornoch Firth, around 50 km directly north from Inverness. To reach the castle, take the A9 north from Inverness and then turn left onto the A836, signposted to Bonar Bridge. Just before Bonar Bridge, in the village of Ardgay, look for signs to Culrain, and take the back roads to Culrian, where there are signs for Carbisdale Castle Youth Hostel. Alternatively, stay on the good road to Bonar Bridge, take a left onto the A836, then another left onto the A837 towards Rosehall. Pass through Rosehall and then after 1.5 km take a left, signposted to Doune/Birchfield/Achnahanat. Then take the next left and this road heads to Birchfield, then Carbisdale Castle, then Achnahanat, in that order. To get to Balblair, simply head west on the A836 from Bona Bridge and turn right after 1.5 km, signed to the Forestry Commission car park.

FORESTRY COMMISSION

Facilities/Overview The Kirk of Sutherland Trails are a long way from even the majority of Scottish riders, and they are not very big (Balblair has a total of 13-km of trails, while Carbisdale is really one 4-km trail with some extensions), so there has to be a good reason to entice people this far north. In fact, there are two: the first is that Rik Allsop, the trail designer at Drumlanrig, has designed Balblair's fantastic Black route, and the amount of features that have been packed into that – and the other trails – is awesome. The second is that Carbisdale Castle offers weekend riders a rare thing: to truly get away from the crowds, while staying in an area of outstanding beauty but without costing a fortune. Of the two centres, Balblair has few facilities except the car park at the start of the trails, while Carbisdale has the impressive Carbisdale

SCOTTISH YHA

Castle, which is a fully-functioning Scottish Youth Hostel and has a café, bike washing, bike hire, toilets, showers, and full accommodation from March through to October, which is bookable through either carbisdale.org, T08701 553255 or reservations@syha.org.uk.

XC There are two routes at Balblair: the Blue: a 3-km classic uphill slog that is still interesting due to the rough ground you have to cover, and quickly rewarded by a sweet descent back to the car park, and the renowned Rik Allsop's Black Trail, a 7.5-km loop (or 11.5 km if you do the extension), that combines the area's outstanding natural terrain of granite and limestone; it and adds enough wooden reinforcements to keep everything flowing, with some brilliantly fun descents including piggybacking on the Blue trail's final section to make a combined total of 4 km of downhill to end on. Carbisdale has a 3-km loop which is graded blue and is virtually all singletrack, including the brilliant Hissing Sid section where a series of switchbacks will vie for your

> Lowdown

Locals do
Know how perfect their natural terrain is.

Locals don't
Worry too much about crowds - this is about as empty as trail centres get.

Pros
Incredible castle, and superb (if a little short) trails.

Cons
It's a very long way from everywhere else.

The trails aren't the longest in the world.

attention against the stunning backdrop (though you'll want to keep your eyes on the track if you're hitting them fast). The Red Trail is essentially the same run as the blue, though it has a 1.5-km added section at the top of the hill that adds some descent and more uphill, and makes the trail 4.5 km in total. It's easy to ride between the two trail starts, and is an enjoyable cruise along the trainline past the beautiful Kyle of Sutherland water.

Downhill There are no specific DH tracks at either Balblair or Carbisdale, but both feature some gentle descents that novice downhillers will definitely enjoy.

Freeride There is no specific freeride area here, though there are a few jumps dotted around the trails. However, this is predominantly natural-feel singletrack on offer.

Easy The Balblair Blue is an absolute classic, and well worth a visit no matter what your riding standard.

Hard The Black route at Balblair has all the makings of a technically difficult, but perfect day out, with approximately one third being natural rock riding, one third hard-packed singletrack and the remaining third being northshore-style additions to the trails that have been painted with a special 'grippy' paint. Worth a journey just to try that out!

Not to miss A stay at one of the world's best youth hostels – Carbisdale Castle.

Remember to avoid Leaving the camera at home – the views across the waters are absolutely stunning.

Nearest Bike/Hire shop
Carbisdale Castle rents bikes, but for the nearest shop you'll have to go to Square Wheels in Strathpeffer, around 40 km to the south, squarewheels.biz, T01997 421000.

FORESTRY COMMISSION

Good local accommodation
Carbisdale Castle is definitely the place to stay, though there are also B&Bs in Bonar Bridge.

Eating Head to the café at the castle, or try the Handmade Crafts and Café in Bonar Bridge, or Lady Ross in Ardgay. The Balblair Whisky distillery is in Edderton, a few kilometres further east from Bonar Bridge.

ⓘ **More info** There are downloadable maps for both Carbisdale and Balblair (as well as how to link the two) found at forestry.gov.uk/cycledornoch.

↘10 Laggan Wolftrax

Train station Newtonmore
Nearest city Inverness
Sat Nav PH20 1BU
Opening times The trails are open 24/7 365 days a year and are free to use

Location Laggan Wolf Trax is just off the A9 main route that connects Inverness to the south and cuts past the Highland centre of Aviemore. From the south, head north on the A9 towards Inverness, turn off at Dalwhinnie on to the A889 towards Laggan Bridge, then turn left on to the A86 towards Spean Bridge. The Laggan Wolf Trax café and parking (called BaseCamp) is located 1.5 km up this road on the left-hand side.

Facilities/Overview Situated on the west side of the impressive Cairngorm Mountains, Wolf Trax (named after the legendary Wolf of Badenoch) is a brilliant all-in-one centre with a bike shop and café at the base, and trails to suit all riders, from absolute beginners all the way through to elite riders. The Black Route features no chicken lines (which suits really good riders and keeps others off the route), while the red-graded route is testing, but fun for most. A blue and green route are perfect for novices, while a skills area and bikepark complete the package. Laggan is a basic set-up, with only one of each graded runs on offer, but the attraction is that each route is absolute perfection. The centre is also just outside Laggan, a village that adopted the fictitious name of 'Glenbogle' during the filming of the BBC drama *Monarch of the Glen*. It's a beautiful part of the world, and a perfect base from which to explore the peaceful countryside and spot a range of wildlife from golden aagle or Osprey to red deer stags and pine martin from the numerous, unofficial XC routes spreading off into the surrounding Grampion hills.

XC Starting off with the obligatory skills area (so you can check which grade you're comfortable on, as well as brush off some cobwebs), the official trails start with the 5-km green route which has been built for all riders – children included – to get out into the forest and enjoy the scenery. The old blue route has actually now been re-graded to orange (though it still works as a blue), as it has a bikepark-style descent with sweeping bends, rollable jumps and plenty of obastacles to keep novice riders through to good freeriders happy. The two main routes are the Red Trail – a 9.4-km (or 15-km loop) incredible run with plenty of rock gardens and northshore additions. It is also home to several granite rides (similar to The Slab in Dalbeattie) and has plenty of areas where you can jump into the Black Trail for a test on some of the obstacles there, before ending in a brilliant raised boardwalk descent (the Wolf Run). That same Black Trail is a 10-km trail of intense riding with lots of rock to negotiate, including some big jumps, hefty drops and serious slabs, and don't forget, there are no chicken lines, so try the red and use the 'opt-in' lines before you hit the black first time! For those looking for a really long XC ramble, ask BaseCamp about hitting the 42-km Corrieyairack Pass. The company can organize a bus for you to the start of the trail so you can leave your car at the BaseCamp car park.

Downhill There are no specific DH trails at Laggan; however, swing your leg over a XC bike and the black route will challenge even the best DH riders, as it contains lots of technical rock features. Plus there's an uplift service run by BaseCamp, so you can DH the red or black runs.

Freeride The bike park has nearly 4 km of obstacle-strewn trails – perfect for those looking to get into the air, especially if you're new to riding and want to improve, as there are plenty of smaller jumps.

Easy Head out on the blue trail, trying the small jumps on the funpark descent; if you easily tackle this loop then after some lunch head out on the red trail, which features more climbing and steeper and more technical descents but most mountain bikers with some off road experience should be able to tackle this...

Hard Only one choice really – head out on the testing black trail, and anything you don't clear first time round you can conquer on our second run after lunch; if you still want some more, look for the uplift bus and go around again.

Not to miss A run down Air's Rock, a steep black optional rock-roll on the red route.

Remember to avoid Riding the black route if you're not technically proficient as it is quite hard.

Nearest Bike/Hire shop
Base Camp MTB (T01528 544786) are based at the Laggan Wolftrax trails. They have a good workshop and hire bikes from Giant and Kona.

Local accommodation
For B&B accommodation try the Rumblie (T01528 544766) in the village, or, if you are looking for a self-catered cottage try Rowan Cottage, (T01226 383258), also in Laggan.

> Lowdown

☺ Locals do
Incorporate all the trails into one loop: ask in the shop and they'll show you how to do it.

☹ Locals don't
Ride long travel machines here, they're overkill for the trails.

✓ Pros
Great compact venue.

Nice, peaceful area.

✗ Cons
The trails are only short so you may exhaust the riding in a few days.

Eating The BaseCamp MTB Café is a great set-up, featuring plenty of home-made soups, cakes and hearty meals, as well as stocking quick snacks for hungry pit-stops. They also have plenty of up-to-date mountain bike magazines, as well as daily papers if you just want to chill out. Nearby Laggan is the nearest town with two hotels/pubs serving food – try the Monadhliath Hotel (T01528 544276) on the Dalwhinnie road, which offers bar meals and a restaurant.

ⓘ **More info** There's a wealth of information online: Laggan village has its own website with pages on the trax at laggan.com, while the Forestry Commission site has specific Wolf trax info at forestry.gov.uk/WolfTrax, but the best site is probably the BaseCamp web pages at basecampmtb.com. New for summer 2009, BaseCamp offer guided wild rides direct from Wolftrax, finishing off on the trails and an optional overnight Bothy trip.

BASECAMP

↘11 Learnie Red Rocks

XC FR N WW

Train station Inverness

Nearest city Inverness

Sat Nav N/A

Opening times The trails are open 24/7 365 days a year and are free to ride

Location Learnie Red Rocks are on the famous Black Isle (not actually an island, but a peninsula) near the town of Rosemarkie, itself around 15 km northwest of Inverness. From Inverness take the A9 heading northeast to Tore, then take the last exit on the roundabout onto the A832, heading in the direction of Cromarty. Pass through the town of Rosemarkie and the trails are signposted off to the right after around 4 km.

Facilities/Overview Learnie Red Rocks are another waymarked Forestry Commission site and started out years ago when local riders recognised the potential of Learnie Forest. However, in 2005, the trails were upgraded by Paul Masson of Cycletherapy – who also designed the Laggan Wolftrax trails – and now include a green route, 5 blue trails, one red trail and a testing black. There's also a bike park and DJ area, as a purpose-built centre. Many of the trickier features have escape lines (or chicken lines as they're known), so you don't have to do the drops or jumps if you don't want to. Good riders should be aware that there isn't a huge amount of vertical drop, and while there are plenty of features, this isn't a DH venue.

XC There are now 16 km of trails here, though all in short loops. The green-graded Home run is 500 m of easy singletrack back to the car park. The blue-graded Callachy Hill Climb is an easy route to the top of the hill, while the Callachy Downhill is a 1.3-km blue back down again. The three other blue-graded trails – Muirhead Climb (1.1 km), Fir Hill Blue (500 m) and Firth View (2.5 km), are all gentle climbs with fun, flowing descents that learners and intermediates will love. The black-graded Learnie Hill is the culmination of years of work, and as such is a very high-standard route with plenty of steep, technical rock sections. The jump between easy and difficult runs is very marked here, so approach with caution.

CHRIS MORAN

Downhill There is no specific DH track here, and the Fir Hill black route (which had DH sections) was recently lost to logging.

Freeride The Fun Park is graded red, but isn't actually that difficult as the bigger jumps are normally graded orange. Again, beginners and intermediates will find much to ride here, though the DJs are of a higher standard and more difficult to ride unless you know what you're doing.

Easy Any of the blue routes here will offer novice riders plenty of challenge, though because of their short length they encourage bravery. You're never too far from the car park! The Firth View is worth it for the view alone, as you might imagine.

Hard The black route is full of stone slaps and rooty switchbacks and not for those out for an easy ride.

> Lowdown

☺ Locals do
Know how to make the most from a smallish area.

Keep their gears tuned - the uphills are short but very technical in places.

☹ Locals don't
Ride around the tougher sections.

✔ Pros
Really good flowing singletrack.

✖ Cons
A good rider could ride every trail in one day.

Not to miss The skills area – a brilliant place to brush up your bike-handling skills.

Remember to avoid Coming here expecting a huge area.

Nearest Bike/Hire shop Mountain Bike Highlands and Islands (T01381 600386) is found in Cromarty, only four miles from the trails and offer bike hire, guiding and servicing.

Local accommodation Denoon Villa (T01381 600297) and the Cromarty Arms (T01381 600230) both offer B&B.

Eating Head to nearby Rosemarkie for the nearest café or supplies, or take everything you need to the trails – there are no facilities on site.

ⓘ **More info** Learnie has a page on the Forestry Commission site, forestry.gov.uk or try the Highland Mountain Bike Association who have a Learnie page on their site, himba.org.uk.

FORESTRY COMMISSION

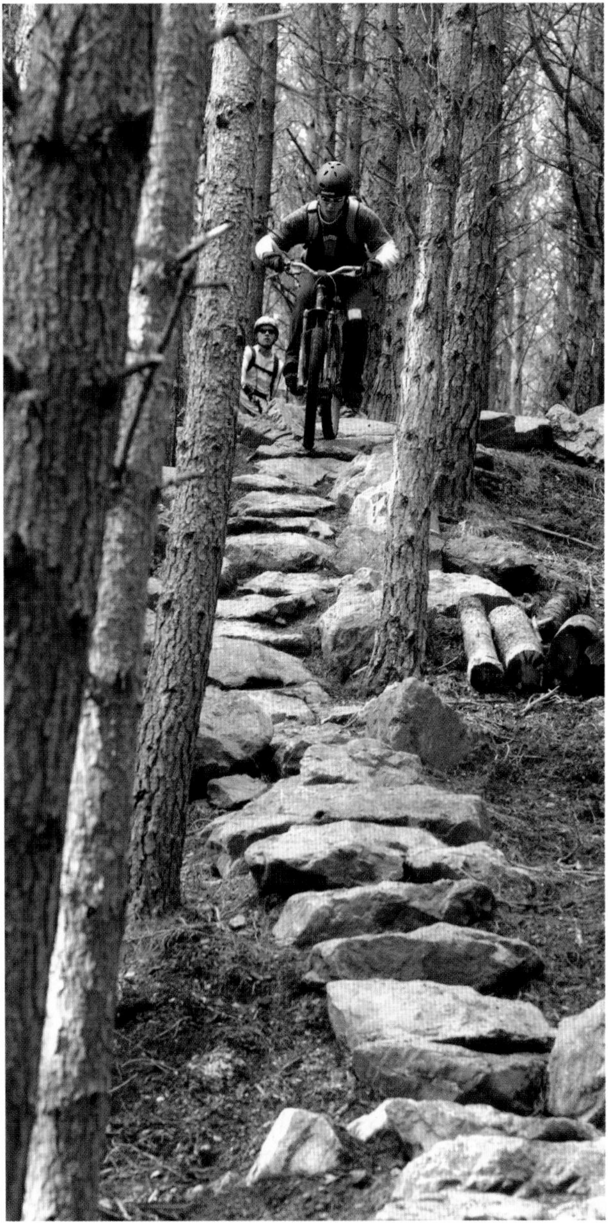

↘12 Moray Monster Trails

XC DH FR N

Train station Keith/Elgin

Nearest city Inverness

Sat Nav N/A

Opening times The trails are open 24/7 365 days a year, and are free to use. However, check the forestry commission site as there are frequent trail closures due to logging

Location The Moray Monster Trails are in a Forestry Commission piece of land which sits within a triangle between the towns of Fochabeers, Keith and Mulben, and is roughly 15 km southeast from Elgin, itself almost equidistant between Inverness and Aberdeen on the road that connects the two cities, the A96. There are three car park starts to the trails: Whitewash, Ordiquish and Ben Aigan. For the Whitewash car park, head to Fochabers and turn onto the A98. Head up this road for a few hundred metres and the car park is signposted on the right. For Ordiquish, start in Fochabers but head in the opposite direction to Whitewash by taking the Ordiquish road out of town in the direction of Ordiquish. The car park is signposted off to the left of this road after 1.5 km. To reach the Ben Aigan car park, take the A96 southwest out of Fochabers in the direction of Aberdeen. After 6 km take a right onto the A95 and follow this road to Mulben (where there is a crossroads in which the B9103 turns off to the right). Take neither the A95 nor the B road, but instead turn right into the un-named minor road and park at the Ben Aigan car park, around 2.5 km up this road.

Facilities/Overview The three car parks each have their own trails, though there are a few forest roads and routes that thread the areas together. Whitewash car park is home to the Fochabers Ring – a red-grade, 8-km XC loop that has some testing uphill and super-rewarding descent; and the Fochabers Freeride route, a 750-m feature-packed loop at the top of the Fochabers Ring, with northshore trickery and a downhill section packed with jumps and berms. The Ordiquish car park has the most routes and is where to access the Soup Dragon (4-km blue-graded loop), and Gordzilla – another blue-graded route of around 5 km. Both feature good uphill sections, followed by controlled descents that should have learners loving the singletrack, while the other blue-graded route here (The Haggis, 6 km), starts and finishes at Ordiquish car park and is full of smaller jumps and interesting features for those who might be getting into their freeriding. Carry on to the top of of the hill and the black-graded route The Gully Monster is a devilish route with some steep switchbacks and a large drop to your left. Don't be fooled by the fact that it starts from the same trail as The Haggis. It is possible to ride from here down to Ben Aigan, where The Hammer is a 7-km red-graded route which boasts being the longest purpose-built bit of singletrack in the UK. Understandably, it's a dream to ride. Also up at Ben Aigan are Mast Blast – a black-graded 1-km descent which is easier than its grade

CHRIS MORAN

suggests, and The (Pink Fluffy) Bunny Trail, an orange-graded 1 km descent which hits the woods and gets steeper, and more technical with every turn. Expert riders only. Ordiquish and Ben Aigan are easily linked, though riders wishing to also hit Whitewash in the same day will have to ride through Fochabers town to do so.

Easy For those looking for an easy introduction into the area, head to Ordiquish first, where The Haggis trail is one of the best blues in Scotland.

Hard The Gully Monster is tougher than you'd expect, especially if you've been surprised by Mast Blast's grading.

Not to Miss The Ben Aigan Hammer section of purpose-built singletrack. It's why many make a long journey here.

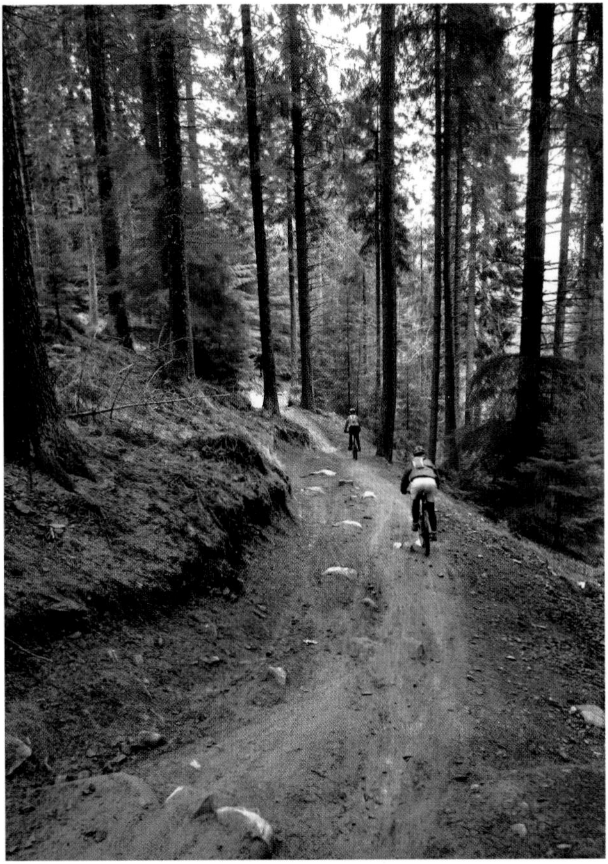
CHRIS MORAN

Remember to Avoid Being fooled by The (Fluffy Pink) Bunny's first section. It gets worse further down the trail.

Nearest Bike/Hire shop Try Bikes & Bowls for simple supplies in Elgin, T01343 549656, or Rafford Cycles for more specialised kit in Forres, T01309 672811.

Local accommodation Castle Cottage is a local B&B, T01343 820761.

Eating Take food and drink into the woods as there are no food or drink stops on the trails. Fochabers is a quaint village with plenty of shops and amenities.

ⓘ **More info** Moray Monster Trails have a page on the Forestry Commission site that is well worth checking for trail closures and news before you head there, – forestry.gov.uk, while Moray Trails have a mountain bike club, moraymountainbikeclub.co.uk.

> Lowdown

Locals do
Link the centres, and get some lunch in Fochabers!

Locals don't
Disrespect The (Pink Fluffy) Bunny trail.

Pros
Lots of different character in a small area.

Cons
Frequent trail closures due to forest operations.

Not as linked as one might imagine.

↘13 Pitfichie Mountain Cycle Trails

Train station Inverurie
Nearest city Aberdeen
Sat Nav AB51 7HJ (for Monymusk village)

Location Pitfichie is a Forestry Commission set-up around 25 km north west from Aberdeen and overlooks some spectacular scenery – most people think they're in the middle of nowhere when they arrive. From Aberdeen, head north west on the A96 towards Elgin/Inverness. Just before Kintore, take a left onto the B994 heading towards Cottown, then another left onto the B993 towards Kemnay and then Monymusk. Carry on the B993 past Monymusk and the road ends at a T junction with the A944 heading left towards Aberdeen or right towards Alford. Here, do a U-turn and head back along the B993 and take the first left. The car park is up this road after around 600 m.

Facilities This is a pretty remote outpost, and there are no facilities at the forest, but if you head back to Monymusk there's a post office/ general store. Otherwise, bring supplies with you.

Overview Pitfichie is well known as being part of the Scottish Downhill Association race series, and is home to one of the most demanding and challenging DH tracks in the country. In addition, there are also a couple of XC trails in the same forest and offer adventurous riders the chance to head out into some of Scotland's wildest hills.

Terrain This is rough, wild terrain, with lots of heather hiding the rocky sections and big jumps on the DH track.

XC There are two routes: the blue-graded Pitfichie Forest Trail, which is a 15-km loop starting from the car park that takes in much forest road and around 10% singletrack, with great views of Bennachie and the Vale of Alford and passes by the Whitehills Stone Circle, and the red-graded Cairn William Trail which starts just off the Pitfichie Forest Trail and is 7 km of trickier riding, including an ascent of Green Hill, then a rocky trail back to the forest road and back up to the top of Cairn William. This is the main thrust of trail building, where there is much slab riding and rocky sections to make the ascent as interesting as possible, the descent includes lots of jumps, the same granite slabs on the way down, and the Devil's Staircase – a rocky section – as well as plenty of bermed corners.

Downhill The Pitfichie Downhill Trail starts at the top of Pitfichie Hill and takes on the heather-strewn hill with plenty of twisting fast turns and big, big jumps. This is no beginners course, with lots of unforgiving rock, hefty jumps and full-on drops to contend with. There are a few chicken lines, but this isn't a place to learn. As part of the SDA race series, expect this to be an elite riders hangout.

ISOBEL CAMERON/FORESTRY COMMISSION

Dirt jumps/Freeride There is no specific bike park or freeride trail, though the Cairn William trail and the DH track have enough drops and jumps to keep those who like being in the air happy.

Conditions There has been a lot of work poured into the trails to keep them interesting and feature-full, and the natural base – mostly a granite bedrock – helps to keep them firm and well-drained. But this isn't a purpose-built area as such, so expect some mud in adverse weather periods.

ⓘ **More info** There is a downloadable route map of Pitfichie's trails available from the Forestry Commission website at forestry.gov.uk.

↘14 Pollock Country Park

Train station Corkerhill/Priesthill & Darnley/Pollokshaws West/Thornliebank
Nearest city Glasgow
Sat Nav G43 1AU

Location Pollok Country Park is on the south side of the Clyde, just to the west of Glasgow city centre. The park is easily accessible by bike from most parts of the city, on either Route 7 or 75 of the National Cycle Network, or by heading to Pollokshaws West train station from Glasgow Central. The M77 dissects the park on its southwest edge.

Facilities Pollok Country Park was Europe's largest urban park until the building of the M77 motorway cut the southwest section of the park off. It was still voted Britain's best park in 2007 though and is home to a variety of facilities, including The Pollok House Tearoom and Restaurant (plus a café in the Burrell House), a herd of Highland Cattle, an orienteering course, picnic areas, woodland gardens, a Go Ape course and stables. It's also home to the Strathclyde Mounted Police and Dog Handling division. Plenty going on then.

Overview Olympic Gold Medalist Chris Hoy opened the three routes of Glasgow Mountain Bike Circuit in 2004, and the area has been incredibly popular with the local riding scene since. There's a green loop, a blue loop and a red, though none offer anything like the terrain you might find if you're heading up to the highlands or to one of the 7Stanes operations. However, for riders who live in the city, the red route offers some challenges, and there are enough jumps and obstacles littered around to make a day here fairly exciting.

Terrain This is an inner-city park with lots of visitors and plenty going on. However, these are purpose-built trails so you should have the run of them without dog walkers and ramblers spoiling the ride.

ⓘ **More info** There has been a huge push in recent years on getting Glasgow's residents out to the park for fun exercise, and as such both Cycling Scotland and Glasgow City Council run courses in the park offering basic through to advanced bike training skills. Call Glasgow's cycling information line T(0141) 287 9171 for a Fit for Life travel map and cycle route information, or visit cyclingscotland.org.

CHRIS MORAN

↘15 Strathpeffer

XC N

Train station Dingwall
Nearest city Inverness
Sat Nav N/A

Location Contin Forest is between the towns of Contin and the larger town of Strathpeffer, itself around 22 km north west of Inverness. From Inverness take the A9 north, then the A835 towards Conon Bridge and on to Contin. Just past the village, around 200 m past the 30 mph speed limit sign, take a right where there's a Forestry Commission Scotland sign in green. At the top of this road is a car park and the start of the Torrachilty Cycle Trail.

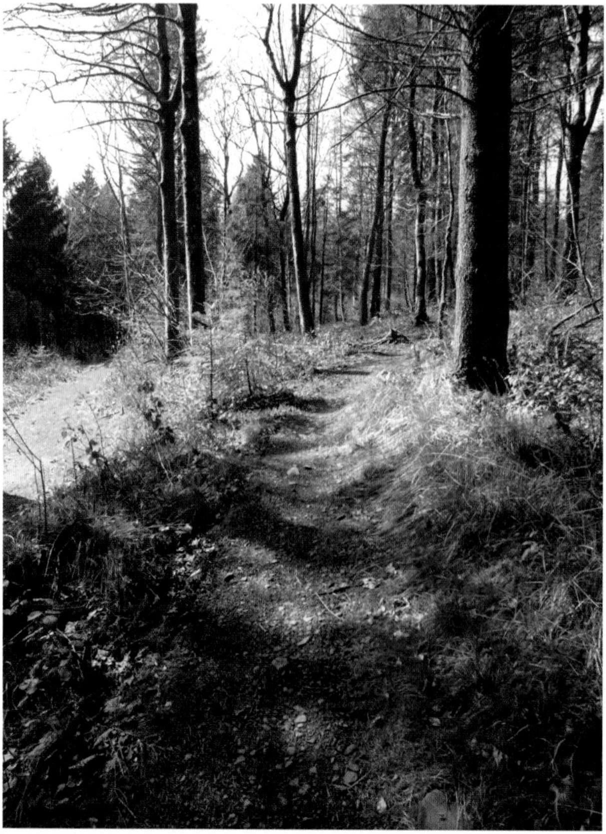
CHRIS MORAN

Facilities There are no facilities at the forest but nearby Contin has shops and Strathpeffer is the bigger town in the area and home to Square Wheels (see below).

Overview There are two routes in the forest – the blue-graded, 4.5-km Torrachilty Cycle Trail which follows the River Blackwater with the 1046 m-high Ben Wyvis in the distant view, and is a perfect family route. The harder, ungraded trail is 12-km natural singletrack route with some reinforced northshore-style wood over the boggier sections, and is home to the hardy 24-hr enduro race, The Strathpuffer 24 (see strathpuffer.co.uk for entry details). Call into Square Wheels in Strathpeffer to get directions and more details on the competition route and others in the Contin Forest. The guys that run Square Wheels have waymarked some of the routes there and have maps available in the shop.

Conditions This is natural terrain with rock drops, rootsy sections and some difficult moss-sections that make the ridge rides quite scary.

ⓘ **More info** The Cycling Scotland website has more info on the forest at cycling.visitscotland.com, or try Square Wheels in Strathpeffer, squarewheels.biz, T01997 421000.

↘16 The Fire Tower Trail

Train station Oban
Nearest city Glasgow
Sat Nav PA31 8RS (for Lochgilphead town centre)

Location As the crow flies, The Fire Trail is around 60 km west of Glasgow, though it's over 120 km by road. From Glasgow, head out on the A82 towards Loch Lomond, then take a left onto the A83, heading to Inveraray and down to Lochgilphead. There are three starting points for the trails: from the Forestry Commission Car Park at Achnabreac, just off the A816 on the Oban to Lochgilphead road; by parking in Kilmichael and riding over the River Add Bridge, then turning right into the forest track; or from Lochgilphead town centre and ride up Blarbuie Road by the golf course.

Facilities/overview There are few facilities on site, save for the Achnabreac Forestry Commission car park, open every day. For cafés, supplies, accommodation and post-riding amenities, ride back down to Lochgilphead, a picturesque town on the banks of Loch Fyne.

Overview This is a very cool hill which has been absolutely filled with incredible features to ride, and has one of the most interesting descents in the UK. The trail takes its name from the Fire Tower at the peak of the hill (it was a forest fire look out), and the ride down takes in a quarry, plenty of jumps, and some brilliant, technical singletrack.

Terrain The main trail takes in everything from northshore to granite slabs, dusty singletrack, and quarry drops. This is a mix of everything.

XC The main thrust here is a 19-km loop starting in Achnabreac (though you can join from Lochgilphead) and heading up to the top of the hill and back down. There are three grades on offer: blue, red and black, though the main route is graded red and the offshoots are either easier or harder. There's something for most riders, but the remoteness means it's not that suited to complete beginners. Starting from the Achnabreac car park, the route heads uphill on the Twisted Fire Starter, before shooting off to the Fire Tower (a black-graded loop around the hill), then into the Quarry Drop – a steep drop down to forest road – before heading uphill again on Murder Hill, ending in a descent down to the Water Splash, then more singletrack to the Swamp Monster and its northshore, before looping back to the start. Also nearby is the Wee Toon Trail in Cambeltown (also known as the Beinn Ghuilean Trail), a lovely XC ramble with plenty of northshore additions. Check out the Forestry Commission site for more info.

Dirt jumps/Freeride/Downhill There's no specific DH or freeride track here, but the riding is technical enough for many downhillers to enjoy and the northshore and plenty of jumps will keep freeriders happy.

JOE MCGHEE/MIDARGYLLTRI-CYCLECLUB.CO.UK

JOE MCGHEE/MIDARGYLLTRI-CYCLECLUB.CO.UK

Conditions Being on the banks of the Loch, avoid in high winds or bad weather, and the swamp areas are clearly prone to bouts of mud.

ⓘ **More info** This is a Forestry Commission Scotland site, and has a page (forestry.gov.uk), while Visit Scotland has a great pages, cycling. visitscotland.com, and the local Mid Argyle cycling club regularly ride here and have created a wonderful page on the trails with downloadable maps and plenty of info (as well as additional XC routes in the area), midargyllcycleclub.co.uk.

↘17 The Kelpies Trail

XC FR N

Train station Inverness
Nearest city Inverness
Sat Nav IV3 8LB

SIMON HARRY/ABRIACHAN FOREST TRUST

Location The Kelpies Trails are in Abriachan Forest, next to the village of Abriachan on the west side of Loch Ness, around 10 km southwest of Inverness. From Inverness (or heading up from the south), take the A82 on the west side of the loch, and turn off near the north end towards Abriachan. In the village, head to the village hall and follow signs to Abriachan Forest Walks, which have a car park and access the start of the trails.

Facilities There are few facilities up at the trails, but Abriachan village is well placed to provide refreshments and is a short ride away. Otherwise, bring supplies with you for a day here.

Overview The Abriachan story is a heartwarming one: in 1998 the village population (all 130 of them), clubbed together to buy the next door forest, and in the years since they have set about re-inventing the town and forest as an ecologically sound, tourist attraction that gives back to their community. It helps of course that they're next to Loch Ness, and recent trail additions by the likes of Rik Allsop (who built much of Mabie Forest and the impressive Drumlanrig trails) have turned this into a fantastic, family-oriented mountain biking destination.

Terrain This is unspoilt, picture-perfect highland scenery with a well-maintained forest and brilliantly quaint village. The trails have been built from locally-crushed rock, and have been designed to work in all weathers and through the winter months.

XC There are four trails, graded green, blue, red and black, as well as a cool skills park. The Green Trail is a 3-km family route which is perfect for showing the kids how to ride in the forest. If they pick it up quick, you can always jump straight from the Green Trail to the Blue, which is 7 km in total and has more interesting features that will test novice riders, as well as 'opt-out' areas to link up to the bikepark. The 4-km Red Trail goes higher into the forest and tops out at the impressive Creag Ard summit, with incredible views over Monadh Liath hills and Loch Ness to the south, and the Affric hills with Ben Wyvis and Ben Bhraggie to the north. There are extensions planned for the Red Trail, and the start of a Black Trail has been high on the agenda throughout 2008. However, all the trails here have been designed to attract families to the area, and so advanced or elite riders might find the grading system a little tame. There is a local mountain bike school (Skills Not Spills), which is accessed through the website below, and they regularly run school holiday-friendly courses for all standards of riders.

Downhill There is no specific DH track here, but the Blue and Red Trails have fun descents.

Dirt jumps/Freeride Kelpies Dare is where you can try out the graded obstacles before taking on the trail of your choice, or stay there and practise your freeride moves.

Conditions These are all-weather, all season trails.

ⓘ **More info** Abriachan has its own village website which includes the Skills Not Spills mountain bike school, abriachan.org.uk.

Best of the rest

↘18 Donkey Hill Dirt Track

FR

Train station Bridge of Orchy/ Fort William
Nearest city Glasgow/Inverness
Sat Nav PH49 4HL

Location This is next door to the Isles of Glencoe Hotel in Ballachulish, a small village on the banks of Loch Leven, around 15 km to the south of Fort William. From either the north or south, the trunk road to Ballachulish is the A82, which cuts straight through the village. The hotel is just to the north west of the village, right on the banks of the Loch, as the road heads to next-door Glencoe.

Facilities Ballachulish is a small, touristy village with plenty of shops and amenities, though there is not a lot specifically at Donkey Hill.

Overview This is a freeride skills practice area suited to beginner and intermediate riders. The local riders built the single-lane BMX-style track with help from pro mountain bikers Greg Minnaar and Sean McCarrol in 2002, and since then have added numerous tabletops, gaps, step ups, doubles and hips. Worth a stop by if you're in the area or fancy a different view other than Fort William, but it is mostly for locals.

Conditions This is a purpose-built little track that drains fairly well, though best avoided after heavy rain.

ⓘ **More info** ridefortwilliam.co.uk has a page on the track.

↘19 Duchany Woods

DH FR

Train station Perth
Nearest city Dundee
Sat Nav PH2 7BH

Location Duchany Woods are just on the western edge of Perth. From the south head towards Perth on the A9, M9 or A90, and exit toards the town centre. Head over the river at West Bridge Street, and up Lochie Brae for 100 m, then take a right into Muirhall Road and head all the way up here to the Kinnoull Hill, where you'll find the Forestry Commission Jubilee Car Park on the right. From the car park, head up the fire-road and the trails should become obvious when you spot the wallride.

Facilities Apart from the car park there are no facilities here, but Perth is a short ride away and full of shops and amenities.

Overview Duchanny Woods are full of trails, mostly DH and freeride-based with a variety of wallrides, jumps, gaps and drops. It's very popular with the local riding scene, and constantly being upgraded. Not particularly worth a long a journey considering the wealth of proper trail centres in Scotland, but for local riders it's a real boon, and for pure downhillers, it makes an interesting day out, particularly the Fanutti Drop, and is a great place to improve your skills if you're an intermediate rider.

Conditions This is an inner-city hill (though a quiet one), so expect the area to also have dog walkers and other forest users, though the atmosphere is mostly friendly.

ⓘ **More info** The guys at Float Productions are often filming at Duchany and have videos of the trials on, xsvideos.co.nr.

↘20 Dunkeld DH

DH FR ⊘

Train station Dunkeld and Birnam
Nearest city Dundee
Sat Nav PH8 0AN

Location Dunkeld is a town around 20 km directly north from Perth on the A9 trunk road that connects the highlands to Perth and Edinburgh. To find the downhill tracks, head along the A9 to Dunkeld, and follow signs for The Hermitage (it's a National Trust garden site with waterfalls etc). When you get to the Hermitage car park, there's a forest road on the right; take that road and go to the end, where there's a gate and a small car park. Hop on the bike there, and go past the gate and take the first right, which should take you to the bottom of the trails.

JAMIE RODDA

Facilities There's nothing up at the downhill, but it's not far from the town centre which is full of cafés, shops and amenities. The Hermitage site has a visitor centre, but you're better off heading into town.

Overview This is one of Scotland's best (and most fierce) downhill tracks, and has been home to plenty of world-class competitions since it was discovered in 2001. It's a mostly-natural downhill track, with horrific rock gardens and rooty sections that have seen some incredible crashes over the years. There used to be an uplift service running, but that seems to have stopped, though there is a new, lesser-graded track coming down the same hill, though this is still of a fairly high standard. Put simply, Dunkeld is definitely one for the elite riders out there.

ⓘ **More info** There are also a number of waymarked XC routes around Dunkeld (mostly forest road, or waymarked estate land). You can get the 'Discover Atholl Estates – Countryside Trails Dunkeld' booklet for 50p from the ranger hut at the Atholl Estate (or online at athollestatesrangerservice.co.uk), or try the cycling page on perthshire.co.uk for other route ideas.

↘21 Kirkhill Mountain Bike Park

XC 4X N

Train station Dyce
Nearest city Aberdeen
Sat Nav N/A

Location Kirkhill Forest is between the village of Blackburn and Aberdeen's Dyce Airport, around 6 km north west from the city of Aberdeen. From Aberdeen, head out on the A96 towards Elgin/Inverness. Pass the exit for Dyce Airport and carry on up the A96 for around 1.5 km, then take a right into the Kirkhill Forest visitor car park. The trails start from here, or the north car park of the forest, which is accessed by heading further along the A96 towards Blackburn, then turning right onto the B979, and taking another right off this road just before the train tracks, then first left. The car park is just off to the right of this road.

Facilities Aside from the car park, there are no facilities at Kirkhill Forest, though head into Blackburn and there are plenty of shops and amenities a short ride away.

Overview Kirkhill Forest is famous for the Kirkhill Mountain Bike Park, a downhill funpark with plenty of jumps, wallrides, switchbacks and berms. You can hit them all without needing to build more speed, which makes it a perfect place to learn or perfect tricks. Most riders come here for the funpark, which has plans to expand, though there is also a waymarked 12-km blue-graded loop to the top of the Tyrebagger Hill and back down (it's a fantastic view, and great if you're into plane spotting – it's right on the flightpath to Aberdeen's airport). There are two other short, singletrack loops – the North and South Spurs, as well as plenty of fire-road and unofficial riding to explore.

Conditions The forest is quite popular with other outdoor users, particularly horse-riders, though there's enough space for all.

ⓘ **More info** Kirkhill Forest (and Mountain Bike Park), has its own page on the Forestry Commission site, forestry.gov.uk.

Best films
Callum Swift

Callum Swift is an up and cmoming UK film maker behind the new DVD release 'The Uprising'. Check out theuprisingfilm.com for more info. Here he gives us his review of the best ever mountain bike films.

Best film ever "Earthed 1 - It really captures the spirit of the sport, plenty of flat out riding by all the top pros. The sountrack fits perfectly with the riding and the shots done on a super 8 camera give it a nice retro feel. Check out Sam Hill and Nathan Rennie rocking to Led Zepplin or when all the Iron Horse lads style it up over the bridge in Bromont.

One for the scenics "It's got to be Roam. There's the stunning cinematography, it's shot on film with beautiful settings, the best riders, the best locations, big film crew, great sountrack....what more could you want? It really makes you want to ride your bike whenever you watch it. Check the bit in Morocco - such a unique location. Or where Jordy Lunn jumps the river gap in Moab. And don't get me started on the cable cam in whistler with Darren Berreclough through all the northshore.

Best downhill film Between the Tape. It's got incredible cinematography and editing. Clay Porter's documentary style is interesting and the gladiatorial voiceover adds drama to the whole thing. The rider sections are all amazing, especially the Athertons section with some amazing cable cam shots. The best shot is of Sam Hill coming into the finish of the World Champs - Clay manages to track him through the crowd perfectly and it looks insane.

Best for watching again and again Illusionary Lines. The sountrack is superb and the split screen race shots with the timer running are an interesting addition. Check out Kovarik ripping up Scuol during the opening credits with his typical destroyer style. Some of his whips are insane.

Best for showcasing Europe Earthed 3. I had to include this for a guide to riding in Europe! It covers the World Cups brilliantly and has some awesome rider sections and a good sountrack. The Megavalanche section is a must see for anyone wanting to do the event. When someone crashes on the single track of the Megavalanche the camera follows his bike from a helicopter as it tumbles about a kilometer down the mountain. Pretty bad news.

Facility breakdown

	XC	DH	4X	DJ	Northshore	Foam pit	Bike hire	Bike shop	Bike wash	Uplift	Map	Waymarked	Family	Visitor Centre	Ac comodation	Cafe/food
Southwest England																
Abbeyford Woods and Goldburn Northshore	✓	✓			✓											
Asham Woods		✓		✓	✓											
Ashton Court (The Timberland Trail)	✓					✓	✓	✓			✓		✓	✓		✓
Aveton Gifford DJs				✓												
Bath BMX Track				✓												
Bradford Hollow	✓			✓												
Blandford UK Bike Park		✓			✓	✓	✓	✓	✓	✓	✓	✓		✓		✓
Bucklands Ring		✓	✓	✓												
Buriton Chalk Pits	✓	✓		✓												
Canford Heath and Pit DH	✓			✓												
Cann Wood Trails		✓		✓												
Cheddar BMX	✓		✓	✓			✓	✓	✓		✓		✓	✓	✓	
Combe Sydenham	✓	✓		✓							✓		✓	✓		
Dartmoor National Park	✓	✓								✓	✓	✓	✓			✓
Decoy BMX				✓												
Forest of Dean	✓	✓		✓			✓	✓	✓		✓	✓	✓	✓		✓
Haldon Forest Park	✓	✓		✓	✓						✓	✓	✓			
Hidden Valley DJs	✓	✓		✓												
Hook DJs				✓												
Hundred Acre Wood	✓											✓	✓			
Island Trails				✓												
JLC Trails				✓												
Leckhampton		✓								✓						
Leigh Woods	✓	✓										✓	✓			✓
Nationwide DJs	✓			✓									✓			
Oasis DJs				✓												
Patchway BMX DJs				✓												
Pines Ridge	✓			✓												
Maddacleave Woods	✓	✓		✓						✓	✓	✓				✓

	XC	DH	4X	DJ	Northshore	Foam pit	Bike hire	Bike shop	Bike wash	Uplift	Map	Waymarked	Family	Visitor Centre	Ac comodation	Cafe/food
Mineral Tramways Project	✓	✓		✓			✓	✓	✓		✓	✓	✓	✓	✓	✓
Poldice Valley Trails	✓	✓		✓												
Portland Bill Quarries	✓			✓												
Portsdown Hill	✓	✓														
Puddletown Woods	✓	✓		✓							✓		✓			✓
Queen Elizabeth Country Park	✓	✓									✓	✓	✓	✓		✓
Randwick DH	✓	✓														
Red Hill Extreme			✓	✓						✓						✓
Rogate		✓		✓	✓											
Sandford DJs and DH	✓	✓		✓												
Sheet DJs				✓												
Still Woods		✓		✓	✓											
Stoke Heights	✓	✓														
Stoughton Trails	✓			✓												
Stoke Woods	✓	✓		✓							✓					✓
The Track			✓	✓	✓	✓	✓	✓	✓		✓	✓	✓	✓		✓
Triscombe DH		✓														
Watchmoor Wood Bike Park	✓				✓		✓				✓	✓	✓	✓		
Woodbury Common	✓						✓				✓	✓	✓	✓		

London & Southeast England

	XC	DH	4X	DJ	Northshore	Foam pit	Bike hire	Bike shop	Bike wash	Uplift	Map	Waymarked	Family	Visitor Centre	Ac comodation	Cafe/food
Aston Hill	✓	✓	✓	✓			✓	✓	✓		✓	✓	✓	✓		✓
A10 DJs				✓												
Bengeo Bumps and Waterford Quarry DJs				✓												
Bedgebury Forest and Freeride Area	✓	✓	✓	✓	✓		✓	✓	✓		✓	✓	✓	✓		✓
Blean Woods	✓															
Bluebell Hill	✓	✓											✓			
Braintree BMX				✓												
Brockwell Park BMX Track				✓												✓
Bushey Park	✓			✓												
Chazey Woods and Northshore	✓	✓			✓											
Chicksands Bike Park				✓	✓						✓	✓	✓			✓

	XC	DH	4X	DJ	Northshore	Foam pit	Bike hire	Bike shop	Bike wash	Uplift	Map	Waymarked	Family	Visitor Centre	Ac comodation	Cafe/food
Crowborough – The Bull Track		✓		✓	✓											✓
Crow Trails				✓												
Danbury Common		✓		✓												
Devils Drop DJs	✓			✓												
Devils Dyke DH and XC	✓	✓											✓			✓
Devils Dyke Nonsuch DJs				✓												
Donkey Island DJs				✓												
Esher Shore				✓	✓						✓	✓				✓
Epping Forest	✓										✓		✓	✓		✓
Friston Forest	✓	✓		✓	✓							✓				
Fearnley DJs				✓												
Gunnersbury DJs				✓												
Harrow Skatepark and DJs				✓												
Hayes Hawkes BMX Track				✓												
Highgate DJs				✓												
Highwoods DJs				✓												
Holmes Place DJs				✓												
Ipswich BMX Track				✓												
Kuoni Trails				✓												
Leith Hill	✓	✓		✓												
Limpsfield DJs				✓												
Look Out Gulley				✓												
M3 DJs				✓												
Mereworth Woods				✓												
Mousehold Trails	✓			✓												
Nature Jumps and Gog Magog XC	✓			✓												
PORC (Penshurst Off Road Club) aka Viceroy's Wood	✓	✓	✓	✓	✓				✓		✓	✓	✓	✓		✓
Normandy Hill DH	✓	✓														
Peaslake	✓	✓														
Peckham BMX Track and Burgess Park BMX				✓												
Rayleigh				✓												
Redlands	✓	✓										✓	✓			

	XC	DH	4X	DJ	Northshore	Foam pit	Bike hire	Bike shop	Bike wash	Uplift	Map	Waymarked	Family	Visitor Centre	Ac comodation	Cafe/food
Shoreham DJs				✓												
Shorne Wood Country Park and DJs	✓															
Sidley Woods				✓												
Slindon Quarry	✓			✓												
Swinley Forest	✓						✓	✓	✓		✓	✓	✓			✓
Sloughbottom Park				✓												
Teddington DJs	✓			✓												
Thetford Forest	✓						✓	✓	✓		✓	✓	✓	✓		✓
Tilgate Forest and St Leonards Forest	✓															
Track 40	✓	✓		✓												
Tring Park	✓	✓		✓								✓	✓			
Warley DJs				✓												
Whiteways	✓												✓			✓
Wild Park	✓	✓		✓												
Willen Lake BMX Track				✓												
Wisley Trails				✓												
Woburn Sands	✓	✓		✓	✓						✓	✓	✓			
The Midlands																
Bringewood		✓								✓						
Brackley DH	✓	✓		✓												
Cauldwell Woods DJs	✓			✓												
Cannock Chase	✓	✓		✓	✓		✓	✓	✓		✓	✓	✓	✓		✓
Cheshire Ghost Riders BMX Track			✓	✓												
Deeping BMX			✓	✓												
Eastridge Woods	✓	✓									✓		✓			
Hopton Castle	✓	✓		✓						✓	✓		✓			
Keele Woods and DJs	✓	✓		✓												
Leamington Spa 4X Track and DJs		✓		✓												
Ribblesford DH	✓	✓								✓						
Perry Park BMX		✓		✓												
Rutland Water Cycle Way	✓						✓	✓	✓		✓	✓	✓	✓		✓

	XC	DH	4X	DJ	Northshore	Foam pit	Bike hire	Bike shop	Bike wash	Uplift	Map	Waymarked	Family	Visitor Centre	Ac comodation	Cafe/food
Sherwood Pines Forest	✓	✓	✓	✓	✓		✓	✓	✓		✓	✓	✓	✓		✓
Swithland Woods	✓															
Tiny BMX Track				✓												
The North																
Carlton Bank DH and XC	✓	✓														
Broomley Trails DJs				✓												
Calverley Woods	✓	✓														
Chesterfield BMX/4X Track				✓												
Chevin Forest Park	✓	✓														
Chester-le-Street spots		✓		✓												
Chopwell	✓			✓							✓	✓	✓			
Delamere Forest	✓	✓		✓	✓				✓		✓	✓	✓	✓		✓
Dalby Forest	✓	✓	✓	✓	✓		✓	✓	✓		✓	✓	✓		✓	✓
Devils Cascade DJs				✓												
Elland Park Wood	✓	✓														
Gosforth Park DJs				✓												
Gisburn Forest	✓	✓		✓			✓	✓				✓	✓		✓	
Greasbrough Trails				✓												
Great Ayton Quarry DJs																
Greenway DJs				✓												
Guisbrough Forest	✓	✓										✓	✓	✓		
Hartlepool 4X			✓	✓										✓		
Hookstone Woods DJs				✓												
Hamsterley Forest	✓	✓	✓	✓	✓		✓	✓	✓		✓	✓	✓	✓		✓
Hulme Park DJs				✓												
Hurstwood Trails	✓	✓		✓												
Ilkley Moor	✓	✓		✓												
Iron Bridge DJs	✓	✓		✓												
Kielder Water & Forest Park	✓	✓	✓	✓	✓		✓	✓			✓	✓	✓	✓	✓	✓
Ladybower Reservoir	✓	✓							✓		✓		✓	✓		✓
Lee Mill Quarry (aka The Adrenaline Gateway)	✓	✓		✓								✓	✓			

	XC	DH	4X	DJ	Northshore	Foam pit	Bike hire	Bike shop	Bike wash	Uplift	Map	Waymarked	Family	Visitor Centre	Ac comodation	Cafe/food
Little Switzerland	✓	✓									✓	✓	✓	✓		✓
Longridge Fell	✓	✓														
Lyme Park	✓												✓	✓		✓
Manchester Road DJs				✓												
Meltham Skills Trails	✓			✓												
Midgley Woods		✓		✓												
Park Bridge 4X		✓	✓													
Ramsden Lane DH		✓								✓						
Roman Lakes Leisure Park	✓										✓	✓	✓	✓		✓
Scratchmere Scar Freeride Bike Park	✓	✓		✓	✓				✓	✓	✓	✓				✓
Silton Forest DH	✓	✓														
Setmurthy DH Trails and Cockermouth XC	✓	✓									✓					
Stainburn	✓	✓		✓							✓	✓	✓			
Sticks Norden	✓	✓		✓												
Storthes Hall DH		✓		✓												
Temple Newsam		✓	✓	✓												
TNF Grizedale	✓	✓		✓	✓		✓	✓	✓		✓	✓	✓	✓		✓
Wassenden DH	✓	✓								✓						
Wiswell Wood	✓	✓									✓					
Woodbank DJs	✓			✓												
Whinlatter Forest	✓	✓		✓	✓		✓	✓	✓		✓		✓	✓		✓
Wooler 4X	✓	✓	✓	✓	✓						✓					
Yeadon BMX Track				✓												
Wales																
Afan Forest Park	✓	✓			✓		✓	✓		✓	✓	✓	✓	✓		✓
Abercarn	✓	✓														✓
Aberhafesp Woods and DH	✓	✓														
Caerphilly DJs				✓												
Brechfa	✓	✓					✓	✓	✓		✓	✓	✓	✓		✓
Betws Y Coed (Snowdonia East)	✓	✓					✓	✓	✓		✓	✓	✓	✓		✓
Clarach DH	✓	✓		✓											✓	

	XC	DH	4X	DJ	Northshore	Foam pit	Bike hire	Bike shop	Bike wash	Uplift	Map	Waymarked	Family	Visitor Centre	Ac comodation	Cafe/food
Clyne Woods	✔	✔		✔												
Coed Llandegla	✔	✔		✔	✔		✔	✔	✔		✔	✔	✔	✔		✔
Coed Trallwm	✔												✔	✔	✔	✔
Coed Y Brenin (Snowdonia West)	✔				✔						✔	✔	✔	✔		✔
Cwm Rhaeadr	✔										✔	✔	✔			
Cwmcarn	✔	✔		✔	✔		✔	✔	✔	✔	✔	✔	✔	✔		✔
Foel Gasnach DH	✔	✔	✔	✔							✔	✔				
Gethin Woods	✔	✔		✔						✔						
Gwydwr Forest	✔	✔		✔	✔						✔	✔	✔	✔		✔
Kilvey Hill		✔		✔						✔						
Henblas/Caersws nr Newton		✔								✔						
Llantrisant Woods DH	✔	✔														
Llanwrtyd Wells	✔										✔	✔	✔	✔		✔
Maindy Road BMX Track			✔	✔												
Moelfre	✔	✔	✔	✔												
Mountain Ash DH	✔	✔														
Ponciau Banks			✔	✔												
Machynlleth	✔			✔						✔	✔		✔	✔		
Nant yr Arian	✔	✔	✔								✔	✔	✔			
Rheola DH Trail		✔								✔						
Rudry DJs				✔												
Sandjumps				✔												
Snowdonia National Park	✔	✔											✔	✔		✔
Wentwood DH	✔	✔		✔												
Southern Scotland																
Ae Forest (7Stanes)	✔	✔		✔	✔		✔	✔	✔	✔	✔	✔	✔	✔		✔
Dalbeattie (7Stanes)	✔			✔	✔		✔	✔	✔		✔	✔	✔	✔		✔
Drumlanrig Castle	✔	✔	✔	✔	✔		✔	✔	✔	✔	✔	✔	✔	✔		✔
Glentress (7Stanes)	✔	✔	✔	✔	✔		✔	✔	✔	✔	✔	✔	✔	✔	✔	✔
Glentrool (7Stanes)	✔		✔	✔	✔						✔	✔	✔	✔		✔
Innerleithen (7Stanes)	✔	✔		✔	✔					✔	✔	✔	✔			

	XC	DH	4X	DJ	Northshore	Foam pit	Bike hire	Bike shop	Bike wash	Uplift	Map	Waymarked	Family	Visitor Centre	Ac comodation	Cafe/food
The Jedforest Trails	✓										✓		✓			✓
Kirroughtree (7Stanes)	✓			✓	✓		✓	✓	✓		✓	✓	✓	✓		✓
Mabie (7Stanes)	✓		✓	✓	✓		✓	✓	✓		✓	✓	✓	✓		✓
Newcastleton (7Stanes)	✓			✓	✓						✓	✓	✓	✓		

Central & Northern Scotland

	XC	DH	4X	DJ	Northshore	Foam pit	Bike hire	Bike shop	Bike wash	Uplift	Map	Waymarked	Family	Visitor Centre	Ac comodation	Cafe/food
Aviemore	✓	✓									✓		✓			
Balnain Bike Park				✓	✓						✓	✓	✓			
Carron Valley Trails	✓	✓			✓						✓	✓	✓			
Comrie Croft Bike Trails	✓	✓		✓	✓		✓	✓	✓		✓	✓	✓	✓	✓	✓
Fort William	✓	✓	✓	✓	✓		✓	✓	✓	✓	✓	✓	✓	✓		✓
Glencoe	✓	✓		✓						✓	✓					✓
Golspie Highland Wildcat Trails	✓	✓			✓						✓	✓				
Isle of Arran	✓	✓									✓		✓			✓
Kyle of Sutherland Trails	✓	✓		✓			✓	✓	✓		✓	✓	✓	✓		✓
Laggan Wolftrax	✓	✓	✓	✓	✓		✓	✓	✓	✓	✓	✓	✓	✓		✓
Learnie Red Rocks	✓			✓	✓						✓	✓	✓			
Moray Monster Trails	✓	✓		✓	✓						✓	✓				
Pitfichie Mountain Cycles Trails	✓	✓									✓					
Pollock Country Park	✓										✓	✓	✓	✓		✓
Strathpeffer	✓				✓						✓					
The Fire Tower Trail	✓			✓	✓						✓	✓				
The Kelpies Trails	✓	✓		✓	✓						✓	✓	✓			✓
Donkey Hill Dirt Track				✓												
Duchany Woods		✓		✓												
Dunkeld DH	✓	✓								✓						
Kirkhill Mountain Bike Park			✓	✓	✓						✓	✓	✓			

KESWICKBIKES.CO.UK
KMB
SINCE'92
IN STORE - ON LINE - INDEPENDENT

PURPLE MOUNTAIN
BIKE CENTRE & CAFE
DALBY FOREST
Quality Mountain Bike Hire
High End Demo Fleet - YETI, KONA, LAPIERRE
Kids Bikes, Tagalongs, and Trailers
MTB Skills Courses - Kids & Adults
Year Round Events Program
Special Rates for Groups
Corporate Events
Great Bikers Cafe with Homemade Grub
www.purplemountain.co.uk
Booking Advisable 01751 460011

WINDERMERE MARINA VILLAGE
the Lake District bike trails on your doorstep...
Luxury Self Catering Accommodation
Onsite Bar & Leisure Club
Secure Bike Storage
Washdown Station
www.wmv.co.uk 015394 46551

GLENKIRK
BED AND BREAKFAST
A HEAVENLY EXPERIENCE!

Set amongst some of the finest Scottish scenery around

Children welcome, travel cot available.

Parking: Private parking for up to 4 cars.

Garage available for motorbikes & pedal cycles

Drumnadrochit,
Loch Ness, IV63 6TZ

Tel/Fax 01456 450802
www.Lochnessbandb.com

Gorsebank Wigwams

01556 611634

Dalbeattie
DG5 4QT

Next to 7 Stanes trails - Drying room
Onsite cycle hire - Great facilities
www.gorsebank.com

TRAQUAIR ARMS
HOTEL & COTTAGES

World-class downhill and cross country mountain bike trails right on our doorstep

Where gaiters, waders and lycra congregate in perfect harmony

Perfect stopover for the weary traveller

Perfect perch to dream over a dram

An idyll to stretch 'trekking-tired' limbs

Traquair Arms Hotel
Innerleithen, Peeblesshire,
EH44 6PD

Tel: 01896 830229
Fax: 01896 830260

info@traquairarmshotel.co.uk
www.traquairarmshotel.co.uk

The Rumblie
A HIGHLAND WELCOME

Our luxury three room Guest House provides warm and friendly accommodation in the village of Laggan and offers a range of organic and fair-trade produce. We are ideally situated for Laggan Wolftrax just 2 miles away with The Witches Trails 35 miles to the west.

Tel. 01528 544766

Email mail@rumblie.com

Web www.rumblie.com

About the author

Chris Moran has spent most of his adult life In and around the mountains, first as a pro snowboarder through the whole of the 1990s and early 2000s and more recently as an action sports journalist for various newspapers and magazines around the world. Through his company ACM Writing - and on behalf of Nike 6.0 - he has managed UCI World Junior Champion Josh Bryceland and fellow UCI World Cup rider Sam Dale.

Chris has been riding bikes since he was five years old and has a collection of BMX mags going back to the late 1980s. He loves riding his freeride/XC bike all over Europe, especially In Lagos, Portugal, and can be found at various trail centres around the UK at weekends. His favourite spots In the UK are Afan Forestin Wales, Haldon Park near Exeter and Drumlanrig Castle In Scotland.

Mountain Biking Britain Is his second book with Footprint, having already co-authored *Mountain Biking Europe* alongside World Cup rider and master trail builder Rowan Sorrell, and freesports journalist Ben Monday.

Acknowledgements

In no particular order I'd like to thank Stacey at The Track, all at MBR Magazine, Andy Heading, Andy Lloyd, Steve Williams, Clive Davies & all at the Forestry Commission, the amazing crew at BGB (Susie Westwood especially!), Danny Milner in the UK, Ian and Dom at DMR Bikes, Gary Ewing & Mat Clark, Gary Williamson, Ian Linton, Jack Beckerson, James Chetwoode, Jamie Rodda, Janet Baxter, Louis Rogers, Pete Derret, Pete Tiley, Phil Young, Rob at Esher Shore, Richard Norgate, Scottish Woodlands, Snowdonia Guides, Steve Behr, The Santa Cruz Syndicate, Tiago Santana, Tore Meirik, Jacob Gibbins, Ali and Ash at Trail Addiction, the Bike Academy, Stuart Tee, Neil Cane, Toby and Jim at the Mountainbike Adventure,

An extra special thanks to: Nick Bayliss at Royal Racing – you're a legend mate. Dan Milner in Chamonix, France (or in cyberspace at danmilner.com), the super snappers Victor Lucas, James McKnight and Steve Jones, Rachel Atherton in Wales, Steve Peat, Sam Dale and Josh Bryceland in England – thanks for taking time out of winning the UCI to help me put this together, the guys at Dirt (Mike and Billy), Callum Swift rom The Uprising, Sam Reynolds and Blake Samson at DMR Bikes and Nike 6.0 and those amazing people that sent in shots and info on the more remote trails. Namely, Dugal D Ross, Greg and Gary Williamson, Andrew Denham, Paul England, Richard Norgate, Jimmy Doyle, Rene Weinberg, Allessandro Marengo, Kenneth Smith, Loic Delteil, Jack Beckerson, Dennis Stratmann, Paul Wurzinger, La Raya Creacions, Alicia Anton, Bruce Taylor, Morven Munro and Andy Boyle. Tim Bell, Jethro Loader, Steve Palmer, Paul Blackburn, Amanda Goller, Roger Knight at the Bike Barn, Malte Iden, Leanne Shipley, Mike at Mountain Bike Brighton, Billy Cheetham in Leamington, John Storey, Steve Cahill, Pauline Sanderson, Julian Williamson, Philippa Clark, Spike at Sqegg, Dan Hendrick, Vicky Chilcott, Rich at Cyclewise Training, Tim Sellors, Peter D'Aguilar, Sam Lattaway, James Colborn, Graham O'Hanlon, Matt Addison, Lyndsey Cheetham, Gail Graham, Julia Strathdee, Ben and Jason Wain , Mike Westphal at Viceroy's Wood, Pete at Roman Lakes, Adrian Taylor, Hilary Carpenter, The Woolybacks! Darren Edwards at Cannop, David Cole at Quench, Stephen Boyd, Arron McGregor, Antony de Hevingham, Tom at Southwales Downhill, Andy Soper, Stephen Garside, Gill Bell, Kate Murray, Alison Kohler, Alice Jell, Colin Williamson, Jeremy Brown, Simon Baxter, Simon Harry, Karl Pugh, Michael O'Connor, Joe McGhee, Michael Marsden, Kirsty Slater at Carbisdale, Gerrard Tattersfield, Ed Daynes, Lyndsey Carruthers,

We couldn't have made this possible without: Alan Murphy, Angus Dawson and the rest of the team at Footprint. Isobel Cameron at the Forestry Commission thanks an absolute million, Rowan Sorrell thanks an unbelievably huge amount, and all the riders and photographers and club members who've helped with info, pictures and maps. You're all legends. If there's anyone we've forgotten, huge, huge apologies, and I'll make sure we put you in the re-print. Oh and please send any errors and omissions to: mountainbikingbritain@gmail.com

Index

SWE = Southwest England; **LSE** = London & the Southeast; **MID** = The Midlands; **NOR** = The North; **WAL** = Wales; **SSC** = Southern Scotland; **CNS** = Central & Northern Scotland

A

A10 DJs, LSE 64
Abbeyford Woods, SWE 18
Abercarn, WAL 178
Aberhafesp Woods and DHI, WAL 179
Ae Forest (7Stanes), SSC 218
Afan Forest Park, WAL 176
Asham Woods, SWE 19
Ashton Court (The Timberland Trail), SWE 19
Aston Hill, LSE 62
Aveton Gifford DJs, SWE 20
Aviemore, CNS 242

B

Balnain Bike Park, CNS 243
Bath BMX Track, SWE 20
Bedgebury Forest and Freeride Area, LSE 65
Bengeo Bumps and Waterford Quarry DJs, LSE 64
Betws Y Coed (Snowdonia East), WAL 182
Blandford UK Bike Park, SWE 22
Blean Woods, LSE 66
Bluebell Hill, LSE 67
Brackley DH, MID 111
Bradford Hollow, SWE 20
Braintree BMX, LSE 67
Brechfa, WAL 180
Bringewood, MID 110
Brockwell Park BMX Track, LSE 68
Broomley Trails DJs, NOR 131
Buckland Rings, SWE 24
Buriton Chalk Pits, SWE 24
Bushy Park, LSE 68

C

Caerphilly DJs, WAL 179
Calverly Woods, NOR 131
Canford Heath and Pit DH, SWE 25
Cannock Chase, MID 112
Cann Wood Trails, SWE 25
Carlton Bank DH and XC, NOR 130
Carron Valley Trails, CNS 244
Cauldwell Woods DJs, MID 111
Central & Northern Scotland 238-269
Chazey Woods and Northshore, LSE 68
Cheddar BMX, SWE 26
Cheshire Ghost Riders BMX Track, MID 114
Chesterfield BMX/4X Track, NOR 131
Chester-le-Street spots, NOR 133
Chevin Forest Park, NOR 132
Chicksands Bike Park, LSE 70
Chopwell, NOR 134
Clarach DH, WAL 183
Clyne Woods, WAL 183
Coed Llandegla, WAL 184
Coed Trallwm, WAL 186
Coed Y Brenin (Snowdonia West), WAL 188
Combe Sydenham, SWE 26
Comrie Croft Bike Trails, CNS 245
Crowborough - The Bull Track, LSE 72
Crow Trails, LSE 73
Cwmcarn, WAL 192
Cwm Rhaeadr, WAL 190

D

Dalbeattie (7Stanes), SSC 220
Dalby Forest, NOR 136
Danbury Common, LSE 73
Dartmoor National Park, SWE 27
Decoy BMX, SWE 27
Deeping BMX, MID 114
Delamere Forest, NOR 135
Devils Cascade DJs, NOR 138
Devils Drop DJs, LSE 76
Devils Dyke DH and XC, LSE 76
Devils Dyke Nonsuch DJs, LSE 77
Donkey Hill Dirt Track, CNS 267
Donkey Island DJs, LSE 77
Drumlanrig Castle, SSC 222
Duchany Woods, CNS 267
Dunkeld DH, CNS 267

E

Eastridge Woods, MID 115
Elland Park Wood, NOR 139
Epping Forest, LSE 80
Esher Shore, LSE 78

F

Fearnley DJs, LSE 82
Fire Tower Trail, The, CNS 265
Foel Gasnach DH, WAL 194
Forest of Dean, SWE 28
Fort William, CNS 246
Friston Forest, LSE 81

G

Gethin Woods, WAL 195
Gisburn Forest, NOR 140
Glencoe, CNS 248
Glentress (7Stanes), SSC 224
Glentrool (7Stanes), SSC 226
Goldburn Northshore, SWE 18
Golspie Highland Wildcat Trails, CNS 250
Gosforth Park DJs, NOR 139
Greasborough Trails, NOR 141
Great Ayton Quarry DJs, NOR 141
Greenway DJs, NOR 142
Guisborough Forest, NOR 142
Gunnersbury DJs, LSE 82
Gwydwr Forest, WAL 196

H

Haldon Forest Park, SWE 30
Hamsterley Forest, NOR 146
Harrow Skatepark and DJs, LSE 82
Hartlepool 4X, NOR 143
Hayes Hawks BMX track, LSE 83
Henblas/Caersws nr Newton, WAL 198
Highgate DJs, LSE 83
Highwoods DJs, LSE 83
Holmes Place DJs, LSE 84
Hook DJs, SWE 32
Hookstone Woods DJs, NOR 143
Hopton Castle, MID 116
How to use the book 5
Hulme Park DJs, NOR 148
Hundred Acre Wood, SWE 32
Hustwood Trails, NOR 148

I

Ilkley Moor, NOR 149
Innerleithen (7Stanes), SSC 228
Ipswich BMX Track, LSE 84
Iron Bridge DJs, NOR 149
Island Trails, SWE 33
Isle of Arran, CNS 252

J

Jedforest Trails, The, SSC 230
JLC Trails, SWE 33

K

Keele Woods and DJs, MID 118
Kelpies Trails, The, CNS 266
Kielder Water & Forest Park, NOR 150
Kilvey Hill, WAL 197
Kirkhill Mountain Bike Park, CNS 268
Kirroughtree (7Stanes), SSC 232
Kuoni Trails, LSE 84
Kyle of Sutherland Trails, CNS 254

L

Ladybower Reservoir, NOR 152
Laggan Wolftrax, CNS 256
Leamington Spa 4X Track
and DJs, MID 118
Learnie Red Rocks, CNS 258
Leckhampton, SWE 33
Lee Mill Quarry (aka
The Adrenaline Gateway), NOR 153
Leigh Woods, SWE 34
Leith Hill, LSE 84
Limpsfield DJs, LSE 85
Little Switzerland, NOR 154
Llantrisant Woods DH, WAL 198
Llanwrtyd Wells, WAL 199
London & Southeast England 56-103
Longridge Fell, NOR 154
Look Out Gulley, LSE 86
Lyme Park, NOR 154

M

M3 DJs, LSE 86
Mabie (7Stanes), SSC 234
Machynlleth, WAL 202
Maddacleave Woods, SWE 36
Maindy Road BMX Track, WAL 200
Manchester Road DJs, NOR 155
Meltham Skills Trails, NOR 155
Mereworth Woods, LSE 86
Midgley Woods, NOR 155
Midlands, The, 104-123
Mineral Tramways Project, SWE 38
Moelfre, WAL 200
Moray Monster Trails, CNS 260
Mountain Ash DH, WAL 201
Mousehold Trails, LSE 87

N

Nant Yr Arian, WAL 204
Nationwide DJs, SWE 34
Nature Jumps and
Gog Magog XC, LSE 87
Newcastleton, SSC 236
Normandy Hill DHI, LSE 90
North, The 124-169

O

Oasis DJs, SWE 35

P

Park Bridge 4X, NOR 156
Patchway BMX DJs, SWE 35
Peaslake, LSE 90
Peckham BMX Track,
and Burgess Park BMX, LSE 91
Penshurst Off Road Club (PORC), LSE 88
Perry Park BMX, MID 120
Pines Ridge, SWE 35
Pitfichie Mountain Cycle Trails, CNS 262
Poldice Valley Trails, SWE 40
Pollock Country Park, CNS 263
Ponciau Banks, WAL 201
Portland Bill Quaries, SWE 41
Portsdown Hill, SWE 44
Puddletown Woods, SWE 44

Q

Queen Elizabeth Country Park, SWE 45

R

Ramsden Lane DH, NOR 156
Randwick DH, SWE 46
Rayleigh, LSE 91